Donald J. Trump's Presidency: International Perspectives

DONALD J. TRUMP'S PRESIDENCY
International Perspectives

Editors
JOHN DIXON
and
MAX J. SKIDMORE

Westphalia Press
An Imprint of the Policy Studies Organization
Washington, DC
2018

Donald J. Trump's Presidency: International Perspectives
All Rights Reserved © 2018 by Policy Studies Organization

Westphalia Press
An imprint of Policy Studies Organization
1527 New Hampshire Ave., NW
Washington, D.C. 20036
info@ipsonet.org

ISBN-10: 1-63391-665-0
ISBN-13: 978-1-63391-665-4

Cover and interior design by Jeffrey Barnes
jbarnesbook.design

Daniel Gutierrez-Sandoval, Executive Director
PSO and Westphalia Press

Updated material and comments on this edition
can be found at the Westphalia Press website:
www.westphaliapress.org

To
Tina, Piers, Aliki, David, and Isabella
and
Charlene

CONTENTS

Preface vii

1. Donald J. Trump: His Public Persona,
   Worldview, and View of the World 1
   John Dixon

2. The Early Days of the Trump Presidency:
   Policy Rhetoric, Vision, and Reality 39
   Max J. Skidmore

3. "I Love Canada": Canada-US Relations
   under Trump's Presidency 69
   Frédérick Gagnon

4. "America First": A Mexican Perspective
   on Trump's Presidency 87
   María Celia Toro

5. Trump's Presidency: United Kingdom
   Perspectives and Responses 119
   Charlie Whitham and Kevern Verney

6. Trump's Presidency: The "New Cold War"
   and US-Poland Security Ties 137
   Karol Bieniek and Grzegorz Nycz

7. The Trump Age of Uncertainty: Grounding
   Central East European-US Relations 157
   Bohdan Szklarski

8. The Trump Effect on Russian Foreign Policy 185
   Maciej Herbut and Karol Chwedczuk-Szulc

9. The Japanese Reaction to Trump's First Hundred Days 209
   Tetsuya Sahara

10. Trump's Presidency: Egypt and the Middle East 217
    Magda Shahin

11. Donald Trump and China 245
    Klaus Larres

12. Stillborn Optimism in Turkey:
    The Trump Presidency 271
    Mustafa Türkeş and Tolgahan Akdan

13. "Out of Africa": Trump's Early Impact
    on US-Africa Relations 291
    John J. Stremlau

14. Kazakhstan Looks at the United States
    under Donald J. Trump 315
    Scott Spehr and Aigul Adibayeva

    Index 331

    About the Contributors 339

PREFACE

> Donald Trump's election victory has alarmed the world: it heralds the end of business as usual in trade, security and much else. Just how serious are the challenges of the Trump era?
>
> Rauhala 2016[1]

Donald J. Trump's foreign policy rhetoric and actions become more understandable by reference to his personality traits, how he constructs his worldview, and his view of the world. He is self-centered and has a very fragile ego. He holds views very firmly, on the basis of what is useful for him to say. His ignorance of his own ignorance permits him to confidently assert "alternative facts" as truths, perhaps supported by conspiracy theories that cannot be negated. He is caught between delusion and denial. This permits a pragmatic approach to policy decision-making, one that makes his decisions impetuous, unpredictable, and certainly not underpinned by a set of well thought through set of principles. He entered the White House with a very naïve view of the office of the Presidency on the world stage. His view of the world reflects his bipolar moral compass, which abides no moral ambiguity; there are just "good" and "bad" *hombres*. This is reflected in his foreign policy agenda, which is aimed at implementing his signature campaign slogans: "America First" and "Make America Great Again."

Trump's campaign rhetoric catered to Americans comfortable with political and economic isolationism and certainly with no appetite for foreign military engagements. So, his foreign policy emphasis was on American isolationism—bilateralism replacing multilateralism—and on economic nationalism—fair and reciprocal trade replacing free trade. His foreign policy perspectives as president are the complete reverse of his campaign promises, particularly with regard to North Korea, China, Russia, Syria, and Mexico. He seems to have discovered that international relations is far more complex than he ever imagined; the world

---

[1] Retrieved from: https://www.project-syndicate.org/focal-points/trump-an-american-horror-story.

is too complex, too unpredictable, too interconnected and too multilateral for simple solutions to be able to solve the global and regional problems faced. It has become obvious that he is not really interested in delving too deeply into some of the substantive issues of international politics, particularly the prevailing quandaries in the East Asia, Middle East and North Africa, and Central and Eastern Europe—their dimensions, causes, implications, or methods of resolution. Why bother when simple solutions will suffice, for his purposes.

Trump's foreign policy objective seems to be the pursuit of American primacy and insistence on America's status and image as the leading world power in the economic, political, and military spheres. His desire is to project the image to his core supporters that it is his will that is directing this pursuit. His global vision, however, is limited to one simple personal desire: that he—and, of course, America—be treated with servile respect and deference. Some countries have already learned how to exploit his rather superficial presidential desires. He can be readily bought with the promise and prospect of some good short-term business deals and with the impression that his frequently impulsive and inaccurate foreign policy statements really matter and so are taken seriously.

Trump is seemingly unaware that if he wants to make America great again by implementing his signature American isolationism and economic nationalism policies, then any domestic economic gains achieved will be at the cost of abdicating its role as a global superpower and leader of the free world. The inevitable power vacuums he would leave by withdrawing from this interconnected and multilateral world would leave regional powers—would-be global powers—free to step into and pick up the pieces. Indeed, China and Russia are taking concrete steps to don the mantle of regional—if not global—responsibility. The status of the US as a global superpower is, of course, multidimensional, and will not disappear overnight—at the whim of a populist president—but it is under threat. The gradual decline of US influence on regional and global policies under Trump seems inevitable.

Much of the results of Trump's rhetoric and actions are, however, yet to materialize. While the worst has not happened, yet, uncertainty prevails—about American multilateral and bilateral security and trade commitments—with traditional allies and neighbor suffering anxiety as a consequence. Taking a position with respect to US foreign and trade policies has never been more difficult for any country. To the rest of the world, Trump is judged to be unpredictable, overhasty, and seemingly disinterested in including his international allies in his decisions, let alone reassuring or even justifying his actions to them. So, the world must come to terms with dealing with a non-traditional US president, one who does not abide by—even rejects—the traditional principles of international relations.

For the international community, dealing with President Trump begs a fundamental question: Does he still want to be a populist and isolationist president dismissive of American exceptionalism, given that his presidential legacy is contingent on achieving successes, which might be easier to achieve on the world stage rather than on a politically polarized domestic stage?

This book's goals are threefold:

- to present a diversity of foreign perspectives on Donald J. Trump and the key international dimensions of his presidential rhetoric and policy initiatives taken since he became president;
- to gauge the alarm, if any, created by the likely or possible impact of Trump presidential rhetoric and policy initiatives at the national level in the international community; and
- to identify the future challenges for the Trump administration that are imbedded in the national, regional, and international responses to the key international dimensions of the Trump presidential rhetoric and policy initiatives taken since he became president.

All editors have their debtors. First and foremost, we are indebted to our contributors who took up the challenge of writing to a predetermined framework. Without exception, they did so with good grace and enthusiasm. We encouraged them to reflect on, and address our goals in whatever way they consider appropriate. So, the chapters present a diversity of styles, voices, and ideas, while retaining a common focus. This difference of voices is, perhaps, an important part of what the book as a whole has to say. We must also thank the editorial team at Westphalia Press. Their professionalism is evidenced by the quality of the end product.

John Dixon and Max J. Skidmore
January 2018

1
DONALD J. TRUMP: HIS PUBLIC PERSONA, WORLDVIEW, AND VIEW OF THE WORLD

John Dixon

INTRODUCTION

Donald J. Trump was elected the 45th president of the United States (US) on November 8, 2016 and inaugurated on January 20. Like any US president, he does not govern alone, for that necessarily involves Congress and the federal executive, not to mention the federal judiciary. He has, nevertheless, considerable authority to make decisions and take actions. So, how he thinks about himself, others, and the world-at-large, and how he perceives and takes the meaning from reality as he sees it, are matters of importance. Trump's rhetoric and actions become more understandable, perhaps even more predictable, in the light of his personality and his worldview.

TRUMP'S PUBLIC PERSONALITY

A person's "[p]ersonality is that pattern of characteristic thoughts, feelings, and behaviors [personality traits] that distinguish one person from another and that persist over time and situations" (Phares and Chaplin 1997, 2). These personality traits influence a person's adaptive capacity in different situation (Allport 1937, Eysenck 1970). As Cattell (1965, 117–118) succinctly remarks, personality is "that which tells what [a person] will do when placed in a given situation." The major—Big 5—behavioral (observable) personality traits have been identified as (Digman 1990):

- *openness*, the extent of openness to new ideas and experiences;
- *conscientiousness*, the extent of carefulness and vigilance;
- *extraversion*, the extent of having a directing interests beyond self;
- *agreeableness*, the extent of having behavioral characteristics

that reflect kindness, sympathy, cooperativeness, and considerateness; and

- *neuroticism*, the extent to which feelings of anxiety, anger, envy, and guilt, and depressed moods are experienced.

The personality traits, discernible from the Trump's public behavior, reveal his public persona. However, one psychologist, Dr. Karl Albrecht[1] has said of Trump:

> Pundits, politicians, people who despise him, and even people who worship him can't seem to grasp the simple truth of this man, which is: **He Is Actually As Simple as He Appears**. He isn't "hard to figure out"—what you see is what you'll get (Albrecht 2017, emphasis in original).

Yet, it may well be that his public persona is a personality he deliberately seeks to portray, rather than being his private persona. As Vladimir Putin, the Russian President, is reported to have said after meeting Trump: "TV Trump is different than the real Trump."[2] Klapp (1964, 36) offers an explanation; a "leader" has to "typify" the wants and desires of his targeted audience, which, thereby, become symbolically significant. These typifications become an essential part of his Jungian "mask"—his front or guise—presented as his public persona for external consumption (Stevens 1990). Jung ([1934] 1981) noted that people with big egos relate to the world-at-large through a flexible public persona, elements of which may eventually be absorbed into their personal persona. The result can be a state of mind that is "utterly unconscious of any distinction between themselves and the world in which they live. They have little or no concept of themselves as beings distinct from what society [their publics] expects of them" (Dawson 1977, 267). The public Trump has, arguably, revealed the following personality traits.

Openness

The first personality trait is his low degree of *openness*, because he is reluctant to accept new ideas that are in conflict with, and so challenge, his

---

[1] See: https://www.psychologytoday.com/experts/karl-albrecht-phd.
[2] Retrieved from: http://www.bb unpicked, dissected, and judged c.co.uk/news/av/world-40545067/putin-tv-trump-is-different-than-real-trump.

own firmly held beliefs, for he does not permit himself any conscious self-doubt or any questioning that threatens his own understanding of world as he sees it. This includes his fantasies about his own brilliance. Indicative is his own assessment of his high IQ: "Sorry losers and haters, but my I.Q. is one of the highest—and you all know it! Please don't feel so stupid or insecure, it's not your fault" (Twitter, May 2013, cited in Piehler 2016, 11). Indeed,

> During the presidential campaign, Donald Trump liked to invoke his late uncle, MIT research scientist John Trump,[3] as evidence of the family's exceptional gene pool, proof should voters need it that Donald Trump is smart, like really smart.
>
> "It's in my blood," he says.[4]

That is as may be,[5] but undoubtedly, "he is sorely lacking in sophistication, knowledge of the world, understanding of government and a rudimentary grasp of economics."[6]

---

[3] See: https://www.aip.org/history-programs/niels-bohr-library/oral-histories/5062.

[4] Retrieved from: http://www.thedailybeast.com/the-good-trump-was-a-genius-and-a-gentleman.

[5] There are, however, said to be five laws of stupidity (Cipolla 1976):

- "A stupid person is a person who causes losses to another person or to a group of persons while himself deriving no gain and even possibly incurring losses."
- "The probability that a certain person be stupid is independent of any other characteristic of that person."
- "A stupid person is the most dangerous type of person."
- "Always and inevitably everyone underestimates the number of stupid individuals in circulation."
- "Non-stupid people always underestimate the damaging power of stupid individuals. In particular non-stupid people constantly forget that at all times and places and under any circumstances to deal and/or associate with stupid people always turns out to be a costly mistake."

Retrieved from: http://harmful.cat-v.org/people/basic-laws-of-human-stupidity/.

[6] Retrieved from: http://www.independent.co.uk/voices/donald-trump-dimmest-us-president-ever-personal-mobile-phone-number-security-concerns-a7766271.html.

Conscientiousness

The second personality trait is his low degree of *conscientiousness*, because he is inclined to act impulsively without deliberation, seemingly unable to resist temptations, urge or impulses even if they may ultimately hurt him or others. One of his biographers, Michael D'Antonio[7]—*Never Enough: Donald Trump and the Pursuit of Success*[8] (2015) and *The Truth about Donald Trump*[9] (2016)—has recently dubbed him the little boy president, because he "acts in a way that would be expected of a 6-year-old boy."[10] And as has been observed:

> When six-year old throws a tantrum because it does not get his own way, everyone except the child's parents may shrug and say thank god he's not my kid.
>
> When the President of the United States throws a tantrum, no one smiles. People tremble.[11]

And another media observation made after a presidential tantrum is even more colorful: "You feel like you've got to give the president of the United States a pacifier and a rattle and put him in the crib."[12] This is the president who told supporters in Youngstown, Ohio in late July.

> Sometimes, they say, 'He doesn't act presidential,' Trump said of his critics. And I say, hey look—great schools, smart guy—it's so easy to act presidential.' But that's not going to get it done. ... With the exception of the late, great Abraham Lincoln, I can be more presidential than any president that's ever held this office. That I can tell you. It's real easy.

---

[7] See: http://www.huffingtonpost.com/author/michael-dantonio.

[8] See: https://www.barnesandnoble.com/w/never-enough-michael-dantonio/1121862017.

[9] See: https://us.macmillan.com/thetruthabouttrump/michaeldantonio/9781250105288/.

[10] Retrieved from: http://google.com/newsstand/s/CBIwkKjv8jQ.

[11] Retrieved from: https://newsstand.google.com/articles/CAIiEGtR133yHzrVaVkPOfeYteIqFQgEKg0IACoGCAowrqkBMKBFMKGBAg.

[12] Retrieved from: http://www.huffingtonpost.com/entry/trump-pacifier-rattle_us_591655f3e4b0031e737dc72e.

Perhaps he is being "modern-day presidential."[13]

Trump gets bored easily, and so has very limited ability to subdue his impulsiveness in order to achieve longer-term goals.[14] Of Trump, Albrecht (2017) suggests:

- He has a very short attention span (Attention Deficit Disorder[15]).
- He is given to acting on his first reaction (Low Impulse Control[16]).
- He might even have a limited proficiency in reading,[17] spelling,[18] and writing[19] (dyslexia[20]).

---

[13] Retrieved from: http://www.bbc.co.uk/news/av/world-us-canada-40746735/do-trump-voters-think-he-s-presidential.

[14] See: http://www.msnbc.com/morning-joe/watch/-no-impulse-control-trump-s-focus-on-the-short-game-891026499969.

[15] See: http://www.healthline.com/health/adhd/difference-between-add-and-adhd. See also: http://www.huffingtonpost.com/george-sachs-psyd/unfit-unfocused-or-is-tru_b_11568002.html; https://www.quora.com/Does-Donald-Trump-have-ADHD.

[16] See: https://www.mentalhelp.net/articles/defining-features-of-personality-disorders-impulse-control-problems/. See also: https://www.entrepreneur.com/article/283480; https://www.washingtonpost.com/business/donald-trumps-most-enduring--and-unbefitting--trait/2016/07/15/f5684848-488b-11e6-acbc-4d4870a079da_story.html?utm_term=.a37e9458a458; http://www.msnbc.com/morning-joe/watch/-no-impulse-control-trump-s-focus-on-the-short-game-891026499969; https://www.ft.com/content/1cf9a2fe-8738-11e6-a75a-0c4dce033ade?mhq5j=e3.

[17] It is known, however, that Trump is not much of a reader. In 2016 he claimed his favorite book was Earnest Hemmingway's All Quiet on the Western Front, although in 2015 it was the Bible. When asked in an interview, prior to becoming president, the name of the last book he read his response was "I read passages, I read areas, chapters, I don't have the time." Retrieved from: https://newrepublic.com/minutes/133566/donald-trump-doesnt-read-books.

[18] Was "covfevfe"—probably "coverage"—in a Trump tweet in late May a typing error or a spelling error? See: http://www.independent.co.uk/news/world/americas/us-politics/trump-ce-tweet-sean-spicer-president-small-group-explanation-a7766141.html; see also: https://www.wired.com/2017/06/asked-lawyers-vet-trumps-controversial-tweets/; http://www.politico.com/story/2016/01/trump-liberty-university-bible-217938.

[19] "It appears that his only out-bound [written] communication channel is Twitter [limited, then. to 140 characters]" (Albrecht 2017). As Trump asserts: "I'm the Ernest Hemingway of 140 characters [Tweets]" (Washington Times, November 2015, cited in Piehler 2016, 35).

[20] This a general term for disorders that involve difficulties in acquiring and

Such deficiencies "would have a huge impact on the way he processes information—and the way others communicate with him. I don't believe he uses a computer or email, or reads very much (his ghost-writers [of his 15 authored books] report that he hasn't read the books they wrote for him)" (Albrecht 2017).

Trump evidences little concerned with any unintended or unexpected consequences of his decisions, as he is indifferent about how they affect others, or, indeed, even himself. He believes that the rules, laws, and norms that apply others do not apply to him. "From his ongoing refusal to release his tax returns to his stonewalling of requests to disclose visitor logs at the White House, he has indicated normal rules do not apply to him."[21] So, they are meaningless and do not deserve forethought. So, nothing stops him doing what he really wants to do. He lacks any sense of remorse, shame, or guilt.

Extraversion

The third personality trait is his low degree of *extraversion*, because his dominant ego has created a grandiose sense of self[22]: as he has said: "The show is 'Trump'. And it is sold-out performances everywhere" (*Playboy*, March 1990, cited in Piehler 2016, 11). This is further evidenced by his proclivity for illeism: "Trump talking about himself in the third person reflects his perception of himself as being a larger-than-life character in the world stage," which is the judgment of Kim Schneiderman,[23] a psychotherapist.[24] John Altman, a contemporary American thriller writer,[25]

---

processing language, which interferes with an individual's ability in read or interpret words, letters, and other symbols, but do not affect general intelligence. See: http://dyslexia.yale.edu/Stu_whatisdyslexia.htm; https://dyslexiaida.org/definition-of-dyslexia/. See also: https://www.youtube.com/watch?v=Lz4gpBH2n-E; https://www.youtube.com/watch?v=bd79UsXSLWg; https://www.youtube.com/watch?v=KXGuJlTVXfw; https://www.youtube.com/watch?v=NXUhcVWOyuI.

[21] Retrieved from: http://www.bbc.co.uk/news/world-us-canada-39724045.

[22] Rosenberg (1979) defined the self-concept as "the totality of the individual's thoughts and feelings having reference to himself [sic] as an object."

[23] See: http://stepoutofyourstory.com/.

[24] See: http://www.bbc.com/news/magazine-33943762.

[25] See: http://www.johnaltman.net/author.html.

in the same vein, considers that Trump is stranger than any fictional character a writer would dare create:

> ... the Age of Trump challenges writers of fiction, and particularly writers of political fiction, to produce work that meets this standard.
>
> For starters: Any day's news supplies plots so fantastic that most make-believe story lines pale in comparison. Elections stolen in collusion with the Kremlin? A White House spokesperson endorsing the Orwellian concept of "alternative facts"[26]? Another denying that Hitler used chemical weapons against his own people? A president firing the Director of the FBI—even as the agency investigates charges of Russian interference in that president's election?
>
> ... And Trump's version of reality feels palpably farfetched. Using a patio at a Florida golf club as a makeshift situation room during a North Korean missile test—as a guest posts pics to Facebook? Really? An author describing this scene risks taxing suspension of disbelief beyond repair. Real and plausible are not the same thing.[27]

Trump is ever likely to exaggerate his achievements and talents, as he is publicly preoccupied with his fantasies about his success, power, and brilliance, even his handsomeness and physical attributes.[28] His domi-

---

[26] This is a reference to Kellyanne Conway, Trump's White House Counselor, who used this phrase, which she considers "a mistake that she has not been allowed to 'brush off.'" Retrieved from: https://www.theguardian.com/us-news/2017/mar/03/kellyanne-conway-alternative-facts-mistake-oscars. See also: https://www.nytimes.com/2017/05/15/business/media/mika-joe-kellyanne-conway.html.

[27] Retrieved from: https://newsstand.google.com/articles/CAIiED4_9nKvcLElp6Rl-mPUtRgqFwgEKg4IACoGCAowjKxcMOvhCzC-kLcB. Definitely see also: https://www.theguardian.com/commentisfree/2017/may/25/is-this-real-life-or-is-this-a-cabaret-of-the-von-trump-family-on-tour.

[28] Retrieved from: http://www.telegraphco.uk/news/2017/05/29/comedy-writer-blocked-trump-gives-hilarious-account-social-media/.

nant requirement is for constant acclaim; his perpetual fear is the loss of self-esteem. But, as Ellis (2005, 3) notes, to

> self-esteem one's self on a global measure of self-worth is unhealthy and dysfunctional. First, it is irrational because there are no objective bases for making global evaluations of one's self. Second, focusing on one's self-esteem will make a person vulnerable to life's little setbacks, rejections or mistakes, so that even people with generally high self-esteem may be predisposed to blow these out of proportion with resultant negative consequences. Third, a concern about self-worth can lead to a preoccupation with comparing oneself with others at the expense of engaging in healthy and productive endeavors and pursuits.

Trump considers everything in life to be a game that he must win—even handshakes.[29] And most importantly, his perceived competitors must definitely lose. So, at the interpersonal level, competition inevitably overwhelms cooperation, particularly when he concludes that he must adopt a hypercompetitive stance toward others—involving incessant and indiscriminate competition—in order to attain personal superiority—power—over them: "The psychic result ... is a diffuse hostile tension between individuals" (Horney 1937, 285–286).

So, Trump's disposition toward interpersonally hostile hyper-competiveness justifies him cheating, lying, stealing, perhaps even using—or encouraging others to use—violence. Adler ([1933] 1973) saw this striving for personal superiority in every area of a person's life giving rise to a destructive lifestyle, one that provides fertile grounds for neurosis.

Trump is also unable to accept responsibility for his actions, so he seeks to shift blame to others for any adverse outcomes his actions may

---

[29] French President Emmanuel Macron bested Trump in their first handshake in Brussels, which apparently irritated Trump. See: https://www.vice.com/en_us/article/j5xq3d/a-frenchmans-firm-handshake-may-have-doomed-the-paris-deal-vgtrn.

cause. He is a convincing—pathological—liar who finds it almost impossible to be consistently truthful.[30] As Professor Dan P. McAdam[31] (Psychology, Northwestern University) has observed: "One possible yield [from Trump's public personality traits] is an energetic, activist president who has a less than cordial relationship with the truth."[32] This makes Trump unreliable and unpredictable, evidencing no commitment to fulfilling or honoring any obligations and assurances he makes, for if he later decides that there is no benefit to him from following through, he will not do so. He will, of course, never apologize; in his own words: "I think apologizing's a great thing, but you have to be wrong. I will absolutely apologize, sometime in the hopefully distant future, if I'm ever wrong" (*The Tonight Show*, September 2015, cited in Piehler 2016, 11).

Agreeableness

The fourth personality trait is his low degree of *agreeableness*, because he considers himself to be superior, which makes him arrogant and conceited:

- "Some people cast shadows [as I do], and other people choose to live in those shadows" (*New York Times*, September 2005, cited in Piehler 2016, 20).
- "You have to treat [women] like shit" (*New York Magazine*, November 1992, cited in Piehler 2016, 117).
- "Cause [sic] I like kids. I mean, I won't do anything to take care of them. I'll supply funds and she [my wife] will take care of the kids. It's not like I'm gonna be walking the kids down Central Park" (Howard Stern Show, 2005, cited in Piehler 2016, 117).

---

[30] See, for example: http://edition.cnn.com/2017/08/03/politics/donald-trump-mexico-boy-scouts-lies/index.html); http://www.politico.com/magazine/story/2017/01/donald-trump-lies-liar-effect-brain-214658.

[31] See: http://www.psychology.northwestern.edu/people/faculty/core/profiles/dan-mcadams.html.

[32] Retrieved from: http://www.theatlantic.com/magazine/archive/2016/06/the-mind-of-donald-trump/480771/.

He can be charming, but behind that facade he is covertly domineering and manipulative. He probably has few intimate relationships and trusts very few people (Albrecht 2017). He expects to be recognized as being superior even without the achievements that warrant that presumption. He demands unquestioning—but unreciprocated—loyalty and full compliance with his wishes, for he does not recognize other people's rights. It seems that he prefers to surround "himself with dim yes men who know little more than he and, in any event, tremble at the prospect of correcting their 'Dear Leader.'"[33]

He presumes that he has a right to manipulate others to get what he wants. He can be envious of important others, believing them to be envious of him. He is unwilling—perhaps unable—to recognize the needs of others and to understand and share their feelings and emotions. This makes him callous and lacking in empathy.[34] He has a limited range or depth of feelings, in spite of displaying signals that suggest he is open and gregarious. This makes him emotionally shallow, for when showing what seems to be warmth, joy, love, and compassion it is feigned and serves only his ulterior motives. This enables him to see others as exploitable opportunities.

Neuroticism

The fifth personality trait is his high degree of *neuroticism*. This is because he is paranoid[35], for he becomes upset or emotional when his

---

[33] Retrieved from: http://www.independent.co.uk/voices/donald-trump-dimmest-us-president-ever-personal-mobile-phone-number-security-concerns-a7766271.html.

[34] See: https://www.psychologytoday.com/basics/empathy.

[35] Those with a paranoid personality disorder "are preoccupied with unjustified doubts about the loyalty or trustworthiness of others," and they are "reluctant to confide in others and tend to blame them and hold grudges even when they themselves are at fault" (Davison and Neale 2001, 360). It "involves intense anxious or fearful feelings and thoughts often related to persecution, threat, or conspiracy. ... Paranoia can become delusions, when irrational thoughts and beliefs become so fixed that nothing (including contrary evidence) can convince a person that what they think or feel is not true." Retrieved from: http://www.mentalhealthamerica.net/conditions/paranoia-and-delusional-disorders.

all-too-fragile ego is threatened.³⁶ So, those who threatened his ego cannot be trusted. Trump's inner feelings seem to fluctuate uncontrollably, driven by his publicly well-suppressed self-doubts and his enviousness of significant others who threaten his vanity, both of which feed his hyper-competitiveness. As Goethe remarked in his classic *The Sorrows of Young Werther* ([1749] 2011, 56–57): "ill-humour arises from an inward consciousness of our own want of merit, from a discontent which ever accompanies that envy which vanity engenders." Trump lives perpetually on the edge—tense, nervous, or irritable—so verbal outbursts and punishments are normal. He has poor behavioral control.

Trump is, then, self-centered, with a strong sense of his own importance, albeit with a fragile ego. This fragility demands that he receives constant expressions of recognition, praise, and appreciation, and unquestioning compliance with his wishes. Criticism—particularly when it is expressed as humor, irony, exaggeration, or ridicule³⁷—must, at all costs, be stopped, where possible,³⁸ otherwise denigrated. Inevitably, this involves him fighting back hard by means of notoriously childish twitter retorts that often involved schoolyard insults that only revealed his immaturity not his strength. He has resorted to banning from accessing his twitter account those he considered who have "replied to his tweets with mocking or critical comments.³⁹ This includes a person who accused him "of having a 'small willy [penis].'"⁴⁰

---

36   See: http://www.independent.co.uk/news/world-0/donald-trump-dangerous-mental-illness-yale-psychiatrist-conference-us-president-unfit-james-gartner-a7694316.html.
37   See: http://edition.cnn.com/2017/04/30/opinions/trump-whcd-contrast-opinion-obeidallah/index.html; see, particularly: http://edition.cnn.com/2013/02/06/showbiz/trump-bill-maher-suit/.
38   In Iran a cartoon contest has been held to mock Trump. See: http://www.independent.co.uk/arts-entertainment/art/news/iran-holds-donald-trump-cartoon-contest-a7822046.html.
39   Retrieved from: http://www.bbc.co.uk/news/world-us-canada-40577858.
40   Retrieved from: http://www.telegraph.co.uk/news/2017/05/29/comedy-writer-blocked-trump-gives-hilarious-account-social-media/.

Speculations

His mental health has been the subject of speculation[41] by numerous mental health professionals. Professor Dan P. McAdam, a psychiatrist, has observed: "Donald Trump's basic personality traits suggest a presidency that could be highly combustible .... Tough. Bellicose. Threatening. Explosive."[42] This is all very much in evidence.[43] To some Trump observers,[44] his public persona evidences personality traits that can be associated with those of a narcissist[45], a sociopath[46], and even a psycho-

---

[41] For a discussion of the appropriateness of such presidential speculation, see: https://newsstand.google.com/articles/CAIiEOiA5NGuxPeSyFSEWtih b7wqGQgEKhAIACoHCAowocv1CjCSptoCMKrUpgU.

[42] Retrieved from: http://www.theatlantic.com/magazine/archive/2016/06/the-mind-of-donald-trump/480771/.

[43] See, for example: http://www.mercurynews.com/2017/08/16/jackie-speier-calls-for-trumps-removal-from-office-under-25th-amendment/; http://money.cnn.com/2017/08/20/media/trump-carl-bernstein-reliable-sources/index.html.

[44] See, for example: https://www.theatlantic.com/magazine/archive/2016/06/the-mind-of-donald-trump/480771/; https://www.nytimes.com/2017/02/17/opinion/is-it-time-to-call-trump-mentally-ill.html; http://www.zerohedge.com/news/2017-04-22/yale-psychiatrists-just-warned-there-something-seriously-wrong-trump; http://www.theblaze.com/news/2017/04/24/psychiatry-experts-claim-that-trump-is-unfit-for-presidency-due-to-dangerous-mental-illness/. For international media speculation see: http://www.bbc.com/news/world-us-canada-38881469; http://www.bbc.com/news/world-us-can71; http://google.com/newsstand/s/CBIwjfyhqjQ; https://www.indy100.com/article/keith-olbermann-donald-trump-psychopath-test-results-gq-resistance-webseries-7657321?utmsource=indy&utm_medium=top5&utm_campaign=i100; http://www.nydailynews.com/opinion/ex-trump-executive-knew-ill-35-years-article-1.2959293; http://google.com/newsstand/s/CBIwzteIzDQ; http://www.salon.com/2017/05/25/psychiatrist-bandy-lee-we-have-an-obligation-to-speak-about-donald-trumps-mental-health-issues-our-survival-as-a-species-may-be-at-stake/.

[45] This is a person with a narcissistic personality disorder. See: https://www.psychologytoday.com/blog/communication-success/201409/10-signs-youre-in-relationship-narcissist; http://www.mayoclinic.org/diseases-conditions/narcissistic-personality-disorder/basics/symptoms/con-20025568; http://dsm.psychiatryonline.org/doi/book/10.1176/appi.books.9780890425596.

[46] This is a person with an antisocial personality disorder. See: https://www.psychologytoday.com/basics/psychopathy; https://www.psychologytoday.com/articles/201305/how-spot-sociopath; http://www.nhs.uk/Conditions/antisocial-personality-disorder/Pages/Introduction.aspx; http://www.

path[47]. Hara Estroff Marano,[48] the Editor at Large of *Psychology Today*, has concluded:

> Donald Trump may or may not be mentally ill. He may or may not have an organic brain disease. Despite those unknowns, a group of prominent mental health professionals today [20 April] agreed that they have an ethical obligation to expose to the public every instance of reality distortion, impulsive decision-making, and violation of presidential norms of behaviors that singularize the Trump presidency.[49]

Indeed, some 60,000 mental health professionals have publicly declared that Trump has a "serious mental illness."[50] Their petition, addressed to US Senator Chuck Schumer[51] (Democrat-New York),[52] declares:

healthyplace.com/personality-disorders/sociopath/signs-of-a-sociopath-are-big-time-scary/; http://www.mcafee.cc/Bin/sb.html; http://www.mayoclinic.org/diseases-conditions/antisocial-personality-disorder/home/ovc-20198975.

[47] This is a person with a psychopathic personality disorder. See: https://www.psychologytoday.com/blog/communication-success/201409/10-signs-youre-in-relationship-narcissist; http://www.mayoclinic.org/diseases-conditions/narcissistic-personality-disorder/basics/symptoms/con-20025568; http://dsm.psychiatryonline.org/doi/book/10.1176/appi.books.9780890425596; see https://www.psychologytoday.com/basics/psychopathy. See also: https://www.psychologytoday.com/articles/201305/how-spot-sociopath; http://www.nhs.uk/Conditions/antisocial-personality-disorder/Pages/Introduction.aspx; http://www.healthyplace.com/personality-disorders/sociopath/signs-of-a-sociopath-are-big-time-scary/; http://www.mcafee.cc/Bin/sb.html; http://www.mayoclinic.org/diseases-conditions/antisocial-personality-disorder/home/ovc-20198975.

[48] See: https://www.bookbrowse.com/biographies/index.cfm/author_number/1554/hara-estroff-marano.

[49] Retrieved from: https://www.psychologytoday.com/blog/brainstorm/201704/shrinks-define-dangers-trump-presidency. See also: https://thepsychologist.bps.org.uk/volume-30/march-2017/psychologists-and-donald-trump.

[50] Retrieved from: https://xk.psychologytoday.com/blog/me-we/201708/60000-psychologists-say-trump-has-serious-mental-illness; see also VXXQQhttps://newsstand.google.com/articles/CAIiEB2nKumhDQJZeyd_7zAEfOQqGAgEKg8IACoHCAowSvrMATC_9SQwxbyWAw; http://www.nydailynews.com/news/politics/shrinks-break-silence-president-trump-exhibits-traits-m-article-1.2957688.

[51] See: https://www.schumer.senate.gov/.

[52] See: https://www.forbes.com/sitesemilywillingham/2017/02/19/psychologist

> We, the undersigned mental health professionals (please state your degree), believe in our professional judgment that Donald Trump manifests a serious mental illness that renders him psychologically incapable of competent discharging the duties of President of the United States. And we respectfully request that you remove the powers and duties of his office.[53]

A debatable issue is whether psychiatrists should speak out against Trump, despite the Goldwater rule[54] in their professional code of conduct? Opinions differ. Dr John Zinner,[55] a practicing psychiatrist, has reportedly suggested:

> ... that, as doctors, who swear an oath to protect their patients, psychiatrists have an obligation to speak out about the menace posed by Trump's mental health. "It's my view that Trump has a narcissistic personality disorder," Zinner said later. "Trump is deluded and compulsive. He has no conscience." He said that psychiatrists have a constructive role to play in advising policymakers to add checks on the President's control over nuclear weapons. "That supersedes the Goldwater rule," he said. "It's an existential survival issue."[56]

Professor Emeritus, Allen Frances[57] (Psychiatry, Duke University School of Medicine), who wrote the defining clinical characteristics for narcissistic personality disorder, has said of Trump:

-calls-on-colleagues-to-sign-petition-for-trumps-removal/#35cd8e9e64f3.

[53] Retrieved from: https://www.change.org/p/trump-is-mentally-ill-and-must-be-removed.

[54] This ethical rule forbids members of the American Psychiatric Association from publicly commenting on "the psyches of living public figures whom they have not personally examined." See: http://www.newyorker.com/magazine/2017/05/22/should-psychiatrists-speak-out-against-trump.

[55] See: https://npidb.org/doctors/allopathic_osteopathic_physicians/psychiatry_2084p0800x/1710044342.aspx.

[56] Retrieved from: http://www.newyorker.com/magazine/2017/05/22/should-psychiatrists-speak-out-against-trump.

[57] See: http://www.psychiatrictimes.com/authors/allen-frances-md.

> He may be a world-class narcissist, but this doesn't make him mentally ill, because he does not suffer from the distress and impairment required to diagnose mental disorder. Mr Trump causes severe distress rather than experiencing it and has been richly rewarded, rather than punished, for his grandiosity, self-absorption and lack of empathy.[58]

And:

> You don't have to be a psychoanalyst to understand Trump. He's the most transparent human being who ever lived. Giving it a name doesn't explain it or change it.[59]

Penultimately, in Trump own words: "Who knows what's in the deepest parts of my mind" (*Buzzfeed*, February 2014, cited in Piehler 2016, 37). And finally, his biographer, Michael D'Antonio, has recently remarked: "Donald Trump is stuck in his own skull ... It's a very cluttered place to be, a fine-tuned machine spewing a torrent of chaos, cruelty, confusion, farce and transfixing craziness."[60]

The Trump's policy rhetoric and actions become even more understandable, perhaps even more predictable, in the light of his worldview.

TRUMP'S WORLDVIEW

A worldview provides the lens through which a person interrogates and judges social reality (Dixon 2003, Dixon, Dogan and Sanderson 2009). It provides insights into how a person prefers to think about the actuality of Marcel's (1952, 164) "world of persons"—the social world or

---

[58] Retrieved from: https://www.nytimes.com/2017/02/14/opinion/an-eminent-psychiatrist-demurs-on-trumps-mental-state.html?mcubz=3&mtrref=www.google.co.uk&gwh=3B404D86E45BF32481BF6863B0FA1708&gwt=pay&assetType=opinion.

[59] Retrieved from: http://www.newyorker.com/news/daily-comment/donald-trumps-state-of-mind-and-ours.

[60] Retrieved from: https://www.nytimes.com/2017/02/18/opinion/sunday/trapped-in-trumps-brain.html.

social reality. It demarcates his preferred social-reality disposition, comprising a set of firmly held propositions about

- how best to describe, explain, and understand social reality (his epistemological disposition), and
- how best to explain and predict the social actions of others and self (his ontological disposition).

Trump's Epistemological Disposition: Existential Epistemology

The Trump's epistemological disposition is clearly grounded in subjectivity (hermeneutic epistemology) based on self-knowledge (existential epistemology). To Sartre ([1946] 1973, 23, 26, 44), this truth grounded "upon pure subjectivity—upon the Cartesian 'I think Thus, "we must begin from the subjective."

Trump individually constructs the meaning and significance of social reality on the basis of pure existential subjectivity. So, in the Nietzschean nihilist tradition,[61] he holds that is there no "objectively true" social reality. Social knowledge—facts about the world of persons—is entirely subjective, and so is relative to the vagaries of a person's thoughts and experiences (Nietzsche ([1886] 1998).[62] This is a foundational presumption of existential epistemology (Kierkegaard [1846] 1941, Nietzsche [1886] 1998, Schopenhauer 1818/1844] 1969). Kierkegaard's related propositions were that "in regard to every other reality external to the individual it can only be known through 'thinking it'" (Stack 1977, 197, n. 19), and that "existence, in its true or authentic form, is a subjective teleological activity for man, an activity characterized by dialectical tension and an intensification of subjectivity" (Stack 1977, 199, n. 40). Thus, the foundation of knowledge is the individual's self-knowledge (Kierkegaard [1846] 1941, Schopenhauer [1818/1844] 1969). The world is, then, a manifestation of will—"the world is my idea" (Schopenhauer

---

[61] Nietzsche, according to Stack (1977, 17), saw nihilism's central concept being that "existence must not be interpreted in terms of 'purpose', 'unity', 'Being', or 'truth.'" For the Nietzschean nihilist there is no 'true' world at all.

[62] This can be extended to the radical form of solipsism, which that holds that nothing at all exists apart from one's own mind and mental states (Russell 1948, Part III, Ch. 2).

[1818/1844] 1969, 1) thus "no will: no idea, no world" (Schopenhauer [1851] 1970, 56). This doctrine of the primacy of will means that what a person believes to be real is the basis for reasoning. The real social world is, therefore, the self who has an idea. All social knowledge is based on immediate personal experience: "Our existence has no foundation on which to rest except the transient present" (Schopenhauer [1851] 1970, 52). To Sartre ([1946] 1973, 26) "we must begin from the subjective [because it] is the absolute truth of consciousness as it attains to itself" (Sartre [1946] 1973, 26). Thus, social reality contains a multitude of subjective truths grounded in first-person mental discernments—intuition,[63] common sense,[64] or revealed wisdom[65] (Warnock 1970, 8-9). Social knowledge is, then, ultimately unique to the individual, such self-knowledge requires the recognition of past determinants, the acknowledgement of present concerns, and alertness to future possibilities (Heidegger [1927] 1967).

Trump is epistemologically elastic. He happily blurs, when personally convenient, the boundaries between:

- *Truths*: propositions that are objectively true—*a posteriori* (empirical) or *a priori* (logical) knowledge (Kant [1781-1787] 1956).
- *Beliefs*: propositions firmly held on grounds short of proof (Mill [1843] 1988).
- *Humbug*: propositions that are deceptive misrepresentations—unavoidable whenever a person is required to talk without knowledge—but just short of deliberate lying—achieved by the use of pretentious words or deeds to express thoughts, feelings, or attitudes (Black 1983).
- *Bullshit*: propositions that are intended to deliberately de-

---

[63] Bergson saw intuition is as an "instinct that has become disinterested, self-, and capable of reflecting upon its object and of enlarging it indefinitely" (quoted in Russell 1946, 821).

[64] These are beliefs that come naturally to mind to all people, as responsible agents, based on memory, reason, moral sense, and taste—carry their own authority, despite accepted perceptual fallibilities, because people, proceeding cautiously, are capable of knowing the world (Grave 1960, Moore 1959).

[65] This is Aquinas' ([1259-64] 1905) truths of revelation: "Wisdom ... conferred by God as a particular endowment" (Rofe 2001).

ceive—in order to misrepresent reality—by conveying false impressions, so as to divert attention away from the alternative accounts of that reality—including the correct one (Frankfurt 2005)—the truth-value of which can be grounded in the charisma of the speaker (Baggini 2017, 22).

- *Lies*: propositions that are known to be not matters of empirical or logical fact. Yet, as Baggini (2017, 102) notes, "falsehood masquerades as truth by retreating into incomplete networks of beliefs where convenient facts are overstated and inconvenient ones ignore or just simply denied." And then there are lies made grand or noble by their civic purpose—the noble lie (Schofield 2007)—"[a] falsehood propagated to serve a higher goal. Sometimes, however, the purpose of such lies is self-interest" (Baggini 2017, 35).

On this, Bacon ([1597–1625] 1972, 7) wryly observed:

> Doth any man doubt, that if there were taken out of men's minds vain opinions, flattering hopes, false valuations, imaginations as one would, and the like, but it would leave the minds of a number of men poor shrunken things, full of melancholy and indisposition, and unpleasing to themselves.

Trump is an intuitive, right-brained thinker.[66] He has the capacity to deny the factuality of information that threaten his fantasies:

> Among his recent fantasies, he asserted that the investigation into possible Russian interference in the 2016 election, headed by the special counsel Robert Mueller,[67] was "not an investigation"; he ventured that Medicaid funding "actually goes up" under a Senate bill that would have cut it sharply; and he said that he had signed more bills "than any President, ever," ignoring Bill Clinton, Jimmy Carter, Harry Truman, and F.D.R., all of whom, the Times noted, had signed more at this point in their

---

[66] See: http://brainmadesimple.com/left-and-right-hemispheres.html.

[67] See: http://www.newyorker.com/news/news-desk/robert-mueller-to-head-russia-trump-probe-first-thoughts.

terms. And finally, this week, Trump seemed to mistake a visit to a crowd of children and teen-agers for a political rally, reminiscing with an audience of Boy Scouts about an election-night event that probably happened past their bedtime: "Do you remember that incredible night with the maps, and the Republicans are red and the Democrats are blue, and that map was so red, it was unbelievable, and they didn't know what to say?[68]

Further evidenced is his insistence, without providing any confirming evidence, that he really won the presidential popular vote—because, he alleged, there was widespread voter fraud orchestrated by the Democrats—and that the former President Barak Obama used the Federal Bureau of Investigation (FBI), or even a British intelligence agency[69]—the Government Communications Headquarters (GCHQ)[70]—to tap his Trump Tower communications system. In his own words: "Terrible! Just found out that Obama had my 'wires tapped' in Trump Tower just before the victory. Nothing found. This is McCarthyism[71]!" (Tweet, March 4, 2017).[72] Of course, as Congressman Ted Lieu (Democrat-California) tweeted: "If wiretap was on Trump Tower, that means [federal] judge found probable cause phone lines used by agents of foreign power."[73]

Trump is, thus, forever caught between delusion and denial.[74] As Kierkegaard (1847, quoted in Marino 2001, 12) remarked: "Indeed, one can be deceived in many ways; one can be deceived in believing what is

---

[68] Retrieved from: http://www.newyorker.com/news/daily-comment/donald-trumps-state-of-mind-and-ours.

[69] See: http://google.com/newsstand/s/CBIw6cLfzDQ; but see http://google.com/newsstand/s/CBIwkv7ezTQ.

[70] See: https://www.gchq.gov.uk/features/welcome-to-gchq.

[71] See: https://www.britannica.com/topic/McCarthyism.

[72] Retrieved from: https://www.theguardian.com/us-news/2017/mar/17/white-house-will-not-be-repeat-claims-gchq-spied-trump-. But see: https://www.indy100.com/article/donald-trump-accuses-barack-obama-wiretapping-twitter-waking-up-breitbart-7611011.

[73] Retrieved from: https://twitter.com/tedlieu/status/838046638065123328.

[74] But his fans do not seem to care if he lies. See: https://www.debatepolitics.com/general-political-discussion/245159-do-trump-supporters-care-if-he-lies-them-29.html.

untrue, but on the other hand, one is also deceived in not believing what is true." This is because "Where ignorance is bliss, 'tis folly to be wise" (Thomas Gray,[75] *Ode to a Distant Prospect of Eton College* (1742)).[76] This means, despite

> [s]itting atop arguably the great resource on the planet—the body of knowledge retained by American government experts on everything from economics to medicine to military history—he remains blissfully ignorant on a range of subjects [worryingly, including American history[77]].[78]

And, of course, there is the convenient willed ignorance: "I've got my mind made up, so don't confuse me with the facts."[79]

Trump's flexibility with the truth suggests he is intellectually shallow. Intelligent he may well be, but he evidences little interest in theories, doctrines, policies, and plans. He disinclination to be truthful certainly makes him unpredictable, even unprincipled. The risk he takes is that people will eventually stop believing what he says. Indeed, some have said his credibility crisis had arrived less than three months after taking office,[80] with a majority of Americans even then thinking that Trump does not keeps his promises.[81]

---

[75] See: https://www.poetryfoundation.org/poets/thomas-gray.
[76] Retrieved from: https://www.poetryfoundation.org/poems-and-poets/poems/detail/44301.
[77] See: http://edition.cnn.com/2017/08/19/politics/trump-history-facts-historians/index.html; https://www.justplainpolitics.com/showthread.php?83637-Trump-s-muddled-view-on-American-history; https://congressionalblackcaucus.com/trumps-muddled-view-of-american-history/; http://www.dispatch.com/news/20170611/is-president-trumps-foreign-policy-strategic-or-simply-muddled.
[78] Retrieved from: http://www.independent.co.uk/voices/donald-trump-dimmest-us-president-ever-personal-mobile-phone-number-security-concerns-a7766271.html.
[79] See: http://www.iep.utm.edu/fallacy/#Willed%20ignorance.
[80] See: https://www.theatlantic.com/politics/archive/2017/03/trumps-credibility-crisis-arrives/520347/?utm_source=feed.
[81] See: http://www.gallup.com/poll/208640/majority-no-longer-thinks-trump-keeps-promises.aspx?g_source=position1&g_medium=related&g_campaign=tiles.

Trump's Ontological Disposition: Existential Individualism

Trump's ontological disposition is clearly grounded in agency ontology, in recognition that individuals are self-determining agents who are ultimately accountable for their own actions. They are free to determine and control their own actions and so "could have chosen or acted otherwise" (Kane 2002, 5). His intuitive proclivity is toward existential individualism. This is the proposition that a person is free to exercise his will to determine his own destiny and character. So, he has the existential freedom to be who he wants to be, and so to be able to engage with social reality—as he imagines it to be—in any way he chooses. Trump, by his drive and determination to pursue whatever goals he sets himself, is exercising Nietzsche's instinct for freedom ([1887] 2006)—his incarnate will-to-power ([1895] 1967)—thereby making possible the Sartrian proposition of seeing "a possibility as my possibility" (Sartre [1943] 1957, 34). So, he is seeking to live in the way he finds most valid and fulfilling.

Insightfully, Frankl ([1948/1975] 2000, 138), an existential psychologist, argued that to be able to exercise the will-to-power requires a person to overcome "a certain inner condition, namely, the feeling of inferiority ... by developing the striving for superiority." A sense of who a person is—and can become—is grounded in the existential notion that an individual simply exists—"existence comes before essence" (Sartre [1946] 1973, 44):

> Man simply is. Not that he is simply what he conceives himself to be, but he is what he wills, and as he conceives himself after already existing—as he wills to be after that leap toward existence. Man is nothing else but that which he makes of himself (Sartre [1946] 1973, 28).

To May (1967, 8), "the human dilemma is that which arises out of man's capacity to experience himself as both subject and object at the same time," a product of simultaneously living in a world of biological needs and drives, a world of interrelationships, and a world of self-awareness and self-relatedness. It is, then, up to him to decide his own fate, and so determines his own destiny—his purpose for being.

A person searching for his own authentic self-identity is required to have what Camus ([1942] 2005, 55, emphasis in original) called "the freedom *to be*." To accomplish this search, according to Sartre ([1943] 1957), requires him to achieve a synthetic unity between his capacity to transcend his knowledge of self in the contemporaneous now—who self is now—so as to be able to project himself into future unrealized possibilities—who self might become—and his knowledge of what it is about him that can be changed as necessary in order to exploit those future possibilities. Exercising the necessary free will to achieve this authenticity involves him engaging in an internal struggle with his subjective interpretations of others' discernments of him, particularly those of significant others. These discernments can ameliorate his capacity to recognize his own unique consciousness, thereby inclining him to self-impose constraints on his exercising of free will. As Greek tragedy suggests, a person who has exercises the will-to-power can face self-destruction (see, for example, Owen 2007). This can occur if the pride and arrogance that follows success become addictive, and gives rise to feelings of invincibility, causing him to construct individually the meaning of reality as he prefers it to be, thereby sowing the seeds of his subsequent ruination—the "Hubris Syndrome".[82]

Trump is a man who never has enough success (D'Antonio 2015), however measured. The yardsticks by which he has measured the success he has achieved—his currency of selfhood—are as follows:

- *Wealth accumulation*: "The beauty of me is that I am very rich" (*Time*, April 2011, cited in Piehler 2016, 18).
- *TV ratings*: "If you get good ratings, they'll cover you even if you have nothing to say" (Dallas Texas, September 2015, cited

---

[82] This a syndrome that affects people who have exercised substantial power over a length of time. Its major manifestations are (Owen and Davidson 2009):

- using power for self-glorification;
- focusing excessively on personal image;
- being excessively self-confident, with a contempt for advice or criticism of others;
- losing contact with reality;
- speaking as a messiah;
- being reckless and taking impulsive actions; and
- having supreme overconfidence that leads to inattention to details.

in Piehler 2016, 75).

- *Popular acclaim*: "People love me. And you know what, I have been very successful. Everyone loves me" (CNN, July 2015, cited in Piehler 2016, 40).

How he measures his success as President is difficult to judge, but his default measure is most likely to be the acclaim of his core supporters—his base.

Trump, despite his past success, evidences a fragility of self-identity—ego. He deals with this existential insecurity by creating a false self. This embodies a set of psychological defense mechanisms—"the ego's struggle against painful or unendurable ideas or effects" (Freud [1936] 1948, 45). There are a wide variety of Freudian and neo-Freudian defense mechanisms (Cramer 1991, PlanetPsych 1999–2006) available for Trump to draw upon to protect his fragile ego:

- *arbitrary rightness*: asserting the rightness of preferred cognitions despite the contrary factual evidence;
- *denial*: refusing to recognize anxiety-provoking contrary factual evidence;
- *repression*: blotting out anxiety-provoking contrary factual evidence by not thinking about it;
- *rationalization*: using plausible but erroneous arguments to reconcile contrary factual evidence with preferred cognitions;
- *compartmentalization*: placing anxiety-provoking contrary factual evidence into categories that conceal their factual inconsistencies or contradictions;
- *fantasy*: channeling anxiety-provoking cognitions into imaginative unacceptable or unattainable desires;
- *displacement*: redirecting thoughts and feelings away from anxiety-inducing cognitions to safer and more acceptable ones;
- *reaction formation*: adopting opposite cognitions to the anxiety-provoking cognitions, so as to make the emotions experienced acceptable;
- *regression*: reverting to an earlier stage of development to avoid facing unsustainable anxiety-provoking cognitions;

- *compensation*: emphasizing strengths to counterbalancing perceived weaknesses caused by sustaining unsustainable anxiety-provoking cognitions;
- *projection*: attributing to others the undesirable behaviors or thoughts attributable to sustaining unsustainable anxiety-provoking cognitions;
- *intellectualization*: rationalizing in a way that dissociates anxiety-provoking cognitions from feelings; and
- *sublimation*: channeling anxiety-provoking cognitions toward activities that are more acceptable.

The fragility of his ego continually drives Trump to strive for—and very frequently assert—his superiority over others. This he achieves by the cultivation of fear,[83] and by never admitting he has been wrong and certainly never apologizing if he is wrong: "I think apologizing's a great thing, but you have to be wrong. I will absolutely apologize, sometime in the hopefully distant future, if I'm ever wrong" (*The Tonight Show*, September 2015, cited in Piehler 2016, 11). This all means that he is able to make decisions on the basis of, in the words of Pascal ([1670] 1966, 34), "pure will free of the perplexities of intellect."

Trump: A Nietzschean Übermensch?

Nietzsche's novel *Thus Spoke Zarathustra* ([1883] 1967) has Zarathustra, his main character, describing his heroic character—an *übermensch* (a super-man or over-man). This is a man who is able to establish his own idiosyncratic values and thus able to exercise—constructively or destructively—the will-to-power in order to create *his* world—perhaps even *the* world—as he believes it should be. To achieve this, he not only has freed himself from all external influences, and, thereby, able to rise above social conventions, but also has dominated the thoughts and values of others—using the power of his will—and thereby, curb or, preferably remove, any of their desires that are in conflict to his vision of the world as it should be. Sometimes, this can result in violent behavior, which, Nietzsche considered, is intrinsic to the nature of men.

---

[83] Retrieved from: http://www.politico.com/story/2017/03/trump-white-house-paranoia-236069; See also: https://www.theguardian.com/us-news/2017/aug/13/donald-trump-white-house-steve-bannon-rich-higgins.

Being a Nietzschean *übermensch*, however, is also about being self-overcoming—repressing any immediate instincts for power by means of cruelty and aggression—so as to achieve a more refined expression of power. This permits the "creator within" to prevail over the "animal within," achieved by self-examination and inner struggle, a process that makes him a deeper and stronger person, one with an independence of mind, able to address his self-constraints. To achieve this, he has to foster an attitude toward life that accepts that there are no absolute truths, merely different perspectives that can be believed at will. Thus, rather than embarking upon a search for the objective and rational truth before taking action, he must be pragmatic and flexible enough to be able to draw upon as many different perspectives as possible. Such a manner of thinking recognizes the importance of not inhibiting and thwarting the passions and emotions that give rise to actions by demanding rational analysis before taking action. This pragmatic approach to truth permits the Dionysian[84] dimensions of life—its irrationalities—to be taken just as they are experienced, without the close examination needed to establish their true nature or causation. On life's irrationalities, Chesterton ([1908] 2007, 97) offers the following insight: "Life is not an illogicality; yet it is a trap for logicians. It looks just a little more mathematical and regular than it is; its exactitude is obvious, but its inexactitude is hidden; its wildness lies in wait." Thus, the will-to-believe (James 1896) becomes a necessary antidote to the will-to-truth (Nietzsche ([1886] 1998), for James was contemptuous of the proposition that knowing the truth produces better life outcomes, thereby acknowledging that there can be dangerous knowledge that can make life unbearable.

Undoubtedly, Trump's president's behavior would suggest that he sees himself as a heroic character intent on changing the presidential politico-administrative landscape. In a speech given in January 2016 at Liberty University (Lynchburg, Virginia), he remarked:

> And you'll say if I am president... 'Please, Mr. President, we're winning too much. We can't stand it anymore. Can't we have a loss?' and I'll say no, we are going to keep winning, winning, winning, ... because we're going

---

[84] Dionysus in ancient Greek mythology is the god of irrationality and chaos, who appeals to emotions and instincts (Nietzsche [1871] 1993).

to make America great again. And you'll say, 'Okay, Mr. President, Okay' (cited in Piehler 2016, 45).

He certainly sees himself as having led a momentous, perhaps even meaningful, life, evidenced by his self-proclaimed mega-success in a family business and as a reality TV star. He considers that this prepared him for his heroic role on the presidential stage. He considers that he has risen above political conventions to establish his idiosyncratic ways of becoming and being president. He believes that he has the independence of mind of a deep and strong person. He imagines that he has the strength of will to create his worlds—his presidential world, his family business world, and perhaps, even *the* world—as he believes they should be, by dominating the thoughts and values of others, so molding them to his will and his world vision. He considers that he has a manner of thinking that does not inhibit and thwart the passions and emotions that give rise to his actions (evidenced by his hasty decision to launch the Syrian airbase missile attack), because he does not demand rational (duty-of-care facts-based) analysis before he acts[85] (evidenced by his criticism of, and unwillingness to engage with, the Washington intelligence community,[86] and by his dismissal of the Congressional Budget Office's critical analysis of the proposed Obamacare[87] repeal and replacement legislation[88]).

The heroic Trump he may be to his faithful followers—some of whom

---

[85] See: https://www.wasingtonpost.com/blogs/plum-line/wp/2017/03/30/trump-has-nothing-but-contempt-for-facts-and-reality-based-policy-now-its-backfiring/?utm_term=.323755276e4a.

[86] See: http://www.huffingtonpost.com/entry/donald-trump-intelligence-agencies_us_58a52530e4b045cd34be99aa?. See also, particularly: http://edition.cnn.com/2017/01/05/politics/russian-hacking-hearing-senate-republicans/?sr=.

[87] Formally, the Patient Protection and Affordable Care Act, 2010. See: https://www.hhs.gov/sites/default/files/ppacacon.pdf; see also: https://www.whitehouse.gov/repeal-and-replace-obamacare.

[88] See: https://www.cbo.gov/publication/52486; https://www.cbo.gov/publication/52939; https://www.google.com.tr/search?q=obamacare+repeal+congressional+budget+office&oq=Obamacare&aqs=chrome.2.69i57j69i60j69i59l2j69i60j0.5468j0j1&sourceid=chrome&ie=UTF-8#q=obamacare+repeal+congressional+budget+office&start=10.

even consider that he has been "anointed by God"[89]—who expect him to do as he promises.[90] In any event, Trump has failed to achieve Nietzsche's demanding heroic standards in relation to self-overcoming. There is no evidence that he has ever embarked on a cathartic self-examination or inner struggle that has made him a deeper and stronger person, able to repress his dominant instinct for power by means of aggression.

Trump's Hermeneutic Agency Worldview

> Man not only strives to perceive his environment as a meaningful totality, but he strives to find an interpretation which will reveal him as an individual with a purpose to fulfill ... pointing up man's distinctive ability to find meaning not merely in what is, but in what can be (Crunbaugh 1973, 29).

Trump's intuitive predilection is for the hermeneutic-agency worldview (Dixon, Dogan and Sanderson 2009). This is the lens through which he interrogates—describes, explains, understands, and predicts—the world of persons as he assumes it to be—his assumptive world. It is grounded on the proposition that social realty is as it is subjectively experienced by those who engage in it, the meaning and significance of which is individually constructed on the basis of self-knowledge, and it exists as a collection of mutually unknowable individuals. This means that that the social actions of those present can never fully predict, so inclining each of them toward self-referentiality in his social relationships, which means acting and interacting in ways each one believes to be necessary. This offers him a distinctive and coherent philosophy of

---

[89] See: www.churchmilitant.com/video/episode/vortex-donald-constantine-trump. But see also: http://www.laciviltacattolica.it/articolo/evangelical-fundamentalism-and-catholic-integralism-in-the-usa-a-surprising-ecumenism/.

[90] See: https://www.usatoday.com/story/opinion/2017/08/24/evangelicals-squander-their-moral-authority-sticking-trump/589241001/; https://www.theatlantic.com/magazine/archive/2017/05/a-match-made-in-heaven/521409/. See also: https://assets.donaldjtrump.com/_landings/contract/O-TRU-102316-Contractv02.pdf. But see also: https://qz.com/971930/trumps-100-days-a-scorecard-trump-made-28-promises-in-a-contract-with-the-american-people/?utm_source=.

life, one that informs and justifies his way he conducts his life. It gives him a stable orientation for decisions and actions, because it justifies his distinctive ways of thinking (acquiring, validating, and using information), feeling (emotional arousals and responses), and acting (personal and social behaviors).

However, this lens gives Trump his blind spots—those elements of social reality that are obscured or denied because of the limitations of his default cognitive dispositions. The first is a knowledge blind spot, caused by his denial that social knowledge can be acquired either by objective investigation or from discourse. This means that the only social knowledge he accepts as valid is that grounded in his own self-knowledge—his opinions—propositions that he finds palatable, and thus, trustworthy. This makes problematic any predictions he may make about the future course of events. The second is a behavioral-response blind spot, caused by his willingness to accept that people's real intentions are unknowable to him and so are unpredicted, which means they can only be presumed. Thus, at the interpersonal level, this means that most people cannot be trusted. This restricts his capacity to anticipate the courses of action followed by others in general. These blind spots are the product because of his *ignorance*, *delusion*, and *denial*. These implications of these blind spots will become very apparent in the chapters that follow.

TRUMP'S VIEW OF THE WORLD

Trump holds a very distinctive set of views of the world-at-large and the role of the US in it. It is clear that Trump has a black and white moral compass—one permitting no hint of moral ambiguity—when it comes to international affairs. Being a man of his time, his moral compass was, no doubt, informed by Hollywood's 1950s Western film genre,[91] which was so dominant in American popular culture in his formative childhood years. In that celluloid world, there were "the good guys"—traditionally those wearing white hats—and "the bad guys"—traditionally those wearing black hats or feathers. The "good guys"—the righteous—were the white male town Sheriffs and roving the US Mar-

---

[91] See: http://www.123helpme.com/characteristics-of-a-typical-western-view.asp?id=170209.

shalls, the upholders of law and order and protectors of property rights, however acquired[92]; the white male ranch owners and their white male cowboys, ever willing to take the law into their own hands as vigilantes posses; and law-abiding and salt-of-the-earth shopkeepers always and ever-willing to serve their community through thick and thin. The "bad guys"—the wicked—were gun-slinging white male drifters, always from other parts and always with trouble-making in mind; raiding parties of native American Indians, ever intent on terrorizing stage coaches and small communities by killing, looting, and kidnapping; marauding bands of Mexican's crossing into the US intent on pillage and rape to terrorize communities and property owners and their families;[93] and, of course, pig-tailed Chinese, with their opium dens and very foreign ways of dressing, behaving, and eating, all of whom disturbed God-fearing Christian communities. Of course, in the Hollywood movies, the "good guys" always won.

Trump's "good-guy" countries—albeit metaphorically wearing off-white rather that white hats—would definitely include:

- The United Kingdom, despite his belief that British intelligence tapped his telephone at Obama's request.[94]
- Europe, despite his evident misgiving about the EU's political integration agenda;[95] Angela Merkel's gender and intelligence, a person with whom Trump has a "fairly unbelievable" relationship";[96] and his frustrations with NATO not pulling its weight

---

[92] Indifferent to the unjustness of the actions of the acquiring individuals in the resource acquisition process (Locke [1688] 1960, Nozick 1974).

[93] See: https://qz.com/934680/donald-trump-wall-with-mexico-america-helped-create-the-racist-myth-of-the-violent-mexican-that-trump-is-exploiting-today/.

[94] See: http://google.com/newsstand/s/CBIw6cLfzDQ; but see http://google.com/newsstand/s/CBIwkv7ezTQ. But see http://www.bbc.com/news/38777762.

[95] See: http://www.bbc.com/news/world-us-canada-38846565; http://www.bbc.com/news/world-europe-38808504;http://google.com/newsstand/s/CBIwp-rC1DQ; http://www.newsweek.com/donald-trump-europe-nato-g7-eu-577321.

[96] This is the judgment of Sean Spicer, the White House Press Secretary. Retrieved from: http://www.independent.co.uk/news/world/americas/us-politics/trump-merkel-sean-spicer-fairly-unbelievable-press-conference-us-germany-relationship-a7764201.html.

financially and in the war against terrorism.[97]

- Japan, despite his evident frustrations with its unfair trade practices[98] and its inadequate contribution toward the cost of its defense, although he loves the Japanese practice of bowing: "In Japan, they bow. I love it. Only thing I love about Japan" (*Washington Post* Interview, September 2004, cited in Piehler 2016, 76).[99]

- South Korea, despite his evident frustration that it not contributing enough toward the cost of its defense,[100] and that it is engaging in unfair trade competition[101].

- Israel,[102] despite his evident frustrations with Prime Minister Benjamin "Bibi" Netanyahu's Palestinian settlements.[103]

- Egypt, despite some concerns about its human rights record.[104]

- Canada, despite being bested by the battle of the handshakes by Prime Minister Justin Trudeau,[105] and his evident misgiving about its unfair trade practices.[106]

- Australia, despite his robust telephone exchanges with Prime

---

[97] See: http://www.bbc.com/news/world-europe-38972695.

[98] See: http://business.financialpost.com/news/economy/donald-trump-to-about-to-order-probe-of-16-countries-to-ferret-out-trade-abuse-and-canada-is-on-the-list.

[99] See: http://edition.cnn.com/2017/04/14/politics/vice-president-pence-trip-asia-pacific/index.html.

[100] See: http://edition.cnn.com/2017/04/14/politics/vice-president-pence-trip-asia-pacific/index.html.

[101] See: https://www.washingtonpost.com/news/wonk/wp/2017/09/02/trump-plans-withdrawal-from-south-korea-trade-deal/?utm_term=.c1d346bb4e36.

[102] See: http://google.com/newsstand/s/CBIw-LHF7zQ; http://google.com/newsstand/s/CBIw36H2zzk.

[103] See: http://edition.cnn.com/2017/03/25/politics/netanyahu-trump-settlements-aipac/index.html?iid=ob_article_footer_expansio; http://google.com/newsstand/s/CBIw1oyN9DQ.

[104] See: http://www.reuters.com/article/us-usa-trump-egypt-idUSKBN17227M.

[105] See: https://www.theguardian.com/us-news/video/2017/feb/14/donald-trumps-strange-handshake-style-and-how-justin-trudeau-beat-it-video-explainer.

[106] See: http://www.bbc.com/news/world-us-canada-38971859.

Minister Turnbull[107] and his evident misgivings about its "dumb deal" with the Obama administration on refugees[108].

Trump during his presidential campaign would certainly have included Russia in this category, given his very apparent fixation on Russian President Vladimir Putin[109], which continued after he became president. As president, such a Russian rapprochement scenario has increasingly become politically untenable, given the disclosures from the FBI and Congressional ongoing investigations of Russian meddling in the 2016 Presidential Election,[110] and the rumors that Russian has compromising information on Trump,[111] and given Putin's intransigent support of the al-Assad regime in Syrian[112] and his continued, albeit recently more constrained, support of the Kim Jong-un regime in North Korea[113].

Trump's "bad-guy" countries—metaphorically wearing the darkest of black hats—include:

- North Korea, because of its nuclear bombs and its intercontinental missile aspirations.[114]

---

[107] See: http://www.bbc.com/news/world-us-canada-38849257.

[108] Retrieved from: https://www.reuters.tv/v/4mF/2017/02/02/dumb-deal-drags-australia-u-s-ties-to-new-low?utm_source=taboola_int&utm_medium=referral&utm_term=eslmedia-theindependent.

[109] See: http://www.bbc.co.uk/news/world-europe-40683083.

[110] See: http://www.zerohedge.com/news/2017-03-20/preview-james-comeys-testimony-russian-hacking-us-elections-trumps-allegedwiretap?utm_source=feedburner&utm_medium=feed&utm_campaign=Feed%3A+zerohedge%2Ffeed+%28zero+hedge+-+on+a+long+enough+timeline%2C+the+survival+rate+for+everyone+drops+to+zero%29; https://thinkprogress.org/this-congressmans-short-speech-crisply-lays-out-the-evidence-of-collusion-between-trump-and-russia-d166801a11fa#.jeep2zcbo.

[111] See: http://www.independent.co.uk/news/world/europe/russia-donald-trump-kompromat-nikita-isaev-new-russia-movement-state-tv-us-president-a7929966.html.

[112] See: https://www.theguardian.com/world/2017/apr/06/postmortems-confirm-syria-chemical-attack-turkey-says.

[113] See: http://edition.cnn.com/2017/04/19/asia/russia-un-veto-north-korea/index.html.

[114] See: http://edition.cnn.com/2017/02/28/politics/north-korea-obama-trump-threat/; http://www.aljazeera.com/news/2017/03/trump-kim-jong-acting-badly-170320043115740.html;http://google.com/newsstand/s/CBIw7YC1zTQ.

- Syria, because of its heinous head of state—Bashar al-Assad[115]—[116] and his despicable use of poisonous gas on his citizens.[117]
- Iran, because of its continued sponsoring of global terrorism and its ballistic missile aspirations.[118]

Trump, when a presidential candidate, rather unfairly, included both Mexico and China in this category. Mexico, he included because he thought it was "sending rapist, criminal gangs, and drugs to the U.S."[119] China, he included because he thought it was using unfair trade practices.[120] These countries now regularly vacillate between the black and white poles of his presidential moral compass.

Conclusion

This chapter has explored and explicated the public persona of Donald J. Trump, and elucidated how he takes meaning from the world of persons as he sees it. He is self-centered, with a strong sense of his own importance, albeit with a fragile ego. He is disdainfully flexible with the truth. He is ever-eager to divert attention away from unpalatable truths about, or related to, himself—what he says and does—making him willing to deceive others by conveying false impressions, perhaps with a hint of

---

[115] See: http://edition.cnn.com/2012/12/06/world/meast/bashar-al-assad---fast-facts/index.html.

[116] See: https://mail.google.com/mail/u/0/#inbox/15b323ed60112324; http://google.com/newsstand/s/CBIw4Yau8zQ; https://www.youtube.com/watch?v=WZ5sZm0pBco&list=UU52X5wxOL_s5yw0dQk7NtgA&index=2.

[117] See: http://www.independent.co.uk/news/world/middle-east/syria-latest-bashar-al-assad-chemical-attack-donald-trump-white-house-claim-a7809641.html.

[118] See: http://www.bbc.com/news/world-us-canada-38868039; http://blink.htcsense.com/web/articleweb.aspx?regionid=3&articleid=84872360; https://www.theguardian.com/commentisfree/2017/may/23/trump-administrations-iran-policy-dangerous-flawed.

[119] Retrieved from: https://qz.com/934680/donald-trump-wall-with-mexico-america-helped-create-the-racist-myth-of-the-violent-mexican-that-trump-is-exploiting-today/.

[120] See: http://www.reuters.com/article/us-usa-china-idUSKBN1792KA; http://google.com/newsstand/s/CBIwjJnPyjQ.

a supportive conspiracy theory. He presumes that he has the freedom to be who he wants to be, and so to be able to engage with reality—as he imagines it to be—in any way he chooses. He sees life as a game; he must win and every other player must lose. So, to this end, any means necessary are justified. This extends to

- making outlandish and unsubstantiated allegations and insinuations about his competitors—political opponents, even their families (notably, Obama,[121] the Clintons,[122] and even his fellow Republican Party members, some of whom were also presidential candidates[123]); and

- making unrealistic, even misleading, promises to win over supporters—promises that raised their expectations beyond those that he could possibly deliver with any certainty (for example, restoring the American manufacturing to its former glory or having the Mexican's finance for his cherished Southern Border wall).

It has also sets an important context for the remainder of this book. Trump's views of the world-at-large, and the role of the US in it, are the product of his black and white moral compass. He sees North Korea, Iran, and Syria as the clear enemies; whom he sees as the US's trusted allies is not at all clear.

References

Adler, A. [1933] 1973. "On the Origins of the Striving for Superiority and of Social Interest." In *Superiority and Social Interest: A Collection of Later Writings* (eds. H.L. Ansbacher and R.R. Ansbucher). New York: Viking.

Albrecht, K. 2017. "Why the Pundits Can't Figure Out Donald Trump." *Psychology Today*, 5 January. Available at: https://www.

---

[121] See: http://edition.cnn.com/2017/06/28/politics/trump-obama-relationship/index.html.

[122] See: https://www.theguardian.com/us-news/2017/sep/08/hillary-clinton-memoir-what-happened-election-trump-sanders.

[123] See: http://www.nationalreview.com/article/449521/donald-trump-republicans-congress-has-failed-adap.

psychologytoday.com/blog/brainsnacks/201701/why-the-pundits-cant-figure-out-donald-trump.

Allport, G.W. 1937. *Personality: A Psychological Interpretation*. New York: Holt.

Aquinas, T. [1259–64] 1905. *Summa Contra Gentiles* [*On the Truth of the Catholic Faith Against the Unbelievers*] (abridged) (tr. and ed. J. Rickaby). London: Burns and Oates. Available at: http://www2.nd.edu/Departments/Maritain/etext/gc.htm.

Bacon, F. [1597–1625] 1972. "Essays or Counsels Civil and Moral." In *The Harvard Classics* (ed. C.W. Elliot). New York: Collier.

Baggini, J. 2017. *A Short History of Truth: Consolations for a Post-Truth World*. London: Quercus.

Black, M. 1983. *The Prevalence of Humbug, and Other Essays*. Ithaca, NY: Cornell University Press.

Camus, A. [1942] 2005. *The Myth of Sisyphus* (tr. J. O'Brien) Harmondsworth, Gt. London, UK: Penguin.

Cattell, R.B. 1965. *The Scientific Analysis of Personality*. Baltimore, MD: Penguin.

Chesterton, G.K. [1908] 2007. *Orthodoxy*. New York: Filiquarian. Available at: http://books.google.co.uk/books?id=W6j4Qx2UF2AC&pg=PA97&lpg=PA97&dq=chesterton+%22the+real+trouble+with+this+world+of+ours+is%22&source=web&ots=yunxnJFil&sig=0zbAi2pTbtupcCvt9JjErodLw2Y&hl=en.

Cipolla, C.N. 1976. "The Basic Laws of Human Stupidity." Available at: http://harmful.cat-v.org/people/basic-laws-of-human-stupidity/.

Cramer, P. 1991. *The Development of Defense Mechanisms: Theory, Research and Assessment*. New York: Springer-Verlag.

Crunbaugh, J.C. 1973. "The Validation of Logotheropy." In *Direct Psychotheropy* (ed. R.M. Jurjrvich). Coral Gables, FL: University of Miami Press.

D'Antonio, M. 2015. *Never Enough: Donald Trump and the Pursuit of Success*. New York: St. Martin's Press.

Davison, G.C. and J.M. Neale. [1976] 2001. *Abnormal Psychology* (8th ed.). New York: Wiley.

Dawson, T. 1977. "Literary Criticism and Analytical Psychology." In *The Cambridge Companion to Jung* (eds. P. Young-Eisendrath and T. Dawson). Cambridge: Cambridge University Press.

Digman, J.M. (1990). "Personality Structure: Emergence of the Five-factor Model." *Annual Review of Psychology*, 41: 417–440.

Dixon, J. 2003. *Responses to Governance: The Governing of Corporations, Societies and the World*. Westport, CT: Praeger.

Dixon, J., R. Dogan, and A. Sanderson. 2009. *Situational Logic of Social Actions*. New York: Nova Science.

Ellis. A. 2005. *The Myth of Self-esteem: How Rational Emotive Behavior Therapy Can Change Your Life Forever*. Buffalo, NY: Prometheus.

Eysenck, H.J. 1970. *The Structure of Human Personality* (3rd ed.). London: Methuen.

Frankfurt , H. 2005. "On Bullshit." Available at: https://www.stoa.org.uk/topics/bullshit/pdf/on-bullshit.pdf.

Frankl, V.E. [1948/75] 2000. *Man's Search for Ultimate Meaning* (for. S. Hunt). New York: Perseus.

Freud, A. [1936] 1948. *The Ego and the Mechanisms of Defense*. London: Horgart and the Institute of Psychoanalysis.

Goethe, J.W. von ([1749] 2011). *The Sorrows of Young Werther* (tr. R.D. Boylan). Istanbul, TR: BS World Classics.

Grave, S.A. 1960. *The Scottish Philosophy of Common Sense*. Oxford: Clarendon.

Heidegger, M. [1927] 1967. *Being and Time* (trs. J. Macquarrie and E. Robinson). Oxford: Basil Blackwell.

Horney, K. 1937. *The Neurotic Personality of our Times.* New York: Norton.

James, W. 1896. *The Will to Believe: An Address to the Philosophical Clubs of Yale and Brown Universities.* Available at: http://falcon.jmu.edu/~omearawm/ph101willto-believe.html.

Jung, C.G. [1934] 1981. *The Archetypes and the Collective Unconscious* (2nd ed.) (tr. R.F.C. Hull). Princeton, NJ: Bollingen.

Kane, R. 2002. "Introduction." In *Free Will* (ed. R. Kane). Malden, MA: Blackwell.

Kant, I. [1781–87] 1956. *Critique of Pure Reason* (tr. L.W. Beck). Indianapolis, IN: Bobbs-Merrill.

Kierkegaard, S. [1846] 1941. *Concluding Unscientific Postscript* (trs. D.F. Swenson and W. Lowrie). Princeton, NJ: Princeton University Press.

Klapp, O.E. 1964. *Symbolic Leaders: Public Dramas and Public Men. Observations.* Chicago, IL: Aldine.

Locke, J. [1688] 1960. "The First Treatise of Government." In *Two Treatises of Government* (ed. P. Laslett). Cambridge: Cambridge University Press.

Marcel, G. 1952. *Men against Humanity* (tr. G.S. Fraser). London: Harvill.

Marino, G.D. 2001. *Kierkagaard in the Present Age.* Milwaukee, WI: Marquette University Press.

May, R. 1967. *Psychology and the Human Dilemma.* New York: Van Norstrand.

Mill, J.S. [1843] 1988. *A System of Logic.* (ed. A.J. Ayer). London: Duckworth.

Moore, G.E. 1959. *Philosophical Papers.* London: George Allen and Unwin.

Nietzsche, F. [1871] 1993. *The Birth of Tragedy* (tr. R.J. Hollingdale). Harmondworth, Gt. London, UK: Penguin.

Nietzsche. F. [1883] 1967. "Thus Spoke Zarathustra." In *The Portable Nietzsche* (tr. W. Kaufman). New York: Viking.

Nietzche, F. [1886] 1998. *Beyond Good and Evil* (tr. M. Faber, intro. R.C. Holub). Oxford: Oxford University Press.

Nietzche, F. [1887] 2006. On the *Genealogy of Morals* (ed. K. Ansell-Earson, tr. C. Diethe). Cambridge: Cambridge University Press. Available at: http://www.mala.bc.ca~joh-nstoi/Nietzche/genealogytofc.htm.

Nietzsche, F. [1895] 1967. *The Will to Power: Attempt at a Revaluation of all Values* (tr. R.J. Kaufmann). New York: Random House.

Nozick, R. 1974. *Anarchy, State and Utopia*. New York: Basic Books.

Owen, D. 2007. *The Hubris Syndrome: Bush, Blaire and the Intoxication of Power*. London: Methuen.

Owen, D. and J. Davidson. 2009. "Hubris Syndrome: An Acquired Personality Disorder? A Study of US Presidents and UK Prime Ministers over the last 100 Years." *Brain*, 132 (5): 1296–1406.

Pascal, B. [1670] 1966. *Pensée*. Harmondsworth, Gt. London, UK: Penguin.

Phares, E.J. and W.F. Chaplin. 1997. *Introduction to Personality* (4th ed.). New York: Prentice Hall.

Piehler, M., ed. 2016. *"Weil ich einfach sehr gut aussehe": Erschreckend wahre Worte von Donald J. Trump*. Hamburg, DE: Rowohlt Taschenbuch Verlag.

PlanetPsych 1999–2006. "Defense Mechanisms." Available at: http://www.planetpsych.com.Psychology_101/defense_mechanisms.htm.

Rofe, A. 2001. "Revealed Wisdom: From the Bible to Qumran." A paper presented at the Sixth Orion International Symposium on "Sapiential Perspectives: Wisdom Literature in Light of the Dead Sea Scrolls," Hebrew University of Jerusalem. Available at: http://orion.mscc.huji.ac.il/symposiums/6th/rofeFullPaper.html.

Rosenberg, M. 1979. *Conceiving the Self.* New York: Basic Books.

Russell, B. 1948. *Human Knowledge: Its Scope and Its Limitations.* London: George Allan & Unwin.

Sartre, J.-P. [1943] 1957. *Being and Nothingness: An Essay of Phenomenological Ontology* (tr. H.E. Barnes). London: Methuen.

Sartre, J.-P. [1946] 1973. *Existentialism and Humanism* (tr. P. Mairet). London: Methuen.

Schofield, M. 2007. "The Noble Lie." In *The Cambridge Companion to Plato's Republic* (ed. G. Ferrari). Cambridge: Cambridge University Press.

Schopenhauer, A. [1818 and 1844] 1969. *The World as Will and Representation* (tr. E.F.J. Payne) (2 vols.). New York: Dover.

Schopenhauer, A. [1851] 1970. *Essays and Aphorisms* (tr. R.J. Hollingdale). London: Penguin.

Stack, G.J. 1977. *Kierkegaard's Existential Ethics* (Studies in the Humanities, 16 Philosophy). Montgomery, AL: Alabama University Press.

Stevens, A. 1990. *On Jung.* London: Routledge.

Warnock, M. 1970. *Existentialism.* Oxford: Oxford University Press.

2
THE EARLY DAYS OF THE TRUMP PRESIDENCY: POLICY RHETORIC, VISION, AND REALITY

Max J. Skidmore

INTRODUCTION

This chapter seeks to capture the spirit of the Trump campaign and the early days of his time in office. Without doubt, his presidency is the most unusual in the history of the United States (US), and it gives no indication of changing. Even as a private citizen, and later as a television entertainer, Donald J. Trump attracted attention, if only as an eccentric. Certainly, he has been a notable presence for decades. It is tempting to say that he changed little, if at all, as a candidate, except perhaps to become progressively louder. Even after his victory, he made absolutely no revision in the direction of gravitas as a result of assuming the highest political office in the US. Memory, though, is fallible.

A review of interviews with Trump over the decades does suggest, however, a change in Trump, and unfortunately it is not one for the better. He was always self-centered and boastful, and has never given any indication of being a deep thinker. Since the 1980s, he has toyed with the notion of running for president. He has appeared many times on television. When questioned, he displayed no knowledge beyond the headline level, but in those early years he did employ normal speech patterns, and did give relevant responses to questions.

Comparing those early Trump conversations with his recent ones is startling. His vocabulary appears to have dwindled. He repeats words frequently, and beyond stock talking points he appears to grope for answers. It is clear that:

- He is unfamiliar (and possibly unconcerned) with the content of bills in Congress based on his own proposals.
- He lacks knowledge of basic elements of American history.

- He has little conception either of the presidential office or of the processes of American government.
- He has an attention span that is dramatically brief.
- He is preoccupied with trivia to the point of obsession, and seems unable to control his responses.

Moreover, he has allied himself with, and receives essential advice from, the most extreme elements from the American right, typified by a key slogan—echoing American fascists from the 1930s— to "Put America First."

Trump as a campaigner repeated several themes constantly.

- He would build a wall between the US and Mexico, and make Mexico pay for it.
- He would "Make America Great Again," and was the only person capable of doing so.
- He would deport all illegal immigrants from the US who did not have proper documentation.
- He would ban all Muslims from entering America.
- He would withdraw from the Paris Climate Accord.
- He would sharply reduce the number of government regulations.
- He would "drain the swamp" in Washington, and eliminate corruption from national politics.
- He would immediately sign a repeal of Obamacare, and replace it with something wonderful—a plan that would cover everyone, greatly reduce costs, and greatly increase services.
- He would not cut Social Security or health benefits.
- He would withdraw from the Trans-Pacific Partnership (TPP).
- He would create vast numbers of jobs, including in coal mining.
- He would embark upon a one trillion dollar infrastructure improvement, which was perhaps his most ambitious campaign promise, but more realistic than many of his generalized proposals.

In office, though, Trump has not accomplished any of his campaign promises that required more than a presidential Executive Order.

- He did withdraw from the Paris Climate Accord and TPP agreements.
- He did issue an order to approve no regulation without eliminating two.
- He has removed much of the restraint on the actions of immigration officials, so permitting more deportations of illegal immigrants.
- He issued orders to ban travel from key Muslim-majority countries, only to have them blocked by the federal courts.

His essential presidential commitment, however, is to destroy, especially with regard to anything remotely related to the suave and capable Barack Obama.

Trump has revealed his attitudes by many of his senior appointments.

- His Secretary of Education is opposed to public schools.
- His head of the Environmental Protection Agency (EPA), the former Oklahoma Attorney General who sued the EPA constantly, has set about immediately diverting it from its key mission, such as to protect the environment, and converting it into an agency working to facilitate the desires of corporations.[1]
- His Secretary of Energy is the former Governor of Texas who, as a presidential candidate, proposed abolishing the department, which assuredly reflects Trump's attitude toward governmental regulation of energy, including nuclear energy.
- His Secretary of Housing and Urban Development is a man who explained that his only background in housing policy was that he "grew up in Detroit."
- His Attorney General came from the Senate; long ago, President Reagan nominated him to be a US district judge, but his racist background caused the Senate to refuse to confirm him.

---

[1] As an indication of the way the Republican Party has changed, but should note that it was a Republican predecessor, Richard Nixon, who established the EPA and in contrast to some of his Republican successors, he considered it vital.

Despite some protests, the Republican Senate confirmed all the Trump appointees with no apparent major concern.

In the previous chapter, Dr. John Dixon goes into considerable detail regarding Trump's public psyche, so that it requires little more attention here. To develop a complete psychiatric profile, competent professionals with access to Mr. Trump would be required. What can be done in this chapter, though, is what this book does throughout: examine the implications of the Trump administration, the consequences of his policies, and the resulting potential for danger.

TRUMP'S ENTRANCE ONTO THE INTERNATIONAL STAGE

Immediately upon assuming office, whether deliberately or as the result of clumsiness, Trump set about antagonizing leaders of many of America's closest allies, including the United Kingdom, Germany, Australia, and France. At the same time, he expressed admiration for harsh dictators, such as Rodrigo Duterte in the Philippines (who brags of personally committing murder), Recep Erdogan in Turkey (who is strongly suppressing the press), and even as he issued threats against North Korea, he praised its totalitarian leader Kim Jong Un (who warns the US that it is a target of his nuclear weapons). The leader with whom he appears most to identify is Vladimir Putin of Russia. His admiration goes so far as to encourage his own Republican Party to ignore any evidence of Russian cyber- attacks on the US (especially since they seem to have been directed at assisting his own candidacy) and during his campaign he had publicly encouraged the Russians to hack into emails of the Democrats.

Trump's notoriously childish retorts on Twitter to slights, according to his staff, are a reflection of his "toughness," and tendency to "fight back hard." Schoolyard insults, however, reflect not strength, but immaturity. In addition to employing insults, his response to any information that he finds unpleasant is to label it "fake news," this coming from one who long insisted that his predecessor, who unquestionably was born in the US, was not. Thus, under the Trump administration, accurate reports become "fake news," while his overt lies become "alternative facts." His administration began immediately to conduct a massive assault on the entire idea of truth, accuracy, logic, or the scientific method. Most threatening to the long-term health of the planet, he dismisses human-induced climate change with its global warming, as nothing but a Chinese "hoax."

Trump, History, and the Reaction of His Support Base

These bizarre times call for an unusual treatment. Thus, the effort here will be to present Trump against the background of American political history, to convey a sense of the strangeness of the times, and to identify their potential for enormous national and world tragedy, thereby "speaking truth to power."

As impossible as it seems to anyone who did not follow Trump's rise to power, there were dozens of highly publicized circumstances that literally would have spelled immediate political destruction for any other candidate for political office, Republican or Democratic, in the history of the US.

- He was recorded boasting of sexual assault, and making lewd comments about his own daughter.
- He was convicted of concocting an enormous swindle "Trump University" that drained the hopeful of their money and provided them with nothing.
- He was notorious for refusing to pay debts he owed.
- He has refused to disclose his tax returns during the presidential campaign.
- He has mocked the disabled.
- He has treasonously urged the Russians to hack into his opponent's systems to assist his candidacy.
- He has encouraged violence against his opponents.
- He has repeatedly attempted to intimidate the press.

None of this had any apparent effect on his support. Indeed, he said, perhaps as a joke, that he could shoot someone on Fifth Avenue, and not lose a vote. In retrospect, it seems literally to have been true.

Yet often his supporters would say, "he's a businessman. That means he would be a good president," as though the skills needed to make money are those required to govern for the good of society. Many of his supporters even accepted his twisted logic. Money, he said, corrupts politics. He said he knew, because he had bribed politicians. People should vote for him because he understood corruption; he had so much money that no one could corrupt him. In effect, he was arguing for eliminating the middleman. Remove politicians who can be bought, he said and replace them with one of those one who did the corrupting.

Yet, Trump supporters seem more than anything else to resent any suggestion that they voted against their own interests. He gave them harsh rhetoric that coincided with their prejudices, but nothing else. He succeeded very inexpensively in buying their loyalty. If he says to them he is the only one who can "make American great again" they act as though that means that he will indeed do so. Forgetting the old saying that talk is cheap, they accept rhetoric for reality, and become infuriated if they hear anyone say that they have been gullible.

Donald Trump had, of course, been prominent in American popular culture for years before he announced his candidacy for president. A perfect illustration of his lengthy period in the public eye comes from the brilliant Garry Trudeau, who for decades has produced the satirical newspaper comic strip, "Doonesbury." In 2016, Trudeau (2016) deftly skewers Trump's lengthy record of idiosyncrasies, boorishness, and wealth without taste.

Despite the notoriety, Trump had achieved what he wanted, to be president of the United States of America. Yet, he had no political experience, no policy expertise, and no record as a serious thinker in any way to suggest that he could be taken seriously as a true candidate for high political office. Regardless of his lack of preparation, in 2016 his sudden self-thrust into the midst of national politics brought him astonishing success.

AMERICA'S SPECIAL CIRCUMSTANCES

The US has long been unusual among political systems in that complete outsiders with no political experience whatever can vie for the presidency, and sometimes can have considerable influence. Examples from recent decades include Ross Perot, Jesse Jackson, Steven Forbes, and Ralph Nader. Prior to Trump, though, no such candidate had a chance at winning. The only time in modern American history in which a candidate without some experience as an office holder, or without high military rank, ever won a major party's nomination was in 1940. That year the Republican National Convention selected business executive Wendell Willkie as its candidate for president. Willkie had served in the World War I, but only as a First Lieutenant who saw no combat. In a sense, however, he was a "public intellectual," and he undeniably had substantial policy experience.

Trump hardly compares. He likes, though, to think of himself as being in the same category as Andrew Jackson, who was the first "outsider" to become president. Jackson was indeed an outsider in that his appeal was populist. It began with his stunning military victory as the general who fought the Battle of New Orleans. The fact that the 1815 battle actually took place after the War of 1812 had been declared over and the news had not reached the participants was irrelevant. Jackson had become "The Old Hero." He was not, however, associated with the "ruling gentry" that had been dominant since implementation of the Constitution (he was neither from Virginia nor named Adams; all previous presidents had been one or the other). Regardless, whatever merits Jackson possessed, or lacked, and despite his controversial history, he was a seasoned politician, a prominent general, and previously had served in several high public offices. He certainly was no Trump, who jumped into office completely unprepared.

Jackson could never be called a political philosopher, but he had, nevertheless, given thought to the substance of government. He redefined the nature of the presidency as fully representative of the people, denying the conventional wisdom of the time that Congress was the only reflection of democracy, and argued for the organic nature of the Union, pointing out that the states—both as they then were constituted, and previously as colonies—had never existed outside of a national umbrella framework—first the British Empire, then the Articles of Confederation, and finally the Constitution. "The states" (37 of which were not in existence when it was ratified by "the people" of the initial 13) did not create the Constitution. Again, Trump is in no real way comparable in that regard. To be sure, though, his harsh immigration policies may be reminiscent in some ways of the "Old Hero's" tragic policies with regard to America's native population.

The Trump candidacy was highly unlikely, even in America. It would literally have been impossible in most political systems, where one must work up inside a political party and assume a position of party leadership in order to seek the highest office. French President Emmanuel Macron might seem to be an exception, because he created a new political party and used it in 2017 to step into the top position, but he had considerable government experience prior to having accomplished this feat, and had served as a minister in the French government.

The ability of an outsider to compete in America's presidential selection system has long been recognized, and Americans have not generally considered it remarkable. This was probably because there are so many obstacles to nomination and election. So, informed observers thought that no completely unqualified person would ever appear able to compete seriously. What Trump's triumph demonstrates—both during his campaign, and even more after he took office—is the fragile nature of the most fundamental political institutions in what had seemed to be an especially stable political system. Immediately upon taking office, Trump began to demonstrate just how vulnerable the system had become. He proceeded to function as he wished, regardless. Sometimes, this was no doubt simple ignorance. He had no idea what he would be facing as president. He had not been aware, for example, that he would need to staff his office, and could not simply take over existing personnel. He even conceded that everything was far more complicated than he had anticipated. Regarding health care, for example, he said that no one could have foreseen how difficult the issue is. Certainly, those who had dealt with it for so long knew, as did much of the public.

Ignorance, though, cannot be an excuse, even though his Republican defenders tried to make it so. "He is new to this," they say, excusing him in ways that they would never have accepted if they were criticizing Democrats. Surely, pure ignorance is not always the issue. He willfully refused to follow what had become customary and release his tax returns, even though he had promised to do so. Neither his voters nor his political party cared. He refused to disconnect himself from his business interests, and immediately began to profit from the activities of government. Neither his voters nor his party cared.

The US is unique in another way—a way that made Trump's victory possible—America chooses its president and vice president by an archaic and now almost assuredly outmoded method, the Electoral College. Trump had a clear victory legally, yet he lost the popular vote by nearly three million. The American procedure for presidential selection thus thwarted the will of the voters. It was the second time in a mere sixteen years that the American procedure for selection its president and vice president ignored "the voters' will" and put in office the minority candidate. It had happened previously in 2000, when George W. Bush narrowly lost the popular vote, and also narrowly won the votes cast by the Electoral College—but he did so in that case only with major assistance from the Supreme Court. Bush did clearly win four years later in 2004, but because of the Court's action—widely seen as partisan—his initial election will never be free from the taint of suspicion. The previous time that the Electoral College had selected the loser of the popular vote was more than a century earlier, in 1888, when the Republican Benjamin Harrison won over Democrat Grover Cleveland.

In 2016, it was not close. The Electoral College massively ignored the preponderance of the popular vote. To be sure, this did not violate the intention of the Founders, who generally were not enthusiastic about "the people" selecting presidents. Times have, however, changed over the past two and a quarter centuries, of course, and popular rule—democracy—now generally is assumed to confer legitimacy on a political regime. Regardless of the Founders' intent, the reality in 2016 makes especially ludicrous Republican claims that "the voters have chosen," that "Republicans all campaigned on repealing Obamacare, and the voters expressed a clear preference," or that "the voters expressed their will about the Supreme Court vacancy."

The much-criticized Electoral College has been in place since the Constitution established it. It assigns to each state a number of electoral votes equal to the number of members that state has in Congress. Since each state has two senators, and regardless of size is guaranteed to have at least one representative, the smallest number of members each state can have in Congress is three. Therefore, the smallest states each have three electoral votes. Currently, there are seven such states: Alaska, Delaware, Montana, North Dakota, South Dakota, Vermont, and Wyoming. The other states range up to California, with fifty-five. Under the Constitution's Twenty-Third Amendment, the District of Columbia is also assigned electors equal to the smallest state, so it, too, has three electoral votes. To win, a presidential or vice presidential candidate has to acquire a minimum of 270 electoral votes, that is, one more than half of the total number of electors, 538.

Trump received 304 electoral votes, far more than the 270 required. His boast that he received an electoral-vote landslide, though, is absurd. Just after the election, the *New York Times* listed all presidents, with the percentages of their electoral votes.[2] Out of the 58 presidential elections in America's history, Trump's electoral-vote percentage exceeded those of only 11 other presidents. Trump was wrong when he boasted that he received a greater electoral vote total than any president since Reagan. Even his two most immediate Democratic predecessors had totals exceeding his. Those were his hated enemies, Bill Clinton in both 1992 (370) and 1996 (379), and Barack Obama in both 2008 (365) and 2012 (332). These totals were far more electoral votes than Trump's 304. This is not simple ignorance; it is a lie. Trump has continued to refer to the "fact" of his electoral-vote "landslide," and has even said that he won the popular vote, "if all the illegal millions who voted had not been counted." What was the source of his "facts"? Trump is known simply to make up facts, but there have been reports that the allegation came from the notorious Kansas Secretary of State, Kris Kobach. Kobach has made a career of trying to prove that undocumented residents have been voting, and thus stealing elections, always for the Democrats.[3] State Secretaries of State are usually the election officials within their states. Despite Kobach, both Republican and Democratic secretaries of state throughout the country, say that there is not, and has not been, any significant level of illegal voting in their states, and many states are refusing to cooperate

---

[2] See: https://www.nytimes.com/interactive/2016/12/18/us/elections/donald-trump-electoral-college-popular-vote.html.

[3] In Kobach's own state of Kansas, Republicans swept the elections, so if there were huge numbers of unqualified voters, they must have been voting Republican.

with the Trump-Kobach effort to collect information on all their voters. A notable exception to this is the Secretary of State of Missouri, a Republican Jay Ashcroft, the son of John Ashcroft—former Attorney General under George W. Bush and Kobach's long-ago mentor on voter suppression. The younger Ashcroft, to no one's surprise, was only too willing to supply the information demanded. Kobach himself, by the way, later remarked that there is no way to be certain whether Trump's allegation is correct.

THE REPUBLICAN BUILD UP TO BECOME THE PARTY OF TRUMP

Did Trump really burst onto the American and the international scene as an unprecedented phenomenon? As a personality, of course, he did. In a key respect, though, he did not. Many traditional Republicans may grumble he is not "really a Republican," and it is correct that he seems to be more purely reactive than ideological, in contrast to the modern Republican Party.

Nevertheless, the Republican Party has been building up to Trump for decades, merely waiting for someone to come along and fill the role. Richard Nixon had pioneered the "southern strategy" and Ronald Reagan built upon it. George Wallace had made the Nixon-Reagan approach possible. Reagan was not as ideologically rigid as his rhetoric had suggested, but he gave force to the inherent Jeffersonian remnant: American tendencies to minimize, and even to disrespect, government. Reagan's anti-tax ideology was sufficiently flexible to make adjustments for pragmatic reasons, and he raised taxes many times to help correct the troubles that his enormous tax reductions caused. Nevertheless, his rhetoric encouraged the irrational anti-tax ideology that under the influence of Grover Norquist grew to permeate the Republican Party. Reagan was not a rigid religious fundamentalist who accepted the harsh authoritarianism of much of the religious right, but he made room among Republicans to accept them into the party, as he did with southern segregationists. Following Reagan came the pernicious tactics of Lee Atwater, who employed "no holds barred" tactics to condemn "liberals," and elect the first George Bush. Then came Newt Gingrich, who deliberately engineered hostility toward Congress as an institution so that the long Democratic dominance would come to an end. A part of his strategy was to treat Democrats not as the loyal opposition to defeat on issues—with whom they then socialized as colleagues—but, rather, they were to be the enemy to be destroyed. Among the casualties was the civility that had marked much of American politics for much of its history. Karl Rove, who engineered the election of the younger Bush, was the next step. A part of the strategy was to convince pundits, and the public, that "they all do it." They succeeded in spreading misinformation. Both parties have become extreme, they say. Thus, politics is evil. To defeat evil, one employs every weapon without restraint. As Senate leader, Mitch McConnell, has demonstrated, the Republican Party does so without apology. This would seem to include, as part of the southern strategy, gerrymandering in favor of the Republican Party (McGann et al. 2016).[4]

The Republican Party Precedents for Encouraging Russian Meddling

The allegation of Russian meddling in the 2016 presidential election and the complicity of the Trump campaign and administration fit into a clear pattern in the modern Republican Party's practice of utilizing a foreign state to advance its political position vis-à-vis the Democrats. When Republican Richard Nixon was running for election in 1968, President Lyndon Baines Johnson (LBJ) received information that Nixon's aides were working with officials in the Government of South Vietnam to boycott the scheduled peace talks in Paris. Nixon feared that a peace agreement would work in favor of his opponent, Democratic Vice President, Hubert Humphrey, and so was willing to prolong the death and destruction until after the election. LBJ confronted Nixon, who strenuously denied that he would ever be complicit in such a scheme. Because there was not clear proof, LBJ declined to go public with that information. Nixon could perhaps have won, regardless, but in that very close election it might have made a difference. At any rate, in 2007 the Nixon Library opened the notes of one of Nixon's key aides, H.R. Haldeman. John A. Farrell, a historian working on a Nixon biogra-

---

[4] See: http://blogs.lse.ac.uk/usappblog/2017/02/08/gerrymandering-the-presidency-why-trump-could-lose-the-popular-vote-in-2020-by-6-percent-and-still-win-a-second-term/.

phy, discovered from these notes that Nixon not only knew of the effort but also he directed it. Indeed, Nixon gave Haldeman a direct order "to 'monkey wrench' the initiative."[5]

Ronald Reagan's campaign aides in 1980 were the subjects of rumors that they dealt with the Iranians, and persuaded them to delay the release of the hostages at the Embassy in Teheran until after Carter left office, offering to supply Iran with arms if they did so. There had been strong circumstantial evidence in support of the allegation, but no solid proof. According Kaufman (1993, 213–214): "In October, 1991, the Senate voted to conduct an inquiry, but the next month Senate Republicans were able to block funding for it." It certainly is not proven that this happened. All that we know definitely is that Nixon was guilty of something similar, that Senate Republicans were able to prevent the investigation, and that Reagan did indeed supply arms to the Iranians who then were able to use them against Americans.

During George W. Bush's administration, on July 6, 2003 Ambassador Joe Wilson wrote in the *New York Times* that he had gone to Niger to examine the charge that Saddam Hussein's Iraq had bought nuclear materials there. He declared that there was absolutely no evidence that this had taken place, and many reasons to doubt that it could have happened.[6] Wilson's findings contradicted statements from the Bush–Cheney administration and undermined its rationale for the Iraq invasion—that Saddam Hussein was working toward nuclear capability. Vice President Cheney was infuriated, and officials from his office leaked to the press the information that Ambassador Wilson's wife, Valerie Plame Wilson, was an undercover CIA agent. This could have put her life at risk, and it did destroy her career, which halted the valuable work that she was doing. At the very least, it was a vindictive action that worked against America's interests.

In March 2015, Republican Senator Tom Cotton penned a letter directly to Iran's leadership, and mailed it with his signature and those from

---

[5] Retrieved from: https://www.nytimes.com/2016/12/31/opinion/sunday/nixons-vietnam-treachery.html.

[6] See: http://www.nytimes.com/2003/07/06/opinion/what-i-didn-t-find-in-africa.html.

46 other Republican senators. Senator Cotton and his colleagues were angry about the nuclear agreement that the US, along with Germany, France, the UK, Russia, and China, was negotiating with Iran to slow down nuclear research with the intention of heading off the development of nuclear weapons. The letter talked down to the Iranian leaders, purporting to school them on the principles of the US Constitution, and urged them to ignore President Barack Obama. There was dispute about whether such action was "treason," or was even illegal under the very old Logan Act. Regardless, it seems clearly to have been extreme and irresponsible. It was perhaps the only time in history when a substantial group of the US senators attempted to deal directly with foreign leaders in an effort to undercut the policy of a president.

The speaker of the House of Representatives, John Boehner, in a related effort, extended an invitation to the head of government of a foreign state to come to the US and address a joint session of Congress. Their purpose was to undermine President Obama's Iranian policy, so as to sabotage the Iranian Nuclear Agreement. That foreign head of government—Benjamin Netanyahu of Israel—foolishly and inappropriately agreed, and he did deliver the address. Boehner had not informed the Obama administration of the invitation, and explained that he asked Israel's ambassador to the US also to refrain from informing the Obama administration. He said he wanted to make sure there would be no interference. Elizabeth Cobbs, writing for *Reuters*, said that there was good reason why such a thing was unprecedented. This bears repeating. It was "for a simple reason. It's unconstitutional".[7] At best, it was unpatriotic, at worst treason. Indeed, there can be little doubt that if the Democrats utilize a foreign state to advance its political position vis-à-vis the Republicans, the cry of treason would sound loud and clear.

Trump, the Truth, Nepotism, and National Unity

It has become increasingly obvious that becoming president has not affected Trump's willingness to lie, even when the truth is simple to check. This was apparent in his campaign, which he based on an out-

---

[7] Retrieved from: http://blogs.reuters.comgreat-debate/2015/03/01/netanyahu-invite-is-a-symptom-of-boehners-grudge-match-against-the-u-s-constitution/.

rageous—and easily disproven—falsehood. Notoriously, he asserted that Barack Obama had been born abroad, and thus had been ineligible to be president. Trump boasted that he had "investigators" in Hawaii, Obama's birth state, and said they were "finding things you wouldn't believe." Presently, he simply ceased to mention these phantom investigators. Later, he conceded nonchalantly, that Obama was, indeed, born in the US. If those non-existent "investigators" were finding anything, they clearly were "things you wouldn't believe," or at least that one *should* not believe.

If anyone expected the boisterous campaigner Trump to become the dignified—unifying—President Trump, the first minutes of his time in office should have demonstrated that it was not to be. Presidents, however partisan they are—however rigidly they may govern—seek to unify the country, and at least to present the image that they are unifiers. Indeed, in their Inaugural Addresses, it was Thomas Jefferson who said in 1801: "We are all Republicans, we are all Federalists."[8] While John Kennedy said, in 1961: "Ask not what your country can do for you, ask what you can do for your country."[9] Trump, however, from the very moment of his inauguration, was belligerent. He presented America as a place of "carnage," and arrogantly implied that his election was a major event in world history that would right all wrongs. Conservative columnist, George Will, in *The Washington Post*, wrote on the day of Trump's inaugural (January 20, 2017) his critique under the headline "A Most Dreadful Inaugural Address."[10] Former President George W. Bush was heard to remark, on leaving Trump's Inaugural Address, that this was "some weird stuff"—or something to that effect.

Trump's disregard of the truth has become notorious. The *New York Times* on June 20, printed a catalogue of what it termed his lies, and in small print it covered an entire page, complete with charts. The *Times* indicated that nearly every day since Trump took office he lied on an important issue. Certainly, no other president has ever received such a

---

[8] Retrieved from: http://avalon.law.yale.edu/19th_century/jefinau1.asp.
[9] Retrieved from: https://www.jfklibrary.org/Research/Research-Aids/Ready-Reference/JFK-Quotations/Inaugural-Address.aspx.
[10] Retrieved from: https://www.washingtonpost.com/blogs/post-partisan/wp/2017/01/20/a-most-dreadful-inaugural-address/?utm_term=.a202175fa784.

dubious distinction, nor has any other president ever faced such sweeping and completely documented charges from anyone.

Apparently feeling uncomfortable without family members close to him, and disregarding prohibitions against nepotism, Trump appointed his daughter and her husband as key—albeit unpaid—advisers. Moreover, he vested each with unprecedented authority throughout government. Despite their enormous portfolios and their potential for powerful influence, they were as notoriously unqualified as the new president himself. Congress, in response to President Kennedy's appointment of his brother, Robert, as Attorney General in 1961, adopted prohibitions on nepotism in 1967:

> A public official may not appoint, employ, promote, advance, or advocate for appointment, employment, promotion, or advancement, in or to a civilian position in the agency in which he is serving or over which he exercises jurisdiction or control any individual who is a relative of the public official.[11]

To be sure, this statute has little force. It provides no penalty for violation, except that if a person is appointed "in violation" of the law, that person may not receive pay. Trump has announced that his daughter and her husband will not receive pay, but the appointment would appear clearly to be contrary to the intent of the law. Neither his voters nor his party cared. Trump disregards any restrictions that he finds inconvenient. Many of these restrictions were constructed over the years for sound reasons, but his disregard of impediments has continued throughout his presidency. As a result, Trump's period presidency has included adverse court decisions overturning his travel ban aimed at Muslim states.

The examination that follows makes plain just how extreme the new Trump administration is, and just how different it is from its predecessors. Many Trump supporters say they wanted change; they wanted something different. They certainly got it, and it may be too late to remedy by the time they recognize that it is not the difference that they had hoped for.

---

[11] 5 U.S. Code § 3110 - Employment of relatives; restrictions. Retrieved from: https://www.law.cornell.edu/uscode/text/5/3110.

Reflections on Trump's Presidency

When a new president takes office in the US, journalists and other analysts—the pundits—begin to compile information in preparation of their attention to—or dissection of—his administration's "First 100 Days." When that 100th day arrives, headlines proliferate concerning accomplishments, failures, and overall speculation as to the remainder of the chief executive's time in office. That happened with Trump as well.

It must be conceded that the "100-day standard" is irrational, but it has a solid historical precedent. Concern with that relatively brief beginning period originated with the new administration of President Franklin D. Roosevelt (FDR). He took office on March 20, 1933, in the midst of the most severe economic crisis the US had ever experienced. His record was astonishing, despite the cumbersome nature of the American national legislative process—with its bicameral Congress divided into powerful committees, and with rigid rules and procedures that had evolved over more than a century and a half. He established the tradition that there must be something special about those initial 100 days.

FDR's first 100 days were notable for a flurry not only of activity but also of solid accomplishment. The Congress passed and the president signed many bills, including some fifteen major pieces of legislation. Scholars marvel at the unprecedented speed with which enormously significant proposals flew through Congress. Some literally arrived in the morning, and returned to the president's desk the same afternoon. Nothing remotely similar had ever happened before, nor has it happened since.

Both FDR's immediate successors, Harry Truman and Dwight ("Ike") Eisenhower, during their first 100 days were preoccupied with war measures, and therefore despite considerable accomplishments they had few legislative achievements during those periods. Eisenhower had gone to Korea as he had promised he would do, but did so before his inauguration. It took him a few months, more than twice the 100 days, actually to bring the Korean War to a close.

John F. Kennedy succeeded Eisenhower, and established the Peace Corps on March 1, well within the 100 days. This enormous accomplishment helped America solidify its reputation around the world.

Kennedy did this by Executive Order, but Congress within that year gave the Peace Corps legislative approval on September 21.

Kennedy's tragic assassination brought to office Lyndon B. Johnson, whose list of legislative accomplishments compiled one of history's greatest presidential records. As described by one of his close aides, Joseph Califano—speaking at the Kaiser Foundation in Washington, DC on May 19, 2008, at the late president's centennial celebration—LBJ's domestic record in barely more than five years overall exceeded even that of FDR.[12] This torrent of accomplishment, though, came after LBJ's first 100 days. He certainly was concerned about his reputation, and wanted to outshine Roosevelt, but he did not waste time on public boasting, nor was he obsessed in besting others even on trivial matters such as the size of inaugural crowds. Trump appeared to be consumed by fear that a predecessor, especially President Obama, might be thought to have attracted larger crowds, or to have been more popular.

Regardless of the 100-day standard, much of the later public comment about LBJ uncritically incorporated Republican efforts to denigrate government action, and thus were completely wrong. As Califano noted, for example, a later president, Ronald Reagan, said snidely "Lyndon Johnson declared war on poverty, and poverty won." The facts, though, say otherwise. "When LBJ took office, 22.2% of Americans were living in poverty. When he left five years later, only 13% were living below the poverty line—the greatest one-time reduction in poverty in our nation's history."[13]

There may be little or no real significance to the "First 100 Days" benchmark, but LBJ deserves credit even here. The accomplishment may have been less tangible than signing an important bill, but it still was vitally important that LBJ succeeded in calming the country immediately after the turmoil of the wrenching Kennedy assassination; he brought the nation together. Although "The First 100 Days" is unlikely ever again to be reliable as an indication of what is to come, the combative Trump's

---

[12] Retrieved from: http://roosevelthouse.hunter.cuny.edu/lbjconference2012/resources/making-washington-work/index.html.

[13] Retrieved from: http://roosevelthouse.hunter.cuny.edu/lbjconference2012/resources/making-washington-work/index.html.

record thus far suggests that whatever his strengths may turn out to be, bringing unity to the country will never be among them.

The president following LBJ was Richard M. Nixon. His presidency certainly was momentous, both for good and for ill, but nothing in particular stands out about his first 100 days. After Nixon's forced resignation, his vice president, Gerald Ford, succeeded to the office.

Ford was an activist, and immediately worked diligently on the economy, and on foreign policy. The most notable action in his first 100 days, however, was his boldest—his pardon of former President Nixon. This caused public outrage, and it may have doomed his presidency to be one of the shortest—only Warren Harding, Zachary Taylor, James A. Garfield, and William Henry Harrison (all of whom died in office of natural causes, except Garfield, who was assassinated) served for shorter periods than Ford's 895 days—certainly the pardon contributed to his loss to Jimmy Carter. In retrospect, however, it almost assuredly seems to have been the right thing to do. However counterintuitive it may be, it was probably necessary to foster public unity.

The remaining presidents of the twentieth century generally were not especially successful in the first 100-day period. Carter came to office with substantial popularity, only to see it decline early, and steadily. Reagan was the victim of a failed assassination attempt. He was seriously wounded, but he appeared to benefit substantially from increasing public sympathy, which encouraged public support. The first George Bush began slowly. President Clinton may be an exception to the generalization. He has been known for a slow beginning with numerous setbacks and controversies, but he did manage to get his budget through Congress—without Republican support—and he did provide essential assistance to Boris Yeltsin after the Soviet Union's dissolution during Bush's presidency. Also, it should not be underestimated that Clinton reflected a more humane, and less ideological, conception of government than his immediate Republican predecessors. He supported, and signed, a law providing family medical leave, and he reversed the Reagan–Bush anti-abortion policies. After the initial fumblesand after the 100 days—he regained his footing, and ultimately demonstrated great political skill.

Proceeding to the twenty-first century, the first president to serve completely in that century, George W. Bush, had a rather slow beginning to his presidency, perhaps owing partly to the controversial circumstances of the election. He lost the popular vote, the first president to do so since Benjamin Harrison in 1888, and was installed after recounts, a judicially mandated a halt to those recounts, and a final decision was made by the US Supreme Court. His major accomplishments, and major failings, all came after the first 100-day period. Just as President Clinton quickly reversed the anti-abortion policies of the previous administration, so, too, did President Bush reverse President Clinton's orders, and he re-instated the restrictions that Clinton had reversed.

Bush's successor, and Trump's predecessor, Barack Obama, became active immediately after assuming office. He followed the precedents of his two predecessors, and again reversed course regarding abortion. He countermanded Bush's order, and returned to the policy that Clinton had adopted. Obama's first two years were extraordinarily successful. In his first 100 days—in fact, in his first month in office—he signed into law the Lilly Ledbetter Fair Pay Act, and his stimulus package, the American Recovery and Reinvestment Act of 2009, to counter the economic damage the country had sustained. This act was largely responsible for preventing the economy from plunging into a repetition of the Great Depression that toppled President Hoover, and elevated President Franklin D. Roosevelt to unquestioned greatness. Also in his first 100 days, Obama's signed into law S-CHIP—the State Children's Health Insurance Program—which expanded the program signed into law by President Clinton. The new law greatly expanded the program, covering far more children. President Bush twice had vetoed expansion, arguing that it would include middle-class children, and not merely the poor.

FDR's New Deal thus suggested something special about the 100-day mark, but as Trump himself complains, that date has no meaning as a benchmark, and should not be considered an important marker. Without doubt the "First 100 Day Milestone" provides an unrealistic standard, and it clearly is unfair to judge any post New Deal president, including Donald Trump, against long-ago circumstances that were unique in the country's history. Admittedly, Trump seems almost devoid of historical knowledge. Nevertheless, with regard to the significance of the initial 100 days, he was correct.

TRUMP'S ACCOMPLISHMENTS IN HIS FIRST 100 DAYS IN OFFICE

Trump, although recognizing that the "First 100 Days" is of limited significance, is so obsessed with setting records, and working so diligently and straining so mightily to be able to present himself as being unusually, if not uniquely, effective, has opened the door to the analysis of his accomplishments. Three examples are worthy of mention:

- Philip Bump in the *Washington Post* (12 June) headlined: "Trump Says He Has Done More by this Point than Anybody Since FDR. Sort of."[14]
- Lauren Carroll in *PolitiFact* (27 April) headlined: "Trump Has Signed More Bills in 100 Days Than Any President Since Truman, [Trump's Press Secretary, Sean] Spicer Says."[15]
- Tamara Keith, headlined her *NPR Politics* broadcast (24 April): "White House Touts 'Historic Accomplishments.'"[16]

But what are his accomplishments?

In a *New York Times*—a newspaper that Trump especially hates—feature "Fact-Checking President Trump Through his First 100 Days" (27 April), Linda Qiu wrote that there had been a "steady stream of falsehoods," from the administration, saying, "The Times has logged at least one falsehood or misleading claim per day on 91 of his first 99 days (Saturday is Day 100). On five days, Mr. Trump went golfing and on two he made limited public statements."[17]

---

[14] Available at: https://www.washingtonpost.com/news/politics/wp/2017/06/12/trump-says-hes-done-more-by-this-point-than-anybody-since-fdr-sort-of/?utm_term=.d39ce23fc8af.

[15] Available at: http://www.politifact.comtruth-o-meter/statements/2017/apr/27/sean-spicer/trump-has-signed-more-bills-100-days-any-president/.

[16] Available at: http://www.npr.org/2017/04/26/525764669/as-president-trump-nears-100th-day-white-house-touts-historic-accomplishments.

[17] Available at: http://www.npr.org/2017/04/26/525764669/as-president-trump-nears-100th-day-white-house-touts-historic-accomplishments.

Thus, Trump's first 100-day period was, at least, highly irregular. The *Washington Post's* Joel Achenbach (10 May) concluded that Trump's was "not the usual presidency. This is something strange, ... Adjectives such as 'unconventional' lack sufficient verve. 'Surreal' comes closer."[18] He went on and said, "Trump has used it himself."[19]

The Trump White House pulled together every bill signing, and every executive order that Trump had issued in the 100-day period. It offered them as a group in order to assert that Trump had been unusually successful. Considering executive orders along with signed legislation is unusual. A president can issue an Executive Order on literally anything, and new presidents routinely issue orders to undo some of their predecessors' actions (as Clinton, Bush, and Obama were quick to do regarding abortion).

For such a group of actions to be meaningful, it should be obvious that the actions need to be significant. Candidate Trump's signature promises were to build—at Mexico's expense—a wall along the country's southern border, to repeal the 2010 Patient Protection and Affordable Care Act—Obamacare—and to halt Muslim immigration and travel, including that of refugees. His first 100 days saw Executive Orders restricting immigration, but no wall, and no repeal of President Obama's signature healthcare law—despite Republican control of all levers of government, and assertion by all Republicans running for national office that they wanted to "repeal Obamacare." His actions on immigration were put on hold by the federal courts, prior to making their way to the Supreme Court. Thus, none of these campaign promises materialized. As for his ambitious plans for infrastructure modernization, he seemed to have forgotten them.

The one action taken during his early period in office that might be considered a significant—and permanent—was his appointment of an associate justice to the Supreme Court. In a talk to the National Rifle

---

[18] Retrieved from: https://www.washingtonpost.com/politics/the-epic-and-bizarre-first-110-days-of-the-trump-presidency/2017/05/10/4d0b85ca-3593-11e7-b373-418f6849a004_story.html?utm_term=.9a4f49c37b8a).

[19] Retrieved from: https://www.washingtonpost.com/politics/the-epic-and-bizarre-first-110-days-of-the-trump-presidency/2017/05/10/4d0b85ca-3593-11e7-b373-418f6849a004_story.html?utm_term=.9a4f49c37b8a).

Association on April 23, Trump boasted with pride that he is the only president of the modern era to appoint a justice to the Supreme Court in his first 100 days. This is correct, but the circumstances surrounding that appointment need to be considered. First, a president cannot appoint a Supreme Court justice unless there is a vacancy to be filled, a situation that for the most part is beyond presidential control. Second, Trump inherited such a vacancy, which should have been filled by Obama.

When the late associate justice, Antonin Scalia died during Obama's presidency, the Senate majority leader, Mitch McConnell, refused even to permit hearings for President Obama's nominee, and McConnell held the vacancy open for nearly a year. He said that he would not consider filling the vacancy so long as President Obama held office. This was a violation not only of tradition but also of the clear intention of the Constitution. Moreover, some other Republican senators, anticipating a victory in the presidential race by Hillary Clinton, said that no Clinton nominee should be considered for confirmation, either. This theoretically could have kept a vacancy on the Court for four, or even eight, additional, years, assuming that Republicans retained Senate control.

The clear signal was that no Republican Senate should ever confirm a nomination to the Supreme Court by a Democratic president. The equally clear signal was that any nomination that Trump sent to the Senate would receive speedy approval. As it turned out, Trump's nominee, Judge Neil Gorsuch, was very well qualified, although in all likelihood he did not have to be, as there were rumblings among Republican senators that the only requirement for confirmation was that there be a Republican nominee from a Republican president. This was, therefore, an accomplishment, but it was a Republican senatorial accomplishment. Only by strained logic should it be considered a triumph for Trump.

Trump, to be blunt but honest, did not have an especially successful first 100 days. In fact, he had an especially high record of failure on his major priorities. In addition to the adverse court decisions, and the continued lack of the border wall, infrastructure rebuilding, or repeal of "Obamacare" Trump faced a major embarrassment in national security.

Disregarding warnings, he appointed as national security adviser, Lieutenant-General Michael Flynn. Flynn, himself, turned out to be a security risk. While he was Trump's adviser, he remained a paid agent for the Turkish government. He also had had improper ties with the Russians from whom he had received payments—all of which he failed to report. President Obama had fired Flynn as head of the Defense Intelligence Agency, and had warned Trump not to trust him. Ignoring this warning, and similar warnings from American intelligence, Trump rashly made the appointment, apparently simply because he liked Flynn. Barely more than three weeks later, Flynn's record had become widely known, and Trump had to request his resignation. This was not only within the first 100 days, but came about within Trump's first month in office. Flynn's 24-day tenure set a record for brevity, and perhaps a record for revealing the extent of the new administration's incompetence.

Trump has been especially tardy in nominating officials for key positions, including ambassadors. This lack of attention extended far beyond the 100 days. The *Los Angeles Times* reported as late as 3 June that only "40 of 1242 positions that require Senate approval had been confirmed as of June 2"[20] Trump complained that the Democrats had been delaying confirmations, but the *Los Angeles Times* said that he "is far behind his predecessors in submitting nominations."

The American Foreign Service Association maintains a record of ambassadorial appointments—Tracker: Current US Ambassadors. It reports that as of June 29, 48 ambassadors had not even been nominated, out of a total of 188.[21] There were other vacancies for which nominees had not yet been confirmed, but those for which there were not even nominations included some especially important positions. Among them were Afghanistan, Argentina, Australia, all five Scandinavian countries, France, Germany, India, Italy, Saudi Arabia, South Korea, and Switzerland.

There have been complaints from abroad, as well as from within the US, that agencies are having trouble performing their functions because of vacancies in key positions. As the *Los Angeles Times* pointed out, a mere 8 of 120 key posts in the State Department have been filled; Veterans' Affairs, it said, is lacking nearly 15% of its authorized work-

---

[20] Available at: http://www.latimes.com/politics/la-na-pol-trump-vacancies-2017 0604-story.html.

[21] Retrieved from: http://www.afsa.org/list-ambassadorial-appointments.

force.²² *USA Today* in an editorial, on May 9 headlined "Trump's 'Help Wanted' Sign,"²³ commented that "Trump has filled fewer than 5% of 556 key executive branch positions in the federal government, well below other incoming presidents and an underperformance that goes to the core of competence." Some cabinet departments, it said, had only one senior position filled, and that was the secretary. "In five of those agencies—Agriculture, Education, Energy, Labor, and the Department of Veterans' Affairs—no one has even been nominated for a key senior executive job beyond the secretary." This affected even the Department of Defense. "The Pentagon has 53 of these top positions," it said, and until a secretary of the Air Force had recently been confirmed, "the only key position filled was that of Defense Secretary."

A businessman recently attempted to justify Trump's tardiness in making appointments by asking, "have you ever thought that this might just be because he thinks it is a good way to reduce the federal work force?" Trump has hinted at the same thing. One of his concerns is that he is expected to nominating officials for top management positions, including ambassadors, without knowing what precisely they do—"I look at some of the jobs, and it's people over people over people ... I say, 'What do all these people do?'"²⁴ Disregarding whether it is wise always to cut the work force—the idea seems always to have a general appeal to Republicans—because if the work is to get done, it means employing far more private contractors, who usually cost far more and perform far less well than federal workers, Trump has put forth his business experience as rationale for his allegation that he is the best possible person to Make America Great Again. Yet, no good business executive would attempt to trim a company's work force by not filling top management positions. A more likely reason for his tardiness is that his new appointments must be, above all, loyal to him, utterly trustworthy; that is, dependably compliant of his wishes when need be.²⁵

---

[22] Retrieved from: http://www.afsa.org/list-ambassadorial-appointments.
[23] Retrieved from: http://www.latimes.com/politics/la-na-pol-trump-vacancies-20170604-story.html.
[24] Retrieved from: https://www.usatoday.com/story/opinion/2017/05/09/president-trump-help-wanted-editorials-debates/101019046/.
[25] See: http://www.businessinsider.com/whos-running-the-government-trump-unfilled-executive-branch-positions-2017-4.

Beyond questions of general competence, the Trump administration is unique for the immediate suggestions that there was Russian influence on American elections, and calls for investigation into possible collusion of his campaign officials with the Russians. Federal Bureau of Investigation (FBI) Director James Comey had played a major role in the election by having violated Justice Department tradition, and twice making major statements clearing Democratic candidate Hillary Clinton of criminal liability, but nevertheless harshly criticizing her. Trump was angry that Comey had not called for prosecution, but later pleased at Comey's continued critical comments about Clinton's use of a private email server.

A few days after assuming office, though, Trump called Director Comey to a private meeting, at which, Comey said, Trump asked for his "loyalty." Comey said that he offered Trump only his "honest loyalty." This meeting, very early in Trump's first 100 days, contributed to Trump's subsequent decision to remove Comey as FBI Director. On May 19, the *New York Times*, in an article by Matt Apuzzo, Maggie Haberman, and Matthew Rosenberg, said that Trump "Told Russians that Firing 'Nut Job' Comey Eased Pressure From Investigation."[26] The investigation to which that headline referred was the FBI's investigation into Russian meddling in the American elections. Apuzzo and his colleagues revealed that a

> conversation, during a May 10 meeting—the day after he fired Mr. Comey—reinforces the notion that the president dismissed him primarily because of the bureau's investigation into possible collusion between Mr. Trump's campaign and Russian operatives. Mr. Trump said as much in one televised interview, but the White House has offered changing justifications for the firing.[27]

Trump was certainly mistaken in assuming that he had eased the pressure. On May 17, the pressure greatly escalated. On that day, Justice Department made an announcement that rattled Trump:

---

[26] Available at: https://www.nytimes.com/2017/05/19/us/politics/trump-russia-comey.html.

[27] Retrieved from: https://www.nytimes.com/2017/05/19/us/politics/trump-russia-comey.html.

Appointment of Special Counsel

Deputy Attorney General Rod J. Rosenstein today announced the appointment of former Department of Justice official and FBI Director Robert S. Mueller III to serve as Special Counsel to oversee the previously-confirmed FBI investigation of Russian government efforts to influence the 2016 presidential election and related matters.[28]

Trump cannot remove a Special Counsel. Only the Attorney General can do so. The current Attorney General—the former Senator Jeff Sessions—has, however, recused himself from the investigation because of conflict of interest. The removal authority, therefore, thus rests with Rosenstein.

So, the judgment must be that Trump did not have a good "first 100 days," nor a good first four months. As of six months into his administration, he not only has failed to be notably successful but also is under investigation. Even so, the first 100 days of Trump in will have to rate, at least in one respect, as among the most important such periods in presidential history.

What he did accomplish of significance was not the number of routine bills he signed, or the number of executive orders that he issued. Rather, he changed the tone in Washington.

- He did move to reduce regulations in order to favor business preferences and reduce environmental protections—for example to permit coal companies to discharge wastes into streams by removing the Stream Protection Rule.
- He did step up the number and speed of deportations.
- He did withdraw from the TPP, although the Senate would probably not have approved it in any case.

He has also adopted the anti-science attitude that has become dominant in the Republican Party over the last few years, even giving legitimacy to the irrational anti-vaccine forces. He says that he favors vaccinations,

---

[28] Retrieved from: https://www.justice.gov/opa/pr/appointment-special-counsel.

but—possibly influenced by his Secretary of Housing and Urban Development, the surgeon Ben Carson—that vaccines should be spread out over a lengthy period to avoid "overloading" an infant's immune system. Despite the strange position taken by Dr. Carson, there is no scientific justification for this, and it would leave children open to infection during the period of delay.

It bears repeating that of all the issues of interest to Trump, he seems to have one overriding concern that supersedes any policy consideration: His determination to look strong and to be seen as being the best at doing anything and everything presidential. This has become an obsession that seems to have far less to do with policy than with destroying everything he can that President Obama had accomplished.

Whatever the significance of his actions, the Trump presidency has been unique in many ways. His constant use of Twitter must rate among the most significant. He justifies it as keeping in touch with the people, but his tweets, by and large, seem to be disorganized reflections of the thoughts that pass through his mind and emerge from his fingers. Never has there been a president who inundates the US—and the world—with his random thoughts. There may be merit to this, but there is also danger. Exposure to a president's undisciplined thoughts can lead to an unsettled situation domestically and internationally as well. When President Reagan carelessly—foolishly, actually—joked accidentally into an open microphone that he was about to bomb the Soviet Union, most people assumed that there was nothing serious about the comment, and were pleased that the Soviets seemed unconcerned as well. Apparently, the joke was not actually broadcast, but the comment became known and it was reported. Later revelations indicated that some Soviets briefly took it very seriously, indeed, and went on alert. The results could have been catastrophic. Trump's Twitter habit, similarly, has the potential for dire consequences.

Additionally, Trump uses Twitter to attack those who have displeased him, from high officials to ordinary citizens. His tendency to lash out reveals his quick temper, and his willingness to use his lofty status to bully even the powerless. It also renders the overly sensitive and insecure Trump vulnerable to manipulation.

What his tweets demonstrate is that America has a president who is deficient in dignity, discipline, vocabulary, knowledge (especially of history), concern for science, devotion to truth, or the ability to engage in logical thought. That this appears not to cause concern to everyone—notably his core base—is, itself, disturbing. Perhaps, the least damning comment that can be made is that the American president seems to be constitutionally unable to be presidential.

Conclusion

The Trump phenomenon was the logical conclusion of the modern Republican Party that had been crafted by Richard Nixon, Ronald Reagan, Lee Atwater, Newt Gingrich, and Karl Rove. George Wallace, who laid the groundwork for the southern strategy, which Trump used so effectively, influenced it. They, in effect, created and legitimized the atmosphere that welcomed Trump the destroyer, even though many of the party's prominent figures found themselves at times appalled by the result. Trump's first year in office is coming to an end, yet it remains impossible to know what will happen thereafter.

One thing, though, is known. As the first 100 days of the administration of Donald J. Trump as president of the US ended, he, in a rare moment of truthfulness, expressed what must have been a heartfelt statement: "I thought it would be easier."[29]

References

Kaufman, B. 1993. *The Presidency of James Earl Carter, Jr.* Lawrence, KS: University Press of Kansas.

McGann, A.J., C.A. Smith, M. Latner, and A. Keena. 2016. *Gerrymandering in America: The House of Representatives, the Supreme Court, and the Future of Popular Sovereignty.* New York: Cambridge University Press.

Trudeau, G. 2016. *YUGE! 30 Years of Doonesbury on Trump.* Kansas City, MO: Andrews McMeel.

---

[29] Retrieved from: http://www.reuters.com/article/us-usa-trump-100days-idUSKBN17U0CA?feedType=RSS&feedName=politicsNews.

3
"I LOVE CANADA": CANADA-US RELATIONS UNDER TRUMP'S PRESIDENCY

Frédérick Gagnon

INTRODUCTION

For Canadians, the 2008 United States (US) presidential race meant envy and yearning. "Why can't we have our own Barack Obama?" was the mood that seized Canadians from all provinces. Roughly at the same time, a federal election took place in Canada and none of the Canadian party leaders—Stephen Harper of the Conservative Party, Stéphane Dion of the Liberal Party, Jack Layton of the New Democratic Party, Gilles Duceppe of the Bloc Québécois, or Elizabeth May of the Green Party—were able to inspire voters. The mood in Canada was quite different eight years later. With Justin Trudeau of the Liberal Party as their new Prime Minister, most Canadians seemed to believe they had finally found their own Barack Obama: a young, progressive, globalist, self-described feminist, social-media-savvy and "hip" leader that could "Make Canada Cool Again."[1] Trudeau's approval rating in Canada stood at 60% in the Summer of 2016[2] and, though the real Barack Obama was about to leave the Oval Office, Canadians took comfort in the fact that most electoral experts were predicting continuity in the White House: Hillary Clinton would win the Presidency against Republican Donald Trump on November 8.[3]

The rest is history and the impact of Trump's rise to the Presidency on Canadians' perceptions of the United States (US) could not be clearer.

---

1 Retrieved from: http://www.nytimes.com/interactive/2016/01/15/style/canada-justin-trudeau-cool.html?_r=0.

2 Retrieved from: http://www.cbc.ca/news2/interactives/leadermeter/index.html.

3 For instance, on November 8, 2016, Nate Silver was giving Hillary Clinton a 71.4% chance of winning the Presidency. Retrieved from: https://projects.fivethirtyeight.com/2016-election-forecast/.

Trump declared "I Love Canada" during his presidential race. However, a June 2017 Pew Research Center report showed that the sentiment was not reciprocal. Only 22% of Canadians had confidence in Trump to do the right thing regarding world affairs, while 83% trusted Barack Obama on these issues.[4] Canadians' negative views about Trump were often linked to particular traits of his personality: 93% thought he was arrogant, 78% dangerous, 72% intolerant, and only 16% believed he was well qualified to be President. The same report showed that Trump's unpopularity in Canada was also hurting perceptions of the US society in general: the percentage of Canadians who saw the US favorably dropped to 43, down from 65 in 2016, and it was the first time in the history of this Pew Research Center survey that "fewer than half of Canadians have expressed a positive view of the US."[5] Other polls tell us that Canadians were particularly distraught about the impact Trump might have on key Canada-US issues: on June 10, for instance, an Abacus Data report showed that 85% of Canadians believed Trump would be bad for the environment, while 79% thought the President would hurt Canada's economy.[6]

Through a study of the main issues of Canada-US relations that have arisen since Trump's inauguration on January 20, 2017, this chapter exposes pessimistic and more optimistic scenarios about how the new President might affect Canada. While Trump's agenda contradicts Justin Trudeau's vision and the wishes of a majority of Canadians on trade and the economy, the environment and energy, and security and the border (Robinson 2017), it can be cautiously argued that Trump's rhetoric might often exceed what he will be able to accomplish with respect to Canada in the remaining period of his presidency. As of July, Fareed Zakaria's expression "a rocking horse presidency" seemed the most relevant to describe Trump's impact on Canada-US relations thus far.[7]

---

[4] Retrieved from: https://www.theglobeandmail.com/news/canadian-mexican-confidence-in-trump-leadership-plummets/article35472343/.

[5] Retrieved from: https://www.theglobeandmail.com/news/canadian-mexican-confidence-in-trump-leadership-plummets/article35472343/.

[6] Retrieved from: http://abacusdata.ca/trump-and-canadians-its-not-going-well/.

[7] Retrieved from: http://www.cnn.com/2017/02/19/politics/fareed-zakaria-trump-take-cnntv/index.html.

Quoting Alfred Montalpert, Zakaria argued that when it comes to the new President, one should not "confuse motion and progress. A rocking horse keeps moving but does not make any progress."[8] While the first section of this chapter describes what the "rocking horse President" has announced regarding Canada—which certainly gives Canadians good reasons to be pessimistic about the future; the second section provides a more optimistic narrative emphasizing key factors that might help Canadians avoid the storm they have feared since November 8, 2016.

The "Rocking Horse Presidency" and Canada-US Issues: Be Very Afraid

Experts of Canadian culture often write that politeness is "at the core" of who Canadians are (Ibbitson 2005, 13), but that did not prevent 68% of them to say Americans, by electing Trump, picked "one of the worst" if not "the worst" President in US history.[9] Such feelings were partly a reaction to Donald Trump's program and official statements on top issues of Canada-US Relations.

Trade Tensions

The "rocking horse president" did not waste time before he targeted Canada on trade. During the presidential campaign, he termed the North American Free Trade Agreement (NAFTA)—a trade deal between the US, Canada, and Mexico launched in 1994—the worst trade deal the US has ever signed.[10] Trump doubled down after his inauguration, declaring that he would pull out of NAFTA,[11] but he ultimately changed his mind when Mexican President Enrique Pena Nieto and Justin Trudeau 'phoned and convinced him to give renegotiation a chance. On May 18, the Trump administration provided a written notice to

---

[8] Retrieved from: http://www.cnn.com/2017/02/19/politics/fareed-zakaria-trump-take-cnntv/index.html.

[9] Retrieved from: https://www.theglobeandmail.com/news/canadian-mexican-confidence-in-trump-leadership-plummets/article35472343/.

[10] Retrieved from: http://fortune.com/2016/09/27/presidential-debate-nafta-agreement/.

[11] Retrieved from: https://www.bloomberg.com/news/articles/2017-04-26/trump-aides-in-raging-debate-over-how-quickly-to-move-on-nafta .

Congress that it wanted to initiate trade talks with Mexico and Canada regarding the modernization of NAFTA.[12] This triggered a 90-day period during which the Office of the US Trade Representative (USTR) solicited comments from the public and held public hearings on NAFTA. The process also required the Trump administration to publish its renegotiation objectives on USTR's website, before it officially commenced the formal talks with Canada and Mexico at the end of the 2017 summer.[13]

Many experts of Canada-US relations painted a dark picture of the likely outcome of the renegotiation for Canada. For instance, fellows at the Peterson Institute for International Economics Gary Clyde Hufbauer and Euijin Jung warned Ottawa of potential "blockbuster demands" Trump might raise: a 20% "border tax adjustment" on imported goods and services from Canada, a reduction of the Canadian goods and services tax (GST) to make US exports cheaper north of the Canada-US border, or a rule of origin for US auto industry that would reduce the trade deficit with Canada in this sector ($10 billion in 2016) and ensure that Americans buy more American cars and auto parts (Hufbauer and Jung 2017).

Justin Trudeau had good reasons to believe Trump would try to change Canada-US trade practices in three additional sectors. First, during a public address he gave in Wisconsin in April, Trump attacked the "very unfair things" that have happened to US dairy farmers trying to export to Canada. This signaled his administration's desire to force Canada to lower or eliminate agricultural trade barriers that regulate its dairy, chicken and egg industries (Hufbauer and Jung 2017, 5).[14] For instance, US agricultural exports to Canada "in excess of quota levels are subject to steep…tariffs, raising prices for Canadian consumers and deterring sales by US farmers. Notable examples include above-quota tariffs of 245% on cheese and 298% on butter" (Hufbauer and Jung 2017, 5). Sec-

---

[12] See the website of the Office of the United States Trade Representative. Available at: https://ustr.gov/sites/default/files/files/agreements/FTA/nafta/NAFTA.pdf.

[13] See: https://ustr.gov/sites/default/files/files/agreements/FTA/nafta/NAFTA.pdf.

[14] See also: https://www.thestar.com/news/world/2017/04/18/canadian-dairy-farmers-being-very-unfair-to-us-counterparts-trump-says.html.

ond, Trump's call to "Buy American and Hire American" might translate into higher restrictions for Canadian companies trying to participate in the US federal procurement market for US government contracts linked to infrastructure and construction projects (Hufbauer and Jung 2017, 10). When the US Congress passed Barack Obama's American Recovery and Reinvestment Act in 2009, Buy American requirements made it more difficult for Canadian producers of iron and steel to compete with the American industry on US soil. In April, Trump's ordering of a "sweeping investigation into whether steel imports are harming America's national security" and assertion that he will not "let Canada or anybody else take advantage and do what they did to our workers" were a sign that this was likely to be a subject at the negotiation table on NAFTA.[15] Third, the softwood lumber dispute that has existed between Canada and US since the 1980s was not likely to be resolved quickly under Trump (Hufbauer and Jung 2017, 8). Former Canadian Ambassador to Washington Raymond Chrétien even predicted that if "lumber is not resolved (before NAFTA) the atmosphere will be ... polluted" when Ottawa and Washington try to come up with a new version of NAFTA.[16] As of July, the problem for Canada was that after a previous softwood lumber agreement expired on October 6, 2016, the US International Trade Commission (USITC) ruled that subsidized Canadian exports represent unfair competition for the US lumber industry and require tariffs at the border (Hufbauer and Jung 2017, 9). The US Department of Commerce imposed a 19.88% duty on Canadian lumber shipments in April 2017 and added another 6.87% in June.[17] This prompted both Ottawa and provincial governments (such as Québec) to promise aid packages and guaranteed loans to protect the softwood lumber industry.[18]

---

[15] Retrieved from: https://www.nytimes.com/2017/04/20/business/trade-canada-trump-steel.html.

[16] Retrieved from: http://www.reuters.com/article/us-usa-canada-trade-idUSKBN17S1IG.

[17] See: http://business.financialpost.com/news/economy/u-s-slaps-more-duties-on-canadian-lumber-shipments/wcm/390653ed-2379-4a98-b072-b2d4407b41fa.

[18] See: https://www.biv.com/article/2017/6/ottawa-announces-softwood-lumber-aid-package/;http://www.cbc.ca/news/canada/montreal/quebec-donald-trump-softwood-lumber-1.4081992.

Environmental and Energy Tensions

Trade and the economy were not the only issues on which the "rocking horse presidency" opposed Canada and the Trudeau government. Environment and energy were also a source of disagreement between Trump and his northern neighbors (Gagnon 2017b). When Justin Trudeau and Barack Obama met in Washington DC (March 2016) and Ottawa (June 2016), they agreed that climate change is a key issue of our time and that measures are needed to speed up the energy transition already under way in the US and Canada (Robertson 2017).[19] For instance, Obama and Trudeau declared their support to the Paris Climate Accord that had been negotiated by close to 200 parties at a UN conference in Paris on December 12, 2015. In accordance with this agreement, the US and Canada respectively pledged to lower their greenhouse gas emissions by 26%–28% by 2025, and by 30% by 2030, based on 2005 levels.[20] In December 2016, a few weeks after Trump's victory in the 2016 presidential election, Trudeau and the governments of all Canadian provinces and territories except Manitoba and Saskatchewan (due to their opposition to the concept of a carbon tax) released a *Pan-Canadian Framework on Clean Growth and Climate Change* aimed at keeping Canada's promise regarding the Paris Climate Accord.[21] Among the pillars of the framework were a plan to price carbon pollution, to tighten energy efficiency standards for vehicles, and to invest in clean technology, innovation and jobs.[22]

However, when Trump met with Trudeau for the first time in Washington on February, he held very different positions on the environment and climate change to those held by Barack Obama. In their remarks at a joint press conference that followed their private meeting, Trump

---

[19] See: http://www.cbc.ca/news/politics/three-amigos-agreements-list-1.3658050.

[20] See: https://www.theguardian.com/science/2016/sep/26/us-climate-change-emissions-miss-2025-target-research; http://www.lemonde.fr/planete/article/2016/12/10/le-canada-adopte-un-accord-a-minima-pour-reduire-les-emissions-de-gaz-a-effet-de-serre_5046688_3244.html.

[21] See: https://www.canada.ca/en/services/environment/weather/climatechange/pan-canadian-framework.html.

[22] See: https://www.canada.ca/en/services/environment/weather/climatechange/pan-canadian-framework.html.

and Trudeau did not even mention the issue of climate change and only the Trudeau stressed the importance of "respecting the environment" when he said Washington and Ottawa should collaborate on "energy infrastructure projects that will create jobs."[23] The ideological gap between them on the environment and energy could not be wider: calling climate change a "hoax," Trump announced, on June 1, the withdrawal of the US from the Paris Climate Accord.[24] After his inauguration on January 20, Trump picked a climate change denier, Scott Pruitt, as the Administrator of the Environmental Protection Agency (EPA), and signed an Executive Order directing him and the agency to withdraw and rewrite Barack Obama's *Clean Power Plan*, which, according to one account: "would have closed hundreds of coal-fired power plants, frozen construction of new plants and replaced them with vast new wind and solar farms."[25] Building on his campaign promises, Trump announced a "new American energy policy" on June 29, one aimed at securing US "energy dominance" by reviving and expanding the US nuclear sector, and by boosting "offshore oil and natural gas drilling and exports of oil, natural gas and coal."[26] To be sure, Trump's emphasis on fossil fuel has been seen in a positive light in some parts of Canada. In the Province of Alberta, for instance, where the President's memorandum inviting the Canadian company TransCanada to "promptly re-submit its application to the Department of State for a Presidential permit for the construction and operation of the Keystone XL Pipeline, a major pipeline for the importation of petroleum from Canada to the United States," was a popular departure from Obama's rejection of the same project.[27] That being said, Trump's willingness to undo Obama's legacy on climate change and to prioritize fossil fuels instead of cleaner energies clearly contra-

---

[23] Retrieved from: https://www.whitehouse.gov/the-press-office/2017/02/13/remarks-president-trump-and-prime-minister-trudeau-canada-joint-press.

[24] Retrieved from: http://www.newsweek.com/trump-global-warming-hoax-paris-berkeley-621073.

[25] Retrieved from: https://www.nytimes.com/2017/03/28/climate/trump-executive-order-climate-change.html.

[26] Retrieved from: http://thehill.com/policy/energy-environment/340135-trump-rolls-out-actions-to-boost-nuclear-fossil-fuels.

[27] Retrieved from: https://www.whitehouse.gov/the-press-office/2017/01/24/presidential-memorandum-regarding-construction-keystone-xl-pipeline.

dicted Justin Trudeau's approach and the vision of a majority in Canada: according to a March 2017 poll conducted by Environics Research Group, 57% of Canadians thought more should be done to fight climate change and 74% believed Canada "needs to generate more renewable energy in order to meet the demands of the future."[28]

Security and Border Tensions

Trump's approach to security and borders is a third issue that has generated concern in north of the Canadian border. First, Trump's "America First" approach to collective security has led him to declare NATO "obsolete" and to call on its members to "pay their fair share" by increasing their military budgets "in order to meet a 2014-set goal of putting two percent of their GDP toward defense spending."[29] Justin Trudeau seemed to respond directly to the demand when he announced that Canada would raise its defense budget to $32.7 billion over the next decade, and by 70% over the same period.[30]

Second, while Trudeau and Barack Obama agreed that the US and Canada had to do their part in finding an international solution to the refugee crisis caused by the Syrian civil war, Trump made a U-turn on this issue. Obama had pledged that the US would welcome 110,000 refugees from Syria for the 2017 fiscal year.[31] This was relatively small number compared to the 400,000 individuals fleeing Syria that the Trudeau government had welcomed to Canada between November 2015 and January 2017 (the total population of Canada is similar to the population of California and ten times smaller than the total US population). However, it was still a higher number of refugees than the one Trump has vowed to welcome since the beginning of his presidency: zero. In his now famous January 27, travel ban Executive Order, Trump wished to suspend the

---

[28] Retrieved from: http://www.newswire.ca/news-releases/majority-of-canadians-support-more-action-on-climate-change-615563183.html.

[29] Retrieved from: http://thehill.com/policy/international/338234-trump-praises-trudeau-for-canadas-increase-military-spending.

[30] Retrieved from: http://thehill.com/policy/international/338234-trump-praises-trudeau-for-canadas-increase-military-spending.

[31] See: http://www.pewresearch.org/fact-tank/2017/01/30/key-facts-about-refugees-to-the-u-s/; https://www.nytimes.com/2017/01/27/us/politics/trump-syrian-refugees.html.

entry of nationals of Syria as refugees for 120 days, to make sure proper changes to the US refugee program could prevent terrorism on US soil.[32] Trump reaffirmed his position in a second Executive Order on March 6, after US federal courts had challenged key provisions of his first travel ban Order.[33] Trudeau and Trump did not emphasize their differences on this issue when the two met in Washington in February.[34] They did not talk about Syrian refugees during their respective remarks but they had to address the issue at a subsequent press conference. When a journalist asked Trump whether he felt "confident the northern border is secure" while "the Prime Minister "hugs refugees and welcomes them with open arms," the President did not take the bait to attack Trudeau like he had lambasted Chancellor Angela Merkel for the "catastrophic mistake" she had made by welcoming too many refugees in Germany.[35] Trump preferred to note the efforts made by his Secretary of Homeland Security John Kelly to get "hardened criminals" out of the US.[36] Trudeau did not attack Trump's position either when another journalist asked him if he believed the President's travel ban "has merit on national security grounds." Said Trudeau: "The last thing Canadians expect is for me to come down and lecture another country on how they choose to govern themselves."[37] Whether this is true or not certainly is a matter of discussion in Canada since various polls have showed that a majority of Canadians would actually like Trudeau to stand up to Trump on progressive values.[38]

---

[32] See: The White House (Office of the Press Secretary), "Executive Order: Protecting the Nation from Foreign Terrorist Entry into the United States," January 27, 2017. Available at: https://www.whitehouse.gov/the-press-office/2017/01/27/executive-order-protecting-nation-foreign-terrorist-entry-united-states.

[33] See: The White House (Office of the Press Secretary), "Executive Order Protecting the Nation from Foreign Terrorist Entry into the United States," March 6, 2017. Available at: https://www.whitehouse.gov/the-press-office/2017/03/06/executive-order-protecting-nation-foreign-terrorist-entry-united-states.

[34] See: https://www.whitehouse.gov/the-press-office/2017/02/13/remarks-president-trump-and-prime-minister-trudeau-canada-joint-press.

[35] Retrieved from: https://www.theguardian.com/world/2017/jan/15/angela-merkel-refugees-policy-donald-trump.

[36] Retrieved from: https://www.whitehouse.gov/the-press-office/2017/02/13/remarks-president-trump-and-prime-minister-trudeau-canada-joint-press.

[37] Retrieved from: https://www.whitehouse.gov/the-press-office/2017/02/13/remarks-president-trump-and-prime-minister-trudeau-canada-joint-press.

[38] See: https://www.theglobeandmail.com/news/politics/canadians-want-

Finally, the remaining Canada-US security/border issue that could potentially force Trudeau to stand up to Trump, even if he would prefer not to, is the security at the northern border. What if the threat of terrorism convinces Trump to increase security at the northern border? The US President has never vowed to "build a wall" between Canada and the US. However, Trump may well change his mind if a serious terrorist attack occurs on US soil, and even faster if the individuals carrying the attack transit into the US from Canada. The 9/11 attacks in New York and Washington showed the kind of impact terrorism can have on how Washington politicians perceive the Canada-US border (Gagnon et al. 2016, 152–155). In the years that followed, the Canadian government not only had to fight the myth that some of the terrorists had slipped into the US from Canada.[39] Ottawa also had to prove to Washington that was doing enough to secure its borders and detect terrorists in Canada. To this end it, for example, created the Canadian Air Transport Security Authority to increase safety on commercial planes, and unveiled the *Anti-terrorism Act*, a Canadian equivalent of the *Patriot Act*.[40] While Senators Ron Wyden (Republican–Wisconsin), Susan Collins (Republican–Maine), and other members of the US Senate Committee on Homeland Security and Governmental Affairs have expressed concerns about Canada's open borders, immigration system and refugee policies, especially since two terrorist attacks occurred in Ottawa and Saint-Jean-sur-Richelieu in October 2014, one can wonder what would be the response of Trump and the Republicans in Congress if unfortunate events convinced them that Canada is not doing enough to protect the US against terrorism (Gagnon 2017a). In June 2017, when a Canadian man who had entered the US stabbed and injured a police officer in the neck at Michigan Airport after shouting in Arabic, Trump said he was "proud of the swift response" from both Canadian and US authorities.[41] However, the US President might have reacted differently had the attack been of a larger scale and caused more victims and deaths.

---

trudeau-to-stand-up-to-trump-but-welcome-a-visit-nanos-poll/article334 34845/.

[39] See: http://www.washingtonpost.com/wp-dyn/articles/A38816-2005Apr8.html.

[40] See: http://ottawacitizen.com/news/national/canadas-post-911-anti-terror-laws.

[41] Retrieved from: http://www.washingtontimes.com/news/2017/jun/21/michigan-airport-evacuated-officer-seen-bleeding-n/.

Why the Storm Might not Sweep Canada: Don't Worry Too Much

The pessimistic scenarios discussed in the first section of this chapter have worried Canadians but at least three factors might help them to avoid the storm they have feared since November 8, 2016.

Benign Neglect and Indifference

A more optimistic account of US-Canada elations focuses on the concept of policy periodicities, which highlight how domestic and international events have imparted Trump's first months in the White House (Nincic 2012, 150). Like any other president before him, Trump has been forced to spend time and energy on a myriad of pressing issues and to react to unforeseen events that have steered his attention away from Canada. At home, he has struggled with hesitant Republican majorities in Congress regarding his plans to repeal and replace Obamacare and to build a wall at the US-Mexican border. Furthermore, the FBI investigation of Russian's role in the 2016 US election, in addition to Trump's decision to fire FBI Director James Comey, has prompted Congressional committees to conduct a series of public hearings where members of the Trump administration—and even the President himself—were suspected of various wrongdoings (such as presidential obstruction of justice and possible Trump Campaign collusion with Russia during the presidential election process). At the international level, Syrian President Bashar al-Assad's chemical attacks on his population and North Korean leader Kim Jong-un's nuclear weapon tests have topped Trump's priorities. While there is no doubt that such world events represent great risks for international and human security, the good news for Canada is that they make Canada-US controversies appear relatively small and unimportant in comparison. As one commentator puts it, Canada-US relations will often seem somewhat "boring" for a President known for his appetite for shocking stories that provoke public excitement.[42]

The historic cordiality of Canada-US ties and America's "benign neglect, indifference or ignorance" towards Canada have often made it difficult for Ottawa to get noticed in Washington (Robertson 2005, 46–50). As

---

[42] Retrieved from: http://ici.radio-canada.ca/nouvelle/1016548/la-tres-ennuyante-relation-commerciale-entre-le-canada-et-les-etats-unis.

a former Canadian diplomat who worked at the Canadian Embassy in Washington puts it: "I'm often asked: 'What do Americans think of us?' The short answer is 'they don't.'"[43] In the first months of his presidency, Trump might have given the impression that he pays more attention to Canada than his predecessors. He might also have provided evidence that he is more convinced than previous presidents that Canada is a threat to US interests. However, the 45th President has often had bigger fish to fry and Canada might find true benefit in the fact that it usually draws little attention south of the 45th parallel.

Rhetoric Without Accomplishment

A second factor that should make Canadians cautiously optimistic about the future is that Trump's personality gives good reasons to believe that his words are not always followed by actions; and his words do not always reveal the true nature of what he wants to accomplish. As a businessman, Trump has often touted the merits of a negotiating style he has crafted and called "the art of the deal" (Trump with Schwartz 1987; see also Feloni 2017): "I aim very high, and then I just keep pushing and pushing and pushing to get what I'm after. Sometimes I settle for less than I sought, but in most cases I still end up with more than I want" (p. 32).

When one looks at what Trump has declared in relation to certain Canada-US issues, he seems determined, as President, to follow the rules of his "art of the deal" strategy. When he promised to rip up NAFTA, lamenting the "very unfair practises" of the Canadian industry, and implied that Canada must pay its "fair share" as a NATO member if it wants Washington to guarantee its security, such strong words worried Canadians. However, what they, above all, illustrate is that Trump has treated Canada-US relations the same way he used to treat his business competitors. In other words, he is aiming very high and is pushing, pushing and pushing to get more from Canada than he actually wants. If that is the case, Justin Trudeau's cautious strategy aimed at downplaying Trump's high-intensity language and at avoiding a verbal escalation with the President could serve Canada well.[44]

---

[43] Retrieved from: http://ici.radio-canada.ca/nouvelle/1016548/la-tres-ennuyante-relation-commerciale-entre-le-canada-et-les-etats-unis.

[44] See: https://www.ft.com/content/5a9ca5da-eb4b-11e6-930f-061b01e23655?mhq5j=e1.

Trump's "art of the deal" strategy reveals an additional reason why Justin Trudeau and Canadians might be well advised not to worry too much about the Trump's words regarding Canada. As one account puts it, Trump's 1987 publication already reveals two predominant traits about the 45th President that have continued to drive his action inside the White House: first, he has an obsession with the press and a constant craving for media attention and visibility; second, he is convinced that the best way to get media attention is to make the most controversy and drama:[45]

> One thing I've learned about the press is that they're always hungry for a good story, and the more sensational the better. ... The point is that if you are a little different, or a little outrageous, or if you do things that are bold or controversial, the press is going to write about you (Trump with Schwartz 1987, 56).

Yet again, it could be argued that Trump's promises to cancel NAFTA, stop protecting Canada's security or punishing Canadian dairy producers do not necessarily reflect the actual policies Trump wants to enact; they rather look like hyperboles Trump has used to catch the attention of the media in a context where the first months of his Presidency have fitted the concept of the "permanent campaign" aimed at keeping the excitement of his 2016 electoral base alive (such as trade protectionists and manufacturing workers in the Midwest, and dairy producers in Wisconsin). Building on Brendan Doherty's seminal work on presidential "permanent campaigns" (Doherty 2012), it could thus argue that, as President, Trump seems to have further blurred the line that already existed between presidential governing and campaigning. He has never really entered in a "governing mode" and has spent most of his time in the "spectacle mode" that helped him secure the White House in 2016—a style he might well continue to use should he seek a second term in 2020. For Canada, what this means is that the Trump administration might be more interested in telling stories about Canada-US issues than in actually changing a relationship that has never had the reputation of being a pressing problem in Washington and, more generally, in the US.

---

[45] See: http://www.businessinsider.com/the-art-of-the-deal-donald-trump-leadership-2017-1/#his-biggest-influence-growing-up-was-his-father-1.

The US Constitutional Impediments

The third factor that should make Canadians more optimistic about the Trump presidency is that power is so decentralized and diffused in the US political system that Canada will often be able to find allies in the US to fight Trump should he go forward with his threatened policies. Trump has had a tendency to praise strong leaders such as Vladimir Putin in Russia, Rodrigo Duterte in Philippines, and Recep Tayyip Erdogan in Turkey. However, by signing the US Constitution in 1787, the Founding Fathers of the US sought to avoid what they called tyranny: "the usurpation of power by a single individual or group, or the circumvention of law by rulers for their own benefit" (Snyder 2017, 10).

The checks and balances and the division of powers within the three branches of government, and between Washington and the 50 state governments embedded in the US Constitution is one of the main reasons why Donald Trump has been unable to attain various presidential goals since his inauguration. The courts have challenged his travel bans on Muslims and Syrian refugees. Congress has refused to fund his proposed wall between the US and Mexico. Some state governments—notably in California and New York—have promised new greenhouse gases regulations to circumvent Trump's decision to withdraw from the Paris Climate Accord.[46] What this means for Canada is that Trump is not the only person in charge in the US. As such, thousands of elected officials up for re-election in the 2018 congressional midterm elections might well be prompted to oppose an unpopular President to boost their chance of keeping their seats.[47] Ottawa, the provincial governments of Canada, and even mayors of major Canadian cities are particularly aware of this and have launched massive campaigns right after Trump's election to establish or reinforce existing links with US governors, state legislators, members of Congress or city mayors who represent local constituencies with strong links to Canada and who benefit from a close relationship with their northern neighbors.[48] On trade for instance, many Repub-

---

[46] See: http://www.aljazeera.com/indepth/features/2017/06/trump-ditches-paris-california-leads-environment-170625141250430.html.

[47] See: http://www.politico.com/story/2017/05/13/trump-2018-midterms-gop-alarm-238342.

[48] See: https://www.durhamregion.com/news-story/7076547-trudeau-reminds-

licans have opposed Trump's protectionist stance on NAFTA, arguing that renegotiating the deal could greatly hurt US interests. Republican Representative of the 21st congressional district of New York Elise Stefanik is one of them.[49] Noting that 15% of the workforce in her district is employed by Canadian or cross-border companies, she has vowed to revive the House Northern Border Caucus on Capitol Hill, a bipartisan panel focusing on Canada-US issues, to put pressure on Trump during NAFTA's renegotiation process, and to make sure Congress will not vote for a revised NAFTA that is detrimental to Americans who benefit from trade with and investment from Canada.

So, the first months of the Trump presidency have shown that Canada still has many allies south of the 45th parallel: elected officials who want to open the Canada-US border more rather than the closing it. For instance, in March, a bill went before Congress aimed at allowing Canadians over the age of 55 who are visiting the US to stay longer in the country—and thus to "spend more of their money while vacationing in Arizona, California, Florida or the like."[50] On energy and the environment, some of Trump's most loyal partisans have challenged his views, including Governor of New Hampshire John Sununu who, during a joint public event with Premier of Québec Philippe Couillard held in Montreal on March, praised Québec's hydroelectric power and described New Hampshire's opportunity to import more hydropower from 'La Belle Province' as a "win-win for both sides."[51]

Conclusion

*The optimist sees the donut,
the pessimist sees the hole.*

Oscar Wilde

---

trump-of-close-canada-us-ties/.

[49] See: http://poststar.com/news/local/government-and-politics/stefanik-discusses-nafta/article_99f19f6c-ead1-591c-9329-a1f3e6b02d0c.html.

[50] Retrieved from: http://www.cbc.ca/news/politics/canadian-snowbirds-8-months-1.4011788.

[51] Retrieved from: http://www.unionleader.com/energy/Gov-Sununu-praises-Northern-Pass-project-during-visit-to-Montreal-03212017.

Oscar Wilde has summed up the Canadian perspective on Canada-US relations in the Trump era. Since Donald Trump's election on November 8, 2016, polls have shown that most Canadians now see the US as "the hole." Canadians have good reasons to worry about the Trump presidency. Indeed, Trump has used high-intensity language on issues that matter to Canada and he has come up with a plan that contradicts most positions of Justin Trudeau, a Prime Minister who has enjoyed a long honeymoon with a majority of Canadians, who saw him as a Canadian version of Barack Obama, a very popular President north of the US border during all of his tenure. A more optimistic outlook of what Canada-US relations might look like under Trump can also be justified. Fareed Zakaria's point that Trump's might be a "rocking horse presidency" seemed to make even more sense. The architecture of the US political system would make it difficult for Trump to unveil the plans he has for Canada-US relations, and Trump's personal style could lead one to believe that he often "talks the talk" without necessarily "walking the walk."

If, however, the pessimism takes precedence over optimism, then Justin Trudeau and Canadians might still find solace in the fact that recent European elections did not go as planned for candidates and parties favored by the 45th President. Trump's ideological clones Geert Wilders and Marine Le Pen respectively lost the Dutch general election (March 15, 2017) and French presidential election (April 23 and May 7, 2017). Theresa May's attempt at strengthening her mandate in order to negotiate a strong Brexit deal with Europe backfired and she lost her majority in the British Parliament on June 9.[52] Over just a few months, Europe thus became more similar to Trudeau's worldview than Trump's. So if Donald Trump's America really ends up becoming "the hole" Oscar Wilde once talked about, the good news for Justin Trudeau and Canadians is that there will likely be a "donut" called "Europe" across the Atlantic for the years to come.

REFERENCES

Doherty, B. 2012. *The Rise of the President's Permanent Campaign*. Lawrence, KA: University Press of Kansas.

---

[52] See: http://www.cnn.com/2017/06/09/world/uk-election-theresa-may-brexit-strategy-backfired/index.html.

Feloni, R. 2017. "8 Key Insights from Trump's Book 'The Art of the Deal' Reveal How the President Thinks." *Business Insider*, February 2. Available at: http://www.businessinsider.com/the-art-of-the-deal-donald-trump-leadership-2017-1/#his-biggest-influence-growing-up-was-his-father-1.

Gagnon, F. 2017a. "De la 'Bromance' au Suspense." *Global Brief*, March 3. Available at: http://globalbrief.ca/blog/2017/03/03/de-la-%C2%ABbromance%C2%BB-au-suspense/.

Gagnon, F. 2017b. "La 'Relation Spéciale' Canado-Américaine à l'Épreuve du Fossé Idéologique Entre Donald Trump et Justin Trudeau." *Revue de Recherche en Civilisation Américaine*, in press.

Gagnon, F. et al. 2016. *L'effet 11 Septembre 15 Ans Après* [The Effect of September 11 15 Years After]. Sillery, QC, CA: Septentrion.

Hufbauer, G.C. and E. Jung. 2017. "17-22 NAFTA Renegotiations: US Offensive and Defensive Interests vis-à-vis Canada." *Peterson Institute for International Economics Policy Brief*, June. Available at: https://piie.com/system/files/documents/pb17-22.pdf.

Ibbitson, J. 2005. *The Polite Revolution: Perfecting the Canadian Dream*. Toronto, ON, CA: McClelland & Stewart.

Nincic, M. 2012. "External Affairs and the Electoral Connection." In *The Domestic Sources of American Foreign Policy: Insights and Evidence* (ed. J. McCormick) (6th ed.). New York: Rowman & Littlefield.

Robertson, C. 2005. "Getting Noticed in Washington: The Hard Part of Canada's Job." Options Politiques, Novembre. Available at: http://irpp.org/wp-content/uploads/assets/po/canada-us-trade-tensions/robertson.pdf

Robertson, C. 2017. "A Primer to the Trump-Trudeau Meeting." *Reports of the Canadian Global Affairs Institute*, February 10. Available at: http://www.colinrobertson.ca/?p=1827.

Snyder, T. 2017. *On Tyranny: Twenty Lessons from the Twentieth Century*. New York: Tim Duggan.

Trump, D.J. with T. Schwartz. 1987. *The Art of the Deal.* New York: Random House.

4
"AMERICA FIRST": A MEXICAN PERSPECTIVE ON TRUMP'S PRESIDENCY

María Celia Toro

INTRODUCTION

On November 8, 2016, the unthinkable happened: Donald J. Trump was elected President of the United States of America (US). The two countries most affected by this, according to a respected Mexican foreign affairs analyst, were the US itself and Mexico (Guerra 2016). This unexpected change in US politics would be "the end of [Mexico's] dream of being part of North America," to quote another seasoned political analyst (Zárate 2017); and for yet another, it represented "a radical change in US-Mexican relations, an epochal watershed, similar to the fall of the Berlin Wall or the disintegration of the Soviet Union" (Rodríguez 2017).

Indeed, Trump—considered to be a threat to Mexico—was expected to unleash major political turmoil in both countries. The Mexican president, Enrique Peña Nieto, was the first to suffer a political setback and many asked how a president whose popularity had declined to less than 20%, would approach a US counterpart who had insulted Mexicans at least since 2014. But if he were to seize the opportunity and strike a favorable deal with the US, he would certainly regain political support not only for himself but also for his party, the Institutional Revolutionary Party (PRI). Thus, coming to terms with Donald Trump became an imperative for Peña Nieto—and for Mexico.

This chapter traces Mexican reactions to Donald Trump during the first 100 days of his administration, as they were recorded by the Mexican press,[1] in order to document and offer a Mexican perspective on an extremely difficult and historic moment in US-Mexico relations.

---

[1] El Universal was reviewed daily, and there were frequent reviews of La Jornada. Other Mexican and US newspapers were also read. All translations are the author's.

The Domestic Political Challenge

Fear was perhaps the first reaction expressed by Mexican elites—in government, business, and society as a whole—to the election of Donald Trump. Mexicans were fully aware that he would have a very negative impact on their country and on US-Mexico relations. It was a matter of anticipating the magnitude of the blow and of assessing what Mexico could do about it.

The priority of the Peña administration was to avoid a political and economic debacle. The government had to quickly ascertain the real intentions of the new US president, and the extent to which he could affect Mexican interests and the bilateral relationship. Equally important, Mexico had to carefully consider its negotiation capacity, and work out appropriate domestic and international strategies. How to face and deal with President Trump thus became an important part of public debate.

Mexico's external vulnerabilities and dependence on the US were well known and, in the short term, impossible to overcome. The night of November 8, 2016, for example, the Mexican peso lost 11% of its value *vis-à-vis* the US dollar,[2] a clear sign of loss of confidence in the future of the country's economy. Capital flight—the traditional Mexican financial nightmare—had to be prevented. In December, the Banco de México raised interest rates, one more time,[3] and the Secretary of Finance announced cutbacks in government spending to avoid further inflation. Projections of economic growth were revised, downward. The head of the Banco de México was asked to defer his resignation—originally announced for June 2017—until the end of the year.[4]

On January 21, the day after Trump's inauguration, Mexican newspapers quoted his famous statement: "From this moment on, it's going

---

[2] Actually, the peso weakened even before the election of Trump. Retrieved from: https://www.bbvaresearch.com/wp-content/uploads/2016/11/161115_EfectosMexico_TriunfoTrump.pdf.

[3] Retrieved from: http://eleconomista.com.mx/sistema-financiero/2016/12/15/banco-mexico-incrementa-su-tasa-interes-575.

[4] Retrieved from: http://eleconomista.com.mx/finanzas-publicas/2017/02/20/agustin-carstens-extendera-permanencia-banxico.

to be America First." A prominent, now retired, Mexican diplomat described this speech as "uninformed," "incoherent," "intolerant and aggressive." In his view, the "terrifying" discourse of "America First" could only mean a "decidedly unilateral foreign policy," one in which "values would not play much of a role" (Navarrete 2017).

True, Donald Trump's agenda focused on mostly domestic issues: trade (for the benefit of US firms and workers), unauthorized immigrants (no longer considered a valuable work force, but a threat to national security and public safety, and, consequently, best deported), and border security (to be guaranteed by a monumental wall along the entire 2,000-mile common border). Except for the North Atlantic Free Trade Area (NAFTA), if indeed it was to be renegotiated and not cancelled, the rest of the presidential agenda with his southern neighbor was strictly unilateral—and detrimental for Mexico.

"Buy American and Hire Americans" was understood as buzzwords against free trade—against NAFTA—and against foreign workers—many of whom were Mexican; they were two of Trump's most frequently repeated and popular stances during, and even before, his campaign. Wilbur Ross (later confirmed to Secretary of the Commerce) had declared two days before Trump's inaugural speech, that "the first thing" he would do once in office would be to change "the nation's free trade agreement with Mexico and Canada," to the advantage of "the American worker and the American manufacturing community."[5]

In Mexico, people from all regions, political convictions, and social classes felt extremely vulnerable. But there was also anger toward their ruling classes, which were held responsible for their country's—and their—plight. A well-known former public official wondered how a once proud and respected nation had become such an easy prey for the new US president (Olea 2017). It seemed as if Mexicans were responsible for Donald Trump's aggressive rhetoric toward their country.

President Peña Nieto was called upon to react to a "parochial" and "nationalist" discourse with courage and dignity. The Mexican press and

---

5   Retrieved from: https://www.washingtonpost.com/news/wonk/wp/2017/01/18/commerce-nominee-ross-says-top-priority-is-renegotiating-nafta/?utm_term=.f99657f029b6.

its editorials insisted on the importance of getting ready to react swiftly and intelligently (Chávez Presa 2017), as the incoming US president's inaugural address had emphasized that his decisions would be only in the interest of the US. (*El Universal* 2017a).

Universities, the media, the Senate, and business groups quickly organized seminars and conferences on Trump and Mexico. But understanding Donald Trump was not easy. Was he simply a unilateralist or an isolationist? Or rather, was he a mercantilist trying to use US power to advance American economic interests? Would he, in the end, follow the advice of the powerful US bureaucracy, always knowledgeable and reluctant to embark on major changes? Would legislative and judicial powers, as well as American civil society, be able to keep Trump within bounds? Pedro Aspe, former Mexican Secretary of Finance, believed they would (*El Universal* 2017b). Would Trump actually fulfill his campaign promises that would seriously impact Mexico or would the traditional US national interest in Mexican political stability prevail? How far was Donald Trump, now president, ready to go?

A Mexican negotiator of NAFTA in the early 1990s, Jaime Zabludovsky, claimed: "We are in a moment of great uncertainty, but it is not that dark" (*El Universal* 2017c). Carlos Slim, the wealthiest and most powerful Mexican businessman, considered that Trump was not "a terminator," but "a negotiator" (*El Universal* 2017d).

It was not difficult, however, to think that Donald Trump's policies and Mexican weaknesses, both internal and *vis-à-vis* the US, would result in very lop-sided trade and border security agreements—favoring the US, of course—and in large-scale deportation of Mexican undocumented migrants (*Milenio* 2017a). (around 5.5 million). Everything seemed possible in those early days of the Trump administration. After all, according to *vox populi*, for Mexico it had always been "America First."

This time, however, it could be worse, and many believed that the Mexican government would be unable to do something about it. Countering this belief and preventing economic and political actors from taking advantage of the delicate international situation became Mexico's most important political challenge.

Preparing for the Worst

A first meeting with Donald Trump was in order. Mexico had to be firm and face Trump. In early January, President Peña Nieto called his former Secretary of Finance, and most trusted collaborator, Luis Videgaray, to head Foreign Affairs and conduct the bilateral relation with the new Trump administration.[6]

On the domestic front, the Mexican president could not take chances. He asked for political support and called for national unity. On the international front, he requested a meeting with Donald Trump. Peña Nieto was convinced that he had not only to elude, by all means possible, a direct confrontation with the US but also to avoid subordination. On January 20, he announced that his diplomacy would strive for a "respectful dialogue with the new US administration" (*El Universal* 2017e). A couple of days later, he established the two priorities of his foreign policy: diversifying foreign relations and establishing a new era of dialogue and negotiation with the Trump administration (*El Universal* 2017f).

On January 21, President Peña called President Trump to congratulate him and express his government's willingness to work for a mutually beneficial agenda, "within a framework of respect for the sovereignty of the two nations and of shared responsibility" (*El Universal* 2017g). The White House press secretary, Sean Spicer, informed, that same day, that the presidents would meet at the White House on January 31 (Briseño 2017a). On Sunday January 22, President Trump said that "Mexico had been fantastic," the Mexican President "had been marvelous" (Briseño 2017b), and that, along with immigration and border security discussions, trade talks would start with Peña Nieto's visit to Washington, and that of Canadian Prime Minister Justin Trudeau would visit shortly thereafter. Only two days after the new president was sworn in, this was a much-welcomed announcement.

But Mexican officials and an attentive public would soon discover that Trump could change his mind from one day to the next, tweet recklessly, and be quite disruptive of bilateral diplomatic encounters only to keep direct communication with his numerous followers alive and remind everyone that he was actively on top of all negotiations.

---

[6] Videgaray had been forced to resign as Secretary of Finance in August 2016, after having organized then Republican nominee Donald Trump's visit to Mexico, which infuriated Mexicans and was considered a major diplomatic blunder.

The day before Trump was sworn into office, the coordinators of five parliamentary groups in the Mexican Senate issued a statement of "support for the Mexican State," demanding fair treatment in the renovation of NAFTA, and rejecting "the construction of a wall, massive deportations, and actions that could affect the human rights of our fellow Mexicans" (*El Universal* 2017h).

Large Mexican business organizations announced, on January 23, that they were ready to increase their investments in Mexico, to support the government, and to participate actively in the negotiation of a new trade deal with the US and Canada (Briseño 2017a, Gascón, Díaz, and Andrade 2017). The President of the *Consejo Coordinador Empresarial* (CCE), one of the country's most important business associations, suggested taking advantage of the opportunity to diversify exports, and to expand the domestic market (*El Universal* 2017i).

Others manifested their worries and anticipated the worst, namely, that Peña Nieto and members of his cabinet would be ready to accept almost anything in order to rescue the trade pact and avoid a costly confrontation with the US. The rightist party—PAN—asked for "firmness with Trump" and for dignity in negotiating issues having to do with security, migration, and trade (Canchola 2017). The left, in particular the highly popular Andrés Manuel López Obrador, expressed concern over the likely content of diplomatic talks and the "lack of transparency": "We don't want dealings under the table" (Zavala 2017).

The Mexican Secretaries of Foreign Affairs, Luis Videgaray, and of Economy, Ildefonso Guajardo, travelled to Washington on January 25, to prepare for the presidential meeting that would take place a few days later. After British Prime Minister Theresa May, the Mexican president would have been the second head of state to visit the White House. But the Trump-Peña Nieto meeting never took place.

As the two Mexican Ministers, together with the Head of the President's Office, were flying to Washington to meet with members of the Trump administration, Donald Trump tweeted "Big day planned on NATIONAL SECURITY tomorrow. Among many other things, we will build the wall!"[7] and signed, a few hours later, an Executive Order mandat-

---

[7] Retrieved from: Twitter, @realDonaldTrump, January 25, 2017; see also La

ing its construction—"Border Security and Immigration Enforcement Improvements."[8] The news traveled quickly. Trump was, once again, toying with Mexico and undermining the authority of high-level foreign officials. Mexicans were outraged. Peña Nieto's envoys "had been ambushed" argued a well-known political analyst (Zubieta 2017); the encounter between the two Heads of State should be cancelled, argued another commentator and former diplomat, as conditions were far from favorable (Filloy 2017). On January 26, President Trump finally instigated the cancellation of Peña Nieto's trip by issuing another of his famous tweets: "If Mexico is unwilling to pay for the badly needed wall, then it would be better to cancel the upcoming meeting."[9] President Peña Nieto tweeted back that he was not traveling to Washington on January 31. This was one of Peña Nieto's best moments, and a much-needed respite. Political parties, congressmen and senators, the Conference of Governors (*Conago*), businessmen, intellectuals, and society at large applauded his decision. Mexicans felt proud of the dignified and patriotic position of their president.

The next day, on the brink of a major US-Mexican diplomatic crisis, only a week after Trump had assumed office, the two leaders held a 20-minute 'phone call' (*El Universal* 2017k). According to Associated Press and a reputable Mexican journalist, during the conversation Trump mentioned the possibility of "helping Mexico" with troops to take care of "the bunch of bad hombres down there," since the Mexican military had not been doing a good job dealing with the drug cartels.[10] Although officials from both countries rushed to deny this, and offered a more nuanced version of the conversation, Mexican media talked about a possible US military intervention (*El Universal* 2017l).

Still, Peña Nieto said the 'phone call was "constructive"'; the presidents agreed not to talk again about the border wall, as it had become a sense-

---

Jornada (2017a).

[8] Retrieved from: https://www.whitehouse.gov/the-press-office/2017/01/25/executive-order-border-security-and-immigration-enforcement-improvements. See also Sancho (2017c).

[9] Twitter, @realDonaldTrump, January 26, 2017; see also El Universal (2017j).

[10] Retrieved from: https://www.theguardian.com/us-news/2017/feb/02/bad-hombres-reports-claim-trump-threatened-to-send-troops-to-mexico.

less source of contention between them, most notably after Trump's visit to Mexico in August 2016. The two would not, however, converse again or meet during the first 100 days of the Trump presidency.

After this souring of the bilateral relation, the US Secretary of State, Rex W. Tillerson, and the Mexican Minister of Foreign Affairs, Luis Videgaray, took full charge of conducting US-Mexican affairs. During ten shocking days, Mexicans could not believe their ears, nor make sense of what was going on. Less than three weeks into the Trump administration, Videgaray declared that "the differences between Mexico and the government of the US are public and notorious, [but we must continue to work together to] address the challenges and common opportunities."[11]

But the sense that Mexico was being bullied by the US and was not responding forcefully lingered on until the end of February (*El Universal* 2017m). Appearing before the Senate, the Secretary of Foreign Affairs had to insist again, "diplomacy is not equivalent to weakness," and explained that President Peña Nieto was not being weak, he was only following diplomatic mores and the rules of international comity (*Reforma* 2017). The following day, in an interview on "Good Morning America," Vice President Mike Pence declared that Trump was determined to make Mexico pay for the wall. As Peña Nieto had said only a week before, with Donald Trump "nothing is certain" and US-Mexican relations are, for the time being, "unpredictable" (*El Universal* 2017n).

A nationalist sentiment began to flourish in Mexico, and its flag, national emblem, or colors proliferated as profile pictures in Twitter, Facebook, and Whatsapp; Peña Nieto's was no exception. While Trump's threats—such as building a wall, abandoning NAFTA, and deporting Mexicans—were first received with great apprehension, they soon became the subject of numerous jokes, quips, and memes, notably in social networks and media. Different political forces were willing to rally behind Peña Nieto, but they were also concerned that he would manipulate Mexican nationalism in his favor. Nonetheless, many people, including religious leaders, were ready to present a unified front against Trump, who had offended Mexicans in many ways, and agreed with the

---

[11] Retrieved from: https://www.insidetheworld.org/2017/02/09/by-us-secretary-of-state-will-go-to-mexico-in-the-coming-weeks/.

powerful businessman Carlos Slim: "We have to back [President Peña Nieto]. The whole country has to, in the face of a special risk in US-Mexican relations that we had not seen in 100 years."[12]

A group of academics and NGOs called for a national march—*Vibra México*—on February 12. One of the main organizers, Enrique Graue, Rector of the National Autonomous University of Mexico (UNAM), stated: "Mexicans are outraged by many things. We're outraged by poverty, we're outraged by inequality, we're outraged by impunity. ... [But] at this time, we're most outraged by the treatment Mexico has received from the president of the US."[13]

Groups that had long been criticizing Peña Nieto felt that marching for Mexico could easily turn into marching for the president. Large segments of the Mexican public were as distrustful of Peña Nieto as they were of Trump. In order to avoid further internal divisions, political parties refrained from participating. In the end, though at least 14 cities participated, the turnout was far from multitudinous (*El Universal* 2017o). Mostly active members of social networks also organized a boycott against American products. Neither the nationalist movement, nor the boycott of US products, lasted more than a few weeks.

With or without a united domestic front, Mexico had to prepare for the worst. By mid-February, it was clear that there were not major differences between candidate Trump and President Trump. Not only was this a moment of great unease and shock, it was also a moment of solitude. Consequently, the Mexican government initiated a systematic outreach for allies in other parts of the world and within the US.

RESCUING NAFTA

A decision by Trump that lent credence to the possibility of seeing the US withdrawal from NAFTA was, on the first working day of his

---

[12] Retrieved from: https://www.washingtonpost.com/world/the_americas/mexicans-march-to-protest-trump--but-also-their-own-leaders-and-politicians/2017/02/12/6cc9b29a-efcc-11e6-a100-fdaaf400369a_story.html?utm_term=.0281dd7de342.

[13] Retrieved from: http://www.razon.com.mx/spip.php?article337462.

presidency, he signed a memorandum to abandon the TPP.[14] After all, abrogating this treaty was one of Trump's most conspicuous campaign promises, and having opened the door to a renegotiation—a day after arriving at the White House—during the telephone call placed by Peña Nieto to congratulate him, Trump wanted to strike a new bargain with Mexico, and presumably Canada, quickly, starting on January 31.

Trying to make virtue of necessity, Mexican officials advanced the idea that, indeed, after more than two decades the agreement had to be modernized, and informed their US counterparts that they were ready to start the talks. At first, it was not clear whether Canada would also be sitting at the bargaining table, and this was yet another source of concern for Mexico.

If threatening to cancel NAFTA was Trump's strategy of choice, Mexico's was to underline its benefits. The policy of finding allies in the US business community and in the Washington-based think-tanks to publicize its advantages, which had begun many months before the US election, was intensified after November 8.[15]

Defending NAFTA in the US, by joining American businessmen and civil society groups with a stake in Mexico, was the first and most visible Mexican tactic to impede the unraveling of a trade accord that represents more than half of the country's GDP in 2014.[16] This seemed to have worked in the past: in 1993, the Mexican government lobbied strongly to persuade US congressmen to ratify NAFTA; in 2001, US businessmen pressed hard to convince their government of the benefits of keeping the US-Mexican border open to trade after 9/11.

Mexico, argued Luis Videgaray, is "an indispensable partner of the US"— "trade between our two countries exceeds 1.4 billion dollars a

---

[14] "Presidential Memorandum Regarding Withdrawal of the US from the Trans-Pacific Partnership Negotiations and Agreement," The White House, January 23, 2017.

[15] Retrieved from: https://www.ft.com/content/84ca9d3c-b327-11e6-9c37-5787335499a0?mhq5j=e2.

[16] Retrieved from: http://www.worldbank.org/en/country/mexico; see also: https://www.census.gov/foreign-trade/statistics/highlights/top/top1512yr.html.

day" (*El Universal* 2017p). Beware—said Peter Schechter, Director for Latin America at the Atlantic Council—withdrawing from NAFTA will affect not only the 28 states of the American Union for which Mexico is their first or second trading partner, but it could have a serious destabilizing effect in Mexico. For the first time, the US could have a southern border, "from Texas to California, radicalized and destabilized," and "we don't want that" (Bugarin 2017).

Secretary of Economy Guajardo declared that the government was considering retaliation, by matching each and every US measure against Mexican exports, like the much-publicized border tax (which, according to Mexican officials, would practically represent the end of the trilateral agreement), or the import tax of up to 35% on Mexican products. Both tariffs were announced as a means to reduce the 60 billion trade deficit with Mexico, one of Trump's most vocal demands (*El Universal* 2017q). Varied US proposals of imposing tariffs on Mexican imports continued until the end of February, despite numerous warnings by both the Secretary of Foreign Affairs and of Economy, that if the US taxed Mexican products, they would walk away from the negotiations (*La Jornada* 2017a). Unless a renovated NAFTA led to a "win-win situation," claimed the newly appointed Secretary of Foreign Affairs, the treaty would be abandoned; furthermore, any agreement that undermined the dignity of the nation was unacceptable *El Universal* 2017r).

Critics in Mexico argued that it would be best to end the accord, and begin an inward reorientation of the country's economy. The expected gains—the narrowing of the gap between per capita income in the US and in Mexico, and the creation of hundreds of thousands of well-paid jobs—were nowhere to be seen. Free trade, they insisted, had not been good for everyone, and this was an opportunity for Mexico to change its development model. As the journalist Felicity Lawrence and many others claimed, Donald Trump was right, NAFTA had been a terrible trade deal: "By 2004 it had become clear that it was a disaster for many poor Mexicans and was driving them to emigrate."[17] The

---

[17] Retrieved from: https://www.theguardian.com/commentisfree/2016/nov/18/trump-nafta-us-workers-not-big-losers-mexican-workers-suffer-most. I thank Nora Lustig for calling my attention to this article.

country, claimed a group of well-known academics at UNAM—*Grupo Nuevo Curso de Desarrollo*—was facing a "serious and clear" threat that demanded "a new development path—one less vulnerable and less dependent."[18]

With an intense travel itinerary, Mexican officials and businessmen reached out to US governors, industrialists, retailers, importers, and exporters (*El Universal* 2017s) and organized various forums to underline the fact that five million jobs in Mexico and six million in the US depended on NAFTA-based foreign trade. The US automotive sector, the core of the agreement, was particularly concerned about the possible disruption of complex cross-border supply chains. So was the US food and agricultural industry, whose huge exports to Mexico led them to address a letter to Trump urging him to "modernize the North American Free Trade Agreement," which they considered to be a very successful "market integration" that had to be preserved and expanded.[19]

Mexican officials and firms were in favor, of course, of a rapid renegotiation and of modest changes, to avoid, as US officials also argued "[casting] a cloud over the investment plans of American businesses and farmers."[20] Pressured by president-elect Donald Trump, two large US companies had announced the suspension of investment projects in Mexico, and the opening of manufacturing plants in the US.[21] While difficult to document, other firms, foreign and national, may have adopted a wait-and-see policy, despite the many offers and efforts of Mexican officials to cajole them into not deferring investments.

In crowded political meetings, Trump kept insisting he would cancel NAFTA (Camil 2017). Just before reaching his first 100 days in office, however, Trump declared that he had decided to renegotiate rather than terminate the trilateral trade agreement,[22] after having said, only a week

---

[18] Retrieved from: http://www.nuevocursodedesarrollo.unam.mx/.

[19] Retrieved from: https://corn.org/wp-content/uploads/2017/01/NorthAmerica_FoodAG-Letter_Pres.Trump_170123-FINAL.pdf.

[20] Retrieved from: http://www.washingtontimes.com/news/2017/jun/21/lighthizer-hopes-renegotiate-nafta-end-year/.

[21] Carrier in November 29, 2016 and Ford in January 3, 2017. See: Ferrer (2017).

[22] Retrieved from: http://edition.cnn.com/2017/04/26/politics/trump-nafta/

and a half earlier, that he was getting rid of it.²³ Uncertainty was negatively affecting the Mexican economy and polity, and time was of the essence. Nevertheless, it was not until the second week in May, a few days after the Senate approved Robert Lighthizer as the new US Trade Representative,²⁴ that the Trump administration was able to inform that negotiations would begin in mid-August. Both governments expressed their desire to finish the talks by the end of the year, before the Mexican presidential and the US mid-term elections of 2018.²⁵

While Mexico concentrated on rescuing NAFTA, the Trump administration preferred to focus first on "security issues"—undocumented migrants, the border, and drug smuggling.

The Wall and Border Security

Constructing a wall on the border with Mexico was at the core of Trump's political campaign, and its very announcement constituted a serious blow to otherwise friendly US-Mexico relations—"I want nothing to do with Mexico other than to build an impenetrable WALL and stop them from ripping off US"— the would-be Republican presidential candidate had tweeted, on March 2015.²⁶ Whether Trump truly believed it would be easy to launch his extravagant project, or was simply tapping into US fears and anxieties for electoral purposes, is not easy to tell. He relished—to be sure—the great applause he obtained every time he gleefully or adamantly reminded his followers of the "big, fat, beautiful, wall"²⁷. Not surprisingly, he invariably talked about it in his public meetings, and in his major speeches. In his remarkable joint address to Congress in February, the president referred to the border more

---

index.html.

[23] Retrieved from: https://www.whitehouse.gov/the-press-office/2017/04/18/remarks-president-trump-buy-american-hire-american-executive-order.

[24] Retrieved from: http://www.reuters.com/article/us-usa-trade-lighthizer-idUSKBN18727C.

[25] Retrieved from: http://www.eluniversal.com.mx/articulo/english/2017/05/31/mexico-and-us-attempt-conclude-nafta-negotiations-end-year-guajardo.

[26] Twitter, @realDonaldTrump, March 5, 2015.

[27] Retrieved from: http://www.latimes.com/politics/la-na-pol-trump-california-campaign-20160602-snap-story.html.

often than to Obamacare.²⁸

On signing the "Border Security and Immigration Enforcement Improvements" Executive Order, Trump declared: "Beginning today the US gets back control of its borders," as "we are in the middle of a crisis in our southern border."²⁹ The US president was adroit at lumping together and associating migrants, criminals, and drug smugglers, with an undefended border. Defining them as threats to US public and national security, he would call to "restore the rule of law," and to erect a physical barrier that would prove to be a "very effective weapon against drugs and crime,"³⁰ and prevent "all unlawful entries."³¹

A few hours after learning of this Executive Order, the Mexican President addressed the nation in a televised message: "I regret and reject the decision of the US to continue building a wall that, for years, far from bringing us together, is dividing us. Mexico does not believe in walls."³²

Trump's insistence on having Mexico pay for the fortification of the US's southern border, which he certainly knew would not happen, put Peña Nieto in a very uncomfortable position. Needless to say, he found the idea not only preposterous but also outrageous, and was bound to answer that Mexico was not, under any circumstance, going to pay for it. As one US journalist commented "Money aside it became a question of national humiliation."³³ Many, including a former Mexican Secretary of Foreign Affairs, considered that Peña Nieto was falling into Trump's provocation by stressing the payment of the wall, "rather [than] its very existence."³⁴

---

[28] See: https://www.nbcnews.com/storyline/trumps-address-to-congress.

[29] Retrieved from: http://www.bbc.com/news/world-us-canada-38740717; see also: Sancho (2017a).

[30] Retrieved from: https://www.whitehouse.gov/the-press-office/2017/02/28/remarks-president-trump-joint-address-congress.

[31] "Executive Order: Border Security and Immigration Enforcement Improvements," The White House, January 25, 2017; see also: Sancho (2017c).

[32] Retrieved from: http://abcnews.go.com/International/mexicos-president-regret-reject-plan-border-wall/story?id=45052352; see also: Twitter, @EPN, January 25, 2017.

[33] Retrieved from: https://www.nytimes.com/2017/02/02/opinion/trumps-mexican-shakedown.html?ref=nyt-es&mcid=nyt-es&subid=article.

[34] Retrieved from: https://www.nytimes.com/2017/01/27/opinion/mexicos-

Indeed, when it came to the wall, the Mexican President had a hard time taking the appropriate stance. At home, Mexicans demanded a more forceful response to the insult, a valiant defense of the nation; the president and his team, according to many, had been silent for too long, and too mild in their disapproval. But, Peña Nieto was determined not to fight with Trump, and was well aware that he could do little to persuade him of cancelling his border plan, which is so dear to him and to his most ardent followers. The Mexican President seemed to be under siege. Mexican officials finally concluded that there was no point in continuing the exchange of rude messages, since the building of the great fence was not, in effect, part of the bilateral agenda (Sancho 2017b).

It was up to the Mexican cabinet and other members of government to address the issue, after the late-January agreement between the two presidents to avoid making any reference to the wall in public discourse, which President Trump subsequently did not honor. Building such a barrier was "not a friendly gesture," said Luis Videgaray on different occasions (*El Universal* 2017t); "a hostile act," according to the Mexican Ministry of Foreign Affairs (*La Jornada* 2017c). In the words of the President of the Committee on Foreign Relations of the Mexican Senate: "The construction of this wall is an affront to Mexico; it reminds us of those who die there" (*La Jornado* 2017b).

Annoyed and incredulous, Mexicans would learn about the many options considered by the Trump administration to come up with the money for the wall, from imposing taxes at the border or on Mexican imports, to confiscating money from drug cartels or migrants' remittances (Gupta 2016, *La Jornada* 2017c). They would also learn about the construction project proposals presented by different firms,[35] which put the Mexican government in the awkward position of publicly disapproving—on ethical grounds (*Milenio* 2017b)—of national firms expressing an interest in participating in the bid (*El Universal* 2017u). From the perspective of the Mexican Catholic church, whoever intend-

---

forceful-resistance.html.

[35] See: http://www.hstoday.us/briefings/grants-funding/single-article/cbp-issues-several-border-wall-construction-conceptrfps/666f6221b5866883dd59a437807c844d.html.

ed to "invest in the wall of the fanatic Donald Trump" would be considered "a traitor" (*El Universal* 2017v).

If Mexican leaders were cautious, trying to prevent a major conflict with the US that could affect their political standing and the bilateral relationship, public opinions reacted more freely, making fun of the wall (some of the jokes were truly ingenious and witty), and this contributed to unifying the country against Trump, and to relaxing the tense political ambience at home.

Fortunately for Mexico, Trump faced many legal and political hurdles to building his fence, as well as little support from important members of his cabinet, most notably, John Kelly, Secretary of the Department of Homeland Security. During his confirmation hearing, Kelly clearly asserted: "A physical barrier in and of itself will not do the job [of] cutting the flow of migrants and illegal drugs."[36] The US Congress refused to fund it, and Trump threatened to "close the government" if he did not get the requested budget; "Trump was flattened by the wall," said a Mexican daily (*El Universal* 2017v).

Trump unwittingly put Mexico back on the global map, as a victim of this offensive proposal. The wall turned into an easy way of mocking Trump and of identifying him as unreasonable. The country garnered international sympathy—often compassionate—and the government tried to bring foreign leaders to talk on Mexico's behalf, in an effort to find support in its lonely resistance to Trump. While not many countries were ready to confront Trump for a policy that did not directly concern them, the most important international newspapers rejected the idea, on moral and practical grounds. The mayor of Berlin reminded Trump that walls were not a good idea.[37] In an interview during his visit to Mexico in 2016, Pope Francis said: "A person who thinks only about building walls, wherever they may be, and not building bridges, is not a Christian," a comment that upset Donald Trump.[38] Similar remarks were heard

---

[36] Retrieved from: http://www.latimes.com/nation/la-na-kelly-nomination-2017 0110-story.html.

[37] See: https://www.theguardian.com/world/2017/jan/27/berlin-mayor-michael -mueller-donald-trump-border-wall.

[38] Retrieved from: http://edition.cnn.com/2016/08/31/politics/donald-trump-

from high-level officials, leaders, and heads of State in Europe, including Spain (*El Universal* 2017w) and Germany,[39] and Latin America (*El Universal* 2017x), including Bolivia, Chile, Argentina, or from international organizations, such as the Organization of American States (*La Jornada* 2017d) and the Delegation to the Euro-Latin American Parliamentary Assembly, which expressed its "solidarity with the Mexican people for Trump's hostile policies and expressions" (*El Universal* 2017y). The most important critic, however, was the US society itself (*La Jornada* 2017e). For example, a group of over 200 philosophers—US Philosophers Against Trump's Policies Toward Mexico—published a letter repudiating Trump for his policies toward Mexico, and expressing their deep concern for the plans to construct a wall—"a direct aggression to a historic economic partner and a cherished friend"—and to massively deport undocumented immigrants, thus compromising "the inherent dignity of these persons."[40]

Trump never explained how the wall would improve US security, nor did he provide evidence to sustain his claim that US borders were "wide open for anyone to cross and for drugs to pour in at [an] unprecedented rate,"[41] but he did not mention the long stretches of fences and walls that already covered one-third of the US-Mexico divide (Toro 2017).

Trump was at his best setting up a political stage, his back to the world, from which to proclaim that he could, with police and a wall, "control the border" —an old but quite effective US political slogan—and "Make America Safe Again."[42] Thus, he manipulated public anxieties about threats that were exaggerated to begin with; addressing a group of followers in Philadelphia on his 100th day in office, he was happy to say:

---

mexico-statements/index.html.

[39] See: http://www.univision.com/noticias/america-latina/analistas-merkel-visita-mexico-para-mostrar-poder-politico-ante-un-trump-no-fiable.

[40] Retrieved from: http://www.filosoficas.unam.mx/sitio/american-philosophers-against-trumps-policies-towards-mexico.

[41] Retrieved from: https://www.whitehouse.gov/the-press-office/2017/02/28/remarks-president-trump-joint-address-congress.

[42] Retrieved from: https://www.whitehouse.gov/the-press-office/2017/02/28/remarks-president-trump-joint-address-congress.

"Don't worry, we're going to have the wall. ... Rest assured. Go home, go to sleep."[43]

MIGRATION AND SECURITY

Another difficult moment in US-Mexico relations came toward the end of February, in the context of bilateral talks on migration and security—always a sensitive matter in Mexico. Different presidential security advisors traveled to Mexico on February 8, to make sure that cooperation between the two countries against organized crime, drug smuggling, and undocumented migration remained unaltered or was expanded. For example, the joint bilateral or regional efforts to prevent Central American migrants from traversing Mexican territory on their way to the US (*El Universal* 2017z). The Mexican Secretaries of Defense and Navy participated in these conversations.

The next day, Luis Videgaray traveled to Washington to continue these negotiations, insisting—as had the Secretary of the Interior, Miguel Ángel Osorio Chong—on the need to implement more effective programs against money laundering and arms smuggling across the common border (*La Jornada* 2017f, 2017g). During that first formal bilateral encounter in Washington between the Mexican Secretary of Foreign Affairs and the US Secretaries of State, Rex Tillerson, and of Homeland Security, John F. Kelly, Videgaray asked for the US to respect for the "civil and human rights of immigrants in the US" and to guarantee the "due judicial process" (*La Jornada* 2017h). The two US secretaries agreed to visit Mexico at the end of the month to continue talks regarding bilateral collaboration.[44]

Mexican public opinion was leery of the likely content of these encounters. Mexican pundits and analysts wondered how much Mexico was ready to offer in exchange for rescuing NAFTA, or put differently, what would be the price the US would exact for maintaining it. In response,

---

[43] Retrieved from: https://www.washingtonpost.com/politics/100-days-in-trump-invigorates-enchants-crowd-during-rally-in-harrisburg-pa/2017/04/29/c656d764-2aa7-11e7-a616-d7c8a68c1a66_story.html?utm_term=.663553115e4f.

[44] See: https://www.state.gov/r/pa/prs/ps/2017/02/267507.htm.

President Peña Nieto declared that he would work with the US in the framework of the deep-rooted principles of defending the dignity of Mexicans abroad and exercising Mexican sovereign prerogatives. "I will put my soul on the line to defend Mexico," he said (*El Universal* 2017aa).

When Tillerson and Kelly visited Mexico City on February 22 and 23, Donald Trump again used Twitter to undermine Mexican officials during their meetings with US envoys. On February 21, Secretary Kelly had published two memos with "wide-ranging directives focused on both interior enforcement and cracking down on security along the US-Mexico border,"[45] seeking to accelerate the implementation of Trump's Executive Orders.[46] In the words of Senate minority leader Chuck Schumer, the White House was planning to "round up and quickly deport anyone who is undocumented."[47] The Mexican government was definitely concerned.

It was then that Trump interfered in the official negotiations with an importunate declaration in a televised interview, attributing gang violence and drug smuggling to undocumented immigrants. He said that the stricter enforcement of immigration laws, to keep "really bad dudes" out of the US, was "a military operation."[48] US—and Mexican—officials learned about the new provocation while sitting at a meeting in the Mexican Ministry of Foreign Affairs. Kelly was forced to explain that there were no plans to militarize the US border with Mexico (*El Univer-*

---

[45] Retrieved from: https://www.dhs.govnews/2017/02/21/secretary-kelly-issues-implementation-memoranda-border-security-and-interior; see also: https://www.theguardian.com/us-news/2017/feb/21/donald-trump-immigration-deportation-guidelines-homeland-security.

[46] See: https://www.dhs.gov/publicationimplementing-presidents-border-security-and-immigration-enforcement-improvement-policies; https://www.dhs.gov/sites/default/files/publications/17_0220_S1_Enforcement-of-the-Immigration-Laws-to-Serve-the-National-Interest.pdf.

[47] Retrieved from: http://www.independent.co.uk/news/world/americas/us-politics/donald-trump-mass-deportation-plan-stop-chuck-schumer-senate-minority-leader-democrat-homeland-a7592661.html; see also: Brooks (2017) and Sancho 2017c.

[48] Retrieved from: https://www.washingtonpost.com/news/post-politics/wp/2017/02/23/trump-touts-recent-immigration-raids-calls-them-a-military-operation/?utm_term=.8f795bb88ade.

sal 2017ab), and that massive deportations would not occur.⁴⁹ Furthermore, the visitors reassured their Mexican hosts that the policy of removing migrants would be respectful of their human rights,⁵⁰ and took note of Mexico's objection to receive non-Mexican deportees while they waited for their removal procedure.

Criticism of the high-level bilateral meeting came from both the Mexican left and right and was geared against Peña Nieto, who, according to many, should not have received the US officials in the first place, and his administration was seen as too eager to please the US in delicate security matters (*La Jornada* 2017j). Members of the opposition parties demanded that the content of the dialogue be made public (*La Jornada* 2017h).

Supporting Illegal Migrants

In Trump's mind, border security and immigration enforcement would work wonders: "By finally enforcing our immigration laws, we will raise wages, help the unemployed, save billions and billions of dollars, and make our communities safer for everyone."⁵¹ If he did, indeed, introduce any significant change during his first 100 days in office, it was in the realm of migration. His rhetoric of fear dangerously opened the door for the harassment of Mexicans—and other Hispanics—in the US. It exacerbated anti-immigrant feelings and helped pave the way for the much-dreaded deportations. It also supported his belief that America is being assaulted by unwanted and dangerous immigrants; coming from different countries and religions, ever ready to harm it.

There were indications—and good reasons to believe—that the number of deportations would be high, higher than those registered during the previous decade, which, at the time, few people opposed—either

---

49   Retrieved from: http://www.independent.co.uk/news/world/americas/donald-trump-us-military-undocumented-immigrants-deport-threat-mexico-border-wall-a7597196.html.

50   Retrieved from: https://www.gob.mx/cms/uploads/attachment/file/195645/INFORME_SOBRE_ENCUENTROS_CON_MIEMBROS_DEL_GABINETE_DEL_GOBIERNO_DE_ESTADOS_UNIDOS.pdf.

51   Retrieved from: https://www.whitehouse.gov/the-press-office/2017/02/28/remarks-president-trump-joint-address-congress.

in Mexico or in the US. Trump's Executive Order of the first days of his term, imposing a travel ban on citizens from seven predominantly Muslim countries[52] had worldwide repercussions and needless to say, resonated in Mexico as well.

Two other Executive Orders—"Border Security and Immigration Enforcement Improvements,"[53] and "Enhancing Public Safety in the Interior of the US"[54]—even if not yet fully implemented, would be the beginning of major alterations in the lives of Mexican, and other, migrants in the US. These presidential Orders expanded both the prerogatives of enforcers and the list of priorities for the detention of "aliens apprehended for violations of immigration law"[55] and other crimes while waiting for legal proceedings. They also allowed for the speedy removal of undocumented migrants. Whether the enforcement crackdown would apply to the "dreamers"—students who had arrived in the US as children with their undocumented parents, and were protected from deportation by since 2012 by Barack Obama's Deferred Action for Childhood Arrivals program[56]—was never absolutely clear, as Trump often changed his mind on this delicate issue.[57] Trump managed to create great confusion, at home and abroad but, more consequentially, in order to intimidate migrants. What Elizabeth Drew observed, certainly applied to Trump's contradictory statements regarding his immigration policy: "He says and does so much that he's hard to keep up with, and this has become a strategy. He's a juggler par excellence" (Drew 2017, 37).

President Trump insisted on deporting or incarcerating "the millions" of undocumented migrants living in the US with criminal records, which,

---

[52] Available at: https://www.whitehouse.gov/the-press-office/2017/01/27/executive-order-protecting-nation-foreign-terrorist-entry-united-states.
[53] Available at: https://www.whitehouse.gov/the-press-office/2017/01/25/executive-order-border-security-and-immigration-enforcement-improvements.
[54] Available at: https://www.whitehouse.gov/the-press-office/2017/01/25/presidential-executive-order-enhancing-public-safety-interior-united.
[55] Retrieved from: https://www.whitehouse.gov/the-press-office/2017/01/25/executive-order-border-security-and-immigration-enforcement-improvements.
[56] See: https://undocu.berkeley.edu/legal-support-overview/what-is-daca/.
[57] See: https://www.vox.com/policy-and-politics/2017/8/31/16226934/daca-trump-dreamers-immigration.

under the expanded list of applicable crimes range from driving without a license to murder. To help him in this endeavor, he appointed Jeff Sessions, well known for his hard stance against unauthorized migrants, and drug smuggling, as Attorney General. On April 11, after visiting the southern border, Sessions announced his new law enforcement strategy to "get rid of the filth of drug cartels and other criminal organizations in US cities and borders" which is, he said, "a new era, the Trump era" (*La Jornada* 2017i).

Confronting opposition from both the federal and state levels to its aggressive deportation policy, the Trump administration emphasized detentions: "All adults apprehended at the border would be detained," announced Sessions.[58] The US government also considered strategies that included separating parents from their children at the border, confiscating remittances, apprehending migrants who had served a prison sentence and deporting them immediately, and detaining or expelling parents with US-born children.

While Peña Nieto felt cornered by Trump and his border policy, he was more comfortable when presenting directives for the defense of Mexican migrants in the US. He directed the Ministry of Foreign Affairs to reinforce long-standing programs for the protection and defense of Mexicans abroad. The fifty Mexican consulates in the US had to become active "advocates for the rights of migrants."[59] The legal defense of migrants in US courts was a fundamental part of Mexican policy toward its diaspora. One billion pesos (around $50 million dollars) were channeled into expanding the capacity of the consulates to offer legal advice and inform migrants about their survival options[60] and the best ways to protect their money and properties. "Our communities are not alone," said the Peña Nieto, "wherever there is a Mexican migrant at risk needing our support, we must be there, his country must be there" (Sancho 2017b).

---

[58] Retrieved from: https://www.justice.gov/opa/speech/attorney-general-jeff-sessions-delivers-remarks-announcing-department-justice-s-renewed.

[59] Retrieved from: https://www.voanews.com/a/pena-nieto-message-to-mexicans/3692860.html.

[60] Retrieved from: http://eleconomista.com.mx/sociedad/2017/01/27/pena-

The return of Mexicans, forcefully sent back as returnees or deportees, or voluntarily returning to the country, received unusual attention in the Mexican press. Every week, a front-page picture with a group of expelled migrants appeared in the newspapers. Articles frequently mentioned that there were 11 million undocumented migrants subject to removal, half of them believed to be Mexican.

Once more, gaining allies in the US was key; and there were many. Their intense and passionate activity was a relief for Mexico and helped reconcile Mexicans with US society at large. Not only philosophers but also economists thought poorly of Trump's immigration policy. A group of 1,470 economists, advocating for a "smart immigration policy," sent a letter to President Trump and congressional leaders, stressing "the broad economic benefit that immigrants to this country bring."[61]

The Mexican government reached out to migrant-friendly civil society leaders and political actors in the US, such as mayors of the "sanctuary cities," that Trump and his controversial Attorney General so furiously opposed. The legal and political defense provided by the American Civil Liberties Union was particularly active and effective, and did not go unnoticed in Mexico (Brooks 2017).

In addition to the work carried out by Mexican consulates in defense of migrants, a large number of prominent politicians traveled to US cities with large Mexican communities to meet with migrants and speak on their behalf. Senators, representatives, governors, mayors of various cities, leaders of the most important political parties (PRI, PAN, PRD and Morena), were seen in the US arguing in favor of the human rights of migrants (*El Universal* 2017ac, 2017ad, *La Jornada* 2017j). Multilateral and human rights organizations, including the United Nations and the Inter-American Commission on Human Rights, issued public statements in defense of migrants, often at the request of the Mexican government.

In addition to governmental actions, many organizations mobilized to best accommodate the return of migrants from the US. The solidarity

envia-1000-mdp-consulados-apoyo-migrantes-mexicanos.

[61] Retrieved from: https://www.usnews.com/news/business/articles/2017-04-12/1-470-economists-send-trump-a-letter-to-support-immigrants. See also: El Universal (2017ae).

expressed toward the plight of fellow Mexicans was unprecedented. Universities, business associations, and churches organized to facilitate the reintegration of the newly arrived into Mexican society. Firms offered employment programs. Mexican legislators hastily approved laws to facilitate the reincorporation of "dreamers" into the national education system. Rumor had it that Trump was not going to maintain DACA, and a few scandalous cases of "dreamers," who were detained or deported, confirmed this possibility. The new legislation offered an expedite revalidation of studies to allow college or university students returning "as a result of the current international context," to continue their higher education (*El Universal* 2017af, *Milenio* 2017c).

News and word of mouth in Mexico pointed at how the lives of the migrant population in the US (Mexicans and others) had become very stressful since Trump was elected. Everybody seemed to have an anecdote at the hands of Mexicans—from different walks of life, documented or undocumented—being insulted in the street, in restaurants, and on the buses.

According to Jorge Volpi, a well-known Mexican author: "In the US, thousands of Mexicans live in a situation of extreme panic. ... At any time they can be forcefully separated from their homen and family ... we are the first line of attack of Donald Trump against human rights" (cited in Morla 2017).

Trump unveiled a dramatic reality for Mexican elites, namely the plight of millions of their countrymen, who had been deported since the 1990s, but reached unprecedented numbers after 2005, in particular, during the Obama administrations. Elites on both sides of the border, in particular those living in Washington and Mexico City, had seemed to ignore what was happening with US-Mexican migration, and at the US-Mexico border. Neither did the average Mexican— public official, legislator, public opinion leader, or businessman—care for migrants in the US until the arrival of Donald Trump, who shed a different light on migrants, one that illuminated their vulnerability to harassment in the US.

Final Remarks

Mexico became an easy target for Donald Trump. It is a concrete and familiar reference for Americans—it is the near abroad—and can be presented as a symbol of two maladies: the loss of manufacturing jobs and unauthorized immigration. In the US, NAFTA became a "dirty word"[62] a few years after its ratification, and Mexican migration to the US over the last three decades, and until 2010, was so large that it changed the face of American society.

The first ten days, perhaps even the three to four weeks, following Trump's inaugural address, will be remembered by many Mexicans for years to come. Donald Trump truly intimidated Mexico. It was shocking. But it was also disheartening to see this from a new US president committed only to himself, feared more than respected, and one whom many considered unfit for the job. Mexicans were upset. Above all, however, they were afraid of this unpredictable individual, who had twitted practically since his political debut that Mexico was not a friend of the US: "I love the Mexican people, but Mexico is not our friend. They're killing us at the border and they're killing us on jobs and trade. FIGHT!"[63]

Donald Trump was pointing at Mexico as a country that had been taking advantage of the US. In his view, it has been displacing US workers through an unfair trade deal. It has been keeping a large trade deficit in its favor, although it does not represent more than 7% of the total US trade deficit. It has been sending millions of immigrants to the US—although since 2010 more Mexicans are returning to Mexico than are going to the US—across an unprotected border, but probably one of the most protected between two friendly nations. Such rhetoric positively resonated in the ears of many of his dissatisfied and angry voters.

Part of public opinion in Mexico blamed its president and politicians for being unable to react with dignity and forcefully protest against Trump's assertions, for not anticipating Trump's victory, and for not having a strategy to deal with a man that after January 20 could move toward implementing his campaign promises.

It soon became evident that Trump's contradictory statements regarding trade, migration, and the border were not only a negotiating strategy

---

[62] Retrieved from: https://www.forbes.com/sites/johnbrinkley/2014/11/03/nafta-still-a-dirty-word-20-years-later/#5f54e1d31d22.
[63] Twitter, @realDonaldTrump, June 30, 2015.

but also part of his peculiar and novice style of practicing politics. He created a turmoil on his arrival at the White House, and impacted Mexico greatly. Trump came across, indeed, as "terrifying" (Drew 2017): anything could happen under his leadership; he could change his mind from one day to the other. The US was no longer a predictable partner for Mexico.

Trump was able to mobilize large segments of Mexican society against his arrogant style and anti-Mexican policies. And nationalism flourished in the face of adversity. But, Mexicans were also confronted with their extreme vulnerability *vis-à-vis* their powerful neighbor. The crash course on Mexico-US relations reminded Mexicans of their painful dependence on the US, and of their country's very little room to maneuver.

Many believed that the US president was not going to push his agenda of withdrawing from NAFTA, deporting various millions of unauthorized migrants, and building a wall along the border with Mexico. After all, Trump's rhetoric aside, American firms and consumers had been the main, if not the only, beneficiaries of NAFTA. Removing millions of migrants, technically an organizational prowess, would deprive US businesses from cheap labor. Building a wall along the US-Mexico divide was extraordinarily complicated, expensive, and useless. Still, Mexico could only hope for Trump to stumble on his way to implementing policies that were so deleterious for Mexico. During 100 days in office, the US president was unable to execute his plans for the US and Mexico. The wall, a clear example of Trump's xenophobia—showing his contempt for his southern neighbor—which were bound to unleash a strong anti-Trump sentiment in Mexico, ended up as a liability for Trump. It has become a project in search of a purpose and without funding. His arrogant and painful insistence on having Mexico pay for the wall, irremediably led to the cancellation of normal communication between the two presidents. Regarding NAFTA, Trump decided it was better to renegotiate. Deportations of unauthorized migrants decreased slightly, although detentions increased, and his administration has been unable to accelerate the strengthening of a national deportation force, which already existed.

Coping with Donald Trump during his first 100 days in office was a complex task for Mexico. While the worst did not happen, US-Mexico relations, as the Mexican Ambassador to Washington warned, were on the brink of "a major derailment."[64] This is not the first instance of erroneous beliefs guiding US foreign policy. However, this time, Mexico, a traditional ally and neighbor, is suffering the consequences.

REFERENCES

Briseño, J.D. 2017a. "Apura Trump negociaciones." *Reforma*, January 23.

Briseño, J.D. 2017b. "Vamos a iniciar la renegociación del TLC con México y Canadá, anuncia Trump." *Reforma*, January 23.

Brooks, D. 2017. "Trump lanza la Guerra contra 11 millones de indocumentados." *La Jornada*, February 22.

Bugarin, I. 2017. "Estamos en un momento de turbulencia." January 20.

Camil, J. 2017. "Dictadura a la americana ...." *El Universal*, February 24.

Canchola, A. 2017. "Pide PAN firmeza ante Donald Trump." *El Universal*, January 23.

Chávez Presa, J.A. 2017. "Trump ya es presidente: ahora a prepararnos." *El Universal*, January 21.

Drew, E. 2017. "Terrifying Trump." *New York Review of Books*, March 9. Available at: http://www.nybooks.com/articles/2017/03/09/terrifying-trump/.

El Universal. 2017a."Trump enarbola nacionalismo." *El Universal*, January 21.

El Universal. 2017b. "Muro y TLCAN serán prioridades." *El Universal*, January 21.

El Universal. 2017c. "TLCAN, prioridad para el gobierno de Donald Trump." *El Universal*, January 19.

El Universal. 2017d. "Trump no es Terminator, es Negotiator: Carlos

---

[64] Retrieved from: http://www.dailymailco.uk/wires/ap/article-4232686/Mexicos-likely-envoy-US-Ties-critical-point.html; see also: Gutierrez, A. (2017).

Slim." *El Universal*, January 27.

El Universal. 2017e. "EPN y partidos cierran filas ante la llegada de Trump." January 21.

El Universal. 2017f. "Ni confrontación ni sumisión." *El Universal*, January 24.

El Universal. 2017g. "Se reunirán Peña Nieto y Donald Trump." *El Universal*, January 22.

El Universal. 2017h. "Relación positiva con Trump: Peña Nieto." *El Universal*, January 20.

El Universal. 2017i. "Plantea Peña estrategia para la negociación con Trump." *El Universal*, January 24.

El Universal. 2017j. "Desata Trump crisis en relación México-EU." *El Universal*, January 27.

El Universal. 2017k. "Distienden Peña Nieto y Trump crisis diplomática." *El Universal*, January 28.

El Universal. 2017l. "El círculo peñista oculta información." *El Universal*, February 3.

El Universal. 2017m. "Videgaray y su diplomacia agachona." *El Universal*, March 2.

El Universal. 2017n. "Con Trump no hay ninguna certeza: EPN." *El Universal*, February 21.

El Universal. 2017o. "Marchas 'vibran' en al menos 14 ciudades del país." *El Universal*, February 13.

El Universal. 2017p "EPN: ni confrontación ni sumisión con Trump." *El Universal*, January 24.

El Universal. 2017q. "Habrá 'medidas espejo' contra Trump, dice la Secretaría de Economía." *El Universal*, January 23.

El Universal. 2017r. "México tiene como opción dejar el TLCAN: Videgaray." *El Universal*, January 25.

El Universal. 2017s. "Para Texas, México es un socio y amigo: Rolando B. Pablos." *El Universal*, March 2.

El Universal. 2017t. "Videgaray: el muro es un gesto no amistoso entre amigos." *El Universal*, February 18.

El Universal. 2017u. "Empresas que apoyen muro, traidores: Iglesia." *El Universal*, March 27.

El Universal. 2017v. "Muro aplasta a Trump: no consigue presupuesto." *El Universal*, April 25.

El Universal. 2017w. "Expresa Rajoy solidaridad de España con México ante posturas de Trump." *El Universal*, February 1.

El Universal. 2017x. "Expresan mandatarios apoyo a México ante Trump." *El Universal*, February 1.

El Universal. 2017y. "Enviado de Trump a México." *El Universal*, February 8.

El Universal. 2017z*El Universal*, February 16.

El Universal. 2017z. "Entregaré el alma para defender a México." *El Universal*, February 14.

El Universal. 2017aa "Kelly niega militarización de la frontera México-Estados Unidos." *El Universal*, February 24.

El Universal. 2017ab. "Economistas destacan aportación migratoria." *El Universal*, April 13.

El Universal. 2017ac. "Inicia Margarita Zavala gira en EU en favor de migrantes." *El Universal*, March 7.

El Universal. 2017ad. "AMLO inicia gira por Estados Unidos. Gira en defensa de los *migrantes mexicanos en Estados Unidos*." *El Universal*, January 30.

El Universal. 2017ae. "Ómbudsman pide apoyo a ONU por política de

EU." *El Universal*, January 30.

El Universal. 2017af. "Propone SEP reforma en favor de deportados." *El Universal*, February 1.

Ferrer, A. 2017. "Quiénes han cedido ante las amenazas de Trump?." *Milenio*, January 3.

Filloy, E.B. 2017. "El viaje a lo desconocido." *El Universal*, January 26.

Gascón, V., U. Díaz, and F. Andrade. 2017. "Afirma IP estar lista para negociar." *Reforma*, January 21.

Guerra, G. 2016. "La última noche." *El Universal*, November 9.

Gupta, A. 2016. "Could Trump Really Make Mexico Pay For The Wall?." *Forbes*, March 9. Available at: https://www.forbes.com/sites/taxanalysts/2016/03/09/could-trump-really-make-mexico-pay-for-the-wall/#1374b8397b29.

Gutierrez, A. 2017. 'Descarrilamiento mayúsculo' en relación México-EU." *El Universal*, February 16.

La Jornada. 2017a. "Mediante tuitazo Trump anuncia el muro para hoy." *La Jornada*, January 25.

La Jornada. 2017b. "México no renegociará el TLCAN si EU insiste en imponer aranceles: Guajardo." *La Jornada*, February 28.

La Jornada. 2017c. "Construir el muro, 'acto hostil': SRE." *La Jornada*, February 23.

La Jornada. 2017d. "'Importantes desencuentros' con EU exhibe México ante OEA; recibe apoyo mayoritario." *La Jornada*, February 17.

La Jornada. 2017e. "Cobrar impuestos a *cárteles, opción* para que México pague el muro." *La Jornada*, January 30.

La Jornada. 2017f. "Tráfico de armas y lavado de dinero, temas que abordarán Osorio y Kelly." *La Jornada*, February 9.

La Jornado. 2017g. "Necesario, detener el tráfico de armas." *La Jornada*,

February 10.

La Jornada. 2017h. "Tillerson visitará México: Videgaray." *La Jornada*, February 9.

La Jornada. 2017i. "Anuncia Sessions nueva era migratoria para limpiar urbes de EU de basura de los cartels." *La Jornada*, April 12.

La Jornada. 2017j. "Líderes de Morena y PRI van a EU a ver migrantes." *La Jornada*, February 9.

Milenio. 2017a. "Apoyo a Dreamers. Entregan iniciativa preferente." *Milenio*, February 2.

Milenio. 2017b. "La deportación masiva: ¡otra mentira de Trump!." *Milenio*, January 30.

Milenio. 2017c. "Videgaray pide examen de conciencia a empresas por muro." *Milenio*, March 17.

Morla, J. 2017. "La decadencia final de mi padre reflejó la del propio México." *El País*, March 4.

Navarrete, J.E. 2017. "Post-verdad-oeste-orden." *La Jornada*, February 23.

Olea, J.C. 2017. "¿Cómo llegamos a este entrampamiento?." *La Jornada*, March 10.

Reforma. 2017. "No confundir diplomacia con debilidad-SRE." *Reforma*, February 28.

Rodríguez, R. 2017. "Focos Rojos, 'El Chapo' y Trump." *El Universal*, January 20.

Sancho, V. 2017a. "Ordena Trump levantar el muro." *El Universal*, January 26.

Sancho, V. 2017b. "La visita fue 'constructiva', dicen Videgaray y Guajardo." *El Univeral*, January 27.

Sancho, V. 2017c. "Refuerza Trump deportación de indocumentados."

El Universal, February 22.

Toro, M.C. 2017. "Bordering on the US." Unpublished manuscript.

Zárate, A. 2017. "Trump, días de miedo." *El Universal*, January 26.

Zavala, M. 2017. "No queremos acuerdos en lo 'oscurito': AMLO." *El Universal*, January 23.

Zubieta, C.H. 2017. "El mensaje de Donald Trump: ¿así o más claro?" *El Universal*, January 26.

5
TRUMP'S PRESIDENCY: UNITED KINGDOM PERSPECTIVES AND RESPONSES

Charlie Whitham and Kevern Verney

INTRODUCTION

In the United Kingdom (UK), the election of President Donald J. Trump came as a traumatic event for a country already painfully divided by its decision in June 2016 to leave the European Union (EU). For "alt-right" politicians like Nigel Farage, the erstwhile leader of the UK Independence Party (UKIP), Trump's victory was celebrated and seen as further evidence of the irresistible rise of right-wing populism on both sides of the Atlantic. Farage, who had campaigned for Trump during the election, was rewarded by a personal invitation to Trump Tower in New York, making him the first British politician to meet with the incoming President. Trump even went so far as to speculate that Farage would be an ideal choice for British ambassador to the United States (US). The suggestion was met with barely concealed contempt by Conservative Prime Minister Theresa May with her office tersely noting that there was "no vacancy" for the post.[1]

For liberals, those on the political left, and the majority of the 48% of the electorate that had voted to remain in the EU, the Trump presidency brought fresh anguish. Their feelings about Trump's election, less than six months after the EU referendum, could be summed up by the words of Charles Ryder in *Brideshead Revisited*: it came as "a blow," unexpected, "repeated, falling on a bruise," with "a dull and sickening pain and the doubt whether another like it could be borne" (Waugh 1962, 161).

Opting for protest over resignation, mass demonstrations were held in cities across the UK to coincide with the first full day of the Trump administration on January 21, 2017. At the flagship event in London up to 100,000 people joined a rally outside the US embassy in Grosve-

---

[1] Retrieved from: http://www.bbc.co.uk/news/uk-38064664.

nor Square chanting "build bridges not walls." Leading Labour Party spokesperson Yvette Cooper addressed a mass crowd that included London mayor Sadiq Khan and British and American celebrities including singer Lily Allen, television presenter Sandi Toksvig, and Hollywood actress Rebecca Hall. Reflecting the particular anger felt by women participants, Cooper told her audience that "when the most powerful man in the world says it's okay to sexually assault women because you are rich and powerful, we have to stand up and say no way."[2]

The presence of Sadiq Khan, a Muslim, reflected an ongoing antipathy between the London mayor and Donald Trump. Khan, who had been an outspoken critic of Trump's presidential campaign pledge to introduce a travel ban on Muslims to the US, stated that he hoped Trump "loses—badly" in the election. When Khan rebuffed the New York property magnate's offer to make him an exception to the ban Trump bizarrely responded by challenging the mayor to an "IQ contest."[3]

In June 2017, Trump rekindled the feud in the wake of a serious Islamic terrorist attack in London. Seeking to reassure residents in the UK capital, Khan promised they would "see an increased police presence today and over the course of the next few days. No reason to be alarmed." Responding in a twitter feed, Trump was sharply critical of Khan, noting, "at least 7 dead and 48 wounded in terror attack and Mayor of London says there is 'no reason to be alarmed!'" Coming in the wake of such a serious incident, the remark led to rebukes on both sides of the Atlantic. New York Mayor Bill de Blasio spoke out in defense of his London counterpart and Prime Minister May commented, "Donald Trump was wrong in the things he has said about Sadiq Khan." At such a time "party politics are put to one side—we work together."[4]

Mayor Khan was not alone in his wish that Trump "loses—badly." The British press and establishment—including the sitting government—

---

[2] Retrieved from: http://www.bbc.co.uk/news/uk-38700123.

[3] See: http://www.bbc.co.uk/news/av/uk-politics-35061953/donald-trump-muslim-comments-sadiq-khan-says-i-hope-trump-loses-badly; http://www.bbc.co.uk/news/av/uk-36299929/donald-trump-challenges-sadiq-khan-to-iq-test.

[4] Retrieved from: http://www.bbc.co.uk/news/av/world-us-canada-40167516/new-york-s-bill-de-blasio-rises-to-london-mayor-s-defence;http://www.bbc.co.uk/news/uk-politics-40172537.

had hoped for and expected a Hilary Clinton victory, which would have spelled a level of consistency in transatlantic dealings.[5] There is no question that Trump's win has raised discussion about the fate of the vaunted "special relationship" to new highs across the country. Much of the divide follows lines similar to those drawn during the Brexit debate. Staunch "UK leavers" point to the ideological similarities between the Trump and anti-EU camps.[6] Indeed, the president-elect claimed to owe an enormous debt to fellow right-wing populist Farage for bringing about the Brexit triumph, which supposedly fuelled hope in his own American brand of nationalism. For conservatives, the apparent convergence between the two versions of right-wing populism indicated the potential for a greater unity of purpose between the two nations. After all, Trump is on record as a profound Eurosceptic.

The US-UK Special Relationship

In a longer historical context, it is an abiding theme of British post-1945 foreign policy that some sort of balance be maintained between relations with the US and the rest of Europe (Dobson and Marsh 2013, Dumbrell 2006, McKercher 2017). However, this Atlanticist vision—Britain as the diplomatic bridge between the two great power centers and independent of them both—has been near impossible to sustain. With few exceptions—the Vietnam War and the 1973 Year of Europe—Britain has, when asked to take sides, favored closeness to the US over Europe at every juncture. Even Prime Minister Tony Blair, perhaps Britain's most pro-European leader, famously turned his back on his European allies and joined forces with President George W. Bush in the vastly unpopular war in Iraq (Arnold 2014, Lindberg 2004, Riddell 2003, Tate 2012). At the heart of this policy conundrum is British fixation with the much vaunted "special relationship" with their transatlantic chums. Time and again, it is argued, the preservation of the cherished "special relationship" of World War II fame has scuppered a more measured, more balanced approach by British policy makers to relations not

---

[5] Some spoke of a "new era" in their relations; see http://www.telegraph.co.uk/news/2016/11/09.
[6] See: https://www.spectator.co.uk/2017/01; https://www.thesun.co.uk/news/2621453; http://www.dailystar.co.uk/news/latest-news/559180.

only with their European neighbors but also with the rest of the world. It should therefore come as no surprise that upon the inauguration of a new American president, whatever the political hue in either capital, the impulse to register closeness with the latest "leader of the western world" was automatically entertained by Downing Street. Still, that Prime Minister Theresa May rushed so quickly to be the first foreign leader to meet America's historically most unpopular president—both inside and outside the US—requires some additional explanation. This is best achieved by understanding Britain's options in a radically changed international landscape brought about not by Trump's ascendancy but by the British public's vote in May 2016 to leave the EU. Much of British media's examination of Donald Trump has been through the lens of the Brexit vote. There is little doubt that the country is in the midst of a critical reassessment of its role in the world, much like, some would argue, the US. The result may be a major recasting of British foreign policy that finally abandons lingering European ties in favor of drawing even closer to the US.

The first and most obvious rationale for Britain to move more closely to the US is economic. Literally, the British government has to engineer some way of making up what is expected to be a significant shortfall in trade with Europe when Britain finally leaves the EU in 2019. The EU, Britain's largest trade partner by far, accounts for exports of around £230 billion a year (2015). Britain's second largest export destination is the USA at £100 billion (2015).[7] If the drawbridge to Europe is being even partially lifted—and no one yet knows just how severe the uncoupling will be—then good relations with the US—in economic terms at least—are at once of greater significance. President Obama warned that if it left the EU Britain would find itself "at the back of the queue"[8] in trade negotiations, and on the campaign trail Trump offered little to calm British nerves about its prospects for a good trade deal under a Trump administration. But as the Minister for Communities and Local Government, Sajid Javid, said on the eve of the November election: "America is our most vital ally, the most important country that we have

---

7   Retrieved from: http://www.parliament.uk/commons-library; see also: The Economist, January 21–27, 2017, 24. http://magazinelib.com/all/the-economist-europe-january-21-27-2017/.

8   Retrieved from: https://www.ft.com/content/63d42778-7273-11e6-bf48-b372cdb1043a.

to work with, both in terms of our prosperity, as our second largest trading partner ... So whoever is installed in the White House, we're going to have to work with them."⁹

Others, who include those who bemoan the lurch away from Europe, questioned whether the accession of Trump would actually undermine the long-standing conventions of the special relationship and even "necessitate their demise."¹⁰ Indeed, relations with the US are further complicated by Trump's substantial unpopularity with much of the British political establishment and a large proportion of the populace, especially those who voted to remain in the EU. Jeremy Corbin, the leader of the British Labour Party and so the leader of the Opposition in Parliaments, would have been supported by most parties outside of the Conservative Party and United Kingdom Independence Party (UKIP) when he warned Trump's victory was a "global wake-up call" for those supporting liberal ideals.¹¹ Going it alone for Britain after Brexit perhaps really did mean cutting the apron strings not only with Europe but also with the US. As Xenia Wickett of Chatham House, an esteemed foreign policy think-tank, and a collection of worried professors meeting in January put it: "The UK is very much between a rock and a hard place."¹² Such counsel points to the risk that, in the eyes of Washington, the Brexit decision had potentially devalued both Europe *and* Britain as partners of the US in any realignment of power between Asia, Europe, and the Atlantic. And Prime Minister Theresa May was just eleventh—after Australia and Ireland—on the list of 'phone calls Trump made after winning in November 2016'.

Dealing with the Trump White House: Trade a Vexing Issue

Whatever the ambitions of the British, dealing with a White House under Trump was clearly not going to be a straightforward task. The president,

---

[9] Retrieved from: https://fullfact.org/economy/uk-trade-usa.
[10] New Statesman, January 20–26, 2017, 5 (editorial).
[11] Retrieved from: http://www.independent.co.uk/news/world/americas/us-elections/donald-trump-us-election-win-jeremy-corbyn-wake-up-call-a7413226.html.
[12] Retrieved from: http://www.standard.co.uk/news/world/usuk-relations-face-biggest-challenge-for -decades-with-donald-trump-as-president-a3444786.html.

himself, has been, not surprisingly, difficult to pin down on his attitude toward Britain. In the same month (January), he declared first "I love the UK,"[13] only to admit on national British television, after criticisms of his anti-immigration stance: "It looks like we're not going to have a very good relationship, who knows."[14] Whatever his real feelings toward Britain, based on his campaign mantra of "America First," it was clear that for the first time in 70 years there was the distinct possibility that Washington could no longer be relied upon to lead the rules-based, liberal political and economic order that Britain and the rest of Western Europe had shared since 1945 and still valued. Open trade, as well as common defense, and security goals, were apparently no longer to be taken for granted in the world according to Trump. Negotiation of the Transatlantic Trade and Investment Partnership (TTIP) was already tough before Britain voted to leave the EU, and would likely not survive a mauling from a self-professed hardheaded protectionist like Trump. Also, the US may loom very large for Britain as a trading partner, but Britain is only the seventh largest for the US. Immigration, regulation, and Trump's "Buy American" mind-set are major stumbling blocks in any deal between the two apparent political bedfellows. Hopes were raised when Trump signaled in January his intention to seek a trade agreement with Britain "very quickly." Yet, as the *Economist*, a champion of globalization and of the UK remaining in the EU, remarked sanguinely: "Mr Trump's proclamations, if of any substance, are encouraging. But Britain is not about to enter a golden era of trade."[15] Yet, beyond trade there are other components of the "special relationship" that Britain is keen to protect.

THREAT TO THE NORTH ATLANTIC TREATY ORGANIZATION

On the campaign trail, Trump made plain his distaste for NATO members not paying their full contribution to Western defense and promised to trim back US commitment to an organization he condemned

---

[13] Retrieved from: https://www.thesun.co.uk/news/2621453/donald-trump-says-he-loves-the-uk-and-reveals-he-wants-a-bumper-transatlantic-trade-deal-to-help-make-brexit-a-great-thing/.

[14] Retrieved from: https://www.theatlantic.com/international/archive/2016/05/trump-cameron/482874/.

[15] Retrieved from: http://magazinelib.com/all/the-economist-europe-january-21-27-2017/.

as "obsolete" (Larres 2017). Trump's position was consistent with his isolationist, "America First" bluster. But it naturally sent shockwaves throughout Europe, when, as president, he indicated that he would retreat on America's post-war commitment to defend the continent, especially worrying in the light of recent efforts by President Putin to assert Russian interests in Eastern Europe.

For Britain, let alone the rest of the continental Europe, the prospect of a shrinking US security presence in Europe raised particularly loud alarm bells. Since 1945, it has been an underlying assumption of British security policy that the Americans undertook responsibility for the overall defense of Europe, a fact that changed little with the ending of the Cold War. Indeed, Britain has always considered its defense relationship with the Americans to be sacred; even when their political and economic relations have been strained, the tight bond between their respective defense and intelligence agencies has remained second to none. In fact, it is in the area of military cooperation with the Americans that the "special relationship" has been most loudly expressed. Britain is also one of the few nations to meet its financial quotient to NATO. But with geopolitical power shifting towards Asia, and Russian-American relations in flux, the maintenance of Britain's traditional attachment to the US defense establishment will be tested just when, as John Bew of the *New Statesman* put it, "our relationship with Washington, DC is arguably more crucial to our security and prosperity than at any point since the 1940s."[16]

The Prime Minister's Visit to the White House and its Aftermath

Given these wider considerations, vagaries and doubts, it is not surprising the British government made immediate plans to be the first in line to meet the new president. The US visit by Prime Minister Theresa May on January 26 and 27 was a very public and very deliberate display of the British government's intent, planned before Christmas by aides from both sides of the Atlantic including Boris Johnson, the British Foreign Secretary, who early tweeted he was "looking forward to continuing [the]

---

[16] Retrieved from: https://policyexchange.org.uk/news/new-statesman-john-bew-considers-the-foreign-policy-implications-of-trumps-election/.

strong UK-US bond"[17] and to working "hand in glove"[18] with President Trump.[19] Speaking before Republican leaders in Philadelphia on the eve of her meeting with Trump, May vowed to rekindle the special relationship "for this new age" and strengthen ties with Britain's "old friends."[20]

The Prime Minister also gave a first rough outline of Britain's post-Brexit foreign policy strategy, which made common cause with Trump's "mission"—whatever that might be—to re-frame US interests in a new world order:

> And as we end our membership of the European Union, we have the opportunity to reassert our belief in a confident, sovereign and global Britain, ready to build relationships with old friends and new allies alike. So as we discover our confidence together—as you renew your nation just as we renew ours—we have the opportunity, indeed the responsibility, to renew the special relationship for this new age.[21]

Bearing a Scottish toasting cup that symbolizing friendship—also acknowledging the birthplace of Trump's mother—and a basket of food for the First Lady, May and Trump discussed matters of trade, security, and the future of NATO.[22]

---

[17] Retrieved from: https://twitter.com/borisjohnson/status/822495306411634689?lang=en; see also: https://www.theguardian.com/world/2017/jan/21/how-world-reacted-donald-trump-inauguration-us-president.

[18] Retrieved from: http://www.independent.co.uk/news/uk/home-news/president-donald-trump-boris-johnson-trade-brexit-deal-extremely-exciting-inauguration-a7538826. Johnson was also the first overseas politician to be called by Vice-President Mike Pence. See: http://www.bbc.com/news/uk-politics-37946420.

[19] But see his negative comments on US immigration order. See: http://www.bbc.co.uk/news/uk-38786576.

[20] Retrieved from: https:/xww.gov.uk/government/speeches/prime-ministers-speech-to-the-republican-party-conference-2017/. See also: The Times, January 21–27 2017, 4. Retrieved from: http://magazinelib.com/all/the-economist-europe-january-21-27-2017/.

[21] Retrieved from: https://www.gov.uk/government/speeches/prime-ministers-speech-to-the-republican-party-conference-2017/.

[22] See: http://www.bbc.co.uk/news/uk-politics-38747979.

May's vision of a reinvigorated special relationship was encouraged by Trump's frequent identification with the Reagan administrations of the 1980s, reflected in his appropriation of the latter's campaign slogan, "Make America Great Again." Press reports hinted that Trump saw May as "my Maggie," invoking images of the close UK-US relations under President Reagan and the then British Prime Minister Margaret Thatcher.[23] This reflected the strong personal rapport between the two leaders. At first sight, the prospects for a similar Trump-May relationship were not encouraging. May was a vicar's daughter, thoughtful and introspective in nature and with a fondness for attention to policy detail. Trump was a brash property magnate and reality TV celebrity with a preference for broad policy generalizations.[24]

Despite their conflicting personalities, the May assault on the White House initially seemed to pay dividends. After a 50-minute private audience with Trump and his aides, Trump proclaimed, on the steps of the White House: "The special relationship between our two countries has been one of the greatest forces in history for justice and peace" and agreed to hold "high level talks" over trade. May also crowed that "[w]e are united in our recognition of NATO as a bulwark of our defence" and later claimed to have asserted her desire on the president for a continued hardline against Russia.[25] These latter remarks naturally carried significance beyond Britain, and as such May could, at least temporarily, claim to have reaffirmed her country's role as a bridge between Europe and the US.

It was not long, however, before attitudes at home and abroad—including those of her new friends in the White House—began to shift the ground from under the May strategy. At home, many viewed May's "excruciating embrace" of Trump as a symbol not of British independence but of quite the opposite.[26] The unpredictable nature of the new presi-

---

[23] See: http://www.bbc.co.uk/news/blogs-the-papers-38708586.
[24] See: http://www.bbc.co.uk/news/uk-politics-38757528.
[25] Retrieved from: https://www.whitehouse.gov/the-press-office/2017/01/27/president-trump-and-prime-minister-mays-opening-remarks. See also: https://www.theguardian.com/commentisfree/picture/2017/jan/29/donald-trump-and-theresa-may-that-special-relationship-cartoon.
[26] Retrieved from: https://www.economist.com/news/britain/21715652-leaving-

dent was highlighted within hours of her departure. Flying home from the US via Turkey, the Prime Minister was clearly taken by surprise at the Trump administration's announcement of a 90-day US entry ban on refugees from seven predominantly Muslim countries. Repeatedly questioned about the initiative at a press conference in Ankara, she refused to condemn the president's action, saying only that "the United States is responsible for the US's policy on refugees."[27]

On her return to London, the Prime Minister was faced with large demonstrations outside Downing Street, which accused her of failing to stand up to Trump over the controversial immigration ban proposals. Leading spokespersons from all political parties spoke out against the action and implicitly or explicitly rebuked May for her silence. In the face of such intense criticism, the Prime Minister's office was forced to issue a statement "clarifying" her position, noting that although the ban was "a matter for the government of the United States," she did "not agree with this kind of approach" and "it is not one we will be taking."[28]

The low regard held by many in the UK for Trump the statesman was further highlighted when news broke that in Washington, May had invited Trump to meet Queen Elizabeth II. The state visit is an honor that has been bestowed upon only two other US presidents since the Queen took the throne, and includes addresses to both Houses of Parliament. Debate within Westminster immediately broke out, with the government facing criticism from all parties[29]—including her own Conservative party—which believed Trump should be denied an audience, both to the Queen and to Members of Parliament. Even the so-called neutral Speaker of the House of Commons, John Bercow, protested at Trump's "racism and sexism."[30] An online petition to withdraw the invitation to

---

european-union-means-country-has-less-not-more-control-over-its.

[27] Retrieved from: http://www.economist.com/news/britain/21715652; see also: http://www.bbc.co.uk/news/uk-38784199.

[28] Retrieved from: http://www.bbc.co.uk/news/uk-38786576; see also: http://www.euronews.com/2017/01/31.

[29] The Labour Party, the Liberal Democrats and the Scottish National Party all supported either postponing or withdrawing the invitation.

[30] Retrieved from: http://www.bbc.news.co.uk/news/uk-politics-38889941.

meet the Queen but to allow Trump's visit to the UK reached over 1.8 million signatories in just a few days. Its sponsor, a concerned Royalist citizen, argued that Trump's visit would cause "embarrassment" to the Queen and that the president's "well-documented misogyny and vulgarity" disqualified him from ever being granted a state visit.[31] White House and Foreign Office officials worked hard to rescue the controversial visit, suggesting even that it could take place outside London where support may be greater—following pro-Brexit demographic fault lines—and easier to police. Such a rally—of say 85,000 people—would help to underscore Trump's faith in the "special relationship" and show that outside the home of the establishment—London—there is much support for the maligned president.[32] This petition, along with a smaller one of some 300,000 signatories that supported Trump meeting the Queen, and two other petitions—one calling for an outright ban on Trump from the UK (some 574,000 signatories) and another asking that he not be banned (13,000 signatories), were sent to Parliament and debated between February 18 and 20.[33] A large coalition of mostly left-wing groups has vowed to mount a huge protest to Trump when he finally arrives.[34] Reason has prevailed, and Trump—always preferring adulation to confrontation—has since postponed his visit so as not to "create a scene."[35]

THE NATO SUMMIT AND ITS AFTERMATH

In European affairs too, British expectations of a softened American stance on transatlantic security were barely realized. Leaders at the EU summit in Malta on February 3 chided Trump for his anti-EU outbursts and flatly rejected May's effort to act as a bridge to the US for Europe, with French ministers pointing out that their country will soon be the only permanent member of the UN Security Council and the

---

[31] Retrieved from: http://www.express.co.uk/news/uk/761541. The petitioner was Graham Guest.
[32] See: http://www.telegraph.co.uk/news/2017/02/11.
[33] For the parliamentary debates, see: https://hansard.parliament.uk/Commons/2016-01-18/debates/1601186000001/DonaldTrump.
[34] See: http://www.telegraph.co.uk/news/2017/02/11.
[35] See: http://www.telegraph.co.uk/news/2017/03/01.

EU.³⁶ Worse still, May's claim to have won Trump over on the matter of collective security was undermined by the comments of Vice President Mike Pence at the Munich security conference on February 18. In his first official trip to Europe, Pence insisted the US remains committed to NATO and would not bypass Western Europe in dealing with Russia, but condemned Germany, France, and Italy for not paying their share toward NATO and that future US support for a threatened nation may be based on how much they had contributed.³⁷

Just as hopes for a Trump reversal on his negativity toward Europe were fading, and consistent with the tenor of his first 100 days as president, Trump struck out against his closest European ally only days after the NATO summit. In March, Trump accused the main British spy center—the Government Communications Headquarters (GCHQ)—of colluding with President Obama in bugging his Manhattan penthouse. The claim prompted an angry and unprecedented public response from Britain's spy agency. It was quick to point out that any allegations it wiretapped Trump Tower were "utterly ridiculous and should be ignored."³⁸ A flurry of meetings between top intelligence officials from both countries followed. The Federal Bureau of Investigation (FBI) and chief of the National Security Agency quickly denied the bugging took place, admitting that the allegation "clearly frustrates a key ally of ours," but he believed the relationship was "strong enough that this is something we will be able to deal with."³⁹ Apparently, the White House apologized for the presidential accusation,⁴⁰ but President Trump, however, stopped

---

[36] See: https://www.scoopnest.com/user/guardian/827633206937649152-guardian-front-page-saturday-4-february-2017-eu-leaders-hit-out-at-trumps-lack-of-respect.

[37] See: https://www.nytimes.com/2017/02/18/world/europe/pence-munich-speech-nato-merkel.html; https://www.theguardian.com/world/2017/feb/18/trump-pence-eu-nato-munich-conference-germany-britain.

[38] Retrieved from: https://www.theguardian.com/us-news/2017/mar/16/gchq-denies-wiretap-claim-trump-obama.

[39] Retrieved from: http://www.independent.co.uk/news/world/americas/us-politics/donald-trump-wiretapping-claims-nsa-director-mike-rogers-denies-gchq-asked-spy-trump-tower-a7639841.html; see also: https://newstand.google.com/articles/CAliEls7hih2E204XssXiT6QSjQqGAgEKg8lACoHCAow5vrMATC_9SQwjcirAw.

[40] See: https://newstand.google.com/articles/CAliEls7hih2E204XssXiT6QSjQq

short of retracting his comment and agreed only not to repeat the allegations.[41]

Trump's Seesaw Approach to Foreign Policy

In what was emerging as a see-saw approach to foreign policy, Rex Tillerson, the US Secretary of State, later helped to calm Europeans, when he met with NATO for the first time on March 31, by reiterating that America was not about to withdraw from its post-war security contract with the continent. Members were glad to hear that "The US commitment to NATO is strong and this alliance remains the bedrock for transatlantic security," the strongest signal of support yet form the Trump administration, but were less than happy at Tillerson's assertion that current levels of European spending on defense was "not sustainable."[42]

The mixed messages over NATO were compounded by an unexpected policy shift from the White House in April. The decision to engage more forcefully in Syria and, apparently, challenge Russia's involvement there came as a surprise to everyone who heard "Trump the campaigner" denounce Obama's policy toward the region and applaud Putin's defense of the Assad dictatorship. On April 7, in a surprising show of force, US cruise missiles showered a Syrian airbase that housed aircraft that dropped chemical weapons on Syrian civilians. The British government, in a pronounced U-turn on the need for military action against the Assad, was among the first and the loudest to announce their support for Trump's very public retaliation against the Syrian forces. "The UK Government fully supports the US action, which we believe was an appropriate response" to the gas attacks, Downing Street stated, and Foreign Secretary Johnson cancelled his scheduled visit to Moscow.[43] Britain, part of the US-led coalition in Syria, was "in close contact" with the US over the strike, but was not asked to join it.[44] The apparent hardening of

GAgEKg8lACoHCAow5vrMATC_9SQwjcirAw.

[41] See: http://www.telegraph.co.uk/news/2017/03/17; http://bbc.co.uk/news/uk-39300191. But see: http://www.telegraph.co.uk/news/2017/03/17.

[42] Retrieved from: http://www.express.co.uk/news/world/787122; see also http://www.dailymail.co.uk/news/article-4367476

[43] See: http://www/telegraph.co.uk/news/2017/04/07.

[44] Retrieved from: http://www.bbc.co.uk/news/live/world-us-canada-39521332.

US policy toward Assad and Russia is consistent with British demands since the conflict in Syria began, yet credit for Trump's turnaround lies not with London, but with the president's troubles in Washington. Besides, Tillerson quickly denied the strikes implied any change to America's wider policy in the region.[45] This did not, however, stop renewed speculation about Britain's global role, with some suggesting "we still have the capacity to shape the world, rather than be shaped by it."[46] Just days earlier, in the wake of the terrorist attack on Westminster in March, Prime Minister May pledged more troops to fight alongside Jordanians against the international jihadist threat, using the kind of bold, assertive "big power" language recently heard out of Washington: "As the UK leaves the EU, we are determined to forge a bold, confident future for ourselves in the world. It is clearly in the UK's security and prosperity interests to support Jordan and Saudi Arabia in tackling regional challenges to create a more stable region" as "Jordan is on the frontline of multiple regional crises."[47] In a post-Brexit world, Britain's prosperity really does depend even more on a stable Middle East which includes many economically vital friends of the west, including Saudi Arabia.[48]

Post-Brexit US Trade Agreement

Over trade, there were signs that pragmatism had prevailed at the White House; but this has not necessarily worked in Britain's favor. May was heartened by Trump's early admission that he would like a trade agreement between the US and Britain "very quickly," yet no timetable has been offered.[49] Worse still, at the International Monetary Fund meeting in April, there were hints that Trump may re-engage TTIP negotia-

---

British Defence Secretary Michael Fallon declared that direct British military action in Syria was anyhow outlawed by Parliament in 2013, see https://buzzfeed.com/rosebuchanan.

[45] See: https://buzzfeed.com/rosebuchanan.
[46] Retrieved from: https://www.spectator.co.uk/2017/04.
[47] Retrieved from: http://www.express.co.uk/news/uk/787075.
[48] Over Saudi Arabia May stated "there is so much we can do together on trade, with immense potential for Saudi investment to provide a boost to the British economy." Retrieved from: http://www.express.co.uk/news/uk/787075.
[49] Retrieved from: http://www.cityam.com/260720/uk-get-us-free-trade-deal-post-brexit-but-donald-trump.

tions over trade with the rest of the EU ahead of any bilateral talks with Britain.[50]

The recent dramatic changes in its relationship with the rest of Europe have pushed Britain into even closer union with the US. This would have been true whatever the outcome of the race for the White House in November 2016. Despite reservations about a Trump presidency, early signs indicate that the basic contours of the long-standing "special relationship"—in defense and security at—have been little altered by the incoming Trump administration. As far as trade is concerned, Trump is keen not to be viewed as anti-trade and is in need of a benchmark bilateral trade deal to satisfy Congressional opponents: though whether that will be with Britain, the EU, or the far more important Chinese market is uncertain.[51]

Concluding Observations

Given the volatility and continued unpredictability of Donald Trump, there is every likelihood that the relationship with the US will continue to be extremely challenging, with potential for another "GCHQ" moment to raise its head at any time. And the bullish, bigoted, and politically ignorant populist president has few supporters among the British public.

Yet, we cannot expect the British government—which is expected to remain dominated by the Conservative Party for at least another five years—to mount any serious criticism of Trump's policies, while Britain detaches itself from its European entanglements and works hard to underscore its adherence to American strength in any global realignment of international power. Even a Labour government, which recently committed itself to buying the latest Trident missiles from the US, would likely represent a change in style, but not substance in its dealings with the US, concerned mostly with achieving a better balance in the relationship than the Conservatives appear capable (Kearns and Murray

---

[50] See: https://www.thetimes.co.uk/article/trump-puts-eu-ahead-of-britain-in-trade-queue-l7t8zwn7k.

[51] See: https://www.theguardian.com/us-news/2017/jan/26/Donald-trump-theresa-may-cracks-special-relationship-trade-talks.

2017). Besides, official criticism of the Trump administration would inevitably be muted under these conditions of heightened political, not to mention economic, dependency.

Whether Trump remains engaged in the conventional instruments of global discourse, or carves a more divisive path, remains to be seen. Though the latter choice would be more troublesome for British foreign interests, the fact remains that the temper of the White House ultimately matters less to a British government desperate not to suffer a calamitous weakening of the remaining western edge of its Atlantic bridge. Walking hand-in-hand into a new era with a president who is vague, inconsistent, untrustworthy, and self-absorbed appears somewhat premature—even desperate.

What is more, Britain has been here before. Some have commented that Britain's predicament resembles that of the 1950s, when Conservative governments under Winston Churchill, Antony Eden, and Harold Macmillan struggled to find a role in what the then US Secretary of State, Dean Acheson, called the new bipolar order of the Cold War (Arnold 2014, Dumbrell 2006, McKercher 2017). It was difficult then, when Britain still owned an Empire and ruled a Commonwealth, to carve a route between overt dependence on the US and a restructuring, resurgent Europe. In the end, it chose *not* to choose but to act as a bridge between the two. Today, after Brexit, such a path is no longer feasible: there is no Empire, the bridge is nearing collapse, and closer alignment with China or Russia is unlikely. This leaves a free-roaming Britain with but one option before it. All hail the "special relationship"!

British public opinion also appeared to endorse this outlook. A survey of global public attitudes toward the Trump administration undertaken by the *Pew Research Center* (between February 6 and May 8)[52] showed that UK respondents had almost uniformly negative perceptions of the new President. Only 22% of Britons questioned stated that they had "confidence in the U.S. president to do the right thing regarding world affairs," compared to 79% for Obama, and only 16% believed that he

---

[52] Retrieved from: http://www.pewglobal.org/2017/06/26/u-s-image-suffers-as-publics-around-world-question-trumps-leadership/; see also: http://www.bbc.co.uk/news/world-us-canada-40409888;

was "well-qualified to be president." In respect to character and personality, 89% of British respondents viewed Trump as "arrogant," 77% as "intolerant", and 69% as "dangerous." There was also strong disapproval of flagship initiatives associated with the new Trump administration; 83% respondents were opposed to Trump's proposed border wall with Mexico, 80% were opposed to the US's withdrawal from the Paris Climate Change Accord, and 53% were opposed to the proposed US entry restrictions on people from Muslim countries. Despite this, 71% of respondents thought that UK's relations with the US would either "stay about the same" or "get better" during the course of his presidency.

More immediately, Prime Minister May ironically failed to learn from what was, perhaps, the most important lesson of Trump's victory, the volatile and uncertain nature of an electoral process. In April, buoyed by double-digit leads in the opinion polls, she called a surprise general election. Over the course of the next six weeks, the prospect of a landslide victory evaporated, reflecting a lackluster Conservative campaign and a stronger than expected performance by Labour Party leader Jeremy Corbyn. In June, May was returned to office as leader of the largest political party, but without an overall majority.[53] The nation was left with an unstable minority government and a Prime Minister whose personal authority was deeply damaged, both within her own party and the country-at- large. At a time when political stability was most needed, as the UK began the negotiations to affect its withdrawal from the EU, the future could scarcely have looked less certain. Such is the nature of politics in the age of Trump.

References

Arnold, G. 2014. *America and Britain: Was There Ever a Special Relationship?* London: Hurst and Co.

Dobson, A. and S. Marsh. 2013. *Anglo-American Relations: Contemporary Perspectives.* London: Routledge.

Dumbrell, J. 2006. *A Special Relationship: Anglo-American Relations from the Cold War to Iraq* (2nd ed.). London: Palgrave Macmillan.

---

[53] See: http://www.bbc.co.uk/news/election/2017.

Kearns, I. and K. Murray. 2017. *The Age of Trump: Foreign Policy Challenges for the Left*. London: Fabian Society.

Larres, K. 2017. "Donald Trump and America's Grand Strategy: US Foreign Policy Toward Europe, Russia and China." *Global Policy*, May. Available at: http://transatlanticrelations.org/wp-content/uploads/2017/05/Larres-Donald-Trump-and-America%E2%80%99s-Grand-Strategy-U.S.-foreign-policy-toward-Europe-Russia-and-China-Global-Policy-May-2017.pdf/.

Lindberg, T., ed. 2004. *Beyond Paradise and Power: Europe, America, and the Future of a Troubled Partnership*. London: Routledge.

McKercher, B.J.C. 2017. *Britain, America, and the Special Relationship since 1941*. London: Routledge.

Riddell, P. 2003. *Hug Them Close: Blair, Clinton, Bush and the 'Special Relationship'*. London: Politico.

Tate, S. 2012. *A Special Relationship? British Foreign Policy in the Era of American Hegemony*. Manchester. UK: Manchester University Press.

Waugh, E. 1962. *Brideshead Revisited*. London: Penguin.

6
TRUMP'S PRESIDENCY: THE "NEW COLD WAR" AND US-POLAND SECURITY TIES

Karol Bieniek and Grzegorz Nycz

INTRODUCTION

While Poland has been an important partner for the United States (US) since the collapse of the Soviet Union, her strategic importance has been tangential, because the Central and Eastern Europe region has been stable and because Poland's geographical location, economy, and natural resources have played only a secondary role. Undoubtedly, the overall good condition of Poland-US bilateral relations should be perceived as one of the biggest achievements of the Polish foreign policy after the collapse of the Soviet Union. Indeed, it is characteristic that Polish perception of US-Poland bilateral relations remains strong, under the influence of assumptions that Poland has a special meaning for the US, as it is one of their most important allies in the region. This is a result of historical and strategic considerations. Both assumptions are justified. Common military and political cooperation has been clearly visible. In the 1990s, the US's support contributed significantly to the normalization of Poland's international position and later its accession into the North Atlantic Treaty Organization (NATO). This had, and still has, a crucial importance for all Polish international security concerns. This support led to almost unconditional Polish support for the American international activities and created a somehow idealistic picture of America among the Polish governing elites, whether right and left wing in political orientation. When the "war on terrorism" started, Poland, despite her European allies, supported American intervention in Iraq and Afghanistan and she was supposed to become one of the US's most important partners in Europe, because the Polish national interest was perceived to be similar to the American interests. This expectation, however, did not become a reality.

Foreign policy, in general, has been the subject of frequent harsh political debates in Poland. For Polish politicians, the characteristic assumptions were that the US has focused on Central and Eastern Europe, and on Poland's special role in the region. In the public discourse, bilateral relations are rather mythologized; the will is to base Polish foreign policy and its international status on an alliance with a world superpower is considered to be fully rational. However, the point being missed is that, for US, Poland is only one of many regular allies.

The ongoing happenings in the region have, however, changed the Central and Eastern Europe situation, resulting in expressions of enthusiasm by members of the right-wing Polish Law and Justice Party Government (PiS) about Trump's winning of the US presidency. But it needs to be understood that the previous, right-wing, coalitional government of the Civic Party (PO) and the Polish Peasants` Party (PS), moved Polish foreign policy toward deepening integration with the European Union (EU). Obviously, it did no harm to the country`s optimistic attitude toward US, but it did encourage some skepticism to be expressed with regard to this generally mythologized relationship. So, the Trump administration was rather warmly welcomed, since it is perceived by some Euro-skeptical Polish politicians, to be an indirect continuation of George W. Bush's foreign policy, which had a purposive focus on terrorism and on international security in general. The latter has become a crucial current concern of Polish political elite, in the context of Russian's aggressive actions in the neighboring Ukraine and the region more general. Thus, for the Polish government, regional security issues are its main international focus and the early days of Trump's presidency should be analyzed within this context, as his initiatives that impact on regional security catch public attention in Poland.

Trump's Defense Policies: The Polish Perspective

In the area of defense policy, Donald Trump can be seen as Ronald Reagan's defense policy successor—his 'Make America Strong Again' theme[1] effectively repeats Reagan's 1980 "peace through strength" motto[2] and his 1981 inaugural address postulated "greater strength around

---

[1] Retrieved from: https://www.donaldjtrump.com/.

[2] Retrieved from: https://www.reaganlibrary.gov/major-speeches-index/10-archives/reference/12-10-19-80;https://www.reaganlibrary.gov/major-speeches-index.

the world."³ The Trump administration is seeking to increase in the defense budget by $25 billion in 2017—to $576 billion—and by a further $54 billion in 2018, secured by decreasing selected non-defense obligations.⁴ Obama's budget outlays for 2017 meant that defense spending would be 3.2% of US GDP.⁵ This included military aid under the US-Ukraine Security Initiative for Ukrainian defense was to be $150 million in 2017 and $250 million in 2018.⁶

One of the key controversial issues in US-Russian relations relates to Poland. President George W. Bush planned to build a missile defense system with elements in Poland and Czech Republic—the Ground-based Midcourse Defense. The US agreement with Poland on the construction of this missile defense system was signed in 2008. It was changed by President Barack Obama's decision to reduce the US engagement from the planned Ground-based Interceptors base targeted against ICBM attack, to the shorter than ICBM targets interception Aegis missile defense components. European Phased Adaptive Initiative, developed in September 2009, led to the construction of Aegis Ashore bases in Poland and Romania. Notably, this brought the beginning of the construction of Redzikowo missile defense base in April 2016.⁷

Polish investments in the area of missile defense—the critically important purchase of PAC-3 Patriot missiles—were, however, delayed, while Trump's positions on Ballistic Missile Defense (BMD) (Hildreth 2017)

---

3   Retrieved from: http://www.presidency.ucsb.edu/ws/?pid=43130.

4   Retrieved from: https://www.whitehouse.gov/sites/whitehouse.gov/files/omb/budget/fy2018/2018_blueprint.pdf; https://www.whitehouse.gov/sites/whitehouse.gov/files/omb/budget/fy2018/amendment_03_16_18.pdf; https://www.congress.gov/115/bills/hr1301/BILLS-115hr1301pcs.pdf; https://www.whitehouse.gov/the-press-office/2017/03/07/hr-1301-department-defense-appropriations-act-2017; https://www.congress.gov/bill/115th-congress/house-bill/1301.

5   Retrieved from: https://www.gpo.gov/fdsys/pkg/BUDGET-2017-BUD/pdf/BUDGET-2017-BUD.pdf.

6   Retrieved from: https://www.congress.gov/bill/115th-congress/house-bill/1301/text;https://www.congress.gov/bill/114th-congress/house-bill/2685/text;https://www.gpo.gov/fdsys/pkg/PLAW-.

7   Retrieved from: https://cnic.navy.mil/regions/cnreurafswa/installations/nsf_redzikowo/news/nsf-redzikowo-officially-becomes-a-command.html.

in Poland were not cognizable (Oswald 2016). During the 2016 presidential electoral campaign, Vice-President Mike Pence supported the George W Bush presidency plan of BMD deployment in Poland and Czech Republic.[8] Under the Trump administration, the US was expected to support a more robust missile defense investment in the National Missile Defense (NMD) follow-up installations. Meanwhile, Russian launchers in Kaliningrad threatened the Polish missile defense base (Bermant and Sutyagin 2016). Trump's early BMD decisions seemed most needed in the light of previous delays in new deployments in Eastern Europe due to Russian pressure (a 2017).

As Hildreth (2017) notes, the National Defense Authorization Act of 2017 increased the role of missile defense (see Kamarck et al. 2017), while placing broader requirements on National Missile Defense than in the 1999 Missile Defense Act, but Trump's position on missile defense remains largely unknown, despite general statements he has made on its upkeep in the light of North Korean threat. The National Defense Authorization for Fiscal Year 2017 Act of 2016 replaced a system against limited strikes (under the "National Missile Defense Act of 1999")[9] with a "robust layered system."[10]

Trump proposed, during the electoral campaign, to build a "serious" missile defense system (cruisers and destroyers)[11] in the context of defense equipment and personnel increases (in the Army to 540,000 soldiers, in the Navy to 350 ships, in the Air Force to 1,200 fighters, in the Marines to 36 battalions).[12] Trump's defense policy included developing missile defense to counter the threat from Iran and North Korea—so

---

[8] Retrieved from: http://www.thenews.pl/1/10/Artykul/274006,Trump-running-mate-supports-missile-defence-shield-in-Poland.

[9] Retrieved from: https://www.congress.gov/106/plaws/publ38/PLAW-106publ38.pdf.

[10] Retrieved from: https://www.congress.gov/114/bills/s2943/BILLS-114s2943enr.pdf.

[11] See: https://www.donaldjtrump.com/policies/national-defense/; https://www.donaldjtrump.com/press-releases/fact-sheet-key-policies-proposed-in-mr.-trumps-military-preparedness-speech.

[12] See: https://www.donaldjtrump.com/policies/national-defense/; https://www.donaldjtrump.com/press-releases/fact-sheet-key-policies-proposed-in-mr.-trumps-military-preparedness-speech.

ending military expenditure cuts—and an investment in the US Cyber Command.[13]

Facing the threat of a "New Cold War," Poland expected more US military engagement, but Trump asserted that NATO members should provide more for their security. Notably, Polish expenditure on national defense reached 2.01% of GDP in 2017 and could rise even to 3% in the future (Wilk 2016). In the 2017 Polish budget, defense expenditures reached 36.8 billion zloty (some $9.5 billion), which is 9.6% of total government expenditure.[14] Owing to Polish 2012 military modernization plans, new equipment sales were to receive funding of $62 billion over the period to 2022 (Grigas 2016). Poland became, in 2015, one of only five NATO countries that have achieved the target defense expenditure quotient (2% of GDP), the others being US, United Kingdom, Greece, and Estonia,[15] with the World Bank suggesting that Poland spent 2.2% of its GDP on defense in 2015.[16] The large growth of Polish defense expenditures in 2015 has been seen as a response to Russian military incursion in Ukraine (Perlo-Freeman et al. 2016).[17] Indeed, it was the 2014 Ukrainian crisis that led to the increased sense of belligerence between the West and Russia, reaching the point of becoming a "New Cold War." This reflects the authoritarian Vladimir Putin's Rus-

---

[13] See: https://www.whitehouse.gov/making-our-military-strong-again (retrieved July 5, 2017).

[14] Retrieved from: http://www.mf.gov.pl/documents/764034/5893644/201701 18_Ustawa_budzetowa_na_rok_2017.zip; http://www.mf.gov.pl/ministerstwo-finansow/dzialalnosc/finanse-publiczne/budzet-panstwa/ustawy-budzetowe/2017/ustawa. Polish defense expenditures stood at 35,4 billion zloties in 2016, while it grew most significantly in 2015 to 38,1 billion from 28,3 billion in 2014. See also: http://www.mf.gov.pl/documents/764034/5257802/20160304_Ustawa_budzetowa+na+rok+2016.zip; http://www.mf.gov.pl/documents/764034/2459648/20140204_ustawa_budzetowa_2014.zip; https://www.nbp.pl/kursy/kursya.html; http://www.nbp.pl/home.aspx?navid=archa&c=/ascx/tabarch.ascx&n=a063z150401; http://www.nbp.pl/home.aspx?navid=archa&c=/ascx/tabarch.ascx&n=a020z160201.

[15] See: http://www.nato.int/nato_static_fl2014/assets/pdf/pdf_2016_07/20160704_160704-pr2016-116.pdf.

[16] Retrieved from: http://data.worldbank.org/indicator/MS.MIL.XPND.GD.ZS.

[17] See: http://www.telegraph.co.uk/news/worldnews/europe/poland/11641852/Poland-increases-military-spending-in-response-to-Russias-belligerence.html.

sian rivalry with the NATO over its admission of former Soviet vassal states (Black 2016, Kalb 2015, Legvold 2014, 2016, Lucas 2014, MacKinnon 2008, Mearsheimer 2014, Rosefielde 2017).

Trump's Engagement with NATO: The Polish Perspective

US Secretary of State, Rex Tillerson, on March 31 in Brussels, emphasized that NATO played a fundamental role in the defense against Russian aggression and stressed that the new US battalion in Poland proved NATO's collected defense capabilities through a forward presence.[18] According to Tillerson, US-Russian relations in the first month of Trump's presidency stood at their worst level since the Cold War, and were worsening further, as he noted during his April conversation with Putin in Moscow, adding that the two strongest nuclear superpowers still had to improve their ties.[19] The Ukrainian war remains a major obstacle to any improvement in US-Russian relations.[20]

On May 2, NATO Supreme Allied Commander in Europe, General Curtis Scaparrotti, told the US Senate that a new defense infrastructure in Europe is needed at a time when there was a need for a "credible deterrence to Russian aggression."[21] The NATO reforms expected

---

[18] See: https://www.state.gov/secretary/remarks/2017/03/269339.htm.

[19] See: https://www.state.gov/secretary/remarks/2017/05/270620.htm. Notably, the time of the US and EU's sanctions against Russia, introduced due to Russian aggression against Ukraine brought a severe recession in Russian economy, suffering also from low oil prices.

[20] Rex Tillerson, US Secretary of State, said in April 2017 in Moscow that the conflict in Ukraine was still hampering improvements in Washington-Moscow relations while Russia could contribute to the Minsk process in ending Ukrainian conflict by its support for the reduction of violence and withdrawal of separatist units including heavy weaponry to make space for OSCE mission. Retrieved from: https://www.state.gov/secretary/remarks/2017/04/270136.htm. See also Rumer, Sokolsky, and Weiss (2017, 12–19).

[21] See: https://www.appropriations.senate.gov/imo/media/doc/050217-Scaparrotti-Testimony.pdf. Scaparrotti stressed that the European Command of NATO had to return to its historic mission as a deterrence and war-fighting body, in place of its security cooperation role. Those changes were introduced in the context of Russian aggressive military policies; see also: https://www.armed-services.senate.gov/imo/media/doc/Scaparrotti_04-21-16.pdf. See also: Gara-

by Trump included greater defense small minority of NATO allies that have increased their military expenditure beyond the minimum NATO-required level of 2%. While the main shifts in East European military equation to be included in Trump's planning related to the future of Obama's European Reassurance Initiative and to NATO's Enhanced Forward Presence plan strengthening the Eastern flank of alliance by the deployments of four US battalions in Baltic states and Poland (Eyal 2017). The strengthening of NATO's Eastern flank received significant German backing because of its 2016–2017 decision to increase troop numbers on NATO's Eastern border in the context of the NATO's new deployments in Poland and Baltic states (Fröhlich, Coffey, and Neubauer 2017, Gramer 2017).[22] Obama's European Reassurance initiative's final contribution included a deployment of 3,500-strong US armored brigade in Poland.[23] NATO's forward presence included moving 36,000 US forces in Germany eastward, near the NATO-Russia borders (Kostrzewa-Zorbas 2017).[24]

US troops came to Poland in January 2017,[25] despite Russian opposition (O'Connor 2017).[26] The deployment plans of the 3rd Armored Brigade Combat Team (4th Infantry Division) led to continued rotational presence of such a force in Poland since early 2017, with the main area of consolidation in West-Polish Drawsko, Pomorskie, and Zagan military

---

mone (2017) and Grady 2017b.

[22] The public support for sending German troops to East European NATO members, Poland and Baltic states, to defend them from Russian invasion reached in Bertelsmann's poll low level of 31%, which due to a Heritage Foundation's report could be attributed to historically-oriented restraints to engage militarily abroad maintained by the German public. See: https://www.bertelsmann-stiftung.de/en/our-projects/strengthening-and-connecting-europe/news/stress-test-for-german-russian-relations/.

[23] See: https://www.defense.gov/News/Article/Article/1048463/eucom-commander-us-armored-brigades-deployment-to-poland-significant. See also: https://pl.usembassy.gov/abct/.

[24] See: http://www.usanato.army.mil/sites/locations/index.html#PL; http://www.dw.com/en/us-forces-in-poland-here-to-stay/a-37130731.

[25] But see: http://www.npr.org/sections/parallels/2017/01/12/509520482/u-s-troops-arrive-in-poland-but-will-trump-keep-them-there.

[26] See: http://www.bbc.com/news/world-europe-38603234; http://www.bbc.com/news/world-europe-38592448.

centers, including Swietoszow, Skwierzyna, and Boleslawiec, from where three battalions would be spread to Baltic nations, Bulgaria, Romania, and Germany.[27] By the end of March 2017 in the framework of the "Atlantic Resolve" operation, US troops deployed Paladin howitzers in Zagan to increase interoperability with the Polish army (Geiger 2017).

After Brexit, the US is expected to receive lower support in the EU, American policy could lead to the increased engagement of Britain in NATO. Moreover, the role of Germany in Europe is likely to increase, thereby increasing the significance of German cooperation with Washington.

A discussion on US-East European policy, which is particularly important from the perspective of the Polish sense of danger coming from Russian military expansion, leads toward two main political concepts: a new containment and a new détente.

Among the leading questions relating to East European security are those referring to Trump's position on particularly important NATO's Eastern flank strengthening in the face of Russian aggression against Ukraine and other threats. A key question arising relates to his ability to keep the *Pax Americana*, at the time of renewed conflicts between the US and Russia, which is at its peak since the fall of the Berlin wall (Jackson 2017), exacerbated by Trump's criticism of Obama for abandoning missile defense plans America had with Poland and Czech Republic.[28]

Trump's Presidency and Polish Foreign Policy

While Hungarian Victor Orban's government shared high expectations of Trump's fortress-building external policies, the Trump administration was not fully understanding of Polish expectations that NATO would provide greater regional security at a time of growing Russian threat and Ukraine security deficit. This came at a time of a Polish revival of the interwar intermarium concept of an alliance of Adriatic, Baltic, and Black Sea countries.[29] Polish fear of Putin's intentions in region

---

[27] See: https://www.army.mil/article/177819/us_army_europe_to_increase_presence_across_eastern_europe.

[28] See: https://www.donaldjtrump.com/press-releases/donald-j.-trump-foreign-policy-speech.

[29] See: http://www.prezydent.pl/en/news/art,352,president-duda-invites-trump-

raised concerns about Trump's desire to establish warm relationship with him.[30] However, Trump's first visit in Poland *en route* to the G-20 meeting in Germany raised very high expectations in Warsaw, building grounds of Central-East European bloc.[31] Trump was well received by the Polish right-wing authorities, including President Andrzej Duda. After the April White House meeting with NATO's Secretary General, Jens Stoltenberg, Trump revoked his previous statements on the alliance being obsolete, but repeated his call for NATO members to pay their "debt"—2% of their GDP to be spent of their defense—and not to count that the US paying for their defense.[32] It was at this time that NATO deployed a new battalion near Kaliningrad district-Polish border in response to new Russia hostilities.[33] During the April meeting with Stoltenberg, Trump emphasized the Tillerson's recent successful visit to Russia, his hope of establishing constructive relations with Putin, and his belief that Syria remains a key issue for NATO.[34] Yet, in February in Brussels, the US Vice-President, Mike Pence, supported the NATO's Enhanced Forward Presence Initiative in Poland and Baltic states as a countering of Russia's attempts to change East-European borders by force and so seen as a NATO contribution to territorial integrity of European countries.[35] At the subsequent Munich Security Conference,

---

to-poland.html; http://washington.mfa.gov.pl/en/news/president_donald_trump_invited_to_visit_poland_by_president_andrzej_duda.

[30] See: https://www.nytimes.com/2016/11/20/world/europe/poland-trump-putin.html?_r=0.

[31] See: http://www.reuters.com/article/us-poland-usa-trump-idUSKBN17F1AV.

[32] See: https://www.bloomberg.com/news/articles/2017-02-14/trump-s-defense-pick-mattis-to-focus-nato-members-on-spending.

[33] See: http://www.newsweek.com/us-soldiers-poland-border-russia-trump-nato-584256; https://www.whitehouse.gov/the-press-office/2017/04/12/joint-press-conference-president-trump-and-nato-secretary-general; https://www.whitehouse.gov/blog/2017/04/13/president-trump-welcomes-nato-secretary-general-stoltenberg-white-house.

[34] See: https://www.whitehouse.gov/the-press-office/2017/04/12/joint-press-conference-president-trump-and-nato-secretary-general; https://www.whitehouse.gov/blog/2017/04/13/president-trump-welcomes-nato-secretary-general-stoltenberg-white-house.

[35] At the same time Mike Pence stressed that the US will continue to press Russia to implement the Minsk agreement on ending violence in Ukrainian conflict. See: https://www.whitehouse.gov/the-press-office/2017/02/20/remarks-vice-

Pence stressed that four new NATO multinational battalions in Poland and Baltic states strengthened the NATO's deterrence capabilities.[36]

Neorealist aspects of Trump's NATO policies—particularly his repeated call to NATO allies to pay their share of their defense costs—could correspond to some extent with Mearsheimer and Walt's concept of offshore balancing—placing more responsibility on regional allies to provide for their security, and supporting regional leaders to defend their region from a rising power—in place of attempts to remake other societies—and lowering support for the promotion of democracy and human rights—as costly liberal hegemony (Mearsheimer and Walt 2016, 71–72, see also Kelemen and Orenstein 2016).

Controversies of US-Polish relations include the possible authoritarian threat emerging from the overarching position of the ruling Law and Justice Party, undermining the autonomy of the Constitutional Court. Critics questioned the stable foundations of Polish democracy under Law and Justice Party from the perspective of European populist-right wing offensive, while Trump's early views saw Poland's political right wing as comparable to the US Republican Party (Karolewski and Benedikter 2016, 2–3, see also Kelemen and Orenstein 2016). The Polish right welcomed Trump victory with an optimism and expectation of not interfering in Poland's domestic developments toward strengthening of the executive branch of government as corresponding with his US governance model.[37]

The Possible Threats and Controversies in US-Polish Relations

In the context of the "war on terror," one controversial issue was Poland's participation in the US-led Iraqi mission. Trump has expressed the view in 2016 that the Saddam Hussein's regime was better for Iraq

---

president-and-european-council-president-tusk.

[36] See: https://www.whitehouse.gov/the-press-office/2017/02/18/remarks-vice-president-munich-security-conference.

[37] See also: http://country.eiu.com/article.aspx?articleid=1585079142&Country=Poland&topic=Politics&subtopic=Forecast&subsubtopic=International+relations&u=1&pid=985139282&oid=985139282&uid=1.

than the present terrorist threat, which has become a "training ground" for terrorists.[38] He described the situation in Libya similarly.[39] Notably, he has talked of the "twisted" US intelligence reports on Iraqi weapons of mass destruction (Trump 2015, 37). In Trump's view, the US made a mistake in Iraq—he thought the intervention was unwise—but judged that the US should "keep the oil" using the occupation period to stop radical Islamic terrorist groups—later ISIS—from benefiting from Iraqi oil reserves.[40] The George W. Bush administration's claim—as justification for military intervention—that Iraq had weapons of mass destruction, however, proved to be false.[41] This leaves open, whether Poland's engagement could affect the future of US-Polish cooperation in the area of "war on terror," including such controversial matters as a secret CIA's prison in Poland.[42] Other elements of US-Polish relations under the George W. Bush administration were the Polish participation in US-led intervention in Afghanistan, the Cracow Proliferation Security Initiative, and, last but not least, the missile defense installations in Poland started as a result of an agreement reached in 2008.

Poland, as a new NATO member (since 1999), remains among those member countries counting on NATO's further enlargement to include other East-European countries, such as Ukraine and Georgia. At

---

[38] See: http://edition.cnn.com/2016/07/05/politics/donald-trump-saddam-hussein-iraq-terrorism/.

[39] See: http://edition.cnn.com/2016/07/05/politics/donald-trump-saddam-hussein-iraq-terrorism/.

[40] See: https://www.whitehouse.gov/the-press-office/2017/01/21/remarks-president-trump-and-vice-president-pence-cia-headquarters. It is seen as a significant issue among the main threats that Iran could attempt to block oil flow from the Persian Gulf, while violating the nuclear deal, which according to Glaser and Kelanic would became more probable in the case of US withdrawal from military engagement in the Gulf (Glaser and Kelanic 2016, 2017).

[41] See: https://www.cia.gov/library/reports/general-reports-1/iraq_wmd_2004/; https://www.cia.gov/library/reports/general-reports-1/iraq_wmd_2004/chap5.html#sect0; https://www.cia.gov/library/reports/general-reports-1/iraq_wmd_2004/chap4.html; http://www.iraqinquiry.org.uk/media/248178/the-report-of-the-iraq-inquiry_section-44.pdf; http://www.iraqinquiry.org.uk/the-report/.

[42] See: https://www.economist.com/blogs/easternapproaches/2012/08/poland-and-america.

the same time, one of the important international topics relates to the reliability of the new NATO members were there are possible threats to liberal democratic political systems, as in Poland and Hungary. The criticism of the EU and, to lesser degree, US, in relation to the threat to democratic standards posed by the ruling right-wing Law and Justice Party's controversial interventions in the structures of the Polish constitutional court was, however, not sustained by the US Republicans, as Rudolph Giuliani confirmed.[43] During the electoral campaign in September 2016, Trump confirmed that the US would remain Poland's firm ally and complimented Poland on meeting its NATO defense expenditure, despite the doubts over the quality of Polish democracy raised by former US President Bill Clinton.

Polish expectations of its special relations with the US are sustained by Obama's European Securitization Initiative and by its new deployments of an Armored Brigade in Poland. Trump has long favored improving US-Russian relations, but Russia saw US troops in Poland as a step toward confrontation.[44] Sanctions against Russia imposed by the Obama administration because of its illegal annexation of Crimea were maintained by the Trump administration, but no information has, however, been provided on the possible US arms sales to Ukraine, perhaps in expectation of closer cooperation with Russia in the campaign against ISIS.[45]

Trump wrote in 2015, seeking support for his policy of burden sharing by US allies benefiting from American military assistance, that he could understand the passive European—German—approach toward Putin's military aggression against Ukraine (Trump 2015, 49–50). Trump's National Security Advisor, Lieutenant-General Michael Flynn received very critical media coverage of his comments made, during his Senate

---

[43] See: http://www.thenews.pl/1/9Artykul/245301,It-is-for-Poles-to-decide-how-to-interpret-their-constitution-Rudolph-Giuliani.

[44] See: http://edition.cnn.com/2017/01/14/europe/poland-us-troops-nato-welcome/.

[45] See: https://www.whitehouse.gov/the-press-office/2017/03/10/press-briefing-press-secretary-sean-spicer-3102017-21; http://www.npr.org/sections/parallels/2017/01/12/509520482/u-s-troops-arrive-in-poland-but-will-trump-keep-them-there; https://www.theguardian.com/us-news/2017/jan/12/doubts-over-biggest-us-deployment-in-europe-since-cold-war-under-trump.

confirmation hearing on NATO, not to mention his statements about his Russian ties.[46]

US-RUSSIAN RELATIONS: THE POLISH PERSPECTIVE ON THE "NEW COLD WAR" CHALLENGES

Historically, the first steps toward the "New Cold War" were taken by Russia after George W. Bush's failure to persuade the US's West European allies, at the 2008 NATO Bucharest summit, to advance the prospects of admission into NATO of Ukraine and Georgia. In the absence of any hope for NATO Membership Action Plans (MAPs) being developed for Georgia and Ukraine, it became possible for the authoritarian Putin's Russia to attack both of those countries (Gallis 2008, 1). First, Russian forces attacked Georgia, using an opportunity posed by Georgia's attempt, under the presidency of Mikheil Shakashvili, to restore its military control over separatist South Ossetia. Shakashvili and his supporters are despised by the Kremlin because their role in the Rose Revolution of 2003 against former Soviet Foreign Minister and then the Georgian President, Eduard Shevardnadze (Kandelaki 2006, Nichol 2013). Russia failed in its attempt to take back control of Ukraine, through the Russia-dependent corrupt-authoritarian Yanukovych's regime, because of a popular rising against Yanukovych's 2013 decision to stop negotiations on accession into the EU,[47] and the subsequent removal of Yanukovych from office by the Ukrainian parliament in February 2014.[48] The Kremlin then decided to invade Ukraine and occupy Crimea, and to support armed paramilitary groups fighting against Ukrainian government in the Doneck and Lugansk districts.[49]

---

[46] See: http://edition.cnn.com/2016/12/12/politics/who-is-michael-flynn/; http://www.chicagotribune.com/news/nationworld/ct-trump-flynn-russia-contact-20170113-story.html.

[47] See: http://www.bbc.com/news/world-europe-25162563.

[48] See: http://www.bbc.com/news/world-europe-26304842.

[49] The UN General Assembly decided that Russian annexation of Crimea was illegal and violated the Budapest Memorandum of 1994 on Ukrainian territorial integrity, guaranteed by Russia in return for Ukraine's decision to give up its nuclear arsenal to Russia. This resolution (A/RES/68/262) was adopted on March 24, 2014 Available at: https://www.un.org/en/ga/search/view_doc.asp?symbol=A/RES/68/262. See also: https://disarmament-library.un.org/

Poland's policy toward Ukraine had a huge impact on the peaceful outcome of the 2004 Orange Revolution, when Ukrainians protested against frauds during the presidential elections, which led to repeated voting and Yushchenko's victory. During the 2013–2014 Ukrainian crisis, Poland, through its Foreign Minister, Radoslaw Sikorski, was pressing pro-Western Ukrainian leaders to resist the temptation of a full-scale confrontation with entrenched Yanukovych regime.[50] Poland became a host of a huge wave of Ukrainian refugees—migrants escaping from the theatre of a Russian-Ukrainian conflict—part of the broader Western-Russian conflict analyzed through the prism of a proxy war, as in the Syrian case (Beehner 2015, Jaroszewicz 2015).[51]

From the perspective of Eastern Europe—including Poland—which is facing an ongoing danger of Russian aggression, it is particularly disturbing, even frightening, that Trump is apparently willing to share confidential intelligence provided by another country to the Russian government.[52]

Conclusion

The main factors of increasing significance in US-Polish relations under the Trump presidency are as follows:

- *The threat posed by Russia's "New Cold War" policies*: This includes Russian aggression against Ukraine and its aftermath;

UNODA/Library.nsf/939721e5b418c27085257631004e4fbf/943f3b2034dc129a852576890070a7c0/$F.ILE/A-49-66-S-1994-91_Russia-Ukraine-US%2014%20Jan%2094%20trilateral%20stmt.pdf. See also http://www.bbc.com/news/world-europe-26304842.

[50] See: http://www.telegraph.co.uk/news/worldnews/europe/ukraine/10654081/Ukraine-protest-leader-warned-youll-all-be-dead.html.

[51] A Proxy war between the West and Russia can be observed in the dynamics of the Syrian conflict, which has lead to an unstoppable wave of refugees to the EU, thus causing a refugee crisis. See: https://www.foreignaffairs.com/articles/2015-11-12/how-proxy-wars-work.

[52] See: http://www.economist.com/newsunited-states/21722161-special-counsel-will-lead-independent-probe-russia-allegations; http://www.economist.com/blogs/democracyinamerica/2017/05/oopshttp://www.economist.com/news/europe/21720493-secondary-casualty-american-attack-was-illusion-rapprochement-after-strike.

Russia's illegal occupation of the Crimea and support of armed pro-Russian separatists in Eastern Ukraine; Russia's threats of attack against Baltic countries; and Russia's military expansionism.

- *Missile defense*: Trump has supported a more "robust" Ballistic Missile Defense–Ballistic Missile Defense system, including the construction of an Aegis base in Polish Redzikowo,
- *US military deployments in Poland*: This relates to the prospects of the Trump administration continuing to commit American military equipment and personnel under the US-Polish military cooperation initiative.
- *Strengthening NATO's eastern flank*: This relates to NATO's deterrence policy and the use of tactical nuclear weapons—the 'Nuclear Sharing' program (Horovitz 2014, 73–89, Schofield 2014, 67–85) and most importantly, the prospects of further NATO enlargement involving Ukraine and Georgia at the time of growing threat of the expansion of authoritarian Russia.
- *Arms procurement*: This includes Poland's procurement of Patriot missiles, F-16/F-35, and Black Hawks.

The key points of US-Polish relations in the second decade of the twenty-first century are numerous and complex. The dominant theme is the Russian threat of military aggression. This brings to the fore the importance of NATO military alliance and Poland's need for US arms procurement. In return, Poland has engaged in US-led Iraqi and Afghan intervention, and has met its NATO defense expenditure obligations. Polish support for stronger ties between US and Europe—the EU and NATO—may also become important in the light of Brexit and Western sanctions against Russia.

References

Beehner, L. 2015. "How Proxy Wars Work and What That Means for Ending the Conflict in Syria." *Foreign Affairs*, November 12. Available at: https://www.foreignaffairs.com/articles/2015-11-12/how-proxy-wars-work.

Bermant, A. and I. Sutyagin. 2016. "Does NATO Missile Defense Have a Future?" *The National Interest*, December 5. Available at: http://nationalinterest.org/blog/the-buzz/does-nato-missile-defense-have-future-18617.

Black, J.L. 2016. "Concluding Remarks." In *The Return of the Cold War. Ukraine, the West and Russia* (eds. J.L. Black and M. Johns). London and New York: Routledge.

Eyal, J. 2017. "The Real Problems With NATO: What Trump Gets Right, and Wrong." *Foreign Affairs*, March 2. Available at: https://www.foreignaffairs.com/articles/europe/2017-03-02/real-problems-nato.

Gallis, P. 2008. "The NATO Summit at Bucharest." *CRS Report for Congress*, May. Available at: https://fas.org/sgp/crs/row/RS22847.pdf.

Garamone, J. 2017. "Eucom Chief Makes Case for Continued Funding for European Reassurance Initiative." *US Department of Defense*, May 3. Available at: https://www.defense.gov/News/Article/Article/1171280/eucom-chief-makes-case-for-continued-funding-for-european-reassurance-initiative/.

Geiger, J. 2017. "US Forces Sustain Interoperability by Relocating to Zagan." *US Army Europe*, March 31. Available at: https://www.army.mil/article/185285/us_forces_sustain_interoperability_by_relocating_to_zagan.

Glaser, Ch. and R. Kelanic, eds. 2016. *Crude Strategy: Rethinking the US Military Commitment to Defend Persian Gulf Oil.* Washington, DC: Georgetown University Press.

Glaser, Ch. and R. Kelanic. 2017. "Getting Out of the Gulf. Oil and US Military Strategy." *Foreign Affairs* 96 (1): 122–131.

Grady, J. 2017a. "Panel: Trump Must Make a Choice in European Ballistic Missile Defense." *US Naval Institute (USNI) News*, February 17. Available at: https://news.usni.org/2017/02/17/panel-question-facing-trump-administration-european-missile-defense-united-state-go-ahead-next-phase-program-says-deter-iran-pause-let-se.

Grady, J. 2017b. "*Scaparotti: Russia Pushing US European Command Back to a Warfighting Focus.*" *US Naval Institute (USNI) News*, March 28. Available at: https://news.usni.org/2017/03/28/scaparotti-russia-pushing-u-s-european-command-back-warfighting-focus.

Gramer, R. 2017. "Amid Growing Threats, Germany Plans to Expand Troop Numbers to Nearly 200,000." *Foreign Policy*, February 23. Available at: http://foreignpolicy.com/2017/02/23/amid-growing-threats-germany-plans-to-expand-troop-numbers-to-nearly-200000-military-nato-transatlantic-security/.

Grigas, A. 2016. "Poland Takes Its Military Might Seriously." *The National Interest*, December 1. Available at: http://nationalinterest.org/feature/poland-takes-its-military-might-seriously-18580.

Hildreth, S. 2017. "Current Ballistic Missile Defense (BMD) Issues." *CRS Insight*, February 21. Available at: https://news.usni.org/wp-content/uploads/2017/02/IN10655.pdf#viewer.action=download.

Horovitz, L. 2014. "Why Do They Want American Nukes? Central and Eastern European Positions Regarding US Nonstrategic Nuclear Weapons." *European Security* 23 (1): 73–89. Available at: http://www.tandfonline.com/doi/abs/10.1080/09662839.2013.846326.

Jackson, V. 2017. "Reading Trump. The Danger of Overanalyzing His Tweets." *Foreign Affairs*, January 25. Available at: https://www.foreignaffairs.com/articles/2017-01-25/reading-trump.

Jaroszewicz, M. 2015. "The Migration of Ukrainians in Times of Crisis." *Centre for Eastern Studies* (Ośrodek Studiów Wschodnich im. Marka Karpia), October 19. Available at: https://www.osw.waw.pl/sites/default/files/commentary_187.pdf.

Kalb, M. 2015. *Imperial Gamble: Putin, Ukraine, and the New Cold War*. Washington, DC: Brookings Institution Press.

Kamarck, K., D. Jansen, L. Kapp, R.C. Mason, and B. Salazar Torreon. 2017. "FY2017 National Defense Authorization Act: Selected Military Personnel Issues." *Congressional Research Service, Report for Congress*, January 23. Available at: https://fas.org/sgp/crs/natsec/R44577.pdf.

Kandelaki, G. 2006. *Georgia's Rose Revolution: A Participant's Perspective* IUSIP Special Report, July. Washington, DC: United States Institute of Peace. Available at: https://www.usip.org/sites/default/files/sr167.pdf.

Karolewski, I.P. and R. Benedikter. 2016. "Europe's New Rogue States, Poland and Hungary: A Narrative and Its Perspectives." *Chinese Political Science Review*, October 2016, 1–22. Available at: https://link.springer.com/article/10.1007%2Fs41111-016-0048-5.

Kelemen, R.D. and M.A. Orenstein. 2016. "Europe's Autocracy Problem. Polish Democracy's Final Days?" *Foreign Affairs*, Janu-ary 7. Available at: https://www.foreignaffairs.com/articles/poland/2016-01-07/europes-autocracy-problem.

Kostrzewa-Zorbas, G. 2017. "Amerykańskie siły lądowe, powietrzne i morskie w Polsce - krajobraz w dniu zmiany władzy w USA." *wPolityce.pl*, January 20. Available at: https://wpolityce.pl/swiat/324151-amerykanskie-sily-ladowe-powietrzne-i-morskie-w-polsce-krajobraz-w-dniu-zmiany-wladzy-w-usa.

Legvold, R. 2014. "Managing the New Cold War. What Moscow and Washington Can Learn from the Last One." *Foreign Affairs* 93 (4): 74–84.

Legvold, R. 2016. *Return to Cold War*. Cambridge and Malden: Polity Press.

Lucas, E. [2008] 2014. *The New Cold War: Putin's Threat to Russia and the World*. London: Bloomsbury.

MacKinnon, M. 2008. *The New Cold War: Revolutions, Rigged Elections and Pipeline Politics in the Former Soviet Union*. Toronto, ONT, CA: Vintage Canada.

Mearsheimer, J. 2014. "Why the Ukraine Crisis is the West's Fault. The Liberal Delusions That Provoked Putin." *Foreign Affairs* 93 (5): 77–89.

Mearsheimer, J. and S. Walt. 2016. "The Case for Offshore Balancing." *Foreign Affairs* 95 (4): 70–83.

Nichol, J. 2013. "Georgia [Republic]: Recent Developments and US Interests." *Congressional Research Service (CRS) Report for Congress*, June 21. Available at: https://fas.org/sgp/crs/row/97-727.pdf.

O'Connor, T. 2017. "US Soldiers Deployed to Poland's Border with Russia as Trump Changes NATO Views." *Newsweek*, April 14. Available at: http://www.newsweek.com/us-soldiers-poland-border-russia-trump-nato-584256.

Oswald, R. 2016. "Trump's Plans for European Missile Defense a Mystery." *Bulletin of the Atomic Scientists*, December 7. Available at: http://thebulletin.org/trump%E2%80%99s-plans-european-missile-defense-mystery10258.

Perlo-Freeman, S., A. Fleurant, P. Wezeman, and S. Wezeman. 2016. "Trends in World Military Expenditure." *SIPRI Fact Sheet*, April. Available at: http://books.sipri.org/files/FS/SIPRIFS1604.pdf.

Rosefielde, S. 2017. *The Kremlin Strikes Back. Russia and the West after Crimea's Annexation*. New York: Cambridge University Press.

Rumer, E., R. Sokolsky, and A. Weiss. 2017. "Trump and Russia. The Right Way to Manage Relations." *Foreign Affairs* 96 (2): 12–19.

Schofield, J. 2014. *Strategic Nuclear Sharing*. London: Palgrave Macmillan.

Trump, D.J. 2015. *Great Again. How to Fix Our Crippled America*. New York: Threshold Editions.

Wilk, R. 2016. "Poland to Spend 2.01% of GDP on Defence in 2017." *Jane's 360*, September 2. Available at: http://www.janes.com/article/63420/poland-to-spend-2-01-of-gdp-on-defence-in-2017.

7
THE TRUMP AGE OF UNCERTAINTY: GROUNDING CENTRAL EAST EUROPEAN-US RELATIONS

Bohdan Szklarski

INTRODUCTION

From a geopolitical perspective, the eastern zone of European countries can be divided into two overarching groups. The first group consists of the Baltic states (Estonia, Latvia, and Lithuania), the Czech Republic, Slovakia, Bulgaria, and Romania. They are strongly pro-European Union (EU) due to the economic benefits, a clear identification with Western democratic values and practices, albeit to varying degrees, and a need to anchor their national security with North Atlantic Treaty Organization (NATO) and other pan-European institutions.

A second group of countries—Hungary and Poland—are pro-Western and see themselves as European, but have become more lukewarm in their views of the EU. This derives from what is perceived as the imposition of liberal social values, as well as economic rules and regulations from Brussels. These are actions that are perceived to have been taken without consideration of national sovereignty. Both Hungary and Poland have elected right-wing governments that have taken a more conservative approach to social issues and, some would argue, civil rights. This has led to some friction with the EU. At the same time, Poland harbors a suspicion of Russia, its traditional geopolitical rival in the east. This has left these countries in a position where they want to be part of the West, but not necessarily as close to the EU as they have been. For Poland, at least, this has made working more closely with the United States (US) a more attractive option. Some commentators interpreted it as quiet condoning of the nationalist-populist policies of Warsaw and Budapest.[1]

The Balkans countries are a third group, which is much more difficult to define due to the long-standing historical feuds, cultural diversity, and

---

[1] See: https://www.theguardian.com/us-news/2017/jul/06/donald-trump-warn-future-west-in-doubt-warsaw-speech.

violent split after the collapse of Yugoslavia, but would include Albania, Bosnia and Herzegovina, Bulgaria, Croatia, Greece, Kosovo, Macedonia, Montenegro, Serbia, and Sloven. Russian penetration into that region is much greater due to historic circumstances and cultural connections. For the same reasons American influence in the Balkans is fresh and lacks firm roots.

The CEE is a region where the old international order has, since the 2014 Russian intrusion to Ukraine, subtly shifted into a more grimy game of power politics and realpolitik. President Donald J. Trump's confusing and inconsistent policy pronouncements, organizational disarray in the administration, personnel shuffling and communication malfunctioning leave conditions conducive to greater economic cooperation and interdependence in limbo, and for CEE region, history has proved too often that, as Scott B. MacDonald notes "limbo is not a good place to be." [2]

US Interests in Central Eastern Europe

The 2016 presidential campaign and political tremors throughout Europe—CEE in particular—over refugees, Brexit, democracy building, fueled by Trump's anti-Obama—anti-continuity—campaign message, raised serious doubts as to the future of European-US cooperation. CEE is certainly not benefiting from such developments.

When we look at American presence in CEE, we must realize that the region is of secondary importance. The US has never had a primary interest in this region, which either belonged to the Soviet sphere of influence (1945–1991) or was a buffer zone between Russia and the West. Historically, after the fall of the Soviet Union, Washington finds itself caught in a difficult position between three competing interests:

- a core of new CEE allies that seek American support for their foreign policy priorities and occasionally for internal partisan conflicts;
- a protective axis of older EU members that are apprehensive about a new Cold War with Moscow; and

---

[2] Retrieved from: http://ayyaantuu.net/eastern-europes-new-geopolitical-fault-lines/.

- Russia is supportive of US anti-terrorist policy but is adopting imperialist policies toward former Soviet satellites.

Balancing these distinct interests is a challenge for previous and current US administrations especially, as when they prioritize the promotion of freedom, democracy, and capitalism as a distinct national interest.

US administrations have been strongly supportive of CCE states and their international aspirations. The military protection of Western Europe and the political liberation of Communist Europe were important legacies of the Cold War and of America's investment in European security. The successful construction of democratic policies and market systems was seen as a major achievement of US foreign policy through decades of intensive diplomatic and material engagement in Europe. In Washington's estimation, at some point, CEE countries have also become valuable role models for political and economic transition whose experiences could be applied to other post-dictatorial systems. That was certainly significant for the Clinton, Bush Jr. and Obama administrations. Now, with populist governments in Slovakia and questionably democratic paths recently taken by Budapest and Warsaw, this role-model factor has lost much of its allure.

The CEE region's views of the US have been shaped primarily by the Cold War and its aftermath. America was recognized throughout the region as the major bulwark against communism and Soviet expansionism, and as the beacon of freedom, democracy, and national independence. Washington was perceived as instrumental in the collapse of communist rule and the unraveling of the Soviet bloc. The US has also been viewed as providing critical political, economic, and security support during the process of democratization and in ensuring that most of the states in the CEE region were integrated into the NATO alliance. The initial hesitation of the Clinton administration regarding the path to the NATO membership for the countries in the region—represented by the idea of Partnership for Peace (1994)—was viewed as an unnecessary delay and a potential gesture of good will to ... Moscow. When, two years later, Washington changed its mind and initiated steps toward full NATO membership for the first three countries in the region—Poland, the Czech Republic, and Hungary—one could hear a sigh of relief throughout region, including countries that were not scheduled to join the alliance any time soon. This promise of NATO membership was received as a confirmation of American commitment to play the role of security guarantor and a democratic mentor for the region.

NATO and EU, while important, still are not considered to have sufficient military power, international prestige, or political will to ensure sufficient security protection against present, and future, Russian pressures and a guarantee that CEE will not return to the status of a no man's land between East and West (Deni 2016, 36). As a result, each CEE government has sought to develop a special relationship or strategic partnership with the US. For CEE leaders, the US is considered to have a more realistic, clear-cut, and consistent policy toward Russia than the EU, though occasionally, as the Czechs or Serbs may not express this with sufficient force. For the populations of former Soviet Bloc countries, the US is the primary Western power that Moscow respects, and CEE leaders calculate that a close alliance with America will help protect these new democracies.

A Conceptual Framework for CEE-US Relations: Non-confrontational Asymmetry And Security Dilemmas

CEE-US relations are a classic example of a non-confrontational symmetry. It is an uneven relation between a senior partner—a hegemon or patron—and the junior partners playing the roles of followers or clients, who recognize their mutual interests and are aware of their limitations. The inequality between these actors is taken for granted (Sylvan and Majeski 2009, 3). It should be treated as an axiom, a fact of life, not as a condition that could be changed. In a way, the recognition of inequalities is a value. It defines the relationship and consolidates it by bonding partners into a long-term relationship or even commitment. Political elites of both partners are responsible for the management of mutual perceptions to legitimize the inequality as a natural condition and sell it as mutually beneficial; otherwise, one inevitably opens the relationship to criticism on both sides. On the side of the patron, people may regard any investment in client states as a waste of resource when clients do not reciprocate to equal extent. On the side of clients, patron supremacy may be seen as a form of big brother's unwarranted intrusion or entanglement and a deprivation of sovereignty.

Equilibrium among partners in the situation of non-confrontational asymmetry is a state of mind of the national elites rather than a condition achieved through negotiations and pressures (Szklarski 2015, 15). Mutual relations create a complex system of norms, principles, institutions, and emotions, which create mutual trust. Junior partners like to believe that such conditions create interdependence, which means that patrons will not exit the relationship and be bound to continue them, in spite of any setbacks.

In established asymmetrical relations, political elites must cope with two types of risk, each requiring an exercise of self-restraint in order to prevent the de-legitimization of the relationship. Patrons must exercise restraint in securing benefits from the junior partner or engaging in their domestic politics to prevent hegemonic domination (alliance dilemma). At the same time, junior partners must position themselves in the relationship in the space between abandonment by the patron (when their demands for sovereignty are taken too far) and entanglement in patron's policies (should they not be in accordance with junior partners' interests) (Dybczynski 2014, 24).

The key to the success of asymmetrical relationship lies in the elites' ability to persuade citizens in both countries to understand reciprocity and equality in non-material, non-tangible terms. Relationship between unequal partners remains sufficiently balanced as long as each side contributes to the relationship based on their best ability to meet mutual expectations (interests). Such a relationship, where both sides are satisfied with what they draw from it, where mutual satisfaction is not measured in material terms and where the reciprocity is not confined to specific time, is called a social exchange transaction (Molm 1997). Patrons provide security and tangible protection to junior partners. Junior partners provide loyalty to patrons and willingness to support its interests when called for.

In practical terms, the US as a patron signs all sorts of agreements of cooperation, sends troops for joint maneuvers, provides intelligence information, constructs military bases, stations troops on permanent or rotational bases, sells necessary military equipment, trains military personnel, makes long-term economic commitments, dispatches public officials to make statements most desired by the clients. These statements are often delivered by Vice-President or Secretary of State, and send clear messages that this particular actor may count on continued US engagement (Falcoff 1984, 27).

Junior partners provide goods and services of no less tangible nature: sending troops to foreign missions where US is active; offering their territory for US intelligence activities; lending diplomatic support; purchasing not-so-new and new military equipment from American suppliers; voting with US in international forums; sharing intelligence information; joining embargoes and other trade initiatives; muting criticism of US policies (such as Prism, Guantanamo, drones, terms of trade, immigration policy); and generally are waiting on the sidelines to step into the center stage with expressions of support for US or critiques of its rivals (Von Hlatky 2013, 43).

There is one very significant product of such transactions—mutual trust. There is one fundamental prerequisite for their success—an extended time frame in which the relationship is balanced—when both parties find it satisfying. Such relations need to be continuous, so that both sides have time to reciprocate for each other's input. The stability of such relations brings predictability and diminished risk of their discontinuation. Translated into the language of international politics, social exchange transactions means that as long as patrons agree to bear greater costs for protecting clients from external threats and as long as clients agree to provide their maximum effort to support the interests of the patrons, then they are allies or partners (Molm 1997, 29). The quality of such alliance depends on the intensity of exchanges and strengths of shared values. What is absolutely necessary for such relations to continue is the commitment of political elites to declare satisfaction from the outcomes of exchanges. Both elites must exercise self-restraint. Patrons must understand the limitations and predicaments of clients to mitigate their demands to avoid exhausting the resources of clients. Clients must mitigate their expectations as to patrons' interest and involvement in their affairs (Sylvan and Majeski 2009, 45). We could risk a supposition that mutual relations under the condition of non-confrontational asymmetry are balanced when the inequality of the partners' military or economic resources is supplanted by emotional and axiological involvements. Since the collapse of communism, the CEE-US relations have been meeting the requirements of that category.

Business approach to politics, as preached by Trump during and since his presidential campaign, sees it as a sequence of independent deals. He views relations with other countries through the prism of the rational calculation of costs and benefits conducted in real time. This meets the criteria of another form of exchange—economic exchange. Such an approach jeopardizes American alliance relations with junior partners. With his rhetoric, tweets, and decisions, Trump signals his preference for economic exchanges, expressed and measured in tangible terms within a shorter time frame that do not bind Washington to continue with them over a longer time frame. Such relations can be terminated as soon as the expected benefits are received. No successive exchange is mandated, each party may exit the relationship and seek other providers of the desired benefits with no penalty. Trump signals his openness to such a philosophy (Hirschmann 1970, 21). For a patron finding another client is much easier than for a junior partner finding another patron. For the latter, even ventilating the exit option is a form of coercion by the patron. This is the essence of unpredictability as a feature increasing the risks in dealing with the US. Unfortunately, it does so both for foes and friends alike. That was unthinkable in the administrations of Trump's predecessors, who understood American patronage of junior allies and a clear commitment to values and alliances as a cornerstone of American leadership in the international arena, despite tensions from time to time that demand restraint (Pressman 2008).

Managing Risk and Uncertainty: Survival Strategies from the Client's Perspective

The strength of the CEE-US links needs to be assessed in a broader context. There are three clear major determinants of the dynamics involved, all of which have an impact on the expectations of the Trump administration:

- the perception of the Russian threat;

- the intensity of conflict (political, ethnic, symbolic) among the countries in the region; and
- the internal EU debates about its future, especially the emerging issues of the Two Speed Europe and Eurozone core, which threaten to sideline other members—particularly members in the CEE region—to the periphery.[3]

The greater the Russian pressure and the greater the cross-border disagreements, the more Washington is sought as a protector, guarantor, or mediator. Whether it is willing to assume any of these roles is another story. The more that politics in the region is permeated by fear and insecurity, the greater the pressure for bipolarity in CEE-US relations. The reverse is also apparent. The less external fears or internal tensions, the more multilateralism and cooperation across central Eastern Europe. Four tendencies have been shaping the CEE-US relations in recent years:

First, the weakening of bipolarity in CEE-US relations was precipitated by the disappearance of a clear Soviet enemy threatening European security, at least until the Russian 2014 military intrusion into Ukraine, something which cemented the NATO alliance. CEE countries have often been on the forefront of Anti-Russian sentiments and warned Western allies of false acquiescence and less vigilance. The 2009 letter from CEE leaders to Washington about Obama's reset announcement was a very visible proof of such sentiments.

Second, the evolving EU is growing to be more than just an economic project, which calls for intensified search for European identity. CEE countries, having freshly tossed off the Soviet control, seem to be infatuated with sovereignty in all aspects of the term and thus less enthusiastic and cognizant of the common European citizenship concept. Though they do not mind at all transfers of structural funds, which are seen as a form of payment for the years of communist enslavement and the forced rejection of the Marshall Fund investment transfers.

Third, the expansion of EU, since 2004, has raised the ambitions of some West European capitals, which saw the opportunity at the end of the

---

[3] See: https://www.theguardian.com/world/2017/feb/14/plans-for-two-speed-eu-risk-split-with-peripheral-members.

Cold War, so as to reduce the American presence and influence in Europe, thereby creating a more Euro-centric structure. In the low-conflict pre-2014 setting, the EU mostly talked about building its own defense capacity to become less dependent on the American protective umbrella. Criticism of Bush Jr.'s foreign policy, especially Iraq, intensified such declarations. Later when Obama's conciliatory and multilateral cooperation rhetoric sprang from Washington, European joint defense policy plans were put on back burner (Legrand 2017). Current uncertainties about Trump's European security commitments have reinvigorated such discussions in the old Western Europe. In CEE, they have, instead, precipitated a turn to more trans-Atlantic bilateralism, which is reinforced by the fact that CEE leaders are not major actors in the joint European defense debates. Their preference for special strategic relations with Washington and an anticipated very high cost of joint European defense plans are both factors that make CEE countries reluctant to endorse such initiatives.

Fourth, the undercurrents of anti-Americanism that have been growing in Western Europe, especially since the 2003 Iraq invasion, are sentiments not exactly shared in the CEE region. Any power that becomes as dominant and predominant as the US invariably breeds resentment and opposition, even among traditional allies. A fusion of resentments has been visible against American military predominance, economic omnipresence, and mass cultural influence, albeit more in Western than Eastern Europe (Keohane 2006, 6). Many Europeans now also equate globalization with Americanization and this has accentuated fears of economic dominance and cultural imperialism. Violent clashes in Hamburg during the G20 summit had clear anti-American tones. In sharp contrast, a day earlier, Polish crowds warmly welcomed Trump. A clear sign that CEE countries, the late entrants to capitalist development, do not share the Western anti-American and anti-globalization emotions.

In short, among the most controversial trans-Atlantic issues that impact on CEE-US relations are the lingering questions of American-European defense cost burden sharing, Europe's emerging defense pillar, NATO's new missions, and the US-led anti-terrorist and anti-rogue-state campaign. The CEE governments became seriously concerned that the US war against international terrorists (ISIS) and the North Korean nuclear belligerence would sideline both Europe and NATO as America's strategic priorities. This is having a negative impact on the security concerns of the CEE countries. For CEE countries, it is not ISIS but Moscow threat that looms on their horizon.

In general, the US needs the EU as a diplomatic and economic player, as a generator of stability within an expanding Europe, and as a supplementary security contributor outside the European zone. The US needs political calm and stability among its European allies to avoid fueling the leave-Europe isolationist sentiments at home, particularly strong in the American interior. CEE countries, as models of transformation to democracy and liberal capitalism, are useful examples of the viability of American commitments in Europe. They are living proof of the viability of American vision of liberal democracy. Recent developments in the region, particularly in Hungary and Poland, have raised doubts their propositions.

What must be taken into account when studying the perceptions and policies of CEE elites is the post-authoritarian paradox. They are torn between the desire to manifest autonomy and sovereignty, so natural for countries that have thrown off external dependency, and the need for shelter in a greater alliance built on shared liberal-democratic values and institutions, which were so desired during the years of communist rule. Sitting astride EU integration (bringing tangible economic benefits but low security guarantees) and US bilateralism (strong security guarantees from the US but lower, though still considerable, economic transfers), CEE countries must juggle the pressures from EU for greater integration and demands from quite numerous domestic Euro-skeptics promoting sovereignty. Finding a balance between these, sometimes contradictory, pressures is a feature of politics in these new democracies.

Although the CEE countries are not economically or militarily powerful, many have made it a national priority to contribute to NATO and US missions, in order to demonstrate that they have graduated from consumers to producers of security. In addition to the participation in NATO missions in Bosnia-Hercegovina (1995–2004) and Kosovo (1999-present), and the Italian-led Operation Alba in Albania after the 1997 crisis, several CEE states made contributions to the US-led coalition missions in Iraq and Afghanistan. By the fall of 2003, the CEE states made up approximately half of the non-American peacekeeping troops in Iraq. However, despite their contributions to recent US-led missions, CEE countries remain hamstrung by limited and costly military capabilities (Bugajski 2006). The annual defense budget of the new CEE members of NATO totals less than $10 billion and their restricted manpower only permits small military contributions. In spite of such economic limitations, two among the four exemplary NATO members who spend 2% of GDP on security expenditures, are CEE countries, namely Estonia and Poland.

From the White House perspective, many of the CEE capitals delivered when it was most needed in Afghanistan and Iraq. The newly announced Trump strategy of American involvement in Afghanistan has received favorable reactions from the region. It has never been simply a question of troop numbers, which remained restricted, but of political commitment based on shared principles and common goals.

The new CEE members of the EU, particularly those bordering Russia, are concerned with the apparent lack of common or effective foreign EU policy toward Ukraine, Belarus, Moldova, or Russia. They fear that such disunity can be manipulated by Moscow to its advantage (Bugajski 2009, 12). Germany, France, and Italy, in particular, are seen as being willing to maintain strong bilateral ties with Russia and not jeopardize these relations for what are perceived as "old fears" by the former Russian bloc countries. Both gas pipelines—the Nord Stream and the South Stream—bypass Ukraine and Poland, thereby providing a direct gas connection between Russia and Western Europe, are a perfect example of CEE worries.[4] American declarations of support for European unity in energy policy—an anti-pipeline stand—were welcomed in CEE. The willingness to sell liquid natural gas (LNG) to Poland and Croatia (since 2018) is a visible sign of pro-CEE sentiments in Washington. Trump reiterated that position at the Warsaw Three Sea Initiative Summit.

Such a position would usually be interpreted as a reinforcement of US commitment to the wellbeing of the region in a global setting. With

---

[4] See: http://www.huffingtonpost.com/julian-popov/who-is-the-loser-from-the_b_6328768.html.

Trump in the White House, however, there is another worry—the separation of economic, political, and symbolic spheres as if they are unrelated. What the CEE countries wish to accomplish is to prevent Trump from deal making in, or even within, each sphere separately. It is one thing to see LNG sale as a form of commitment to CEE security by lessening dependence of Russian supplies. Yet, another interpretation is also feasible: the LNG contract is a way of advancing US economic interests—simply good business—that challenges the Russian competitor.[5] CEE countries interpret it as an element of a bigger commitment to regional security, while Trump may see it primarily as a business transaction.[6] Similarly, the promise of a sale of modern anti-missile technology—Patriot Launchers—to Romania and Poland may be a sign of commitment to strengthening the defensive posture of CEE countries and a security enhancing measure. Yet, it is equally possible to see it as a good business for American corporations and a delegation of responsibility for the security to CEE partners. There is simply no way of knowing whether such security enhancing measures (LNG and Patriots) will be followed by other similar actions, or whether they will be treated as isolated transactions disjointed from any broader considerations and from policies based on shared values.

CEE countries, at first, watched with satisfaction as the US promised to provide the most modern THAAD equipment to South Korea, a desired security enhancing measure in response to Kim Jong-un's aggressiveness, but were stunned by Trump's follow-up tweet questioning why South Koreans are not paying for the equipment on their own because it was their problem.[7] Even more anxiety among US allies and partners, and not just from CEE countries, resulted from the Trump administration's decision to suspend around $300 million of military aid to Egypt, a key ally in the Middle East, as a punishment for violations of civil rights by the Sisi government, a move that could be taken straight from the catalog of Obama liberalisms. What is particularly significant

---

[5] See: https://www.euractiv.com/section/europe-s-east/news/trump-to-promote-us-lng-exports-at-warsaw-summit/.

[6] See: https://www.bloomberg.com/news/articles/2017-04-27/u-s-lng-expands-to-eastern-europe-as-poland-avoids-russian-gas.

[7] See: https://www.nytimes.com/2017/04/28/world/asia/trump-south-korea-thaad-missile-defense-north-korea.html?mcubz=0.

in this case is the fact that the *de facto* hostile decision was announced by the State Department in August while Jared Kushner, the president's son-in-law and advisor, was in Cairo as the Trump's emissary praising Egyptian president for his strong leadership.[8] It is a classic case of dual policies executed simultaneously and organizational chaos in the Trump administration, which raise confusion and increase uncertainty as to actual intentions. Such uncertainty is exactly what junior partners in asymmetrical relations with the US wish to avoid. The Egyptian or South Korean cases send one more disturbing signal: they clearly raise doubts about whether the Trump administration will respect long-term commitments and value-based arrangements if even two of the principal American allies are treated instrumentally, in accordance with the deal-making, bilateralism, and rational-business criteria, as parts of the "America First" view of the world.

CEE elites are, to say the least, confused by such mixed messages. When one adds Trump's reluctance to confirm unambiguously Article 5—on collective defense—of the NATO treaty, and his repeated insistence on 2% burden sharing (Zyla 2016) as a prerequisite for good alliance, the message for CEE countries is clear: one can no longer take American commitment to the region for granted. So far his words or tweets, which reveal his, disquieting for many, view of the world are followed by explanations and interpretations from his national security team in order to try to reassure partners that prior American commitments are not endangered, no matter how Trump's message is constructed. We have not yet seen any serious policy change with regard to the region, but the seeds of trepidation have been sown by the Trump White House's inconsistencies.

THE CEE APPROACH TO THE HANDLING THE RISKS OF UNCERTAINTY

In order to deal with the risks stemming from uncertainty, CEE countries have started seeking special relations with Washington. There have, however, not been any particular tangible accomplishments that would

---

[8] See: http://www.independent.co.uk/news/world/middle-east/egypt-snubs-jared-kushner-meet-after-us-cuts-300m-in-aid-over-human-rights-concerns-a7910091.html.

bear a Trump stamp. There is little action coming from Washington. The White House is preoccupied with bigger issues. Under ordinary circumstances, such lack of interests would not disturb CEE partners, as they were certain of continued American commitments and interests. However, never in the past did a change at the helm in the White House precipitate a major policy shift. These usually came as a reaction to the developments in the region itself.

Unsettled by Trump's rhetoric and political philosophy, CEE countries have been trying to position themselves in search of some measure of predictability. CEE countries send offerings to Washington mostly in the form of signals and declarations of availability and willingness. When such signals do not evoke desired reactions from the Trump administration, then, for the domestic and regional audiences, the CEE elites resort to a well-known tactics of highlighting small actions, such as brief encounters and casual contacts with the administration officials as signs of American commitment to continue friendly relations. The NATO Summit 2012, the UN Nuclear Security Summit in New York 2016 and the Three Seas Initiative Summit in 2017 served that purpose very well. Trump seemed to play along by delivering verbal remarks, making himself available for photo ops, or having brief encounters with CEE diplomats.

Trump's visit to Warsaw for the Three Seas Initiative Summit, his meeting with Romanian president in the White House, and his meeting with the Czech President all seem to confirm that the Trump administration respects continuity in foreign policy and wants to ensure that it has dependable and predictable partners, and sufficient areas of commonality with CEE. Good relations with CEE countries may be seen as a potential leverage for Washington in dealings with old EU countries that are growing impatient with American unpredictability.[9] In which case, the US could use its favorability among CEE countries to try and actively disaggregate the EU through a modern-day version of divide and rule.[10] This would involve dealing selectively with European partners; favoring some

---

[9] See: https://www.nytimes.com/2017/06/29/world/europe/angela-merkel-trump-group-of-20.html.

[10] See: https://www.newyorker.com/news/news-desk/trump-is-taking-advantage-of-europes-divides-not-causing-them.

states over others; promoting political disputes between the European allies; rewarding the most loyal capitals; and undercutting any emerging common EU foreign and security policy. Such an approach assumes that Washington wishes to intensify its unilateralist approach. Trump's political philosophy of bilateralism, deal making, and a balanced commitment to alliance will be utilized by some of CEE countries to seek special relations with Washington. Weak EU team spirit and European consciousness among CEE countries make such developments likely.

Which way Trump will go is uncertain. On the one hand, Washington could more resolutely support CEE's drive toward EU and help implement lasting solutions to the frozen conflicts in Moldova, Georgia, and Ukraine. NATO and US military bases in CEE could be tied to the development of major infrastructure projects that can benefit wider sectors of the population. The anti-terrorist pact could involve a host of US assistance programs, such as civil emergency training, technical modernization for border guards, and the development of intelligence capabilities. US defense companies that have shown a renewed interest in the CEE's military sector, as its modernization process intensifies, should be encouraged to invest there. For instance, the LNG sale could become a regional security enhancement by providing Europe with energy diversity if US decides to make long-term commitment or it could be a reward for good behavior to give a divide and rule mentality if no long-term contracts are signed. Such instrumentalization of continued support would be a break from prior axiological commitments.

It is particularly important to avoid unrealistic expectations from any special relations achieved with the US. Public expectations of material and military benefits should not be raised too high, as they were before the 2003 Iraqi war or in the midst of negotiations over the emplacement of American military units before the Newport NATO summit. Such heightened and often unrealistic expectations about the benefits of bilateral relations with Washington are a fact of life in CEE (Szklarski 2015, 7). Every American president has to confront them, and practically can do little to scale them down to realistic levels. Such unrealistic expectations are often a product of domestic conflicts in which the ruling elite uses the special relations with the US as a proof of their effectiveness in promoting their national interests.

CEE in the International Arena

By no means is there a uniform group of countries in the CEE region, even when it comes to the issues of security. The Russian invasion of Ukraine may have created a cohesive bond of fear among former Soviet satellites and republics. In response to the changing security situation in Europe, NATO troops have become more active in joint maneuvers in member states that border Russia, and more consideration is given to upgrading eastern militaries. At the Newport NATO summit in 2015, NATO decided to initiate a European Reassurance Initiative (RNI) and place a brigade of troops (4,200 soldiers) on its eastern flank on "permanent rotation" and move sizeable military equipment into Poland that could be manned in case of urgent need by troops from the US or Western Europe (Deni 2016, 37–38). In spite of these symbolic and tangible developments one is left wondering about the ability of the alliance's forces to deter a determined Russia if it opted to take control of one or more of the Baltic states.

The sphere of military cooperation seems to be the one where continuity from previous administration is most prevalent. Although undermined by inconsistent rhetoric revealing wavering alliance commitments, the sphere of security remains relatively least vulnerable to America First isolationism. Several issues in the sphere of military East-West cooperation provide both credible (deterrence) and effective (real military) US capabilities in a variety of situations. The common security architecture that has remained in place includes not only enhanced allied participation but also emphasis on ensuring control of the battlefield across all domains of possible conflict (land, air, sea, cyber, and space).

What usually followed the formulation of recommendations for American allies were offers of military equipment transfer (some of it dated), or credit assistance (on very favorable terms) for the procurement of new weapons systems. In some way, this is what Trump offered in this Warsaw speech when he encouraged the countries of the region to invest in common security and defense (Bartosiak 2015). Reality, however, is much more complicated.

The Visegrad Group, in pursuit of a cohesive CEE foreign policy, is now moribund, given the reluctance of three members—Hungary, Slovakia, and the Czech Republic—to apply more rigorous sanctions against Russia for its attack on Ukraine. Russian business investment and energy dependence corrodes institutions and corrupts politicians. Hungary, for instance, despite its historical confrontations with the Soviet Union, is inviting Russian investment in nuclear energy development. Vladimir Putin spent five days in Budapest during the judo world championships working hard on his Hungarian partners, who seem to follow Moscow's footsteps when dealing with undesired civil society and independent media. Serbia and Bosnia-Hercegovina, for religious reasons, are inclined to seek Russian support and welcome economic investment.

The progress of several Balkan states into NATO and the EU has been sabotaged by Moscow to prevent further Western institutional enlargement. The Kremlin has focused on Serbia and Bosnia-Herzegovina, in particular, by playing on ethno-nationalist and revisionist sentiments, but it also uses the sizeable Russian diaspora in Latvia and Estonia as potential sources of disruption, similar to hybrid war situation in Ukrainian Donbas region.

Understandably, the three Baltic states are guarding their territory and sovereignty from persistent irredentist pressures from Moscow. Poland is also building up its defenses against regular threats from Russia and the consequences of the Ukrainian war. Romania is preparing for a potential spillover of conflict from Moldova if that country is further destabilized by Moscow's subversion. In the western Balkans, Albania, and Kosovo, there will always remain bastions of pro-Americanism and resistance to Russia's inroads. Small Montenegro, a recent new member of NATO, is an object of heavy Russian economic pressure.

As usually, the Kremlin has many levers of political and financial influence and can capitalize on ethnic disputes in the region. The US has never been able to undermine Russian penetration in the region due to deep partisan bickering and conflicts driven by historical, cultural, and ethnic factors, especially in the Balkans.[11] American support for Kosovo against Serbia in 1999 was a significant yet short-lived attempt to play a more active role in the Balkans. Moscow's backing for nationalism, ul-

---

[11] See: https://www.theguardian.com/world/2017/feb/27/balkans-foreign-policy-headache-trump-kosovo-serbia-bosnia-montenegro.

tra-conservatism, and Euro-skepticism throughout the continent—not only CEE—is a profitable way of undermining the EU from within. The Trump administration, with its hesitant stands on alliance cohesion, confirms American weakness in dealing with culturally, religiously, and ethnically diverse region of South Eastern Europe in particular.

At the same time, the region has limited resources to conduct systematic lobbying in Congress and the White House. Particular ethnic lobbies may become active, or even act together, as it was the case with the first wave of NATO expansion in 1999. On regular basis on matters of lesser urgency, however, coming up with coherent demands is not easy. The Central and East European Coalition (CEEC), representing more than 20 million Americans whose heritage lies in that region, tries to share, despite its internal diversity, its concerns, and ideas with the US Congress and administration. Frankly speaking, as a lobby group it is not known for its particular influence. It takes positions that, in the first place, represent the fear of Russian expansionism in the region, resisting any thinking in terms of Yaltan "spheres of influence" and promoting democratic nation building in the region. It favors appropriations for defensive military support and eventually welcoming Ukraine into Euro-Atlantic structures. It gives highest priority to the preservation, or in some cases, restoration and advancement of regional democracies through effective deterrence of Russian interference on all levels, support maintenance of current sanctions to achieve withdrawal of Russian forces from Ukraine. Its members support the Magnitsky Act and any actions that undermine Russia's ability to expand its influence into CEE countries.[12] Most of their activities are symbolic in nature, and are targeted at US Congress. Their access to the White House is insignificant. Trump may treat the CEE Lobby as a useful tool of pressure on Congress when such a need comes.

Trump and Key CEE Countries

It is time to leave the broader regional perspective and look at the CEE-US relations from more specific national perspectives. To facilitate this

---

[12] See: http://www.huffingtonpost.com/michael-haltzel/trumps-east-european-achi_b_11951906.html.

analysis, the following options are available to junior partners in a situation of non-confrontational asymmetry. These represent potential behaviors or tactics that junior CEE partners can use when dealing with the uncertainties produced by the Trump administration:

1. Wait for clear position from the US.
2. Use access points in the US to get information about the American moves.
3. Position themselves to signal willingness to follow.
4. Seek preferential positioning in a US special relationship.
5. Become useful in spheres signaled by Trump administration as priorities.
6. Support controversial measures adopted by the Trump administration.
7. Downplay policy differences with the Trump administration.
8. Comply with US wishes.
9. Build multilevel relations with the US (cultural, economic, political, military) to compensate for lack of any big success.
10. Develop spheres of autonomy.
11. Build a shared axiological space.
12. Re-define interests so as to avoid conflict with US interests.
13. Prioritize the promotion of their national interests in the US.
14. Provide rhetorical support for US initiatives.
15. Support other US allies.
16. Avoid the adoption of conflictual positions to those of the US, but only when it does not affect the principal interests of their other allies.
17. Search for *any* possible confirmation of American commitment.
18. Search for confirmation in the *words* of the US president or any of his advisers.
19. Read and over-interpret signals from Washington in a way that gives rise to hope, even if it is delusional.

20. Attempt to maintain relations at *any* level, by, for example, inviting engagement by representatives from the Trump administration or Congress.
21. Attempt to build bilateral relations if the bigger multilateral alliance is questionable.
22. Attempt to join in a larger cooperative scheme if bilateral relations are doubtful.
23. Redefine roles in the leader–follower relationship by, for example, undertaking a role that is useful to the leader.
24. Adapt to the new levels of risk in the new relationship.
25. Search for replacement relationships to compensate for new risk (EU in the first instances, but Russia is a possibility).
26. Deny that any relationship problem exists.

There has not been much activity in the CEE-US relations in the first months of the Trump administration. Its attention was devoted to more important issues such as Muslim refugees, the probe to Russian interference in the presidential election, defeating ISIS, and the Syrian and Afghan war, and, of course, the North Korean nuclear threat. None of these issues position CEE countries to play a key part in US foreign policies. Many CEE leaders and representatives who took part in the annual UN General Session boasted, as a sign of US recognition, of meetings with Trump or with high-ranking members of his administration, a typical compensatory behavior. Similar press announcements could be seen after the Three Seas Initiative summit in Warsaw attended by Trump.

Following is a summary of the events and declarations with respect to the contacts made, and/or relationships established, between key CEE countries and Trump since his inauguration on January 20, 2017.

Hungary

Its Prime Minister Viktor Orban welcomed Trump's inauguration as the end of multilateralism, and praised Trump's inaugural statement as a big change that would usher in an era of bilateralism. The Trump administration seems to be warming to Orban's cheerleading. In a sign of closer ties, Hungarian Foreign Minister Peter Szijjarto spoke by 'phone with Secretary of State Rex Tillerson in March". Meanwhile, former Hungarian government official and one of Orban's advisor, Sebastian Gorka became one of Trump's senior White House advisors on counterterrorism. Gorka's links to Hungarian extremist and anti-Semitic groups, however, have come under increasing scrutiny. He resigned in late August.

Orbán has a lot in common with Trump. He has long pursued policies that he claims put his country first. His speeches are laced with anti-immigrant rhetoric. And he has backed up his hardline nationalist rhetoric with actions—for example, by erecting fences along the country's southern borders with Serbia and Croatia. That must have pleased Trump. What may have been unwelcome was Budapest's signing a deal with Russia's Gazprom—to link the country with the Turkish Stream pipeline by the end of 2019—one day ahead of Trump's trip to Poland, where he promoted US LNG exports. By joining the Turkish Stream enabled Hungary to import 8 billion cubic meters of gas a year, which is close to its total consumption. This move probably undermined American support for an LNG terminal in Croatia in 2019.

The largest anti-government demonstration in Hungary for years occurred when tens of thousands of people protested in Budapest in April against the closing of the Central European University (CEU), known for its academic independence. Orban was counting on Trump's support, but he miscalculated. First the State Department and then Trump, in a forceful letter to the Hungarian government, urged Hungary not to shut down George Soros's CEU, describing it as a premier academic institution. That was unexpected in Budapest (Müller 2017).

Even the Orban's close ties with *Breitbart* (the alt-right on-line news service that supports Trump's presidency) and Steve Bannon (Trump's initial Chief Strategist, who resigned in August), and his ideological proximity to Trump, with similar policy positions on immigration and refugees, did not protect Hungary, as a junior partner in a US relationship, from being scorned by Trump and his administration. Poland, it should be noted, suffered a similar fate when its nationalist-conservative Law and Justice Party government undermined the separation of powers and challenged the autonomy of the Constitutional Tribunal.

Croatia

No significant bilateral issues are looming on the horizon for Croat-American diplomatic relations. The White House cautiously views Zagreb's ability to play a role in stabilizing the Balkans and to act as a counterbalance to Russian presence in the region. Trump, in a meeting with Croatian President Kolinda Grabar-Kitarovic in Warsaw, urged him to do everything possible to advance regional reconciliation in the western Balkans. He also expressed his support for timely completion of the Krk Island liquefied natural gas facility, which is scheduled to be ready to accept its first tankers in 2019. This is seen by the White House as a good effort to diversify its energy sector.

Slovenia

Slovenia's most significant asset in America is ... the First Lady, Melania Trump. She was born as Melanija Knavs in Sevnica, a small Alpine town located 30 miles east of Ljubljana, with a population 5,000. Their son, Barron, is being taught both English and Slovenian, mostly thanks to his grandparents spending six months a year in the US. Melania left Slovenia in the 1990s to pursue fashion modeling in the US. She has not been back in more than a decade.[13] Trump has accepted an invitation extended by Slovenian President Borut Pahor to visit Slovenia, but when the visit is to take place is unknown. Such a visit would make Trump only the second American president ever to do so.[14]

Romania

Romania views itself as the US's closest ally in CEE, along with Poland. Both countries host American troops, buy American military equipment (F16 fighter jets, Patriot missiles, and host parts of anti-ballistic missile shield). Romania plans to buy Patriot missiles to help protect its airspace. The defense budget of Romania—a NATO member since 2004 and one of Washington's staunchest allies in Eastern Europe along with Poland—was 1.7% of gross domestic product in 2016 and was set

---

[13] See: https://www.nytimes.com/2016/07/19/us/politics/melania-trump-slovenia.htmlJason.

[14] See: https://www.reuters.com/article/us-usa-trump-poland-slovenia/trump-to-visit-slovenia-country.-of-wife-melanias-birth-idUSKBN19R1Q5.

at 2.0% in 2017—a move that will please Trump. Romania, a country of 20 million people, hosts a US ballistic missile defense station and has contributed troops in Iraq and Afghanistan.

During his brief visit to the US, Romanian President Klaus Iohannis confirmed the strategic partnership that existed between Romania and the US. As a significant part of Romanian defense spending is going into strategic acquisitions, he expressed hope that he and "President Trump, will find good ways together to make good use of this money" (Tamkin 2017). Such words and the symbolic honor of being the first CEE leader to be received in the Trump White House demonstrate the degree to which Romania and the US share common views of the world. They also illustrate a classic junior partner contribution to a non-confrontational asymmetrical relationship.

Czech Republic

Its President Miloš Zeman was the first European head of state to endorse Trump as a presidential candidate and has aligned himself with Trump's approaches to immigration as well as terrorism. Zeman has fanned anti-immigrant sentiments at home, claiming there is no such thing as a moderate Muslim and has opposed Western sanctions against Russia. Trump, in kind, invited the Czech president to the White House in April. He has told Zeman, "You're my type of guy."[15] Soul communion between Trump and Zeman is confirmed in several other ways, many of which would, no doubt, please Putin.[16]

Zeman has denied the presence of Russian forces in Ukraine, stating "I take seriously the statement of [Russian] foreign minister Sergei Lavrov that there are no Russian troops [there] and calling the Russian invasion of Ukraine, conveniently for the Kremlin, a 'civil war.'"[17] He even proposed the "Finlandization" of Ukraine, meaning that Ukrainian defense

---

[15] Retrieved from: https://www.politico.com/story/2017/02/trump-foreign-leaders-phone-calls-234770.

[16] See: http://www.politico.com/story/2017/02/trump-foreign-leaders-phone-calls-234770 (13.08.2017)

[17] Retrieved from: http://www.radio.cz/en/section/curraffrs/president-zeman-proposes-finlandization-of-ukraine. See also: http://www.politico.com/story/2017/02/trump-foreign-leaders-phone-calls-234770.

and foreign policy would be subject to control by Moscow.[18] In 2015, Zeman broke ranks with Western leaders to visit Moscow on Victory Day, despite other leaders boycotting and refusing to support a Russian public show of force in the wake of aggression against Ukraine. This was a huge public relations win for the Kremlin. Zeman's visit to the Trump White House is another big win for the Kremlin. Russian propaganda will surely spin their favorite story of Russia-friendly President Trump meeting with another Russia-friendly EU leader. Zeman has opposed EU assistance to Ukraine, even advocating for the EU recognition that Crimea is part of Russia and doubling down on that position in 2016, claiming that the world's politicians have acknowledged that Crimea cannot be given back to Ukraine. Zeman also actively opposes sanctions against the Russian Federation, calling them ineffective and stupid, and advocates for them to be lifted immediately.

Much like his Visegrád Four counterparts, Zeman has opposed mandatory relocation by the EU of refugees and has voted whenever possible against this scheme, which is still yet to be implemented in most EU countries.

Zeman, just a few days after Trump's inauguration, let it be known that Trump's ex-wife—Ivana Trump—would make an ideal ambassador to the Czech Republic.[19] Ivana Trump—born Ivana Zelnickova—comes from Zlin in south Moravia. She married Donald Trump in 1977 and divorced in 1992. Zeman told the Czech-born socialite in a 'phone call that the US "could not send a better US ambassador to Prague."[20] When she shunned this idea, Zeman floated, he "was furious," allegedly telling her that she was avoiding her responsibility "like a coward."[21] He is said to have told Ivana Trump that she should feel responsible for her homeland and abide by her statement that she would like to be the ambassador. Clearly, Zeman is a likely verbal match for Trump.

---

[18] See: http://www.radio.cz/en/section/curraffrs/president-zeman-proposes-finlandization-of-ukraine.

[19] See: http://praguemonitor2017/06/23/ivana-trump-annoys-czech-president-not-being-us-ambassador.

[20] Retrieved from: http://praguemonitor.com/2017/06/23/ivana-trump-annoys-czech-president-not-being-us-ambassador.

[21] Retrieved from: http://praguemonitor.com/2017/06/23/ivana-trump-annoys-czech-president-not-being-us-ambassador.

Serbia

Serbs were generally delighted with Trump's election victory, if only because he defeated the wife of Bill Clinton, their 1990s nemesis who led the NATO bombing campaigns against Serb forces in Bosnia and Kosovo. Serbian's historically pro-Russian sentiments also predispose them favorably to Trump. Indeed, Belgrade expected him to lower the level of tensions in US-Russian relations. The EU, hamstrung by its own existential woes, has cooled on expansion into the western Balkans. The Trump administration's approach to this region is, however, still not entirely clear. Russia, meanwhile, attempts to project power across the region, which it sees as within its sphere of influence. Serbia is eagerly looking for support over the issue of Kosovo, which for them remains an unsettled problem. In northern Kosovo, streets are lined with Serbian flags, the Serbian dinar is the currency, Serbian government companies provide many utilities, and the language spoken on the streets is generally Serbian. Trump's anti-Islamic initiatives are viewed favorably in Belgrade, because a majority of Albanians and Kosovars are Muslims.

Serbian EU aspirations, however, make them reluctant to offer too blunt an endorsement of Trump's anti-Islamic policies. When Trump congratulated Kosovo on the anniversary of the proclamation of its independence (see Morina 2017), he seemingly disappointed those in Serbia who allegedly expected that America, under his rule, would change its policy in the Balkans—in favor of the presumed Serbian interests.[22] When Trump met Kosovo's Parliamentary Speaker Kadri Veselji in February, he got a cold shower. Their disappointment grew even bigger when Nikki Haley, Trump's American ambassador in the UN, made a statement that "Kosovo deserves to take its rightful place in the international community, including full membership in the UN."[23] For Serbs, hoping to retain their control in Kosovo, it came as a warning sign that predicting the Trump administration's policies based on Trump's campaign rhetoric and reading his ideas is problematic, even misleading.

---

[22] See: https://www.theguardian.com/world/2017/feb/27/balkans-foreign-policy-headache-trump-kosovo-serbia-bosnia-montenegro.

[23] Retrieved from: http://www.balkaninsight.com/en/article/trump-administration-maintains-us-support-for-kosovo-02-28-2017-1.

Conclusion

Central Eastern Europe is a region in waiting. Some countries are more hopeful, especially those that are less pro-EU (such as Poland, Hungary, and Slovakia). Some are more anxious and confused, torn between EU skepticism and fear of isolation (such as Czech Republic). Still others are quite happy to see security concerns and Russian sanctions continue (such as Romania and Croatia). In Washington, there seems to be little indication as to the direction of US policies with respect to CEE. What is heard and seen is rather a clear signal that the CEE should not expect to figure prominently in American strategic thinking. It is viewed as a bargaining chip—the pessimistic scenario—or a potential thorn in the bigger picture of US-Russia relations. The other scenario, one that is equally instrumental, sees CEE as a factor in US-EU relations, should US decide to employ a divide-and-rule strategy. At the same time, Trump is eager to develop good bilateral relations with the countries of the region, especially economic relations (such as US LNG exports, American investment, and military transfers). Continuingly, it will seek diplomatic support from CEE countries in international forums and endorsements and material contributions to military missions across the world. CEE countries usually were quite eager to offer their assistance in this last regard hoping to score points in Washington and position themselves in some imaginary favorable situation with their powerful patron ally (Poland) or partner (Romania). The first months of the Trump administration have alleviated anxieties about the American multilateral and bilateral security commitments, but have also raised doubts regarding the political philosophy and strategies of the new Trump administration. Taking a position with respect to Trump's Washington has never been more difficult.

References

Bartosiak, J. 2015. "As Air-Sea Battle Becomes JAM-GC … Don't Forget Central and Eastern Europe." *The National Interest*, November 24. Available at: http://nationalinterest.org/blog/the-buzz/air-sea-battle-becomes-jam-gcdont-forget-central-eastern-14429.

Bugajski, J. 2006. "American Interests in Central-Eastern Europe."

The Analyst. Available at: https://www.euractiv.com/section/enlargement/opinion/american-interests-in-central-eastern-europe/.

Bugajski, J. 2009. *Dismantling the West: Russia's Atlantic Agenda.* Washington, DC: Potomac Books.

Deni, J.R. 2016. "Modifying America's Forward Presence in Eastern Europe." *Parameters* 46 (1): 35–42.

Dybczynski, A. 2014. *Sojusze miedzynarodowe.* Warszawa, PL: Scholar.

Falcoff, M. 1984. *Small Countries Large Issues: Studies in U.S.-Latin American Asymmetries.* Washington, DC: AEI Press.

Hirschmann, A.O. 1970. *Exit, Voice, and Loyalty.* Cambridge, MA: Harvard University Press.

Keohane, R. 2006. *Anti-Americanism in World Politics.* Ithaca, NY: Cornell University Press.

Legrand, J. 2017. "Common Security and Defence Policy." *Fact Sheets on the European Union* (06/2017), European Parliament Think Tank. Available at: http://www.europarl.europa.eu/ftu/pdf/en/FTU_6.1.2.pdf.

Molm, L. 1997. *Coercive Power in Social Exchange.* Cambridge: Cambridge University Press.

Morina, D. 2017. "Trump Administration Maintains US Support for Kosovo." *Balkan Insight,* March 1. Available at: http://www.balkaninsight.com/en/article/trump-administration-maintains-us-support-for-kosovo-02-28-2017-1.

Müller, J.-W. 2017. "Hungary: The War on Education." *The New York Review of Books,* May 20. Available at: http://www.nybooks.com/daily/2017/05/20/hungary-the-war-on-education-ceu/.

Pressman, J. 2008. *Warring Friends. Alliance Restraint in International Politics.* Ithaca, NY: Cornell University Press.

Sylvan, D. and S. Majeski. 2009. *U.S. Foreign Policy in Perspective: Clients, Enemies and Empire*. New York: Routledge.

Szklarski, B. 2015. *Niekonfrontacyjna asymetria w relacjach Polsko-Amerykańskich*. Warszawa, PL: MSZ.

Tamkin, E. 2017. "The Romanian President is in D.C. to Talk Defense, But ...." *Foreign Policy*, June 7. Available at: http://foreignpolicy.com/2017/06/07/the-romanian-president-is-in-d-c-to-talk-defense-but/.

Von Hlatky, S. 2013. *American Allies in Times of War: The Great Asymmetry*. Oxford: Oxford University Press.

Zyla, B. 2016. "NATO Burden Sharing: A New Research Agenda." *Journal of International Organization Studies* 7 (2): 5–22.

8
THE TRUMP EFFECT ON RUSSIAN FOREIGN POLICY

Maciej Herbut and Karol Chwedczuk-Szulc

INTRODUCTION

The United States (US)-Russia Federation relations under President Donald J. Trump's administration were widely and intensely discussed even before his inauguration on January 20, 2017. The question of Russia's alleged involvement in the 2016 presidential campaign has gained a lot of traction, but addressing this issue is beyond the scope of this chapter.

A sheer quantitative analysis of the official documents of the US Department of Defense (DoD) shows that the relations with Russia and Russia-related issues are one of the most important questions for the new Trump administration during its first 100 days. The words "Russia," "Russian," and "Lavrov" (the last name of the Russian Foreign Minister) account for over 34% of all words used in DoD's press releases and remarks.[1] We treat this as evidence that Russia is an important reference point for the Trump administration's foreign policy.

This chapter focuses on the way in which Trump's presidency has affected the conduct of Russian foreign policy and its implications for the Trump administration. It comprises three parts. The first provides a systematic Foreign Policy Analysis framework. The second scrutinizes Russian foreign policy objectives. The final part seeks to answer answering the following questions:

1. In what ways does the conduct of US foreign policy reflect the declarations introduced by Trump during the presidential campaign?

2. Can we perceive the shift in American foreign policy as beneficial from the Russian perspective (as perceived by the elites,

---

[1] This is the results of a word frequency query of DoD's press releases and remarks since January 20, 2017.

not the society)?

3. What are future challenges and implications for the Trump administration of Russian foreign policy?

Methodology

The methodology used in this chapter is a systematic Foreign Policy Analysis model, confined to a specific time and context. Our model takes into account two states—the Russia Federation and the US—and is built around the issue of how the Trump presidency influences the Russian Foreign Policy (see Figure 1).

Figure 1: The impact of US Foreign Policy on Russian Foreign Policy.

Although Russian foreign policy priorities and behaviors are relatively easily identifiable, this is not the case of the US. Thus, we are only considering the impact of the first 100 days of the Trump's presidency focusing on Foreign Policy and Foreign Policy Behaviors. According to Hudson (2012, 14):

- a Foreign Policy of a state is "the strategy approach chosen by a national government to achieve its goals in its relations to external entities. This includes the decision to do nothing"; and
- Foreign Policy Behaviors are the "observable artifacts of foreign policy—specific actions and words used to influence others in the realm of foreign policy ... [and] may include behavior that are accidental or unintended ...."

In this paper, we will introduce a two-stage framework which will be loosely based on Kaplan's (1975, 5) "coupled systems" concept: "When an input leads to a radical change in the relationship of the variables of the system—it is said to transform the characteristic behavior of the system. Such an input will be called a step-function." If we treat the US and Russia as "coupled systems" in which "the output of one system affects the input of the other system" (Kaplan 1975, 5), it is, then, logical to consider American foreign policy as an input (from the Russian perspective) that alters the parameters of the Russian foreign policy. This relationship between Russian foreign policy objectives and the actions and behaviors of Trump as a presidential candidate as well as Trump as the US president will be illustrated by the concept of *Foreign Policy Clusters*.

Thus, we analyze both Foreign Policy and Foreign Policy Behaviors during the first 100 days of the Trump administration, including Trump's declarations during his presidential campaign, with respect to the Russian Federation, but we focus mostly on its preferable Foreign Policy outcomes. This enables us to evaluate whether Trump's changes in US Foreign Policy are preferable or not from the Russian perspective.

RUSSIAN FOREIGN POLICY OBJECTIVES AND THE TRUMP PRESIDENCY

Russian Foreign Policy Objectives

Being a leader of one of the most powerful country in the world comes with great expectations from the Russian elites and Russian society. In this paper, we treat the legitimacy issue[2]—the necessity of constantly reassuring the popularity of the leader (and the government)—as a central feature of Russian politics determining both Russian Foreign Policy and its Foreign Policy Behaviors. The Trump administration must realize that the survival of the Russian regime comes first, the overall development of the country—whether economic and societal—is of secondary importance for the Russian regime. This affects Russia in many ways, but we focus only on two issues. The first is human rights and freedom of

---

[2] The legitimacy issue may be considered as the priority of regime survival over other considerations. This is a feature of any regime, democratic or otherwise. However, due to the lack of a system of checks and balances, authoritarian regimes are more often affected by the legitimacy issue.

the press, which are severely restricted as official state propaganda aims at keeping the Russian society unaware and docile.[3] The second is the lack of a strong middle-class, a pillar of private entrepreneurship, which contributes to the overall poor performance of the Russian economic sector.[4] However, Russia's access to natural resources, such as natural gas and oil, allows it remain a relatively strong and influential actor on the international arena.[5] This over-reliance on the energy sector, however, comes as both a blessing and a curse. On the one hand, Russia's weak domestic economic performance is compensated by the income generated by the export of natural resources. On the other hand, there is less incentive to modernize the underdeveloped infrastructure and the weak manufacturing sector. This relationship between the development in one sector (natural resources) coupled by the underperformance of other sectors (such as agriculture and banking)—gives rise to the Dutch Disease[6], which was responsible for the economic breakdown of Russian economy in 2008 (Mironov and Petronevich 2015). In short, the reliance on the energy sector, accompanied by the legitimacy issue, may influence Russian foreign policy-making in the following ways:

---

[3] The functioning of the Russian propaganda apparatus according to Darczewska (2014, 27) follows the following rules:
1. focus on messages that are repetitive and constantly present in the media;
2. follow the rule of selecting the information that is convenient for the proper time or place;
3. target the emotions of the receiver;
4. follow the rule of simplicity;
5. refer to myths, historical realities that are well known in the public; and
6. do not use extensive resources.

[4] Poor performance of the regime has also been reflected in the statistical data provided by the Bertelsmann Transformation index report (BTI) of 2016 as well as the International Monetary Fund (IMF) country Report No. 15/211 from August 2015. Retrieved from: https://www.imf.org/external/pubs/ft/scr/2015/cr15211.pdf; https://www.bti-project.org/fileadmin/files/BTI/Downloads/Reports/2016/pdf/BTI_2016_Russia.pdf.

[5] Russia is the world's "fourth largest producer of electricity, second largest exporter of crude oil, fourth largest producer and largest exporter of refined petroleum products, the second largest producer and largest exporter of natural gas" (Kuznetsova and Kuznetsova 2015, 160). As Kazantsev (2009, 201) states, thanks to its energy policy, Russia, as a "petrostate" can preserve its status as a superpower.

[6] The "Dutch Disease" has been well depicted by Elkhan and Zada (2016, 85–115).

- Shifts in the prices of gas and oil decrease the country's income and societal support may force the regime to resort to alternative sources of legitimacy, which may take the form of aggressive or war-like actions.
- Russia may try to preserve its monopolistic position as a gas and oil supplier in its near abroad, any signs of breaking this monopoly may be met with a decisive Russian response;[7]
- Russian energy hegemony has been and most likely will be a political tool in achieving preferable foreign policy objectives.[8]

Another factor influencing Russian foreign policy is, in general, Russia's negative perspective on globalization. Russian leaders see globalization as unfavorable, since it promotes economic openness, democratization, and cooperation in fields such as environment, migration, or human rights, which, in general, limit states' sovereignty and control over their own territory.[9] Russian policy-makers would prefer to see the world as multipolar and comprised of independent states with which Russia can individually do business.[10] This means that Russia will welcome eco-

---

[7] This can be exemplified by the policies to which Goldman (2008, 152–153) refers to as "pipeline poker games"—punishing disloyal states by manipulating the prices of gas supplies. This happened in Ukraine in 2006 and 2009 and Belarus in 2007–2010.

[8] Gazprom negotiates prices with its EU partners, differentiating in accordance to political preferences; Germany receives oil from Russia at lower prices than Poland and the Baltic states (bloomberg.com/news/articles/2017-07-03/german-addiction-to-russia-gas-raises-alarm-in-merkel-s-backyard). As further evidence, both the Nord Stream (I and II) projects bypassed Eastern European States. Because the Baltic States are almost completely dependent on Russian gas supplies, they very vulnerable to Russian gas prices manipulation and economic and political blackmail. See: http://www.clingendaelenergy.com/files.cfm?event=files.download&ui=9C1DEEC1-5254-00CF-FD03186604989704.

[9] Russian approach towards any form of supra-national coordination is, in general, not preferable since the government's authority is undermined by such enterprises. Enhancement of cooperation in within any of four freedoms of movement—goods, people, services, and capital—decreases the political grasp of the authorities over the citizens and resources (Bordachev 2014, 29).

[10] We can consider Russia's foreign policy priorities as driven by neorealist priorities, where relative gains dominate absolute gains. The difference between absolute and relative gains has been a subject of debate between the neoliberal and neorealist schools of thought. While the focus on absolute gains means that a

nomic growth, but not at the expense of other international actors benefitting more than itself. Such a trend is visible in terms of Russian near abroad and globally.

Another factor that Trump should not underestimate is the importance of Former Soviet Union (FSU) region to the Russian regime. As long as countries like Georgia or Ukraine remained under the influence of Moscow, a certain degree of independence was tolerated. However, once these states began economic and military cooperation with EU and the US, they threatened Russian interests. The Russian leadership has not taken this lightly. The war with Georgia in 2008 (for cooperating with NATO), as well as the involvement in Ukraine in 2014 (for cooperating with the EU), can serve as examples of how Putin is determined to keep these states in the sphere of Russian influence.[11] The FSU region, including the Commonwealth of Independent States (CIS), therefore, remains of strategic importance and Russian policy-makers will do all they can to ensure Russia's continued domination of the region.[12] This control can take the form of

state favors cooperation, regardless of the "ratio of benefits." The focus on relative gains means that the authorities of a state perceive the gain of another country as not preferable, even if their own country could benefit from the agreement (Powell 1991, 1303).

[11] The Russian Federation treats international organizations and bilateral treaties as instruments for preserving its domination both regionally and globally. According to Willerton and Slobodchikoff, and Goerts (2012, 61–65), the Russian Federation initiated over 1,300 treaties with its neighbours in order to exert Russian influence. The same goes for multilateral projects initiated by Russia, such as the Collective Security Treaty Organization (CSTO) or Eurasian Customs Union (ECU), which, in general, were supposed to preserve Russian domination in the Region. What is worth mentioning is that as long as Russia remains richer from its neighbor—Russian per-capita income is three times higher than Ukrainian, 5.5 times higher than Moldova and 11 times higher than Uzbekistan and Kyrgystan)—it remains an economic integrating center in the region (Trenin 2011, 146). However, as Russia's neighbors are becoming economically stronger, they have started to slip away, slowly, from Moscow's control (Arakelyan 2013, 1–2).

[12] The term "strategic" requires some explanation. In general, we can divide Russia's neighbors into two categories when it comes to Russian energy policies. The first are counties that are important transit countries (such as Georgia, Ukraine or Belarus). The second are countries that are possible competitors (such as Turkmenistan), which can, due to oil reserves, sell resources at more competitive prices, thereby undermining the Russian position (Trenin 2011, 167).

- financing Russian-friendly institutions promoting Russian culture (Russian "soft-power" or compatriot policy), such as NGO diplomacy, culture, media and language promotion, repatriation programs, and citizenship and passport policies (Laruelle 2015, 10–11);
- making these countries dependent on Russian oil, then, when necessary, punishing them by increasing oil prices or rewarding them by decreasing it (Ukraine, Georgia, Belarus) (Goldman 2008, 152–153);[13] or
- initiating military intervention, which can be direct (invasion) or indirect (supporting separatist movements, as in South-Ossetia, Abkhazia (in Georgia), Transnistria (in Moldova), or Donetsk and Donbas (in Ukraine) (Hikari 2015).

Thus, from Russian perspective the most preferable situation is a multipolar world in which Russia can act freely because there is no global hegemonic power or regional powers to inhibit its leadership. The EU and the US spreading "Western values"—democracy, institutional development, liberalization, and human rights—are generally seen as unfriendly activities. So is American involvement in the Middle East or FSU region (for instance, US cooperation with Georgia). Russia will do all in its power to weaken EU or NATO influence in its near abroad, which it considers to be its privileged sphere of interest. In short, Russian global foreign policy objectives are twofold:

- to secure Russian domination as a "petrostate" and a major exporter of gas and oil; and
- to weaken the economic and political position of both the US and the EU.

After defining the main objectives of Russian Foreign Policy, we come to the question: what are the Russian expectations of Trump's presidency? Contemporary Russian policy objectives seem to be less ambitious than the ones of the former Soviet Union, as they are mostly restricted to its closer and further abroad (the FSU-CIS region, Europe and Asia). However, their achievement requires Russia's global involvement and, just as during the Cold War, the US remains its main protagonist.

[13] See also: https://www.theguardian.com/world/2013/dec/17/ukraine-russia-leaders-talks-kremlin-loan-deal.

Donald Trump's presidency creates an opportunity for Russia, because he could bring chaos and disorder in the "Western camp," which is exactly what the Russian leadership has long wanted. This hoped-for chaos and disorder follows from the style and orientation of the Trump presidency, a product of Trump's personality traits, his anti-establishment approach to governance and government, his signature campaign slogans—"America First" and "Make America Great Again"—and his promotion of American isolationism. What is more, Trump not only questions the conduct of American foreign policy making but also presents himself as an anti-establishment politician who is willing to reform the US political system. For his controversial speeches, Trump was criticized both inside his country and abroad.

In order to assess how much Russia has benefited from the ascendancy of Donald Trump, we will introduce the concept of a *foreign policy cluster*, which is reflected a two-stage process of foreign policy making:

(a) the declarative stage, during which Trump as a presidential candidate expressed his vision of American foreign policy.

(b) the implementation stage, when Trump as president and his administration conduct their foreign policy.

This is depicted in Figure 2.

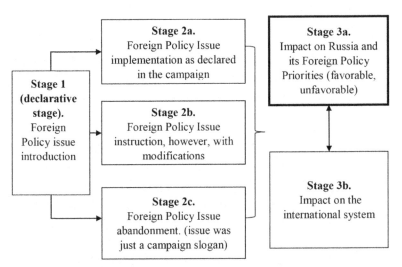

Figure 2: The lifespan of an American "foreign policy cluster" and its impact on Russian Foreign Policy.

We will then:

1. identify the most important foreign policy clusters;
2. consider in what ways the foreign policy clusters that were beneficial from the perspective of the Russian Federation at the declarative stage, were modified at the implementation stage once Trump became president; and
3. judge how the conduct of American foreign policy has been beneficial to Russian interests, from the perspective of Russian foreign policy.

Policy clusters, for practical reasons, will be divided into two categories: issue-based systems and geography-based systems.[14] While the former are restricted to certain foreign policy domains that are not bound to any specific territory, the latter are geographically defined. The clusters are therefore as follows:

- *Issue based*: environmental policy, migration policy, human rights and democratization, and trade policy; and
- *Geographic based*: Europe, FSU-CIS, the Far East, and the Middle East)

Trump's Foreign Policy Campaign Declarations and Presidential Actions

Issue-based Policies

Environmental Policy

Trump seems to be have been coherent in terms of the presentation of his environmental policy. His presidential campaign declarations and his presidential actions are compatible. The Trump administration's environmental policy is presented in the White House's "America First Energy Plan."[15] This plan focuses on supporting fossil-fuels-based industries, ignoring the renewable sources of energy. Its main aim is to lift the environmental restrictions imposed on the American economy—Paris

---

[14] This division was introduced by Rosenau (2006, 187–195), according to whom the two types of systems coexist and actively interact with each other.

[15] Retrieved from: https://www.whitehouse.gov/america-first-energy.

Climate Accord being one of the most important sources of these restrictions. That is why Trump declared as a presidential candidate that the US will withdraw from that Accord in 2020.[16]

The reactions around the world to Trump's declaration were more than skeptical, not excluding those from the Russian Federation. The Russian government traditionally perceives environmental agreements, especially the ones limiting the emission of greenhouse gases, as a burden for Russian economy, which is anything but energy efficient. It could be expected that the moves from Trump's administration would not bring any significant Russian reaction, as both have currently seemingly similar environmental agenda. Nevertheless, even though Vladimir Putin has publicly stated that climate change doubters may be right (Banerjee 2017, McDonald 2017),[17] the Russian government officially supported the Paris Climate Accord and still declares its willingness to adhere to achieving its targets.[18] What may be the reason for this change of a long-standing Russian skepticism toward multilateral environmental agreements vis-à-vis US withdrawal? The most reasonable answer seems to point to a divide-and-rule policy. When Trump attracts international criticisms at his policies, it seems like a good time for Putin to settle the score and present himself as a more reliable political leader. In other words, the fact that Putin officially denounces American withdrawal from the Paris Climate Accord does not mean that he considers it as unfavorable. On the contrary, the Trump environmental policies and actions seem to be compatible with the foreign policy priorities of the Russian Federation.

Migration Policy

The hallmark of Trump's immigration policy, both as a presidential candidate and as president, is the wall that he wants to build, at Mexico's

---

[16] According to article 28 of the Paris Climate accord, this withdrawal can happen not earlier then November 2020, just after the next presidential election.

[17] See also: http://www.independent.co.uk/news/world/europe/vladimir-putin-russia-climate-change-not-caused-by-humans-echoes-us-trump-a7660941.html; https://inews.co.uk/essentials/news/world/vladimir-putin-climate-change-real-good/.

[18] See: http://www.upi.com/Russia-sees-growing-support-for-Paris-climate-deal/5241498211620/.

expense, along US-Mexico border. While the wall still remains in the sphere of policy declarations, the travel ban from some countries and refugee suspension are declarations that became US policy by presidential executive order (no. 13769[19]). This sought to suspended entry into the US for 90 days of the citizens of Iraq, Iran, Libya, Somalia, Sudan, Syria, and Yemen. Following its suspension by a federal court, in March 2017, another executive order was issued, which excluded, from the travel ban, Iraqi visa-holders and permanent residents. Ultimately, the US Supreme court supported this executive order, albeit with some technical changes.

The actions of Trump's administrations brought wide international criticism, with one significant exception: Russia. Officially, the Kremlin was indifferent toward the controversial executive orders issued by Donald Trump.[20] It is quite widely assumed that there are two main reasons for this stance. First, Putin did not want to alienate Trump from the very beginning of his presidency, as he was counting on fruitful cooperation with him. Nevertheless, this immigration policy position posed a considerable difficulty for the Russian regime. Second, Putin did not want to support such extreme actions by Trump, given that there are round 20 million Muslims living in Russia, and given the on-going conflicts in the Russian region of the Caucasus and his close ties with Ramzan Kadyrov, the Head of the Chechen Republic.[21] Even the Russian government's it's-none-of-our-business stance was troublesome, as the Muslim world expected Russian condemnation of the new American policy. In short, the Kremlin remained largely neutral toward the new US migration policy and probably will continue this course in the future.

Assessing the general context surrounding the immigration policies of the Trump administration, and looking at it from the perspective of Russian interests, it can be considered as favorable for two reasons. First, there is overt international criticism and tensions between the US and other countries, thereby weakening the "Western camp" and American

---

[19] Retrieved from: https://www.whitehouse.gov/the-press-office/2017/01/27/executive-order-protecting-nation-foreign-terrorist-entry-united-states.
[20] See: https://ria.ru/world/20170130/1486762276.html.
[21] Kadyrov presents himself as a good paternalistic Muslim leader.

relations with the rest of the world. Second, the issue is widely contested and, to some extent, destabilized the US internal policies.

Democratization and Human Rights

Russia traditionally perceives the Western focus on democracy and human rights just as an excuse to interfere with sovereign states around the world and to promote Western interests. One example of such a perception is the crisis in Ukraine, where Russia directly blames the West, especially the US, for inciting the Revolution of Dignity and anti-Russian sentiment.

We do not have any tangible material on the policy direction of Trump's administration democratization and human rights. What we can take into account, however, are his related declarations, his meetings with other leaders, and statements of his inner-circle of policy advisors. On the one hand, Trump, Vice-President Mike Pence, and Secretary of State Rex Tillerson, have all declared that freedom, human dignity, and democracy are the most important values in the US and underpinning its foreign policy.[22] Additionally, bombing of al-Shayrat airbase in Syria as a retaliation for the assumed use of chemical weapons by the Assad's regime against its own citizens—including women and children—could be used as an argument that Trump is prepared to go beyond rhetoric in defending human dignity and human rights. On the other hand, Trump is described as having a business-like attitude, where he would reach any agreement with anyone, as long as it is a "good deal."[23] One example of this is the invitation to visit the White House Trump extended to Rodrigo Duterte, the President of Philippines. Duterte has been accused of massive human rights violations, including mass murder,[24] but he may be a valuable ally against China in the Southeast Asia region. The bottom line, however, is that the Trump administration has not yet significantly embraced either the democratization or the human rights issues. The outlook presented by the activists dealing with

---

[22] See: https://www.state.gov/secretary/remarks/2017/05/270620.htm.

[23] Retrieved from: https://www.washingtonpost.com/posteverything/wp/2017/05/15/donald-trump-desperate-dealmaker/?utm_term=.0083ae17a6e7.

[24] See: https://www.nytimes.com/2017/04/30/us/politics/trump-invites-rodrigo-duterte-to-the-white-house.html.

the issues is rather grim.²⁵ Nevertheless, this does not mean that it will remain this way.

From the Russian perspective, most promising is the "deal-based" approach to international relations. If both Trump and Putin can treat democracy and human rights as a part of more complex deal, then it may be that Putin will be satisfied in the end. Trump, however, may use this issue as a bargaining chip, when there is a deal at stake. This bargaining chip may be used either to criticize Russians for not following the basic rules of democracy and human rights or to forget about them. These issues will be subordinate to others, more relevant for both sides (from example with respect to Ukraine and Syria) and will be raised or ignored, according to what will serve Trump's interests better.

Geographic-based Policies

Europe and FSU-CIS Region

Europe, including Russia,²⁶ has traditionally been very interested in the US presidential elections and the change in president. The 2016 elections were especially of interest to Europeans because of significant changes in the foreign policy pronounced by Trump on the campaign trail. And, with the exception of Russia, most of Europe was rather skeptical and full of concerns, to say the least. The list of these possibly difficult issues between the European Union (EU) and the Trump administration is long and contains, among others, the following key issues:

- Trump's negative rhetoric on the feasibility of the EU political project (McNamara 2017);²⁷

---

²⁵ See: http://www.huffingtonpost.comentry/trump-human-rights-100-days_us_590220d0e4b0af6d718c9779;https://www.theguardian.com/law/2017/apr/04/donald-trump-xijinping-abdel-fattah-el-sisi-human-rights;http://www.independent.co.uk/news/world/americas/donald-trump-praises-totalitarian-leaders-human-rights-advocates-putin-duterte-kim-jong-un-a7712931.html.

²⁶ It should be noted that Former Soviet Union countries are included with Europe, and that the most important country issue to US-EU-Russia triangle is Ukraine.

²⁷ See also: https://www.cnbc.com/2017/08/14/how-trumps-criticism-of-the-

- Trump's support for populist Eurosceptics like Jean Marie Le Pen in France;[28]
- Trump's negative rhetoric on the "obsolete" NATO and his assuming of a more assertive role toward US allies, especially in terms of military budgets (the famous 2% of GDP target);[29]
- Trump's protectionist leanings in terms of transatlantic trade, especially in the context of the Transatlantic Trade and Investment Partnership (TTIP) and trade deficit with the EU,[30] most of all with Germany, plus the aversion to multilateralism, as in the case of the World Trade Organization or Paris Climate Accord;
- Trump's pre-presidency rhetoric on Ukraine, justifying (or at least expressing a degree of sympathetic understanding toward) the Russian position, and the fact that a quite few members of Trump's campaign and administration teams had close ties with the Kremlin (Calamur 2016).

Taking into account all these issues and the very strained relations between the EU and Russia, it could be thought that this is a very simple recipe for rapprochement between the US and Russia, as Trump and Putin share many views on the EU and foreign policy. The reality, however, is more nuanced:

- The Pro-Russian Michal Flynn (Trump's initial National Security Advisor and Steve Bannon (Trump's initial Chief Strategist)[31] have both left Trump's administration.
- The US has stressed its support for Ukraine and confirmed its recognition of Crimea as Ukrainian soil.

---

eu-makes-the-region-stronger.html; https://www.cnbc.com/2017/08/14/how-trumps-criticism-of-the-eu-makes-the-region-stronger.html.

[28] See: https://www.theguardian.com/us-news/2017/apr/21/donald-trump-marine-le-pen-french-presidential-election.

[29] See: http://blink.htcsense.com/web/articleweb.aspx?regionid=3&articleid=86304083.

[30] See: https://www.cnbc.com/2017/08/14/how-trumps-criticism-of-the-eu-makes-the-region-stronger.html.

[31] See: http://www.newsweek.com/steve-bannon-donald-trump-jared-kushner-vladimir-putin-russia-fbi-mafia-584962.

- Trump has cited the infringement of human dignity and human rights to justify bombing al-Shayrat airbase under the control of the Russian-supported Syrian regime.
- The US Senate has voted to accept Montenegro into an alliance and has expanded sanctions against Russia.

It seems, as many commentators put it, that "the honeymoon is over" in US-Russian relations. Initial "bromance" of both leaders has remained largely hypothetical. That does not mean that it cannot be revived, but it seems that certain rootedness of US in the transatlantic international subsystem is too strong to be completely altered within the first 100 days of the Trump presidency. These arguments obviously do not change the fact that there are many convergences between Donald Trump and Vladimir Putin, both in their assumed personal traits and political actions.

Asia

US policy toward Asia can be described as almost revolutionary declarations during Trump's presidential campaign becoming mellow outcomes achieved during the first months of his presidency. The world expected an all-out trade war with China and all it received was more rhetoric and some trade talks, both marked by caution. There are some traditional tensions (South China Sea) and even some mutual understanding (China's influence on North Korea and its ballistic and nuclear program). One spectacular and almost immediate move from Trump when he became president was the US withdrawal from Transpacific Trade Partnership (TPP) negotiations. This has permitted China to assume the novel role of a global free-trade promoter (Solis 2017).

As for US-Russia relations in the Asian context, there is not much to say after the first 100 days of Trump's administration, except perhaps that it is a work-in-progress. It might be suggested that Trump is subject to pressure from the so-called "deep state" in the US intelligence community and military-industrial complex. They need an existential threat, which they see as Russia. Therefore, they push Trump into the direction of Kissingerian divide and rule policy, aimed at separating Russia from its allies in Asia, mainly China and Iran.[32] But until now,

---
[32] See: http://www.scmp.com/week-asia/opinion/article/2064005/trump-will-

there is little evidence to support that thesis. The only salient issue in Asia, where we can be more or less sure of US stance, is North Korea. A famous sentence from Trump to Xi Jinping—"if China doesn't deal with North Korea, we will"—epitomizes the US position on that issue (Weaver, Haas and McCurry 2017).[33] The deployment of anti-missile THAAD system in South Korea to counter a possible strike from North Korea is an issue with tangible tensions between US and China and Russia. Both Russia and China are against it, but until now, they were unable to contain Pyongyang, so some developments around this issue can be expected.

Middle East

Middle East is the first region visited by Donald Trump, with some decisions and actions being taken by his administration. Therefore, we can say more about US policy, not only just about Trump's declarations. First, the US seems to be really strengthening its ties with traditional allies: Israel (Aronson 2017) and Saudi Arabia.[34] Second, the US seems to have recognized the role of Russia in the Syrian conflict; therefore, the fate of Bashar al-Assad is no longer clear (contrary to the stance of previous Obama administration). Rex Tillerson stated that al-Assad's fate is up to Syrian people, but, at the same time, Assad's reign is coming to an end.[35] The attack on the al-Shayrat airbase seems to be a message conveying the assertiveness of the US rather than a move aimed against Russia or the al-Assad's regime. Third, in spite of a quite aggressive, anti-Iranian rhetoric, the deal with Iran remains in force, perhaps only for the time being. There are even some talks between Americans and Iranians taking place (US citizens detained or missing in Iran, and Boeing-Aseman Airlines deal).[36]

try-smash-china-russia-iran-triangle-heres-why-he-will.

[33] See: https://www.theguardian.com/us-news/2017/apr/02/donald-trump-north-korea-china.

[34] See: https://www.wsj.com/articles/on-saudi-arabia-trip-trump-to-woo-muslims-he-once-sought-to-block-1495186208.

[35] See: http://foreignpolicy.com/2017/07/03/tillerson-ready-to-let-russia-decide-assads-fate/; http://www.newsweek.com/are-trump-and-tillerson-letting-syrias-assad-hook-578571; https://www.state.gov/secretary/remarks/2017/07/272371.htm.

36 See: http://www.reuters.com/article/us-iran-aseman-boeingidUSKBN1910HT.

To some extent, the Middle East policy of the Trump administration follows the same pattern as in the case of other policies, especially in the context of Russian involvement in the region. US declarations seemed to show American understanding of the Russian position and plans, but in the end the perspectives of both parties are incompatible. Russia sees Iran as a part of the solution of the Middle East problems (and a close ally); the US sees it as a part of a problem. US administration has strengthened its traditional ties in the region and it looks like they are not willing to change that, even at the cost of ignoring Saudi Arabia's sponsorship of Islamic extremist groups. *Ergo*, it seems that even though the Middle East is a very unstable region, the political configuration of allies will remain largely unchanged in a short term.

DOMESTIC AND INTERNATIONAL CHALLENGES FACING TRUMP'S PRESIDENCY

Elements of US domestic institutional constraints, societal pressure, and opposition from within the Republican Party have a substantial influence on the conduct of Trump's foreign policy. First, it turns out that some controversial policies presented during the presidential campaign cannot be implemented. The idea of building a wall on the Mexican border (paid by the Mexico) and full implementation of immigration policies are two examples of promises that Trump will most likely not deliver to his followers. Trump's defiant tweets, such as "see you in court" after the Federal San Francisco Appeals Court upheld the suspension of the immigration order, show how helpless a president can be in the face of judicial constraints.[37] Second, the Republican-dominated Congress does not seem to be making life easier for Trump. This is visible in terms of the Senate's willingness to extend the sanctions against Russia.[38] Last, but definitely not least, the allegations that the Trump campaign team colluded with Russia to influence favorably the

---

[37] See: http://abcnews.go.com/Politics/government-lawyers-call-delay-trump-immigration-order-case/story?id=45467116; http://www.foxnews.com/politics/2017/02/09/appeals-court-upholds-ruling-blocking-trumps-immigration-order.html.

[38] See: https://www.nytimes.com/2017/07/27/us/politics/senate-russia-

presidential elections, and the rising threat of impeachment, are by no means advantageous for Trump's presidency and the conduct of US foreign policy (Osnos 2017).

Trump's declarations during the presidential campaign as well as his actions during the first months in office seem to pose some serious problems for his administration. First and foremost, Trump started his relations with some of the most important partners disastrously. Declarations about quitting the Paris Climate Accord, the questioning of the importance of NATO and the EU, as well as leaving the TPP negotiations, made partners suspicious of Trump's foreign policy. If the US wants to pursue an active foreign policy on a global scale and reassure its position as a global leader, Trump has to start improving relations with established US partners, mostly the allies from the EU. The Syrian crisis and the war with ISIS, the refugee crisis, war in Ukraine, North Korean and nuclear ambitions, and the Iranian nuclear deal, as well as global challenges such as global warming, can only to be effectively addressed when dealt with multilaterally. It seems clear that Trump has not made any new allies and has damaged and destabilized relations with the old ones. Such a foreign policy is clearly unsustainable under current conditions.

US-Russian Relations and its Implications for the Trump administration

The two major questions we have sought to address are as follows:

- Is Trump's foreign policy favorable or unfavorable from the Russian perspective?
- What are the implications for the Trump administration of its policy toward Russia?

As to the first question, American withdrawal from global politics in all fields, both issue and geographic based, would be welcomed by Russian policymakers. A more isolationist US would ultimately increase the significance of regional powers, which is in line with the Russian under-

sanctions-trump.html?mcubz=1.

standing of multipolarity. Such an isolationist desire is apparent under Trump's presidency. Still, it is questionable how durable any withdrawal from global politics will be and which policy areas it will mostly likely affect. The US is a global (if not *the* global) player that defines the shape of the world politics.

US withdrawal from issue-based policies would significantly affect the process of building the global governance order, embedded in common set of principles and values. Any US withdrawal—or at least indifference—will ultimately undermine such attempts and the formation of a more multipolar world order. For now, it is difficult to say what the long-term outcomes of the Trump presidency may be. Withdrawal from the Paris Climate Accord can mean Trump is, to some extent, true, to his words, which is good for Russia. The US trade policy becoming more protectionist (for example, the "America First Energy Plan") can also be considered as preferable for Putin's regime. What is certain, a step backward on the path of multipolar world has already been taken. For now, Putin's Russia seems to benefit from these processes.

Focusing on geographic-based policies, it seems that Russian expectations of the US being less involved in different parts of the world are not being met. The US has not only increased military spending but also presented a more assertive policy. For instance, Trump's declarations to stand firm with US's NATO allies—despite all his prior negative rhetoric—are by no means a positive outcome as far as Russian interests are concerned. Still, what may be beneficial for Russia is that the US, although officially denouncing the Russian annexation of the Crimea, seems to show less interest in the protection of states with a problematic or unclear future—such as Ukraine or Georgia. This may actually be a sign that Trump will unofficially recognize Russian domination in the FSU region. Considering the Middle East and Far East, the US is not likely to withdraw. The decisive US acts against the regimes in Pyongyang and Syria are not a welcome change for Putin, same with the rebuilding of traditional alliances with South Korea, Israel, Saudi Arabia, and Egypt.

Figure 3 summarizes our assessment.

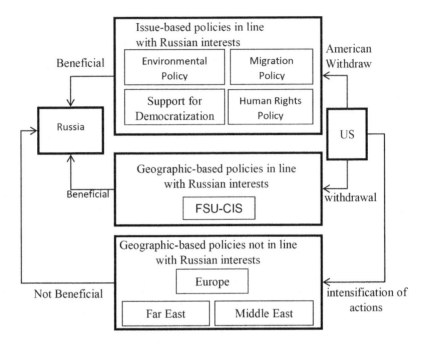

Figure 3: Russian policy expectations from the rise of Donald Trump.

Beneficial to Russian interests is the US's visible withdrawal in all issue-based policy clusters and, most likely in one geographic-based policy cluster, namely the FSU-CIS region. US actions in other geographic policy clusters are not, however, in line with Russian interests.

As to the second question, four implications for the Trump administration of its policy toward Russia can be identified. First, in order to conduct an effective foreign policy, Trump has to secure his domestic political position. As long as he continues to fight the Washington politico-administrative system, the US position as a global hegemon will be weakened, which Putin is eagerly awaiting. Second, if the US is to remain influential, Trump should look for the improvement of the relations with traditional allies, such as the EU. Russia will continue to obstruct European integration and play EU and NATO members off against each other. Third, Trump should reconsider his approach to the issue- based policies, which historically have integrated the Western World of which the US is a cornerstone. Additionally, focusing on these policies would be helpful in silencing activist groups as well as political opponents who accuse Trump of violating human rights or promoting authoritarianism. Fourth, what Trump's administration has to realize is that Russian interests are intrinsically contradictory to those of the US. This is not related to leadership personalities or their likes or dislikes. The US and the Russia Federation are states that differ in nearly every important aspect of governance, particularly the position and power of their leader, the role of civil society, their economic outlook, and their approach to globalization. Trump has to acknowledge this simple fact in order to conduct an effective policy toward the Russian Federation.

Conclusion

The future of US-Russia relations remains unclear. On the one hand, it seems that Trump—to the dissatisfaction of Putin—turned out to be less anti-establishment and isolationist than he presented himself to be during the presidential campaign, and more internationalist and so more involved in world affairs once he became president. On the other hand, there are certain aspects of US foreign policy that actually may benefit Russian interests, for instance environmental or economic policies. Still, as far as American global engagement is concerned—reflecting Trump's geographic-based policies—it is visible that the focus is rather on a hard-power strategy than on the soft one. This means that the US is increasing its military presence and following a more protectionist trade policy. The withdrawal from the TPP exemplifies this. What this means that the space left by Trump's new emphasis on American isolationism and its move away from free trade vision embedded in globalization may be filled by regional powers—particularly Russia and China. Is this in then the US national interest? Definitely not. The US's status as a global superpower is multidimensional and will not vanish overnight at the whim of a populist president.

References

Arakelyan, A. 2013. "CIS Frontier Countries, Economic and Political Prospects." *Deutsche Bank Research*, July 16. Available at: https://www.dbresearch.com/PROD/DBR_INTERNET_EN-PROD/PROD0000000000317261.PDF.

Aronson, G. 2017. "US-Israeli Relations in the Trump Era." *SETA Alalysis, No. 32*. Available at: http://setadc.org/wp-content/uploads/2017/05/Analysis_32_US_ISR_rv02.pdf.

Banerjee, N. 2017. "Russia and the U.S. Could Be Partners in Climate Change Inaction." *Inside Climate News*, February 7. Available at: https://insideclimatenews.org/news/06022017/russia-vladimir-putin-donald-trump-climate-change-paris-climate-agreement.

Bordachev, T. 2014. "Eurasian Russia in the Twenty-First Century." In *Russia Pivot to Eurasia* (ed. K. Liik). London: The European Council on Foreign Relations.

Calamur, K. 2016. "Donald Trump Appears to Back Russia's Annexation of Ukraine's Crimea." *The Atlantic*, July 27. Available at: https://www.theatlantic.com/news/archive/2016/07/trump-crimea/493280/.

Darczewska, J. 2014. "Anatomia Rosyjskiej wojny informacyjnej. Operacja krymska—studium przypadku *OSW*." *Center for Eastern Studies, Ośrodek Studiów Wschodnich* 42: 5–33.

Elkhan, R. and S. Zada. 2016. *Oil Abundance and Economic Growth*. Berlin: Logos Verlag.

Goldman, M. 2008. *Petrostate: Putin Power and the New Russia*. New York: Oxford University Press.

Hikari, M. 2015. "Shifting Russian Policies Towards Allied Separatist Regions." *The Central Asia-Caucasus Analyst*, June 10. Available at: https://www.cacianalyst.org/publications/analytical-articles/item/13227-shifting-russian-policies-towards-allied-separatist-regions.html.

Hudson, V. 2012. "The History and Evolution of Foreign Policy Analysis." In *Foreign Policy, Theories, Actors, Cases* (eds. S. Smith, A. Hadfield, and T. Dunne). Oxford: Oxford University Press.

Kaplan, M. 1975. *System and Process in International Politics*. New York: Robert E. Krieger.

Kazantsev, A. 2009. "Russian Policy in Central Asia and the Caspian Sea

Region." In *Power and Policy in Putin's Russia* (ed. R. Sakwa). London and New York: Routledge.

Kuznetsova, N. and E. Kuznetsova, 2015. "Energy Strategy of the Russian Federation." *Mediterranean Journal of Social Sciences*, 6 (5): 160–168.

McNamara, K. 2017. "Trump Takes Aim at The European Union." *Foreign Affairs*, January 24. Available at: https://www.foreignaffairs.com/articles/europe/2017-01-24/trump-takes-aim-european-union.

Mironov, V. and A. Petronevich. 2015. "Discovering the Signs of Dutch Disease in Russia" (BOFIT Discussion Papers, 3). Helsinki, FI: Bank of Finland, Institute for Economies in Transition. Available at: http://www.suomenpankki.fi/bofit_en/tutkimus/tutkimusjulkaisut/dp/Documents/2015/dp0315.pdf.

Osnos, E. 2017. "How Trump Could Get Fired." *The New Yorker*, May 8. Available at: https://www.newyorker.com/magazine/2017/05/08/how-trump-could-get-fired.

Powell, R. 1991. "Absolute and Relative Gains in International Relations Theory." *The American Political Science Review* 85 (4): 1303–1320.

Rosenau, J. 2006. "Pre-theories and Theories of International Politics. In *The Study of World Politics: Theoretical and Methodological Challenges* (Vol. I), (ed. J. Rosenau). London and New York: Routledge.

Solís, M. 2017. "Trump Withdrawing from the Trans-Pacific Partnership." *Brookings*, March 24. Available at: https://www.brookings.edu/blog/unpacked/2017/03/24/trump-withdrawing-from-the-trans-pacific-partnership/.

Trenin, D. 2011. *Post Imperium*. Washington, DC: Carnegie Endowment for International Peace, United Book Press.

Willerton, J., M. Slobodchikoff, and G. Goerts. 2012. "Treaty Networks, Nesting, and Interstate Cooperation: Russia, the FSU, and the CIS." *International Area Studies Review* 15 (1): 59–82.

9
THE JAPANESE REACTION TO TRUMP'S FIRST HUNDRED DAYS

Tetsuya Sahara

INTRODUCTION

On January 20, 2017, the global civil society greeted Donald J. Trump's inauguration as the 45th President of the United States (US) with massive protest and demonstrations denouncing his chauvinist-protectionist stances. In stark contrast to the rest of the world, Japanese society showed only the slightest sign of complaint and generally remained calm. The reason for this response lay in Japan's complicated political ethos.

Japan had long pursued bandwagoning diplomacy with its "big brother" over the Pacific, in the hope that aligning with the US will advance its own national interests. So, a trivial event like a change of presidency should not affect the most important principle of Japan's foreign policy. Thus, the Liberal Democratic Party (LDP) government, led by Prime Minister Shinzo Abe, the third-longest serving post-war Prime Minister, greeted the event with utmost flattery, suppressing its resentment over Trump's willful intent to withdraw the US from the Trans-Pacific Strategic Partnership Agreement (TPP).[1] The opposition parties were also circumspect in their reaction, despite their concern over Trump's xenophobic militarist campaign discourses, perhaps because they owed him their gratitude for his strong commitment to withdraw from the TPP, which they had unsuccessfully tried have Japan do in the previous summer.

In this way, the Trump's presidential inauguration ceremony was a prelude to a turbulent period of love–hate fluctuation between Japan and US that follow over the next 100 days. The remainder of this chapter describes the Japanese reactions to the Trump administration, mainly focusing on the tumult and wobble within Abe's LDP government.

---
[1] Nikkei, January 21, 2017.

Context: Japan Prior to the Trump Presidency

Since the start of his second term of office on December 26, 2012, Prime Minister Shinzo Abe has enjoyed unexpectedly high popularity that made his political position unprecedentedly formidable. Though he owed this enhanced formidability mainly to his predecessor Yoshihiko Noda's misrule and personal stupidity, Abe believed his success has been grounded in his new economic policy. Discarding Japan's prudent monetarist tradition, the newly appointed governor of the Bank of Japan, Haruhiko Kuroda—a loyal Abe supporter—poured immense amount of money into the capital market though a zero-interest rate policy and monetary easing of different dimension. Though, ostensibly, this policy was aimed at exiting Japan from its deflationary spiral, it was actually a means of increasing stock market prices, achieved by currency devaluation. In a few months, the Japanese Yen (JPY) devalued against US Dollar by 20%, and stock price, on average, rose accordingly. So, investors and exporters were the main beneficiaries. Abe was proud of his handling of economy, labeling it "Abenomics." But, the overall net result was a general pauperization of the population, as most of workers suffered from constant falling real wages.[2]

To balance this popular discontent, Abe tried to stir up the chauvinistic sentiment widely shared by the younger population, who had been alienated from the progressive wealthy life-style—the symbol of postwar era of Japanese democracy. Helped by the anti-China and anti-Korea propaganda orchestrated by the mainstream media, Abe disseminated hostile rhetoric exaggerating the threat of nuclear missile projects in the Democratic People's Republic of Korea and border dispute with the People's Republic of China. He declared that Japan's—imagined—"enemy" neighbors are besieging it, so justifying fascist-style militarist reforms in national security and education.

Abe revealed, paradoxically, that he is an economic liberal and a political reactionary, the sustainment of which necessitated friendly, if not cordial, relations from Washington. This is the reason why Abe hastily visited New York to meet Trump on November 17, 2016, to become the

---

[2] See: https://www.forbes.com/sites/michaelauslin/2016/03/09/tradition-and-innovation-battle-in-japans-economy/.

first head of state to salute the president-elect in person. Overconfident of Hillary Clinton's victory, Abe had neglected to prepare any channel of communication with the Republican candidate. His main objective was to persuade Trump to change his mind about withdrawing the US from the TPP. Abe's visit gave Trump an air of sanction amidst fierce dispute over his presidential legitimacy, but Trump did not treat his guest kindly, for he made no concession. After the meeting, Abe emphasized "his confidence in future friendship" with the future president, but did not mention any concrete result.[3]

THE INITIAL PHASE OF TRUMP'S RELATIONS WITH JAPAN: A JAPANESE SIGH OF RELIEF

The Obama administration's Asian-Pacific shift—and Japan's central position in that regional strategy—had provided a convenient context for Abe's foreign policy. Its main objectives were to check China and to keep Koreans under Tokyo's control. Thus, he provoked China over the Senkaku/Diaoyu islands, supported the US claim over the Spratly islands, and stepped up sanctions against North Korea.

Toward the end of Obama's terms, Abe was stepping up his hardline policy. He persuaded the Americans not to take part in the China-led Asian Infrastructure Investment Bank—to the chagrin of the Wall Street—and launched a rapprochement with the Russians amidst the Ukrainian crisis. He realized that the plight of Moscow gave him a rare chance to gain territorial concessions in the South Kuril Islands, which had been Tokyo aspiration since the end of war. However, Trump's ascendency to the presidency caste ominous clouds over Abe's political visions.

Trump's appeasing gesture toward Vladimir Putin emboldened him to reject any territorial concession at the Tokyo meeting on December 15–16, 2016.[4] Trump's stated intention of downsizing of the US Forces in Japan would expose Tokyo to direct military pressure of China. Trump's reproach on Japan's cheap Yen, and his demand for the US to attain a larger share of Japanese market, coupled with his protectionist stance,

---

[3]   See: http://www.kantei.go.jp/jp/97_abe/actions/201611/17usa.html/.
[4]   See: http://news.livedoor.com/article/detail/12559784/.

threatened the future prosperity of the Japanese economy, and so would eradicate the base of an already faltering "Abenomics."[5]

Therefore, the Japanese government took a deep breath of relief, when US Defense Secretary, James Mattis assured the *status quo* of US Forces Japan (USFJ),[6] and applauded Japan' contribution as "a model."[7] Vey soon after, Abe paid an official visit to Trump in Washington, and the two leaders agreed on the following issues.

- The US-Japan security treaty covers the Senkaku/Diaoyu islands.
- A commitment to making joint efforts to block the unacceptable:
  - Chinese expansion over the Spratly islands; and
  - North Korea's nuclear-missile project.
- A commitment to work together to create a "free and fair" market without the interference of "state capitalism" in the Asian-Pacific region.[8]

Finally, in exchange for Trump's assurance of the protection of Japanese interest, Abe underlined he would support the US immigration policy, including the "Muslim ban."

THE SECOND PHASE OF TRUMP'S RELATIONS WITH JAPAN: A HEIGHTENING OF JAPANESE FEARS AND EXPECTATIONS

Though the initial contacts with the Trump administration suggested nothing but a vague consensus on the present state of affairs, the Japanese government conceived an optimistic idea about the US having a wider role in East Asia. Abe promised that Japan would take a "larger roles and responsibility" in the alliance in exchange for the US's commitment to putting joint pressure on North Korea "to freeze nuclear and

---

[5] See: http://www.jiji.com/jc/article?k=2017020100013&g=eco.
[6] See: http://www.usfj.mil/.
[7] See: http://jp.reuters.com/article/mattis-inada-china-idJPKBN15K0TW.
[8] Nikkei, February 21, 2017; https://www.nytimes.com/2017/02/10/world/asia/trump-shinzo-abe-meeting.html.

missile projects and to refrain from further provocative acts."[9] The US's plan to deploy THAAD missile system in South Korea[10] and Rex Tillerson's remarks on an aggressive shift of the US policy toward North Korea further encouraged the hawks in Tokyo.[11] Japan decided to send a large contingent—including its largest warship—to a joint drill with the US navy in the East China Sea, despite Beijing' strong warnings about the conduct of this joint drill.[12]

In the meantime, Pyongyang stepped up its brinkmanship by displaying its military prowess. On February 12, Kim Jong-un, Chairman of the Workers' Party of Korea and supreme leader of North Korea since 2011, launched a medium-range missile to the direction of Japanese sea. Considering this act to be in open defiance to Trump-Abe summit, Yoshihide Suga, Chief Cabinet Secretary, strongly condemned Pyongyang's grave breach of the UN Security Council resolutions and warned "Japan would never tolerate such provocations."[13] His protest fell on deaf ears. Less than a month later, Kim shot four missiles, and three of them travelled more than 1,000 kilometers and dropped into the Japan's self-proclaimed but disputed Exclusive Economic Zone. Suga was so furious that he warned of Japan taking "strong action" if necessary.[14] The climax came in the next month. In the early morning of April 5, Kim Jong-un launched a medium-range ballistic missile. The test was apparently set to send a warning message to the Sino-US summit that was to discuss the preventive measures to Kim's missile project. Trump was so upset that he assured Abe of pre-emptive measures was already "on the table."[15]

What Trump actually did, however, was to launch Tomahawk cruise missile strikes not against Pyongyang but against Syria. The attack might

---

[9] Retrieved from: http://www.nikkei.com/article/DGXLASFS11H1Y_R10C17A2PE8000/.
[10] See: http://archive.fo/7i7w6.
[11] See: https://www.nytimes.com/2017/03/17world/asia/all-eyes-on-china-as-us-signals-new-tack-on-north-korea.html.
[12] See: https://www.rt.com/news/381012-china-japan-warship-response/.
[13] Retrieved from: http://www.kantei.go.jp/jp/tyoukanpress/201702/12_a.html.
[14] Retrieved from: http://www.kantei.go.jp/jp/tyoukanpress/201702/12_a.html.
[15] Retrievedfrom: http://www.kantei.go.jp/jp/97_abe/actions/201704/06kaiken.html.

have been a show of force, in order to urging the Chinese President Xi Jinping to take harsher measures to curb North Korea. Xi did not tolerate such an insult and no joint communiqué was issued after the summit, even though the two leaders shared "deep concern" over Pyongyang's nuclear potentials. Abe, however, interpreted the action differently. He believed the Tomahawk power show in Syria was a rehearsal for a coming war against his northern neighbor. The Japanese media embarked on a massive campaign exaggerating the "Northern threat," and speculated that the US would take immediate military action.

THE THIRD PHASE OF TRUMP'S RELATIONS WITH JAPAN: AN ORGY THEN THE APATHY

In the weeks that followed, the Japanese media was full of surmises and rumors of imminent US military action against Pyongyang. It was reported that Trump had set the red line as either a nuclear test or ICBM blastoff, and that the Pentagon was preparing its list of targets for its pre-emptive military intervention. Self-styled analists and military experts stipulated the "madman in Pyongyang" would carry out a nuclear test to celebrate his grandfather's birthday, the most important national holiday, on 15 April.

North Korea did, indeed, launch a missile on April 16, but it did not cause any harm as it exploded almost immediately. Notwithstanding, the Japanese government stirred up popular fear by deploying its anti-missile system in civilian zones. Amidst this high tension, US Vice-President Mike Pence visited Japan, and added fuel to the fire by his remark that the era of "strategic patience" was over, and "all options are on the table."[16] He even assured: "We will defeat any attack and meet any use of conventional or nuclear weapons with an overwhelming and effective American response."[17]

The Abe government claimed the North Korea had developed its ballistic missile technology smart enough to reach Japan, and started the na-

---

[16] Retrieved from: https://www.stripes.com/news/pacific/pence-in-japan-all-options-are-on-the-table-regarding-north-korea-1.464217#.WXmQs2U2tEI.

[17] Retrieved from: https://www.stripes.com/news/pacific/pence-in-japan-all-options-are-on-the-table-regarding-north-korea-1.464217#.WXmQs2U2tEI.

tionwide alarming system—"J-Alert"—ostensibly to provide first-hand information. It also disseminated manuals instructing people how to defend their lives in case of North Korean attacks.[18] The media started to mention the coming of a nuclear war, and, by so doing, stirred up even more fear among the population. Journals were discussing the scale of damage if a nuclear bomb exploded at the center of Tokyo. Even popular talk shows, which were willing to give up their inherent mission to convey celebrities' gossips, as well as comedians and clowns were engaging in serious debates over the possible X-day scenario. The most probable date was April 25, when the North Koreans would be celebrating Military Foundation Day. The popular fear was so strong and real that there was smaller traffic on some daily commuter trains on the day.[19]

An abrupt end of this orgy of paranoia came on 28 April, when Tillerson and Mattis issued a joint statement referring to the "new" US approach to North Korea. As a result of "thorough review of the US policy pertaining to the Democratic People's Republic of Korea," they said, the Trump administration has adopted a new approach "to pressure North Korea into dismantling its nuclear, ballistic missile, and proliferation programs by tightening economic sanctions and pursuing diplomatic measures with our Allies and regional partners."[20] So, there would be no change, after all, to the "strategic patience" strategy of the Obama administration. The next day, North Korea launched a ballistic missile that fell into its own territory after a few minutes of flight. The Japanese government denounced the act, but no international reprisal followed.

Conclusion

For all the stipulations declared by Trump the candidate that would drastically reshape US trade and defense relations with Japan, Trump's presidential diplomacy has not brought about any change in US policy with respect to Japan. It is true that the repeal of TPP agreement was a serious blow to Abenomics, but the Japanese economy remains intact, thanks, perhaps, to the very failure of that new tariff union. Likewise,

---

[18] See: http://www.kantei.go.jp/jp/tyoukanpress/201704/21_a.html.
[19] An observation made by the author.
[20] Retrieved from: https://www.state.gov/r/pa/prs/ps/2017/04/270464.htm.

Trump's aggressive gesture has not modified Abe's reactionary security policy. Because of the Russia election interference and collusion scandal are undermining Trump's presidency, is now not likely that he can bring about any significant change in East Asian politics in the near future. For the time being, the present situation—the gradual decline of US influence and collateral isolation of Japan—will continue unabated.

10
TRUMP'S PRESIDENCY: EGYPT AND THE MIDDLE EAST

Magda Shahin

INTRODUCTION

Despite expectations that, as a political novice, President Donald J. Trump would use his first months in the White House as a learning phase to establish a solid presidential base, he chose to approach this timeframe aggressively. Convinced of his popularity and the veracity of his mandate from the American people, Trump's prime objective was to project authority from day one. Much to his satisfaction, the Middle Eastern states, many of which carry a grudge against his predecessors, provided Trump with a fertile ground to undermine former President Barack Obama's posture, and portray him as a weak and ineffective president incapable of acting.

Governments and peoples in the region welcomed Trump's election with open arms, revealing their annoyance and disappointment with the Obama administration. Trump, by his actions, clearly indicates his intention to reverse much of his predecessor's foreign policy in the region, particularly with regard to human rights. Already, the United States (US) State Department has pursued a major arms deal with Bahrain, which had been formally suspended under President Obama due to human rights concerns. Similarly, Secretary of State Rex Tillerson signaled his intent to lift the US freeze on sales of cluster munitions to Saudi Arabia, which Obama had similarly blocked due to their purported role in civilian casualties in Yemen. Finally, Trump's energetic embrace of Egyptian President Abdel Fattah el-Sisi drastically contrasts the adversarial position of the previous president.

This chapter discusses the rhetoric and actions of the new Trump administration in the Middle East region. It addresses whether or not Trump has succeeded in combining military actions with diplomacy. His maneuvering by surprise bombing strikes and troop deployment, along with his cordial meetings with the leaders of the major Arab countries in the White House, is reviewed. The conclusion drawn is that much of the results of Trump's rhetoric and actions are yet to materialize.

The Reactions to the Trump Presidency

The government of Egypt takes pride in having reconstituted some of its regional statute after the long overdue visit of President el-Sisi to the White House. Yet, Egyptians act more cautiously, dreading a repetition of the experience they had with President Obama following his speech in Cairo on June 4, 2009. Though ecstatic and overjoyed at President Obama's praise of Islam and the clear attempts toward rapprochement with the Islamic world, Egyptians soon after realized that it was more rhetoric than reality. Their disappointment with the Obama administration was all the greater after the so-called Arab Spring and its support of the Muslim Brotherhood, even after Egyptians had rebutted the legitimacy of that regime with a march of over one million people. Cairo has made it no secret that it perceives the Trump administration as presenting new vistas for a revamped relationship between the two countries.

Similarly, the Gulf States, led by Saudi Arabia, have found in President Trump a potential ally to rebuild the historic relationship with Washington after years of apathy. Unlike the Obama administration, President Trump seems to consider Saudi Arabia and Gulf States as key partners in his regional foreign policy plans. Under the previous administration, the Gulf States were disappointed with the US policies toward the region, which they felt marginalized their role in favor of other regional actors (Boghardt and Henderson 2017, 2). For example, one particular issue was not engaging them in the primary rounds of the political dialogue that led to the nuclear deal with Iran (Boghardt and Henderson 2017, 3)

Even Israel, which has always relied on bipartisan support and levied its legislative allies to convince Barack Obama to provide a lavish military assistance package, was content to see a change of guards. Prime Minister Benjamin Netanyahu was among the first international leaders to visit his American friend in the Oval Office.

The Middle Eastern Reaction to the Style of the Trump Presidency

The Middle East's reaction to the Trump presidency should not cause anyone to overlook the commonly held perception that President Trump is unpredictable, overhasty, and seemingly uninterested in including his international friends and allies in his decisions, let alone reassuring or even justifying his actions to them. The airstrikes on regime installations in Syria, which occurred while the Egyptian president was still in Washington, is illustrative. The hastiness of Trump's decisions has led to ill-conceived executive orders, as evidenced by its repeated failure to stop citizens from seven then six Muslim-majority countries (Iraq was excluded from the second list) to enter the US.

Moreover, the President's tweets give the region and its leaders much to scrutinize. The international community is ignorant of this new type of presidential diplomacy, its bluntness, and the extent of its seriousness. The challenge is that Trump comes to the presidency with ideas outside the box, which are unfamiliar to the traditional, often parochial, Arab thinking. When coupled with missile attacks on Yemen and Syria and use of the "mother of all bombs" on Afghanistan, presidential tweets underlining the US resolve to pursue its own solutions have indeed raised some misgivings. It is surprising that ten days after striking Syria, Trump chose to drop the world's largest non-nuclear bomb on a desolate stretch of Afghanistan. Ultimately, the strategic and military significance of the US's deploying that particular bomb, at a cost of $16 million, against "one of the smallest militias it faces in the world [in ISIS-Khorasan Province]"was minor to its symbolic importance (Wright 2017). Bombing Afghanistan was more an attempt by Trump to seek validation from the US media, and his desire to appease the US, military, which is institutionally predisposed to testing its weaponry, and temperamentally conditioned to validate US presidents who pursue the use of military force over diplomacy. How can the Arab World, which experienced major vicissitudes with past US administrations, deal with the policies of this new administration as predicated thus far? Should they understand Trump's tweets as setting diplomacy aside, and expect his new administration ready to bomb without room for dialogue or compromise? Alternatively, should they understand his tweets as political rhetoric, divorced from the actions the Trump administration will take to secure its foreign policy objectives? Despite appearances to the contrary, the intricacies of the Middle East region require the US diplomatic apparatus to remain robust, healthy, and engaged.

Trump has made his foreign policy preferences quite clear: a policy of deterrence and diplomacy with muscle, thus far making the military choice in the Middle East region the prevailing arm of his diplomacy. Verification and engagement were off the table. Acting swiftly and decisively left many of his aides confused, and without a rationale. They have been forced to ineptly justify such actions, notably his first drone attacks on Yemen.

Though the overwhelming majority of people in the region welcome the bombing of so-called Islamic terrorist groups and yearn for a return to stability, they also recognize the need for diplomatic efforts to address intractable conflicts.

The Implications of the Successive White House Visits

It is unprecedented that an American president meets with three Arab leaders during the first 100 days. Trump also extended an invitation to Palestinian President Mahmoud Abbas and met with him on May 3, shortly after his first 100 days. It would be premature to assess the results of these meetings, as the main ideas discussed involve contentious issues, which still need time to develop. Apart from the attempt to establish a so-called Sunni alliance against Iran, there is the much-talked-about Middle East conference in July. However, the Palestinian President still needs to be convinced to come on board in the light of the hard pro-Israeli stance of the Trump administration.

The meetings between Trump and Arab leaders have instigated a better sense of the president's priorities and objectives. Most Arabs have reacted positively to his reception of these leaders in the White House and are hopeful that the US will adopt a more constructive approach to the region's problems. Many experts in the region advocate for the necessity of dampening expectations and shying away from building castles in the sand, as the US strategy in the region remains unpredictable and in flux. The many controversies that surround Trump and his decision-making process, however, do not undermine the fact that the Middle East region falls within his sphere of interest. Trump is keen on a hands-on approach to managing affairs in the Arab world.

Above all things—perhaps even above his desire to be perceived as being physically powerful—Trump wishes to be viewed as a powerful businessman—and by extension—as a powerful negotiator.[1] It is, therefore, not surprising and quite natural that Trump has made solving the Palestinian-Israeli conflict an early priority of his presidency. For Trump, it is the ultimate deal, which, if he is successful, will render him the world's greatest negotiator—and by extension—the world's greatest businessman. In his approach to conflict in the Middle East, Trump's desire to project power will, therefore, compete against his desire to be seen as a powerful negotiator.

ISRAEL: THE BIGGEST WINNER

It can be easily claimed that the biggest winner is the Israeli Prime Minister Benjamin Netanyahu, whose relationship with Obama soured considerably. Throughout its two terms, the Obama administration had suffered constant abuse from the Israeli government, which refused to stop building settlements in the West Bank, calling into question the practicability and feasibility of the two-state solution. The Obama administration routinely appeared impotent to counter constant Israeli defiance. This did not prevent it from signing the largest pledge of military assistance to Israel three months prior to the Security Council Resolution. The Memorandum of Understanding between the US and Israel regarding security assistance, signed on September 14, 2016, covers the period 2019–2028. The agreement provides Israel with military assistance to the tune of $33 billion in military financing funds, in addition to $5 billion for missile defense programs.[2] However, in an act of apparent retaliation against the Netanyahu regime, Obama acquiesced and chose not to veto the landmark UN Security Council Resolution 2334 (December 23, 2016), which called on Israel to halt all settlement expansion in the

---

[1] See: http://fortune.com/2016/07/19/donald-trump-negotiating-the-art-of-the-deal/.

[2] The existing MOU from 2007 to 2018 provided Israel with $3.1 billion annually plus $3.1 billion for missile defense programs in the same period.

Occupied Territories. This unprecedented move angered Israel, which had grown accustomed to its powerful patron protecting the country from the Security Council's criticism.

In contrast, Candidate Trump did not hide his unyielding support for Israel on the campaign trail, and stressed his determination to move the US Embassy from Tel Aviv to Jerusalem (Schaefer 2016). Despite Netanyahu's prior knowledge of President Trump and his administration's supportive policies, his White House exceeded all expectations. President Trump's retreat from the commitment to a two-state solution, conditioned by an apparent acceptance of the two parties, exceeded even the hopes of Netanyahu (Shapiro 2017). Retraction of such a long-standing principle, which represents the internationally agreed upon cornerstone of the Palestinian issue, comes as an unpleasant revelation to the region.[3] While the Trump's actions so far, particularly David Kushner's appointment as Special Advisor to the Middle East and David Friedman's confirmation as US ambassador to Israel, clearly indicate resolute support for Israel, relations with Saudi Arabia, contrastingly, have fluctuated considerably.

Saudi Arabia: Another Winner

A successful visit to the White House by the Crown Prince of Saudi Arabia, coming after the apparent chill in the relations between Washington and Riyadh during Obama's final term, and support for certain Saud positions have encouraged the Saudi side to usher in a new phase of relations with the US. This, however, has not prevented the President Trump from reverting to the campaign trail rhetoric and complaints that Saudi Arabia abuses the US by relying on Washington to fund the Kingdom's defense.[4]

The most important outcome of the meeting between Trump and the Crown Prince was the reiteration of their common stance against Iran. Throughout the campaign, Candidate Trump caustically criticized the

---

[3] See: https://www.youtube.com/watch?v=WEX7S8j8DUM.

[4] See: http://www.breitbart.com/video/2016/01/04/trump-im-not-going-to-tell-what-id-do-with-disaster-iran-deal-people-dont-have-right-to-know-how-far-id-go/.

Iranian Deal—the Joint Comprehensive Plan of Action (JCPOA)—that he viewed as naïve, and swore to renegotiate. Speaking to the American Israel Public Affairs Committee (AIPAC) in March, Trump declared, "my number-one priority is to dismantle the disastrous deal with Iran,"[5] a position shared by Riyadh (Begley 2016). In addition, the two states identified common language on Iran, which provides support to Saudi Arabia in its engagement in Yemen. Such language transpired without any delay and subsequently has resulted in strikes on Yemen and Syria, escalating the war in Iraq, all of which are clear attempts to abate the pro-Iranian resistance in the region. Additionally, the Crown Prince and Trump agreed to form a military force of 40,000 soldiers to fight terrorism under the umbrella of the so-called Islamic Sunni Alliance and also implicitly directed toward Iran. Despite the ongoing tensions over Saudi's financial contributions toward its own security, the Crown Prince's visit to Washington set the stage for Trump's landmark visit to the Kingdom a few months later and helped reset the relationship between the two traditional allies.

The Islamic Sunni Alliance

The Islamic alliance initiative conceptualized by Washington and Riyadh, however, does not bode well for many countries in the region and is viewed unfavorably by sectors of Arab society. Leaks about forming a Sunni alliance, with a certain kind of unofficial association with Israel and co-sponsored by the United States, are offensive to the people in the region, to say the least. Not to mention, Egypt and Turkey, which remain at loggerheads over President Recip Taiyap Erdogan's open hostility toward President el-Sisi, following the overthrow of the Muslim Brotherhood. Turkey and its president continue to godfather the Muslim Brotherhood and provide safe haven for its insurgents and fugitives from Egypt and the Arab world. Saudi Arabia is keen on reconciliation between Cairo and Ankara to pave the way for the establishment of the so-called Sunni bloc, but the rift between the two countries runs deep. For Egypt, fighting Islamists remains the top priority, and Turkey's adoptive child, the Muslim Brotherhood, tops the list. Moreover, Egypt

---

[5] Retrieved from: http://time.com/4267058/donald-trump-aipac-speech-transcript/.

is firmly convinced that Turkey harbors manipulative and devious ambitions *vis-à-vis* the region, which are detrimental to Arab countries and their people. The relationship between Egypt and Turkey is illustrative of the geopolitical challenges of creating the Islamic Sunni Alliance.

Despite these concerns, President el-Sisi's visit to Washington depicted the considerable common ground between Egypt and the US. The two most important outcomes of el-Sisi's visit were the consensus that fighting terrorism is a top priority and the resolve to end the Arab-Israeli conflict. Regarding the latter, the parties agreed to hold a five-nation summit next July in Washington, including Egypt, Jordan, Palestine, Israel, and the US, in an effort to reach a deal on the Palestinian issue. These two goals, if fulfilled, would undeniably portend a new beginning for the Arab world and the entire Middle East region. Indeed, Trump's meeting with el-Sisi has been characterized as part of a pattern in which Trump "[showcases] his determination to reshape America's relationship with a number of Middle Eastern countries regardless of their human rights concerns."[6]

Implications for Russia

Despite the accomplishments of successive visits by Middle Eastern leaders to the White House, and the clear understandings they cemented with Trump, the practical results remain contingent on many variables, foremost among them being Russia's reaction and its relations with the US. The Obama administration, and its apparent detachment from the Middle East as part of its pivot to Asia, provided Russia with the opportunity to exert ever-growing power and influence in the region. Trump's rhetoric on the campaign trail and his upfront admiration to President Putin further nurtured this situation. Trump's strategy, however, left Russia with many question marks. The world had to wait some six months for Trump and Putin to meet. Will there be a new Sykes-Picot Agreement[7] for the region? Will the non-Arab emerging

---

6   Retrieved from: https://www.nytimes.com/2017/04/03/world/middleeast/-egypt-sisi-trump-white-house.html.

7   The Sykes–Picot Agreement was a secret 1916 agreement between the United Kingdom and France partitioning the Arab provinces of the Ottoman Empire, after its defeat in WW I, into areas of British and French control. The terms, nego-

powers of Iran and Turkey act as spoilers, as they have no interest in staying on the margin as the equation shifts? There is also the question of Trump's personality itself, and the known sharp fluctuations and apparent contradictions that make it difficult to predict his next steps. The decision to launch airstrikes on a regime airbase in Syria came as a surprise and drastically contradicted his campaign rhetoric. Most ironically, Trump previously counseled Obama against striking al-Assad in 18 separate tweets, describing any US military intervention in Syria as fundamentally dangerous, and unlikely to produce tangible economic or security benefits (Hoffman 2017).

Furthermore, the decisiveness in the American domestic situation and the evolving tensions in Trump's relationship with Congress must be foreign policy considerations. Will Congress be a source of support or hindrance to the Trump's military decisions and policies, particularly in the light of the fact that all the military strikes undertaken so far were unilateral decisions? Not only does Congress appear divided and marginalized, but it re-raises questions over whether a president constitutionally needs Congressional authorization for any military action.[8]

TRUMP RHETORIC VERSUS ACTION IN THE MIDDLE EAST

Although on the campaign trail Candidate Trump's rhetoric catered to Americans comfortable with isolationism and certainly with no appetite for foreign military engagements, President Trump soon unraveled his promises and, unexpectedly, rushed to use force even in unsubstantiated and highly controversial circumstances. In the Middle East,

---

tiated by British diplomat Mark Sykes and a French counterpart, François Georges-Picot, defined agreed sphere of influence between the two countries. France received control of Syria and Lebanon, while Britain gained control of Iraq, Jordan and the coastal strip between the Mediterranean Sea and the River Jordan.

[8] In this context, the military strikes have prompted a serious discourse on the war powers of the executive branch. According to Article II of the Constitution the president, as Commander in Chief of the Armed Forces, is already entrusted to take military action, including directing the country into battle without necessary reverting to Congress. Article I of the Constitution, however, gives only Congress the authority to declare war—and to appropriate funds to the Defense Department to wage it. No doubt, President Trump will hold tight to Article II in his future military actions and continue bragging about his authority as Commander in Chief.

Trump's policy has reversed 180 degrees from his campaign rhetoric and promises, particularly in regard to Syria and Yemen. Trump wanted to demonstrate that he was in charge at both the domestic and international levels, which he did by a show of force. He provided no explanation to Congress, or, for that matter, the international community, about his strategic insight and underlying reasons to attack Yemen or Syria. It was clear that the decision was solely his, and he did not even attempt to engage the Congress or even an inner circle in his administration. It was incumbent upon the White House spokesperson to justify the consecutive military actions in the region and deviation from campaign promises by explaining that it is normal for people to change their minds as they receive more information, as Trump had done.

The Strike on Yemen

Controversy has surrounded the Trump's early decision to initiate excessive military airstrikes against Yemen without explicitly linking the strikes to a full-fledged strategy against the Islamic State (McLeary 2017). Unlike Western public perceptions, the Yemen dilemma is tribal rather than religious. The rift between the Sunnis and Shias is less distinct than in other countries in the region. Saudi Arabia, in search of an enhanced regional role, believed that handling the problem in Yemen would elevate the Kingdom to a regional power to be reckoned with. Saudi Arabia has plunged itself and its allies into a quagmire, with no easy way out according to many veterans in Yemeni affairs (AUC 2017). Former Yemeni President Abdullah Saleh, a shrewd politician and a major adversary of the Saudi Kingdom, is the one pulling the strings and remains the make-or-break player at the heart of the Yemeni impasse. In contrast, the Saudi-backed president, Mansur Hadi, presents as a weak leader and the Yemeni people question his legitimacy. The Houthi insurgents, siding clearly with Abdullah Saleh, are in control of the most populated areas, including the capital Sana'a and the second largest city of Taez. The situation is further compounded by resurgent Al-Qaeda presence in the south, particularly around Aden. At some point, the Saudis will have to accept that their original ambitions in Yemen will not materialize. Iran, though a significant supporter of the Houthis, is a bystander with immense *schadenfreude* from draining the Kingdom's financial and military resources and to continuing to muddy its image abroad.

It is highly debatable whether additional US involvement in Yemen at this stage serves its interests and its national security. The US military strikes and increased drone attacks on Yemen, at first sight, appear to be simply the product of White House havoc. However, the attacks in Yemen affirm the US relationship with Saudi Arabia and prove its support for the Saudi military option, antagonize Iran, and abandon the Obama administration's attempt to promote a political solution in Yemen. Gaining tangible victories in the fight against the Islamic State and Al-Qaeda as a result of the strikes in Yemen seems less of an objective than regional signaling. However, the new Trump administration needs to be cautious about sinking into the Yemeni quagmire. Yemen is an internal conflict, exacerbated but not created or imposed by outside forces. The entry point for peace in Yemen is neither through a premature mediation attempt nor by using missile strikes to intimidate the Houthis and/or the Sunnis.[9]

The Bombing of Syria

Yemen does not seem to have been a stand-alone military adventure during President Trump's first 100 days, as other strikes followed in Iraq and Syria. Whether these moves are strategic, with the objective of defeating the Islamic State, or merely a tactic to provoke Iran and irritate Russia, leaves room for speculation. However, Trump must be aware that Russia is adamantly committed to not losing control over its ally and allowing an Iraq-Libya-type power vacuum to recur once again.

Nowhere has Trump contradicted his most fundamental campaign promises regarding US foreign policy more than in Syria. "We should stay the hell out of Syria; the rebels are just as bad as the current regime,"

---

[9] *A peace-building strategy should begin with staged negotiations between key Yemeni stakeholders and politicians, and be conducted without external manipulation or influence. At a later stage, regional and international parties could join the process to safeguard and guarantee a durable peace in Yemen. One could even envisage establishing peace in Yemen as an integral part of a comprehensive settlement to the region's crisis, including Iraq, Syria and maybe even Libya. Such a settlement may entail exchanging concessions pertaining to Syria and Yemen on the part of the regional powers, notably between Saudi Arabia and Iran. The US and Russia, as the major international powers, having a stake in the region, should be willing to guarantee the final settlement (AUC 2017).*

reads Trump's tweet from June 16, 2013, articulating his opposition to the use of the force in Syria. Though this was a 2013 tweet, his opinions had not changed much prior to the campaign, during which he stipulated again in a campaign rally on October 5, 2016, in Reno, Nevada "You're going to end up in World War Three over Syria if you listen to Hillary Clinton. You're not fighting Syria anymore; you're fighting Syria, Russia, and Iran."[10]

However, on April 3, his shift in approach to Syria became apparent. Reports emerged alleging that the President al-Assad's regime had used chemical weapons on civilians, killing at least 80 people, including women and children.[11] In the two to three days that followed, Trump quickly condemned the attacks through an official statement stipulating that al-Assad crossed the red line by killing innocent babies. Yet. the White House also spoke of the need to acknowledge the Syrian political realities, insinuating, admittedly, the power of the al-Assad regime (Rahim 2017). Without the slightest attempt to verify why al-Assad, who had gained momentum to the extent of convincing the new Trump administration to consider his potential usefulness, would throw himself into an abyss, Trump ordered airstrikes against the Syrian regime, exactly what he had warned Obama against doing three years earlier.

The attack on Syria also served as an affirmation of former President Bill Clinton's doctrine of unilateral intervention for humanitarian reasons, coupled with former President George Bush's preemptive war doctrine. The 2005 Right to Protect (R2P) consensual UN summit resolution provided Trump with the legitimization of unilateral action, and the Trump administration has found no reason to resort to cooperation with the international community or even to show that it contemplated doing so. Neither the Organization of the Prohibition of Chemical Weapons (OPCW) nor the OPCW Joint UN Investigative Mechanism has released their final report, nor have they pronounced themselves on any perceived result. Both are still collecting and analyzing information from all available sources and they refuse to position themselves prema-

---

[10] Retrieved from: https://www.reuters.com/article/us-usa-election-trump-exclusive/exclusive-trump-says-clinton-policy-on-syria-would-lead-to-world-war-three-idUSKCN12P2PZ.

[11] See: http://www.bbc.com/news/world-middle-east-39500947.

turely. It is worth noting, however, OPCW is investigating the events of April 4, upon direct request by the Syrian government. Despite the lack of verification, the Trump administration decided to act directly against the regime. Such an approach recalls memories of other US rash military intervention; when Secretary of State, Colin Powell accused the Saddam regime of acquiring nuclear weapons prior to the 2003 invasion of Iraq.

Following the missile strike, President Trump told the media that the strike was an "emotional and impulsive reaction" and said "that attack on children yesterday had a big impact on me—big impact… That was a horrible, horrible thing. And I've been watching it and seeing it, and it doesn't get any worse than that."[12] On the contrary, Trump's advisers do not view this move as neither emotional nor impulsive.[13] They insisted that it was carried out according to a well-thought-out strategic calculation.[14] Commenting on the strike in Syria, Secretary of State Rex W. Tillerson said, "Mr. Trump had looked back on Mr. Obama's decision not to carry out a strike and decided that the US could not yet again turn away, turn a blind eye" (Lander 2017). Both versions of the official explanation for the attack on Syria come up short if the purpose is to understand its underlying rationale. To bomb a Syrian airstrip with 59 tomahawk missiles, under the pretext of being moved by the death of children, sounds false. Nor does it seem realistic that he is principally committed to halt the use of weapons of mass destruction or engaged in a calculated battle plan. A more likely explanation is that the chemical attack provided Trump with a pretext to make a show of force. Not only has he succeeded in demonstrating that he is willing to act where Obama had not, he also showed unpredictability in acting so decisively in a matter that he, himself, had urged Obama not to act. In doing so, Trump effectively showed that he was willing to respond violently in unexpected cases where he had formulated no red lines and given no warning. This unpredictability and decisiveness seems to be central

---

[12] Retrieved from: https://www.nytimes.com/2017/04/07/world/middleeast/syria-attack-trump.html.

[13] See: https://www.nytimes.com/2017/04/07/world/middleeast/syria-attack-trump.html.

[14] See: https://www.nytimes.com/2017/04/07/world/middleeast/syria-attack-trump.html.

to Trump's foreign policy. Regardless of whether it was an emotional or strategic act, the missile strike has certainly marked an unexpected policy shift that established some new benchmarks in the new Trump administration's policy toward handling conflicts and wars in a region sending few messages worth considering.

THE CONCEIVABLE REASONING BEHIND THE SYRIAN ATTACK

The hasty arranged attack on Syria contains a number of messages, seemingly none addressed particularly to Syria. The Trump administration simply politicized the situation in an attempt to assert itself at the international level and to send messages to China, Russia, and Iran.

Message to China

At the time of the bombing, Trump was preparing for the Chinese President Xi Jinping's visit to the White House and he wanted to exude strength and authority. Attacking Syria prior to his meeting with Xi, and right after some tough talks on North Korea, seemed convenient, and served to further Trump's desired strong-man image. Such an approach is not without precedent in American domestic politics, and was popularized by former President Ronald Reagan. His decision to fire all 11,000 striking Air Traffic Control employees in August 1981 changed the Soviet's perception of the former actor-turned president. After this show of strength, Moscow considered Reagan a more serious adversary. During his campaign, Trump emphasized, particularly with regard to Reagan's legacy, that leadership style Trump experiences when it comes to managing foreign affairs. Like Reagan before him with Gorbachev and the Soviet politburo, President Trump had to prove to Xi Jinping that he is a man of action to ensure a balanced discourse on trade and North Korea. The Syrian attack signaled clearly that Trump, unlike his predecessor, would translate his threats into actions on the ground and that he had the resolve to carry his threats through to the end. In turn, he expects President Xi to give that same message to North Korea.

Message to Russia

The attack provided Trump with way of directly warning Russia, Syria's protector and ally. His warning had two objectives: he wanted to set the record straight that the US intends hereinafter to be an integral player in the Syrian conflict, and he wanted to let Putin know that he must contain Bashar al-Assad or the US is ready and willing to expand its military action. Under Trump, the US will no longer accept a peripheral role in Syria, nor will it allow al-Assad to flaunt openly Washington's red lines. Trump clearly intends to pursue a major change in the balance of power on the ground in the US's favor, by signaling that it, and not an alliance between Moscow and Tehran, will drive the solution.

Message to Iran

The attack sent a message directly to Iran. The US military strike on Syria coincided with the escalation of US pressures on Iran in response to its ballistic missile tests, which convinced the US that Iran is not acting in good faith. The message of the new US strike, which targeted Iran's closest regional ally, highlights that undermining Iran is one of the Trump administration priorities as they move forward. Convinced that it lacks the international support to abrogate the nuclear deal with Iran or reinstate international sanctions, the Trump administration is employing a range of tactics to pressure Iran into submission. However, the US strike, itself, has precipitated counter-warning signals from Iran and Russia. In their eyes, the US has crossed a red line by directly targeting the regime, and both states will respond to any future attack and continue to intensify their support for the Syrian regime.

The linkages between US actions in Syria and the previous attacks on Yemen, together with the new sanctions on Iran, have not escaped the attention of Tehran. Iranian political elites have repeatedly accused Washington of destabilizing the Middle East, which suggests that conflict between the two states will continue.[15] Such statements will only undermine the moderates in Iran and turn public support in favor of the hardliners, to the detriment of the nuclear deal.

In this context, the Trump administration must attempt to reconcile with Russia. The two powers need an understanding—a *déjà vu* of the Sykes-Picot carve-up of the Middle East into spheres of interest—created by the major power without the interfering voices of Iran, Saudi Arabia, and Turkey. Such an approach is not without risks, as Iran has

---

[15] See: http://sana.sy/en/?tag=iranian-shura-council.

invested too many military and financial resources in Iraq and Syria to accept exclusion from the endgame. However, Tehran's fears extend beyond the consequences of the US strike, and the regime has its eyes on the outcome of a potential rapprochement between the US and Russia concerning Syria and its implications on Iran's position in the region.

Though the strikes were meant to strengthen the US bargaining position at the negotiating table on Syria and to eliminate the emerging regional powers from the equation, the Trump administration has put at risk its number one regional priority: fighting ISIS. To achieve this goal, the Trump administration will need to rely on the help of Russia and Syria, two of the strongest foes of the Islamic State with the utmost dedication to exterminate it. The recent strikes in Syria risk alienating these crucial allies.

More important are the regional implications of the Trump administration's hasty and difficult-to-comprehend military actions. Many in the region remain suspicious of US intentions, regardless of which party controls the Executive Office, and the Trump's bellicose statements, could lend credence to those fears. Whether Trump has taken these daring steps merely in accord with his business risk intuitions or whether they are based on sound military and international relations tactics is debatable. It remains to be seen whether his foreign policy is on solid ground or whether it is a leap in the dark, the consequences and implications of which are unknown, perhaps even unknowable.

The Fight Against the Islamic State

It is critical to note first that Washington has been fighting its "War on Terror" since 9/11 without a long-term bipartisan strategy. It is needless to recall now that the US's arming of opposition forces in Afghanistan in the 1980s actually gave rise to the Taliban. By President Reagan calling the Taliban freedom fighters and comparing them with the anticolonial movements in their own war for independence, he gave them a holy mission to win over the Soviet Union. The copious military and financial support the Reagan administration provided the mujahedeen in Afghanistan, coupled with their apparent military success over the so-called evil empire confirmed the image of the rising Islamist movement, Al Qaeda. The narrative of Islamists as victorious freedom fighters quickly became the *raison d'être* for marginalized Islamists groups in Saudi Arabia and Egypt. This apparent victory over the Soviet Union galvanized extremist organizations, prompted the creation of transnational Islamist movements, and encouraged competing organizations to attempt increasingly spectacular attacks, culminating with the heinous 9/11 attack. The 2003 invasion on Iraq further exacerbated the situation by creating a power vacuum in the center of the Middle East and inciting public outrage across the Western world. Matters may have turned out differently had the Bush administration helped establish an effective Iraqi government, one commanding support from both the Sunni and Shia communities, instead of presenting Iraq on a silver plate to Iran. It is in this context that the demobilized and marginalized Sunni army emerged as the nucleus of the Islamic State.

Ironically, it seems that the havoc created by US support for the Taliban is not a lesson that has been learnedt from history. Today, prominent journalists advocate leaving the so-called Islamic State (ISIS) undefeated so as to make it al-Assad's, Iran's, Hezbollah's and Russia's headache—the same way the mujahedeen fighters were encouraged to bleed Russia in Afghanistan.[16] The idea of leaving Islamic State to become the final nail in al-Assad's coffin borders naivety, as the US will fail to contain the Islamist movement afterward, inasmuch as the world is still fighting the Taliban.

The intensified pressure on the Islamic State in Mosul (Iraq) and the missile attacks on Syria have prompted two Islamist organizations—the Islamic State and the El Sham Liberation Front (the "Victory Front" loyal to Al Qaeda in Syria")—to fall in each other's arms. Traditionally, they were hostile toward each other, but recently their leaders reached an agreement antithetical to past interactions. This reorganization of forces between the two extremist groups reflects pragmatic assessment of their shared objectives. First, this will reduce their losses and improve resilience in the face of the war of attrition to which they are exposed on numerous fronts. In addition to the well-publicized advances of Iraqi troops on the Islamic State stronghold in Mosul, the Syrian army was

---

[16] See: https://www.nytimes.com/2017/04/12/opinion/why-is-trump-fighting-isis-in-syria.html.

conducting its own successful war against Al Qaeda on its territory. Second, while facing a losing battle against Iraqi and Syrian forces, the two groups were keen to streamline the deployment their forces in the field, focusing on the most pressing enemy, and positioning troops so as to minimize their losses. It is no longer a war for supremacy between the two groups, but a war for their mutual survival against the US and its allies. This pragmatic and tactical agreement between the Islamic State and the El Nusra Front means an expansion of Al Qaeda's power and strengthening of its influence not only in Syria but also in Libya and Yemen, without any domestic competition between the two major Islamist factions. The new Trump administration will certainly have to acknowledge these changes on the ground and be prepared to adjust policy decisions accordingly.

In his inaugural speech, President Trump pledged: "We will reinforce old alliances and form new ones—and unite the civilized world against radical Islamic terrorism, which we will eradicate from the face of the Earth."[17] He vowed that defeating the Islamic State would be one of his key priorities and he heavily criticized the Obama administration for not taking serious measures against it.[18] Once *in situ*, Trump ordered his Secretary of Defense to put together a new strategy to defeat the Islamic State forces in Syria and Iraq.[19] The new secret plan submitted by the Pentagon is said to be including different military, diplomatic, and financial tactics.[20] The Trump administration seems to embrace the five-point plan—the Five Lines of Effort—set by the NATO back in 2014. This plan includes:[21]

1. Providing military support to our partners;
2. Impeding the flow of foreign fighters;

---

[17] Retrieved from: https://www.washingtontimes.com/news/2017/jan/20/donald-trump-we-will-eradicate-radical-islamic-ter/.

[18] See: http://www.washingtontimes.com/news/2017/jan/20/donald-trump-we-will-eradicateradical-islamic-ter/.

[19] See: http://edition.cnn.com/2017/02/27/politics/thepentagon-has-sent-isis-options-to-the-white-house/.

[20] See: http://edition.cnn.com/2017/02/27/politics/thepentagon-has-sent-isis-options-to-the-white-house/.

[21] See: https://www.defense.gov/OIR/.

3. Stopping foreign financing and funding;
4. Addressing humanitarian crises in the region, and
5. Exposing the true nature of the Islamic State.

On Monday May 8, Trump authorized the Department of Defense to arm the Syrian Kurdish militia—the Syrian Kurdish Peoples' Protection Units (YPG)—to fight against the Islamic State in Syria and recapture Raqqa.[22] This announcement has greatly upset the Turkish government that considers the YPG as terrorist organization in its own right. This move is expected to shake the long-term American-Turkish relations over the question of the Kurds.

It is still debatable whether the Trump administration has shown any signs of defeating Islamic State during its first 100 days. It is true that in Iraq, Islamic State has lost much of its land, reducing the territory it controls from one-third of the country to a mere 7%.[23] According to the same source, however, this retreat is *a priori* not attributable to Trump, as his administration only followed through with plans originally implemented by the Pentagon during the Obama administration. On the contrary, the feeling is that Trump, with his strike on Syria, has detoured from the priority of defeating the Islamic State. In doing so, he has also antagonized the Syrian regime and Russia, two solid supporters in the fight against the Islamic State. Nowadays, even Turkey seems less preoccupied with fighting the Islamic State and more invested in facilitating Erdogan's rise to become the most powerful Turkish leader since Atatürk, under the purported justification of giving the civilian government control over the military. Moreover, Turkey's actions, in contrast to the US approach, focus on Kurdish militias in Iraq and Syria, which are viewed by the US as the most effective partners for countering the Islamic State.

The Trump administration is yet to articulate a military strategy to defeat the Islamic State, decrease the number of jihadists, or undermine the group's ability to recruit. It will have to explore new and more effec-

---

[22] See: http://edition.cnn.com/2017/05/10/middleeast/syriaus-turkey-trump-arms-kurds/.
[23] See: www.cnn.com/video/world/2017/28/president-donald-trump-track-record-fighting-isis-100-days-pkg-walsh-cnn.

tive multi-faceted polices to weaken the appeal and capacity of the Islamic State. Escalating drone attacks and taking out the so-called leaders of different extremist movements do not dislodge their organizations or lessen their support. It is true that the Trump administration has flexed its muscles, intensified its counter-terrorism deployments, and carried out air strikes in Yemen, Iraq, and Syria. However, it remains open to debate, to what extent these policies have deterred the Islamic State or decreased its capacity.

EGYPT: AN IMPORTANT PARTNER TO THE US

Long gone are the days when Egypt was considered the make-or-break player in the region, when both Kissinger's and Carter's Middle East diplomacy relied on Egypt as the lynchpin. Egypt was an essential player and the "key to war and peace in the Middle East. If Egypt chose peace, other Arab states would eventually follow, and if they did not, at least there would be no full-fledged wars" (Quandt 1986, 358). As the Arab Spring unleashed disorganization and created political voids, the regional power equilibrium tilted toward outside forces, particularly Iran and Turkey. Yet, Egypt has shielded itself from the lingering violence of the Arab Spring syndrome and rebuilt the political system without disintegration or civil war. Egypt did not shy away from its fight against Islamic extremism, even when the name of the political game was inclusiveness. There should be no doubt in the minds of the international community that Egypt is, and always will be, a staunch ally in the War on Terror.

It is important for Egypt to think independently, to charter its own political course and evaluate what is best for itself and the region. The differences between Saudi Arabia and Iran are at the heart of many conflicts in the region and present one of the largest and thorniest challenges. Many political commentators and academics have come to believe that Iran is part of the regional equation.[24] At no time, however, does this condone or tolerate egregious Iranian actions in the Arab World, but it does seek to emphasize the importance of understanding Iran's intentions. In an interview reported in *Al-Masry Al-Youm* (January 17), the Egyptian

---

[24] For a more in depth discussion on Iran's role in the region, see: Karagiannis (2016) and Modell (2014).

Foreign Minister has recently not ruled out a dialogue between Cairo and Tehran, if the latter changes its approach.

Iran will need to reorient its foreign policy approach to gain regional acceptance. Indeed, Egypt will need to come to terms with Iran sooner rather than later if it is to play a role in the emerging regional order. When the time is ripe and the Islamic State is defeated, there will be a dire need for a political solution to the region's conflicts. Egypt, with the cooperation of countries known for their independence, most notably, Oman, can set a new trajectory for dialogue and understanding toward ending this continuing drift into sectarianism and proxy conflicts.

Yet, the question of who would support Egypt's mediation role and how Cairo would position itself remain wide open. First, it is not too far-fetched to consider the US, or even Israel, as potential behind-the-scene partners, since they both have a stake in the stability of the Middle East. Second, Egypt will have to coordinate closely with Saudi Arabia, which is an ally that Egypt cannot afford to lose. Finally, Egypt will have to lure small but crucial regional players, such as Jordan, to play a part in order to pave the way for a new trajectory. There is a need for a new discourse between the Arab countries, one that accepts Iran as a new regional power; yet, not a power that interferes in the Arab region.

It is also evident that President Trump is a political realist who sees international relations through a transactional lens. Egypt can be a partner in the battle against international terrorism, if in Trump's calculation, that is more important to the US than concerns over any suppression of domestic dissent. On this issue, Trump does not differ from previous American presidents or other political leaders who pursued the same approach regardless of their political rhetoric. To allege that Trump differs from his predecessors in this regard is to misunderstand fundamentally both US presidential history and the realist paradigm of international relations. Moreover, describing Trump's human rights policies as representing a fundamental shift in US foreign policy toward support of authoritarian dictators is to ignore Washington's decades of support for authoritarian regimes in the region, particularly in the Gulf.

After the meeting between Presidents el-Sisi and Trump, Egypt could become more proactive and refrain from the wait-and-see approach, which characterized its policy toward Turkey during the Obama era. Egypt is capable of returning to its historic role as a regional mediator and power player, but Egypt's top two priorities should be fighting the Islamist insurgents and securing assistance for its economy, both of which will decide upon its future stability and regional power. In this context, the new Trump administration realizes that there is no alternative but to help Egypt reclaim its traditional role in the region. In a turbulent region, Egypt will have to calibrate very prudently and sensibly its future steps between conflicting poles and critical impasses. In that regard, Egypt should also be prepared to deal with the more dangerous objectives of Turkey in the region.

THE PALESTINIAN-ISRAELI CONFLICT

The Palestinian-Israeli conflict remains close to Egypt's heart and mind. This conflict, perpetually relegated to the backburner, continues to be the cornerstone of the regional order. In spite of some apparent attempts by Presidents Sadat and Carter at Camp David to bring the Palestinian issue to the negotiating table, Israel would not agree to any meaningful concessions to the Palestinians. The American Jewish lobby was also not helpful, thereby allowing the Palestinian issue to fall out of the priorities of US leaders, as they did not want to compromise their domestic support (Quandt 1986, 361). Indeed, until now, the Palestine question still hangs over the Middle East.

Trump has spoken of his ability and willingness to negotiate a deal between the Israelis and Palestinians. One cannot but take such eagerness with a grain of salt because of the intricacies of the conflict and the taboos set by the parties involved. Revealing his personal preference for a one-state solution to the Arab-Israeli conflict few weeks after taking office indicates that Trump had begun the process on the wrong foot. Taking Netanyahu's side and contradicting two decades of US support for a two-state policy (Shapiro 2017) does not augur well for a neutral mediator. However, a positive sign seems to have emerged from his meetings with Egypt's President el-Sisi and Jordan's King Abdullah II. The decision to hold a summit in Washington for regional actors, including Israel and the Palestinians, in order to reach a deal to solve the

Palestinian issue, is a giant step after years of stalemate and a total breakdown in the negotiations under the Obama administration. If the Arab League Summit held in Amman this past April succeeded in anything, it was mandating King Abdullah of Jordan to share with Trump the Arab position on the Palestinian issue. The King clearly reiterated that the basis of any solution remains the establishment of a Palestinian state within the 1967 borders, with East Jerusalem as its capital, living in peace alongside the State of Israel. It reaffirms the principle of all land in exchange for a durable, equitable peace, and the inevitability of a two-state solution. It ensures normal, peaceful relations between Israel and the Arabs to achieve peace and security for all the countries of the Middle East. Both el-Sisi and King Abdullah confirmed this clearly articulated position during a time when the new Trump administration is still in the process of crystallizing its policies in the Middle East.

If Trump is determined to reach a durable solution to the Palestinian-Israeli conflict, he will have to deal directly with the remaining four contentious issues: security, refugees, territory, and Jerusalem. Much of the solution will depend on the alliance forged between the Secretary of State, Rex Tillerson, and Trump's Middle East adviser, his son-in-law Jared Kushner. While the State Department will cater to Tillerson's more traditional position, the expectation is that Jared Kushner will push in the opposite direction, in the light of his well-known Jewish background and his support for Israel. In this regard, Egypt, as well as Jordan, can serve as the US partner and intermediaries. Egypt was the first in the region to recognize Israel, and today the two countries have established a relationship based on mutual and successful cooperation in the Sinai in order to counter terrorism and to fight the Islamic State. At the same time, Egypt is a staunch supporter of the Palestinians and also has solid relations with the Palestinian leadership, which mandated el-Sisi to speak on their behalf in his encounter with Trump. Egypt has also a considerable sway with the new leadership of Hamas, an organization viewed as a potential spoiler for any peace process. After 22 years of imprisonment in Israeli jail, Yehia Sinwar has taken over from Ismail Hanniya in the Gaza Strip and now must make a tough decision between relying more heavily on Iran to strengthen the military power of Hamas, or heeding to the sufferings and misery of the people in the

Gaza Strip and deciding to reconcile with Egypt. If Hamas chooses conciliation, this means another winning card and the indispensable Egyptian role in the region.

Conclusion

There is no doubt that President Trump has reinvigorated US policy in the Middle East and has distanced himself from Barack Obama's approach. The people and leadership of the Middle East are firmly convinced that President Trump has shown interest and resolve in the region, but all remain cautious after their experience with his predecessor. The new Trump administration has expressed interest in finding solutions to the many intractable conflicts, which are exacerbated by a twofold problem: the Islamic State and the growing confrontational ambitions of Iran and Turkey. The Trump administration has also resolved to be part of the solution in Syria, by rejecting Russia's attempts to sideline it. Though policies undertaken in the region are still fresh and need to be tested, the one matter that is clear is that the US will readily disengage from the Middle East in favor of other regions. This said, the impact of Trump's rhetoric and actions in his first 100 days on the Middle Eastern region cannot be assessed in isolation of the changing environment around the world—including the mainstream populism now spreading in Europe, potentially to the detriment of a strong and stable European Union, which includes political fallout that could follow the United Kingdom's Brexit, and the rise of China and Russia, and, of course, the existential threat posed by North Korea. Closer to home in the Middle East, the change of heart in Turkey and its decision to grant the power of dictatorship to its leader is yet another daunting challenge. If excluded or denied a voice in the region, Turkey will not hesitate to play an irritating role and, of most concern, Turkey's authoritarian regime allegedly asserts that it is entitled a leadership role in the region. With an antagonized Iran, a disappointed Turkey, and a frustrated Russia, the region now faces a new triangle of opposition to a more engaged US administration. This has already diminished Russia's goodwill and Iran's readiness to participate in the fight against the Islamic State. The endgame of the two powers—the US and Russia—has reversed. Instead of managing the region together, each is now competing to exclude the other.

After 100 days into the Trump presidency, ambiguity and bewilderment continue to frame US foreign policy in general and its policy in the Middle East in particular. It is bordering on naive to think that it is possible to anticipate or predict future foreign policies of the Trump administration on the basis of Trump's parochial rhetoric and erratic presidential actions over his first 100 days. His two campaign foreign policy priorities—defeating the Islamic State and dismantling of what he saw as the catastrophic Iranian nuclear deal—have taken a backseat, overtaken by the firm resolve to destroy his predecessor's foreign policy positions. Though the early signs of his presidency indicate some successes in the region—notably, his positive meetings with regional leaders and his decision to at least forestall moving the embassy to Jerusalem—his major disappointments—notably, his heavy-handed bombing campaigns and his disorganized approach to combatting ISIS—do not augur well. It is unprecedented that a Republican President and a Republican-controlled Congress have failed to bond on any major foreign policy issue. Little that has happened in the first 100 days of the Trump presidency has matched Candidate Trump's rhetoric or his supporters' expectations. On the contrary, his administration has acted where least expected, leaving much room for speculation as to where he is heading and why.

In many ways, Trump is resistant to traditional ideological constraints that could limit his actions. If we can define Trump's initial foreign policy doctrine, it is by his commitment to unilateral interventionism and his willingness to change his mind about fundamental political issues. It is still too early to tell whether the protean nature of Trump will be established as the foundation of his foreign policy strategy and future doctrine, or whether it will prove that he has no doctrine. Experts and analysts are still looking for a Trump strategy in the Middle East, especially after his erratic attacks in Syria, Yemen, and for that matter Afghanistan. All three countries are facing unique and complex crises, where local tensions are intertwined with regional and international tensions. But the region must come to terms with dealing with a non-traditional US president, one who does not abide by—even rejects—the traditional principles of international relations. Moreover, his first 100 days cannot confirm that President Donald J. Trump has a clear vision about the prevailing crises in the Middle East, or their dimensions, causes, implications, or methods of resolution.

References

American University of Cairo. 2017. *Roundtable Discussion (April 26): "Is a Coherent Policy in Yemen Still Possible?"* Speakers: Mohamed Badr Eldin Zayed, Former Egyptian Ambassador to Yemen, and Shoki Maktary, Yemen Country Director. Cairo: American University of Cairo.

Begley, S. 2016. "Read Donald Trump's Full Speech to AIPAC." *Time*, March 21. Available at: http://time.com/4267058/donald-trump-aipac-speech-transcript/.

Boghardt, L. and S. Henderson. 2017. "Rebuilding Alliances and Countering Threats in the Gulf." Washington, DC: The Washington Institute for Near East Policy. Available at: http://www.washingtoninstitute.org/policy-analysis/view/rebuilding-alliances-and-countering-threats-in-the-gulf.

Hoffman, A. 2017. "Syria Missile Attack: What Donald Trump's Old Tweets Say." *Time*, April 7. Available at: http://time.com/4730219/syria-missile-attack-donald-trump-tweets/.

Karagiannis, E. 2016. "The Rise of Iran as a Regional Power: Shia Empowerment and Its Limits." *NATO Review*. Available at: https://www.nato.int/docu/review/2016/Also-in-2016/iran-regional-power-tehran-islamic/EN/index.htm.

McLeary, D.D. 2017. "Trump's Ramped-Up Bombing in Yemen Signals More Aggressive Use of Military." *Foreign Policy*, March 9. Available at: http://foreignpolicy.com/2017/03/09/trumps-ramped-up-bombing-in-yemen-signals-more-aggressive-use-of-military/.

Modell, S. 2016. "Iran's Destabilizing Role in the Middle East." *Testimony before the US House Foreign Affairs Committee on 16 July 2014*. Available at: http://docs.house.gov/meetings/FA/FA00/20140716/102496/HHRG-113-FA00-Wstate-ModellS-20140716.pdf.

Quandt, W.B. 1986. "Camp David and Peacemaking in the Middle East." *Political Science Quarterly*, 101 (3): 357–377.

Rahim, Z. 2017. "President Trump's Syria Policy Changes in a Week:

Timeline." *Time*, April 7. Available at: http://time.com/4730494/trump-syria-chemical-weapons-idlib-intervention/.

Schaefer, B. 2016. "Where Does Donald Trump Stand on Israel? *Haaretz*, November 10. Available at: http://www.haaretz.com/world-news/u-s-election-2016/1.720213.

Shapiro, D. 2017. "Trump Sounds Like Obama on Israeli Settlements." *Foreign Policy*, February 3. Available at: http://foreignpolicy.com/2017/02/03/trump-sounds-like-obama-on-israeli-settlements/.

Wright, R. 2017. "Trump Drops the Mother of All Bombs on Afghanistan." *New Yorker*, April 14. Available at: http://www.newyorker.com/news/news-desk/trump-drops-the-mother-of-all-bombs-on-afghanistan.

11
DONALD TRUMP AND CHINA

Klaus Larres

INTRODUCTION

Presidential candidate Donald J. Trump shouted at a campaign rally in Fort Wayne, Indiana, on May 1, 2016, "We can't continue to allow China to rape our country and that's what they are doing," with their unfair trade policy. With this rather inappropriate phrase, which Trump had first used in 2011,[1] the 2016 presidential election campaign reached its ugly high point.[2] China remained a foreign policy focus throughout the long electoral battle. Critical and frequently hostile comments about Beijing's policies continued to be heard from almost all presidential candidates, but most frequently from Donald Trump. He kept saying that he wanted to "Make America Great Again" and for him it was clear, "America First." The rather unrestrained Trump never grew tired of accusing Beijing of currency manipulation and of "killing" the US with its trade practices that had resulted in America's huge trade deficit with China. The latter, he claimed, had also been the reason for US firms moving jobs from America to China to exploit the country's much cheaper labor market. Trump, of course, eventually obtained the nomination of the Republican Party and went on to become the 45th US president.

This chapter analyzes China's ambitious strategies, as they have been advocated by Xi Jinping since 2012–2013, may help to understand its goals, objectives, and responses to Donald J. Trump's China policy since taking office. It considers Trump's frequently overblown rhetoric but mostly focuses on his objectives and still developing strategy of how to deal with China geopolitically and in terms of trade relations and the intractable North Korea problem. China is the country that has pre-occupied US foreign policy for some time.

---

[1] See: http://www.nytimes.com/2011/04/28/us/politics/28trump.html.
[2] See: http://www.mid-day.com/articles/china-is-raping-our-country-says-donald-trump/17189185.

Chinese President Xi Jinping's Dream

It is wrong to assume that relations with China sharply worsened because of Trump's election campaign and his eventual move into the Oval Office. It was in the course of President Barack Obama's two terms in office that relations with China deteriorated and, at times, were rather tense, particular since 2012–2013 when Xi Jinping became President of the People's Republic of China,[3] and soon embarked on his own assertive and proactive policy of making China great again. Xi worked "tirelessly," as he claimed in 2017, "for the great success of socialism with Chinese characteristics for a new era." His prime objective was to realize the "Chinese Dream for national rejuvenation," as he was fond of saying.[4]

From an early stage of his leadership, Xi expressed the view that China had evolved into a "major power."[5] Already in 2012, Xi had referred to a "new type of great power relations," which seemed to be all about China sharing global leadership with the US and putting Beijing on equal terms with Washington. But, establishing a "constructive partnership" with Washington might entail dividing up the world into spheres of influences, as the Obama administration thought. Xi's dream, officials in Washington feared, might entail pushing the US gradually out of the Pacific and making China the hegemonic power in Asia within a short period of time (Chen 2014, Zeng 2016). Observers in Washington and other Western capitals were becoming increasingly doubtful that, in the long run, Beijing would be happy with continuing to play second fiddle to the global leadership role that the US has assumed since World War II. This particularly applied in China's own backyard—the Asia-Pacific region, including the South China Sea—where China was unlikely to accept continued US dominance. Trump therefore frequently refers to the region as the Indo-Pacific area to include India, a US ally, and so

---

[3] He also became General Secretary of the Communist Party of China Chairman of the Central Military Commission.

[4] See the beginning of Xi's long opening speech (work report) to the 19th Party Congress in November 2017 as published in translation by Xinghua press agency on November 4, 201. Retrieved from: http://www.chinadaily.com.cn/china/19thcpcnationalcongress/2017-11/04/content_34115212.htm.

[5] Retrieved from: https://www.nytimes.com/2014/12/01/world/asia/leader-asserts-chinas-growing-role-on-global-stage.html.

demonstrate to China that there are other strong and important powers in the region.[6] Whether or not this accounts for a new American vision or grand strategy for South-East Asia, as some commentators believe, remains to be seen.[7]

Already in the early years of his chairmanship of the Communist Party and his presidency, Xi and his colleagues in the all-powerful seven-member Standing Committee of the Politburo believed they could detect clear signs of hubris, incompetence, indecision and a lack of will in the White House. The global financial and economic crisis that had begun in the US in 2008 made a deep impact on the leaders in Beijing. Wan Qishan, one of China's most experienced statesman who would become Xi's anti-corruption czar, told US Treasury Secretary Hank Paulson, in the same year, with an air of triumphalism "'You were my teacher,'" but "Look at your system, Hank. We aren't sure we should be learning from you anymore"[8] (see also Paulson 2015). Xi seems to have concluded that the US was a declining power and that the world was inevitably moving toward an era of multi-polarity with China playing a dominant—if not *the* dominant—role in the future. Xi became convinced that the twenty-first century was the Chinese century."[9] In various speeches and statements, he made it clear that by 2049—at the latest—the hundredth anniversary of the Chinese communist revolution, China aspired to have become the world's leading power. But China's ambitious industrial plan—"Made in China 2025" was unveiled in 2015.[10] By the mid-2020s, China intends to become the world leader in a number of important new technologies, such as in the semiconductor and chip industry, the Artificial Intelligence

---

[6] See: https://www.politico.com/story/2017/11/07/trump-asia-indo-pacific-244657; https://www.ft.com/content/e6d17fd6-c623-11e7-a1d2-6786f39ef675; http://www.businessinsider.com/trump-indo-pacific-asia-pacific-china-asia-trip-2017-2017-117.

[7] See, for instance: http://www.scmp.com/news/china/diplomacy-defence/article/2120521/opinion-donald-trump-needs-more-words-make-his-vision.

[8] Retrieved from: https://www.ft.com/content/d82964ba-6d42-11e7-bfeb-33fe0c5b7eaa. See also: http://foreignpolicy.com/2015/04/16/xi-jinpings-problems-are-monumental-henry-paulson-interview/.

[9] See: http://nationalinterest.org/feature/does-china-think-america-decline-15042?page=show.

[10] For an excellent overview see: https://www.nytimes.com/2017/11/07/business/made-in-china-technology-trade.html.

industry and the post-fossil-fuel car industry with its focus on electric or battery driven cars (known in China as new energy vehicles).[11]

Although by 2025 Xi will have been long retired, he clearly wants to go down in history as the founding father of China's coming new global importance. To achieve this goal, it appears that Xi's method consists of, as Hines (2015) put it, "creeping assertiveness in the maritime domain, conciliatory rhetoric, and economic engagement," in the developing world, such as in Africa, or with the help of his grand Belt and Road Initiative. This new Silk Road, proposed in 2015, envisages huge infrastructure projects and the construction of a vast new network of transcontinental roads and railway tracks. The development of a maritime silk road is part of this scheme. This massive new transportation and infrastructure program is expected to connect China to Europe via much of Central Asia, the Middle East, and Southeast Asia.[12] In addition, Xi's China has also discovered the value of "soft power" and has begun to focus on enhancing China's cultural and spiritual appeal.[13]

Xi Jinping's most detailed outline of his objectives occurred in his long opening speech to the 2,300 delegates of the 19th National Congress of the Communist Party of China in the Great Hall of the People in Beijing on October 18. The Party Congress would approve Xi's appointment to a second five-year term, and his elevation to almost-equal status with Mao and Deng, which is the beginning of a personality cult, as well as the positioning of his confidants in important party jobs. He spoke about reinforcing the role of the Communist Party in all aspects of China's life and promised to continue his anti-corruption drive. In his

---

[11] See, for instance: http://money.cnn.com/2017/07/21/technology/china-artificial-intelligence-future/index.html; http://www.news.com.au/technology/innovation/design/china-announces-goal-of-ai-leadership-by-2030/news-story/331bf2fc0994b0f3c68a87280fdc33e1; https://www.computerworld.com/article/2491172/computer-processors/china-wants-to-be-the-global-leader-in-chip-manufacturing-by-2030.html.

[12] See: https://www.theatlantic.com/international/archive/2017/10/china-belt-and-road/542667/; https://thediplomat.com/2017/10/the-belt-and-road-initiative-and-the-future-of-globalization/; https://www.economist.com/blogs/economist-explains/2017/05/economist-explains-11.

[13] See: https://www.economist.com/news/china/21719508-can-money-buy-sort-thing-china-spending-billions-make-world-love-it; https://thediplomat.com/2017/09/why-chinas-soft-power-solution-lies-in-its-past/.

opening work-report speech, Xi explained that, above all, he wished to "accomplish the three historic tasks of advancing modernization, realizing China's reunification, and preserving world peace and promoting common development."[14]

Quite rightly, Xi recognized at the beginning of his speech that both "China and the world are in the midst of profound and complex changes." He believed that his country was "still in an important period of strategic opportunity for development." He was convinced that "the prospects are bright but the challenges are severe." In his speech, Xi proudly lists all the many impressive economic, social, and not least strategic and military achievements and bureaucratic reforms that China made during the last five years, when he was at the helm. He referred to over 1,500 reform measures. The "Chinese dream of national rejuvenation," Xi proclaimed, "will be an era that sees China moving closer to center stage and making greater contributions to mankind."[15]

In his speech, Xi did not hesitate to taunt Trump about his economic nationalism policy by explaining "openness brings progress, while self-seclusion leaves one behind. China will not close its door to the world; we will only become more and more open." Harking back to his acclaimed speech at the Davos Global Economic Forum in January, just a few days before Trump was inaugurated, Xi explained that the Belt and Road Initiative was part of China "going global." This also included the expansion of foreign trade, the development of "new models and new forms of trade," that would "turn China into a trader of quality."[16]

Xi, however, appears to have listened to the great deal of outside criticism regarding China's trade practices. Beijing, he pronounced in his speech, would "significantly ease market access, further open the ser-

---

[14] Xi's speech (work report) to the 19th Party Congress in November 2017 (as published in translation by Xinghua press agency on November 4, 2017), 64. Retrieved from: http://www.chinadaily.com.cn/china/19thcpcnationalcongress/2017-11/04/content_34115212.htm.

[15] Xi's speech (work report) to the 19th Party Congress in November 2017, 9. Retrieved from: http://www.chinadaily.com.cn/china/19thcpcnationalcongress/2017-11/04/content_34115212.htm.

[16] Xi's speech (work report) to the 19th Party Congress in November 2017, 30. Retrieved from: http://www.chinadaily.com.cn/china/19thcpcnationalcongress/2017-11/04/content_34115212.htm.

vice sector, and protect the legitimate rights and interests of foreign investors." Western businessmen were certainly delighted to hear that "all businesses registered in China will be treated equally." Great skepticism remains, however, whether or not these words will be implemented in practice.[17] Still, Xi was attempting to position China "as a stable alternative to the United States," as the *New York Times* observed.[18] Beijing wants to come across as "willing to take on the obligations of global leadership and invest in big infrastructure projects across Asia and Europe much as the United States did after World War II."[19]

Xi felt that emphasizing China's strong support for globalization was so important that he came back to the topic at a later stage in his long speech. "China adheres to the fundamental national policy of opening up and pursues development with its doors open wide," he said. "China will actively promote international cooperation through the Belt and Road initiative. In doing so, we hope to achieve policy, infrastructure, trade, financial, and people-to-people connectivity and thus build a new platform for international cooperation to create new drivers of shared development." Xi emphasized, "China will support multilateral trade regimes and work to facilitate the establishment of free trade areas and build an open world economy."[20]

Xi also briefly referred to matters of war and peace in his speech. While "no one should expect us to swallow anything that undermines our interests," he thundered ominously, but then continued by saying that "China pursues a national defense policy that is in nature defensive. China's development does not pose a threat to any other country. No matter what stage of development it reaches, China will never seek hegemony or engage in expansion."[21]

---

[17] Xi's speech (work report) to the 19th Party Congress in November 2017, 30. Retrieved from: http://www.chinadaily.com.cn/china/19thcpcnationalcongress/2017-11/04/content_34115212.htm.

[18] Retrieved from: https://www.nytimes.com/2017/11/06/world/asia/trump-xi-jinping-visit-china.htm.

[19] Retrieved from: https://www.nytimes.com/2017/11/06/world/asia/trump-xi-jinping-visit-china.htm.

[20] Xi's speech (work report) to the 19th Party Congress in November 2017, 54. Retrieved from: http://www.chinadaily.com.cn/china/19thcpcnationalcongress/2017-11/04/content_34115212.htm.

[21] Xi's speech (work report) to the 19th Party Congress in November 2017, 53. Re-

Naturally, these words were widely welcomed, but skepticism about China's assertive foreign policy has been on the rise in the US and elsewhere in the West since at least 2014–2015. In the Western world, the China hawks dominate the discussion at present. Comparing the rise of China with the rise of other countries in centuries past has almost developed into a cottage industry.[22] It is, however, too simplistic to juxtapose the US-Chinese economic competition and geopolitical rivalry in Asia and worldwide with the battle for hegemony between Athens and Sparta in the ancient world or between imperialist Germany and Britain in the early twentieth century. The existence of a "Thukydides Trap" may only exist in the lively imagination of Graham Allison who has coined this term (Allison 2017). The phrase refers to a rather black and white battle for economic and military supremacy between Beijing and Washington that may well end up in a military conflict between the two great powers.

A military clash, therefore, between the US and China in the twenty-first century is by no means unavoidable or likely. Despite all the tension that has been slowly increasing over the last 10 years or so, China and the US are keen on the escalation of their economic and geopolitical rivalry. So, when Trump became President in January 2017, this did not suddenly open a new era of friction in US-Chinese relations. Although his hostile rhetoric during the 2016 election campaign had not helped to improve matters, bilateral relations between Washington and Beijing had already developed in a rather difficult and tense way under Trump's predecessor.

THE US AND CHINA RELATIONS BEFORE TRUMP: THE OBAMA ADMINISTRATION AND ITS WORLD VIEW

It has been difficult to discern Obama's view on America's future position in global affairs, including his vision for US-Chinese relations (see Chollet 2016, Dueck 2015, Greenberg 2016). Initially, Obama can be characterized as quite idealistic. After a few years, however, toward the end of his first term and certainly by the beginning of his second term in

---

trieved from: http://www.chinadaily.com.cn/china/19thcpcnationalcongress/2017-11/04/content_34115212.htm.
22 See: http://www.nybooks.com/articles/2017/10/12/chinese-world-order/.

2013, he grew increasingly cynical. He soon began to believe in a much more neorealist conception of America's role in global affairs. He certainly moved toward a much more pragmatic approach. He focused on what is doable rather than on all his many desirable objectives. He, however, continued to share the long-standing belief of the Washington foreign policy establishment that the US was the indispensable country in global affairs—a benign hegemon—even despite exceptions to the rule such as America's ill-advised and unnecessary wars in Vietnam and Iraq. He stopped viewing the US as the world's omnipotent policeman. This, he believed, would overstretch the country's resources. Trump would agree with his reasoning.

For Obama, a multilateral world had arrived, particularly with the rise of China and India. It was crucially important, therefore, to understand that no country could possibly fulfill the role of global policeman in view of the ever more complex and intricate problems facing the twenty-first century world. Consequently, he decided to focus US foreign policy on those issues that were absolutely essential for America and the West's future wellbeing, such as the environment and dealing with Russia and China.

Obama and his first Secretary of State, Hillary Clinton, had become convinced that the Asia and the Pacific region were of the highest relevance for the future of US power, influence, and security. This gave rise to his so-called Asian pivot (Campbell 2016, Southgate 2017,). Clearly, it was the rise of China that motivated Obama's foreign policy shift. But, this change in policy was only hesitatingly followed up by concrete action on the ground (Bader 2012). In practice, it turned out to be much less of a shift than the rhetoric implied. As a concept, the pivot was meant to allow Washington to "manage" Beijing's increasingly influential global role. Not least China's assertive claims on the sea, reefs, rocks, and islands within the so-called nine-dash-line, and thus over 80% of the South China Sea, which worried the US and many of America's Southeast Asian allies. The July 12, 2016 decision by the UN arbitration court in The Hague that went almost entirely against China's long-standing legal and historically grounded positions on the South China Sea question, but it did not have a decisive impact. Most countries in the area soon felt they had no choice but to accommodate China's assertive behavior in the South China Sea. China was simply too important both as a geopolitical factor and as a trading partner.

This, however, was an unexpected development for America. After all, part of the "pivot to Asia" was Obama's intensive wooing of a significant number of China's fourteen neighbors in Asia. His administration attempted to channel the genuine security fears of these countries regarding Beijing's potential hegemonic role in the region into a pro-American direction. The successfully negotiated 12-nation Trans-Pacific Partnership (TTP) had a similar function in the economic realm. It was meant to prolong US influence as the dominant and most influential trading partner for Asia that would continue enabling it to set trade rules and standards well into the future. Of course, from the point of view of the Obama White House, it would also have positive geopolitical implications. While many Asian countries signed up to the trade deal finalized in October 2015—and Washington made sure that China was not among them—it was never ratified by the US (Elms 2016).

Obama's overall strategy in the Asia-Pacific, thus, consisted of his attempt to "manage" China's increasingly dominant role in Asia. He wanted to steer that important country into a more cooperative way in both security and economic affairs, which he considered necessary if a constructive working relationship with China was to be achieved.

Donald Trump's Conceptual Foreign Policy Objectives

In contrast, it has been difficult to discern the conceptual principles and strategies that have guided the Trump administration's foreign policy in general and toward China in particular. The one overriding driving force for Trump's domestic and foreign policies has proved to be his election campaign slogans—"Make America Great Again" and "America First." However, precise definitions of these rather vague and all-encompassing terms are difficult to come by though, they clearly correspond well with the mood and desire of Trump's core support base. Nevertheless, the loose phrases do not provide any conceptual clarity; in fact, they muddy the water. Anything and everything can be subsumed under them on the spur of the moment. And. it often is (see, for example, Mills 2016, Nehlen, 2017).

One of the few more concrete driving forces that can be detected in Trump's global political agenda is the importance he attaches to his and his country's status and image, and its right to act according to its sovereign national interests. During his first speech to the UN General Assembly on September 19, for instance, Trump focused on the idea of national sovereignty and declared that the conduct of all nations on earth ought to be governed primarily by this idea. It appears his is a rather simplistic notion of global affairs and how the world ought to be run: "I will always put America first, just like you, as the leaders of your countries, will always and should always put your countries first," he pronounced. "As long as I hold this office," Trump told the assembled global luminaries, "I will defend America's interest above all else." He expressed the belief that US success in the world "depends on a coalition of strong, independent nations that embrace their sovereignty, to promote security, prosperity, and peace for themselves and for the world."[23]

Instead of having developed a global vision for America, Trump is limiting his objective to the simple desire that he and his country are treated with servile respect and indeed deference. He also believes that the US is entitled to undertake unilateral action. While abhorring multilateral structures, he is keen on bilateral negotiations and deals with other nations that Washington can more easily dominate.

Many countries have learned to exploit Trump's rather superficial desires. This became most obvious during his state visit to Saudi Arabia in mid-May 2017, a visit some commentators have viewed as a rather "bizarre" diplomatic episode.[24] Trump's 12-day visit to five Asian nations in November 2017 also demonstrated this inclination. It has become obvious that Trump is not really interested in delving too deeply into some of the hard-nosed substantive issues of international affairs. He also never inconveniences his authoritarian counterparts by espousing the values of democracy and human rights.[25] Trump has both a value

---

[23] For the text of Trump's UN speech, see: https://www.politico.com/story/2017/09/19/trump-un-speech-2017-full-text-transcript-242879.

[24] Retrieved from: https://www.washingtonpost.com/news/global-opinions/wp/2017/05/21/trumps-bizarre-and-un-american-visit-to-saudi-arabia/?utm_term=.879849cd6f00.

[25] See: http://time.com/5016665/trump-asia-trip-highlights/; https://www.

and an ego-problem, it seems. He can be easily accommodated with the offer of some good but short-term business deals and by giving him the impression that his words and frequently impulsive and inaccurate statements are taken seriously and really matter. Trump wishes to come across as relevant, although, in fact, he actively contributes to the impression that US importance and relevance in global affairs are on a downward slope.

For Trump, his prime foreign policy objective seems to be the pursuit of American primacy and insistence on America's status and image as the leading power in the world, be it in the economic, political, or the military sphere. This also applies to his relations with China. In fact, it appears that for Trump maintaining and perhaps even increasing America's status as the world's only superpower is of particular relevance in the struggle for primacy with China in Southeast Asia. He wishes to demonstrate that America cannot be pushed about, neither by a big power like China, a rogue nation such as North Korea, nor allies such as South Korea, Japan, or the NATO countries.

Beyond this kind of emotional foreign policy, the Trump administration has not attempted to design anything approximating a coherent foreign policy strategy. It seems, in fact, that the Trump administration disdains a comprehensive framework for US foreign policy. Trump's approach is a transactional, piecemeal approach, one that is focused on trade deals and on emphasizing his personal friendship with other world leaders for the sake of it. There is, it appears, very little more strategic substance to it. Thus, "amidst all the chaos of Trump's presidential executive orders, political uncertainty, the Russia investigation crisis, and the shrill rhetoric that has engulfed the US capital since his inauguration, the new administration has hardly had the time or inclination to begin thinking about the formulation of a 'grand strategy'" for the nation's foreign relations (Larres 2017a). Indeed, Trump's search for a comprehensive "new global order" is unlikely to succeed. In any case, the world has become too complex, unpredictable, interconnected and perhaps too multilateral for this to happen.

---

theguardian.com/news/2017/nov/08/what-will-happen-on-donald-trumps-state-visit-to-china.

Organizing global affairs in terms of a G2 world with China, for instance, as first proposed by the former National Security Advisor Zbigniew Brzezinski in 2009, has found little support in Trump's Washington. Originally, the G2 idea referred to a US-China forum to achieve a bilateral consensus between the two countries. Such a consensus would then be useful to steer more effectively issues of global governance. Yet, this requires cooperation and above all mutual trust rather than insistence on maintaining global hegemony.[26] Sharing primacy, however, is not what the Trump administration has in mind. And China is not fond of the idea either.[27] In any case, primacy appears to come China's way much faster than anyone could have hoped for in Beijing. US global strategic deficiencies so far in Donald Trump's presidency are increasingly obvious and have opened up a number of geopolitical vacuums, some of which China intends to fill with a vengeance.

TRUMP AND CHINA: THE EARLY DAYS

Within a few months of his inauguration, there was very little left of Trump's aggressive verbal attacks on China during the election campaign. The turning point came during the 'phone conversation with Xi Jinping on February 9. Already prior to this call, Trump had agreed to Beijing's request not to question the One-China policy, as he appeared to have done when he accepted a congratulatory 'phone call from Taiwanese President Tsai Ing-wen in early December. This was the first time since 1978 that a US President-elect had had direct contact with his Taiwanese counterpart. China interpreted it as a challenge to one of its core national interests—the maintenance of the unity of the nation that for Beijing includes without question Taiwan, Hong Kong, and Macau. During the 'phone call with Xi in early February, however, Trump confirmed Washington's adherence to the One-China policy. This provided the basis for an improvement in US-Chinese relations.[28]

26 See: https://www.ft.com/content/d99369b8-e178-11dd-afa0-0000779fd2ac; http://bbs.chinadaily.com.cn/forum.php?mod=viewthread&tid=633271#lastpost.

27 See: http://bbs.chinadaily.com.cn/forum.php?mod=viewthread&tid=633271#lastpost.

28 See: https://www.politico.com/story/2017/02/trump-china-xi-jinping-call-234887.

Two months later, during the bilateral meeting with Xi Jinping at Trump's Mar-a-Lago resort in Florida on April 6–7, relations were stabilized further. In particular, the Florida talks dealt with trade and Trump's interest in reducing America's huge trade deficit with China. The discussions do not seem to have focused on climate change, human rights, or the South-China Sea dispute. Instead, Trump and Xi agreed on a 100-day plan to work out trade compromises to increase US exports to China, which would help chip away at America's $347 billion trade deficit with China. Xi even claimed that he welcomed such a development as reducing the Chinese trade surplus would allow Beijing to better control its own inflation.[29]

To improve relations with the US, Xi suggested rescinding the 2003 ban on US beef exports to China. He also talked about better market access for American financial investments, particularly securities and insurance. But the Chinese President also indicated that the US trade deficit could be significantly reduced if Chinese companies were allowed to make major investments in the US and purchase high-tech companies. Beijing hopes that in the future the US will impose fewer restrictions on the purchase of US high-tech products and firms, such as the transatlantic chipmaker, Aixtron, the purchase of which by a Chinese company blocked in 2016 (Larres 2017b). Yet, this hope is optimistic, as the US has serious security concerns about allowing China to purchase crucial knowledge industries that are often of military importance.

The "new harmony" in US-China relations that developed during the Florida talks bore fruit when, on May 12, a 10-point trade deal was announced with great fanfare by the Trump administration, although the actual agreements were quite minor in substance. For instance, China agreed to allow US credit rating agencies and credit card companies to commence business in China from mid-July. The long-halted US beef exports to China could also be resumed. Washington, in turn, started exporting liquid natural gas to China and accepted imports of cooked poultry meat from Beijing. Still, the overcapacity of steel production in China, concerns about the new Chinese cyber security law that came into effect in June 2017, about the new Non-Government Organiza-

---

[29] See: http://www.dw.com/ new-trade-talks-in-sight-as-trump-xi-meeting-closes/ a-38348675en/.

tions law of January 2017, and abut continuing barriers to economic activities by Western companies in China, such as joint venture requirements, including the theft of intellectual property in the process, were not addressed in the new trade deal.[30]

Nevertheless, the agreement demonstrated an improvement of US-Chinese relations and the readiness of both sides to tackle disputed aspects constructively. In an interview with *The Economist*, Trump confirmed that he liked Xi Jinping "a lot" and that he thought, "he likes me a lot." The President expressed his view that Xi was "a great guy."[31]

During the Florida meeting in early April, Trump accepted Xi's invitation to visit China before the end of the year. The two leaders also agreed quite sensibly to establish a "US-China Comprehensive Dialogue" consisting of four strands—diplomacy and security, economy, law enforcement, and cyber security. This new dialogue replaces and upgrades Obama's "Strategic and Economic Dialogue." Partially, it will take place at presidential level and is perhaps not altogether dissimilar to the annual high-level German-Chinese Government Consultations (Larres 2017c).

Another major topic at the Florida meeting was North Korea. Both Presidents agreed that North Korea's nuclear development has "reached a very serious stage," though they parted ways on how to deal with it. During the talks, Trump repeated that Washington was prepared to take unilateral action if China did not pressure North Korea into a change of policy. This could include a potentially very dangerous military strike on North Korea or perhaps the re-introduction of nuclear weapons in South Korea.

The Florida meeting between Trump and Xi Jinping was surprisingly successful and led to constructive personal relations between the two men and a number of moderate compromise agreements. In the summer of 2017, the "new harmony" in Chinese-American relations was

---

[30] See: https://www.ft.com/content/9a5ee6b8-36c0-11e7-bce4-9023f8c0fd2e; https://www.washingtonpost.com/opinions/trumps-china-trade-deal-is-artless/2017/05/15/79437666-39a3-11e7-8854-21f359183e8c_story.html?utm_term=.bfb9b5b399f2.

[31] Retrieved from: https://www.economist.com/Trumptranscript.

rightly viewed as a promising development. Trump's turn from being the China basher as a presidential candidate to being a president ready to constructively engage and deal with China's economic and geopolitical challenges certainly deserved credit. Still, the South China Sea dispute continued to loom on the horizon and was hardly addressed in Florida. So far, the Trump administration has downplayed this issue and has also referred to China's alleged unfair trade practices much less emphatically and less often than could have been expected. The explanation for this is Trump's desire to obtain Xi's cooperation in dealing with the North Korea question.

During most of his time in office, Trump is fortunate that the forthcoming 19th Party Congress that commenced in Beijing in mid-October influenced Xi's policy thinking. Prior to this all-important Party Congress, Xi required a period of stability and calm. Volatile relations with the US would only damage his carefully nourished image of being a wise and thoughtful leader. The forthcoming Congress made him perhaps more ready than he would otherwise have been to avoid serious tension in relations with the US. He even tolerated the surprise attack on a Syrian airbase the US executed—in the middle of Trump's dinner with Xi at his Mar-a-Lago resort—to punish Syrian President Assad for an alleged chemical attack on civilians. While Xi was clearly not pleased by the surprise attack, he decided to go along with and downplayed its importance.[32] Cleary it was to Xi's domestic advantage if he could demonstrate his superior global leadership capabilities and his ability to deal with the unpredictable new US President and thus manage China's foreign relations calmly and wisely.

Yet, China also recognized an opportunity during the early days of the new Trump administration. With the ascent of the disorganized and inexperienced Trump White House, a vacuum had arisen in global leadership that Beijing might usefully be able to fill. Xi Jinping's speech at the World Economic Forum in Davos on January 17 was an early attempt to position China in such a leadership role. The speech about the importance of globalization and free trade, which would normally have been given by the US President, was in fact given by the President of China,

---

[32] See: http://www.dailymail.co.uk/wires/afp/article-4389586/China-warns-deterioration-Syria-Xi-US.html.

a most unlikely scenario. And the assembled international business elite rewarded him with much applause.[33]

It was agreed as part of the new 10-point-trade deal announced on May 12 that Washington would send the capable National Security Council-China Director Matthew Pottinger to the Belt-and-Road summit in Beijing in mid-May 2017, thereby indicating its support for Xi's grand scheme. The summit turned into a massive spectacle and was attended by over 29 heads of state. During the two-day meeting, China announced substantial funding for the expansion of economic links between Asia, Africa, and Europe to "uphold and grow an open world economy."[34]

Still, since the launch of the 100-day economic plan, agreed at the Mar-a-Lago talks in April, there has been no progress in US-Chinese trade relations regarding US market access and improvement of trade relations with China. The first meeting of the economic strand of the new US-China Comprehensive Dialogue mechanism that occurred on July 19 in Washington, DC, was, therefore, of great importance. It proved, however, to be a failure. No meaningful headway regarding new trade agreements was made and both the envisaged press conference and final joint statement were cancelled. Apparently, the US pushed the Chinese delegation very hard and attempted to make China agree to precise "numerical benchmarks for reducing its trade surplus with the US and to reduce steel overcapacity."[35] In his blunt opening speech, the US Commerce Secretary Wilbur Ross had blamed China's huge excess capacity for a global steel glut that was damaging American producers. The Chinese, however, were not impressed by this rather robust approach. They

---

[33] For the reaction to Xi's speech as summarized by the Chinese news agency Xinhua, see http://news.xinhuanet.com/english/2017-01/18/c_135991364.htm.

[34] Retrieved from: https://www.reuters.com/article/us-china-silkroad-africa/china-pledges-124-billion-for-new-silk-road-as-champion-of-globalization-idUSKBN18A02I; on Pottinger's presence, see https://qz.com/983477/trump-just-gave-china-what-it-wanted-for-its-new-silk-road-a-credibility-boost-from-the-us/.

[35] Retrieved from: https://www.forbes.com/sites/insideasia/2017/07/21/after-100-days-and-much-hype-u-s-china-talks-fall-flat/#56b415b82010; see also: https://www.cnbc.com/2017/07/19/us-china-comprehensive-economic-dialogue-disagreement-over-how-to-reduce-trade-deficit-official-says.html.

did not budge either on granting Washington greater access to Chinese financial markets or on a reduction of tariffs on cars. There also was a dispute over Chinese data localization requirements. The Chinese, in turn, complained about "outdated US regulations on export controls," in particular those relating to exports of "advanced technologies, key equipment and critical parts to China."[36] The Hong-Kong-based *South China Morning Post* concluded that the economic talks in Washington had brought the US and China on the "verge of a trade war."[37]

Thus, by July, trade and investment concerns had indeed come to the forefront again. The failed first US-China Comprehensive Economic Dialogue contributed to this. Trump came to realize that nothing had really changed substantially, despite his strong personal relationship with Xi and his apparent willingness to compromise on market access issues and China's export practices. The huge US balance of trade deficit with China—some $347 billion annually—remains and does not seem to be decreasing. In particular, Trump was annoyed that, despite his constraint in trade questions, Xi had proved unwilling or incapable of containing North Korean dictator Kim Jong-un's nuclear ambitions. So, by July, both the North Korea question and the uneasy trade relationship with China were once again at the forefront of Trump's China policy. To Trump, it seemed that China had done relatively little to address America's concern about these two vital issues.

THE NORTH KOREAN PROBLEM

During the election campaign and early in his administration, Trump had made clear that he would pay special attention to the North Korea problem. His was driven by impatience, as he had given up on the notion of "strategic patience" that had characterized Obama's North Korea policy. This, essentially, meant that Washington would patiently wait until North Korea was ready to return to the six-power denuclearization process that had characterized the 1990s but whose failure had become

---

[36] Retrieved from: https://www.forbes.com/sites/insideasia/2017/07/21/after-100-days-and-much-hype-u-s-china-talks-fall-flat/#56b415b82010; see also: https://www.cnbc.com/2017/07/19/us-china-comprehensive-economic-dialogue-disagreement-over-how-to-reduce-trade-deficit-official-says.html.

[37] Retrieved from: http://www.scmp.com/news/china/policies-politics/article/2117695/china-us-headed-significant-outcomes-trade-and-north.

obvious by the mid-2000s. The Obama administration had, essentially, based its policy on the expectation that the negotiation process with North Korea could be revived and would eventually lead to Pyongyang giving up its nuclear weapons in return for a number of security and economic assurances. For Trump, this represented a naïve and failed approach.[38]

Yet, once Trump had moved into the Oval Office, he discovered that there were very few alternative options available. Like Obama, he has largely had to rely on the imposition of sanctions to contain North Korea. Trump, however, introduced two new elements to America's North Korea policy. First, he employed much harsher rhetoric and essentially threatened Pyongyang with an invasion and even a nuclear attack. Second, he anticipated China would intervene, believing that by adopting a constructive, restrained, and respectful policy toward China he could persuade Xi Jinping to put massive pressure on its North Korean ally. Already in some of his election campaign speeches, he had made China responsible for containing North Korea and bringing about the elimination of its nuclear weapons program.[39]

The surprisingly harmonious relationship with China at the Florida talks at Mar-a-Logo Resort developed partially due to Beijing's readiness to cooperate in trade questions and deal more energetically with North Korea. Subsequently, Trump emphasized several times that if Beijing was unable to deal successfully with North Korea, then the US would have to act on its own, possibly by military action. But he clearly is relying on China to resolve the North Korean nuclear problem. According to both Trump and Secretary of State Rex Tillerson, not only the US and its allies but also China were in favor of a de-nuclearized Korean peninsula.[40] This was a misreading of the situation. It explains, however, the subsequent disappointment with China.

---

[38] See: https://www.politico.eu/article/donald-trump-north-korea-the-era-of-strategic-patience-is-over/.

[39] See: https://www.theguardian.com/world/2017/jul/11/china-tells-not-responsible-north-korea-nuclear-program.

[40] See: https://www.washingtonpost.com/news/post-politics/wp/2017/09/26/trump-thanks-china-for-help-on-north-korea-claims-diplomacy-is-working/?utm_term=.bd921f2cfc2c.

After all, Beijing knows that for North Korea the atomic bomb is an insurance policy for the survival of the regime. Pyongyang and its young leader Kim Jong-un would, therefore, be unwilling to agree to the denuclearization of North Korea. For Kim any US assurance not to invade, or otherwise undermine his hold on power, and to help North Korea economically in return for denuclearizing his country counts for little. Such is the skepticism about Washington's reliability.[41]

During the Florida talks, however, Trump succeeded in persuading Xi Jinping to put greater economic pressure on North Korea to stop conducting atomic and ballistic missile tests. Yet, China can only go so far. Beijing has clearly no interest in bringing about the collapse of its difficult North Korean ally. This, after all, might lead to the presence of American or South Korean troops on China's border and might also lead to many thousands of North Korean refugees streaming onto Chinese territory. No wonder that Beijing appreciates the buffer state role North Korea plays (Mount 2017, Yi 2016).[42]

The war of words between Kim Jong-un and Donald Trump escalated into aggressive rhetoric, further escalating an already dire situation. Beijing would seem to be greatly frustrated, but does not seem to know what to do. It appears to be unable to de-escalate the situation.

Trump was asked at a press conference if he could imagine being friends with North Korea, he said:

> That might be a strange thing to happen but it's a possibility. If it did happen it could be a good thing I can tell you for North Korea, but it could also be a good for a lot of other places and be good for the rest of the world. It could be something that could happen. I don't know if it will but it would be very, very nice.[43]

---

[41] See: https://www.nytimes.com/2017/10/09/opinion/iran-deal-trump-mistake.html.

[42] For background the Chinese-North Korean relationship see: https://www.cfr.org/backgrounder/china-north-korea-relationship.

[43] Retrieved from: https://www.reuters.com/article/us-trump-asia-northkorea-friend/trump-being-friends-with-north-koreas-kim-is-possible-idUSKBN1DC03B.

Xi Jinping's reaction to Trump's public overture to North Korea is unknown, but could not have been impressed. In the admittedly quite unlikely scenario of the development of a US-North Korean rapprochement, China would find itself rather isolated. The buffer state role that North Korea plays for China, keeping South Korean and US troops and the influence of Western democratic ideas at bay would become dangerously porous. China is clearly uneasy about America's alliance and partnership system in the region. Adding North Korea to this system would be a rather disconcerting development from the Chinese point of view.

US relations with Abe's Japan—China's traditional archenemy—have become rather close. It is unlikely that China will succeed prying them apart. Trump's visit to Japan in the second leg of his Asia tour demonstrated this once again. US relations with South Korea, however, are much less close. Shortly before Trump's arrival in the region, China attempted to exploit this and upgrade China's relations with South Korea after a prolonged crisis. Xi Jinping proceeded to bury its conflict with Seoul over the THAAD anti-missile system deployed near Seoul. The dispute had not only pushed the conciliatory new South Korean leader, President Moon Jae-in, more firmly into the arms of his American ally than would otherwise have been the case. The crisis had also led to a Chinese boycott of South Korean goods and stores with very negative economic consequences for the South Korean state and not least the Lotte department store empire. Lotte had provided the government with the land on which the THAAD anti-missile system was deployed. The cessation of Chinese tourists visiting South Korea had also proved financially very painful for Seoul. Overcoming the crisis in Chinese-South Korean relations clearly was part of Beijing's attempt to prevent Trump from being able to cement too firmly America's alliance with South Korea.[44]

Trump's Caution when Dealing with China

By the late summer of 2017, the Trump administration had once again begun to view trade relations with China as highly unsatisfactory. Trump

---

[44] See: https://www.nytimes.com/2017/11/01/world/asia/china-south-korea-thaad.html; https://thediplomat.com/2017/11/china-and-south-korea-examining-the-resolution-of-the-thaad-impasse/.

was personally very disappointed that the intervention of Xi Jinping had been insufficient to make North Korea change its policy. North Korea did not stop or freeze its nuclear program, nor did it cease its missile test and its underground atomic tests. In fact, it speeded them up. Angrily, Trump began to focus on his earlier complaints about China's unfair trade practices and the huge balance of trade surplus it was running with the US, prompting him to investigate whether steep tariffs should be imposed on Chinese steel products arriving at the US borders. The US also intensified its investigations of Chinese investment practices.[45]

This sounded like tough action, but it was a far cry from imposing tariffs on cheap Chinese steel exports. It was a warning shoot, no more no less, although it might impress his domestic audience. But it was clear; Trump was still shrinking from getting into a tit-for-tat trade war with China. He fully realized that US companies and US businesses would severely suffer from such a development. He was also clearly under pressure from US lobbyists not to antagonize China too much and to avoid getting into a fully-fledged trade war.[46] Instead of doing something drastic to make Beijing reconsider its trade practices, the Trump administration embarked on a rather cautious and much wiser course of action. This was replicated four months later.[47]

Trump asked his Trade Representative Robert Lighthizer to launch an investigation into whether or not China was stealing intellectual property when insisting on certain rules foreign companies have to adhere to get market access in China, such as joint ventures.[48] The White House resorted to using Section 301 and 302(b) of the Trade Act of 1974 for this investigation. The Statute enables the US to unilaterally impose tariffs on exports from a country or restrict access to the US market if a country discriminates against American exporters. Since the creation of

---

[45] See: https://nypost.com/2017/09/13/trump-admin-blocks-chinese-buyer-from-taking-over-us-tech-firm/.

[46] See: https://www.bloomberg.com/news/articles/2017-08-13/trump-trade-push-on-china-faces-challenges-as-ip-takes-spotlight.

[47] See: https://www.theguardian.com/world/2017/aug/15/donald-trump-china-trade-war-investigation.

[48] See: https://www.whitehouse.gov/blog/2017/08/14/president-trump-takes-action-intellectual-property-rights.

the World Trade Organization (WTO) in 1994, Section 301 has hardly been used; instead, cases were referred to the WTO trade dispute system. The Trump administration, however, decided that this would take too long. Instead, Washington launched its own investigation. Still, this also is essentially an investigation to decide whether or not a proper investigation into Chinese discriminatory trade practices should be launched.

China views the process with disquiet but, so far, has not come out fighting it strongly. Instead in September, China's National Development and Reform Commission announced a number of reform measures. These included the removal of the investment cap on some foreign financial service companies and the foreign ownership caps, and the joint venture requirements of 49%, 50%, or 20%, depending on the industry in question, were loosened, particularly in those sectors where Chinese companies already have a competitive edge.[49] These measure were clearly meant to impress—if not appease—the Trump administration. Still, Beijing realizes that a Section 301 investigation is a long-drawn out process and much can happen within a year. The Section 301 investigation may not end with any results, be it for political or other reasons.

Still, as far as the Trump administration is concerned, the investigation demonstrates that Washington is serious in tackling Chinese market access abuses while proceeding cautiously and legalistically and without imposing new tariffs or other restrictions on China, which would clearly lead to counter-action. This is a determined but also fairly subtle and skilful approach to make the Chinese respect the notion of "reciprocity" in market access. And on this issue, the Trump administration enjoys the support of the transatlantic allies. Countries such as Germany also have a strong interest in obtaining much better market access in China and basing Western trade relations with Beijing on reciprocity.

Conclusion: The Outlook for the Future

It is difficult to predict the further development of Sino-US relations during the remainder of Trump's years in office. Owing to the volatility

---

[49] See: http://www.scmp.com/business/banking-finance/article/2119300/china-ease-ownership-limits-foreign-joint-ventures-finance.

and unpredictability that has, so far, characterized Trump's foreign policy, he has squandered much of America's global leadership image and potential. It will be difficult to reverse this course, even if Trump wanted to. And, to all intents and purposes, Trump has no interest and ambition to do so. He appears to mix up warm and effusive superficial welcoming gestures with real personal relationships and strategic substance. He may not even be fully aware of the fact that the global leadership of the US, as it has been for the last six decades, and certainly Washington's predominant position in Southeast Asia and the Pacific, will soon be a thing of the past. In the world of global politics and complex strategic thinking and planning, Trump is clearly out of his depth. The real, quite unforeseen and self-imposed "tragedy of American diplomacy"—to borrow William Appleman Williams' famous book title from the mid-twentieth century—is about to unfold in the twenty-first century. China is ready to step into the vacuum and pick up the pieces—certainly in Asia and perhaps beyond. Roles have been reversed. The Trump administration has embarked on a number of unpredictable and self-defeating policies while China attempts to don the mantle of global responsibility.

References

Allison, G. 2017. *Destined for War: Can America and China Escape the 'Thukydides Trap'?* New York: Houghton, Mifflin, Harcourt.

Bader, J.A. 2012. *Obama and China's Rise: An Insider's Account of America's Asia Strategy.* Washington, DC: Brookings Institution Press.

Campbell, K.M. 2016. *The Pivot: The Future of American Statecraft in Asia.* New York: Twelve.

Chen, D. 2014. "Defining a 'New Type of Major Power Relations." *The Diplomat*, November 8. Available at: https://thediplomat.com/2014/11/defining-a-new-type-of-major-power-relations/.

Chollet, D. 2016. *The Long Game: How Obama Defied Washington and Redefined America's Role in the World.* New York: Public Affairs.

Dueck, C. 2015. *The Obama Doctrine: American Grand Strategy Today.* Oxford: Oxford University Press.

Elms, D. 2016. "The Origins and Evolution of the Trans-Pacific Partnership Trade Negotiations." *Asian Survey*, 5 (6): 1017–1039.

Greenberg, J. 2016. "The Obama Doctrine: The US President Talks Through his Hardest Decisions about America's Role in the World." *The Atlantic*, April. Available at: https://www.theatlantic.com/magazine/archive/2016/04/the-obama-doctrine/471525/.

Hines, R.L. 2015."Xi Jinping's New Foreign Policy." *NBR: The National Bureau of Asian Research*, January. Available at: http://www.nbr.org/research/activity.aspx?id=516.

Larres, K. 2017a "Donald Trump and America's Grand Strategy: US Foreign Policy Toward Europe, Russia and China." *Global Policy*, May. Available at: http://transatlanticrelations.org/wp-content/uploads/2017/05/Larres-Donald-Trump-and-America%E2%80%99s-Grand-Strategy-US-foreign-policy-toward-Europe-Russia-and-China-Global-Policy-May-2017.pdf.

Larres, K. 2017b. "China and Germany: The Honeymoon is Over." *The Diplomat*, November 16. Available at: https://thediplomat.com/2016/11/china-and-gemany-the-honeymoon-is-over/.

Larres, K. 2017c. "Germany Courts China: Leading from the Middle." *Foreign Affairs*, May 3. Available at: https://www.foreignaffairs.com/articles/2016-05-03/germany-courts-china.

Mills, D.Q. 2016. *The Trump Phenomenon and the Future of US Foreign Policy*. New York: World Scientific Publishing.

Mount, A. 2017. "How China sees North Korea." *The Atlantic*, August 29. Available at: https://www.theatlantic.com/international/archive/2017/08/china-military-strength-north-korea-crisis/538344/.

Nehlen, P. 2017. *Wage the Battle: Putting America First in the Fight to Stop Globalist Politicians and Secure the Borders*. Los Angeles, CA: WND Books.

Paulson, H. 2015. *Dealing with China: An Insider Unmasks the New Economic Superpower*. New York: Headline Book Publishing.

Southgate, L. 2017. "The Asia Pivot as a Strategy of Foreign Policy: A Source of Peace or a Harbinger of Conflict?" Paper presented at the International Studies Association Conference, Hong Kong, June 2017. Available at: https://dspace.lib.cranfield.ac.uk/bitstream/1826/12071/1/ISA%20Paper%20Asia%20Pivot%202017%20%281%29.pdf.

Yi, K-H. 2016. *China's Neighborhood Diplomacy and Policies on North Korea: Cases and Application*. Seoul, KR: Korea Institute for National Unification.

Zeng, J. 2016. "Constructing a 'New Type of Great Power Relations,' the State of Debate in China (1998–2014)." *British Journal of Politics and International Relations*, 18 (6): 422–442.

12
STILLBORN OPTIMISM IN TURKEY: THE TRUMP PRESIDENCY

Mustafa Türkeş and Tolgahan Akdan

INTRODUCTION

It is no secret that Turkey's President, Recep Tayyip Erdoğan, was enthusiastic about opening a clean page under a new United States (US) administration given the further straining of US-Turkey relationship during the Obama administrations. At issue were US policy toward the Syrian Kurds and its unwillingness to extradite Fethullah Gülen. He is the US-based self-proclaimed cleric whose followers the Justice and Development Party (JDP) government blames for orchestrating the failed *coup* attempt in July 2016, which resulted in some 270 deaths.[1] However, according to the JDP leadership, this clean page was not expected to be opened if Hillary Clinton had been elected, because it was considered that her US foreign policies would continue as before under the Obama administration. Hence, they hoped that relations with the US could and would improve under the presidency of Donald J. Trump.[2]

Yet, any improvement in the relations between Erdoğan's Turkey with Trump's America appears not to be not so easy, given Trump's deeply suspicious view of Islam, as promoted by several of his senior aides, notably retired Lieutenant-General Michael T. Flynn, his first but short-lived National Security Adviser, and Stephen K. Bannon, who was his Chief Strategist until August.[3] In this respect, Turkey's enthusiasm for

---

[1] Retrieved from: www.tccb.gov.tr/assets/dosya/15Temmuz/onsorudafeto_tr_en.pdf.

[2] See: https://www.dailysabah.com/diplomacy/2016/11/10/turkey-hopes-to-turn-page-on-us-relations-after-trumps-unexpected-victory-1478722878.

[3] See: https://www.nytimes.com/2017/02/01/us/politics/donald-trump-islam.html?_r=0; http://www.bbc.com/news/world-us-canada-38886496; https://www.usatoday.com/story/news/2017/02/09/how-some-trump-advisors-see-islam-their-own-words/97662862/.

embracing Trump's presidency can be considered bizarre for a country where Muslims constitute an overwhelming majority of its population, and where the ruling Islamist political party aspires to make Turkey a leading Muslim power, particularly in the Middle East.

However, Erdoğan's enthusiasm for Trump the candidate was not without its reasons. Erdoğan's optimism about Trump's candidacy is based on, as Steven A. Cook puts it, their shared dislike of the existing political establishment in the US.[4] Erdoğan may have come to think that the way Trump would govern the US as more akin to his own governance style. Indeed, he seems to share a pragmatic understanding of doing business with the new "dealmaker" American president.[5] Erdoğan may have decided that even though Trump has said nothing about the Syrian Kurdish issue, this uncertainty creates an opportunity to persuade Trump in favor of Turkey's thesis regarding the question of how to deal with the ISIS and Kurdish People's Protection Units (YPG) militia. In contrast, the Democratic nominee, Hillary Clinton, has expressed a commitment to supporting the Kurdish Syrian militia, which put her at odds with the Turkish government.[6] In this regard, Clinton's statement about the arming the YPG militia was considered to be a signal that the Obama administration's policy over Syria would continue under her administration. Erdoğan may have decided that Trump has no connections, financial or otherwise, with Gülen, whereas Hilary Clinton has documented financial connections with him,[7] which put her at odds with the Turkish government. Erdoğan and his JDP government had established covert ties with Michael T. Flynn, who became Trump's campaign adviser on national security from August 2016,[8] which appear to have played a de-

---

[4] Retrieved from: http://www.politico.com/magazine/story/2016/11/why-turkey-is-salivating-for-president-trump-214481.

[5] Retrieved from: www.tccb.gov.tr/haberler/410/29719/gelecegin-turkiyesine-mevcut-sistemle-ulasamayiz.html; https://www.washingtonpost.com/news/politics/wp/2017/03/27/trumps-idea-to-run-the-government-like-a-business-is-an-old-one-in-american-politics/?utm_term=.94543f8293ed.

[6] Retrieved from: www.aljazeera.com/news/2016/10/debate-clinton-trump-clash-syrian-war-161010093723691.html.

[7] Retrieved from: http://dailycaller.com/2016/07/13/new-ties-emerge-between-clinton-and-mysterious-islamic-cleric/; www.star.com.tr/dunya/hillary-clinton-ve-fethullah-gulen-baglantisi-belgelendi-haber-1125504/.

[8] Retrieved from: http://dailycaller.com/2016/11/11/trumps-top-military-

cisive role in shaping Erdoğan's general positive expectation of toward a Trump presidency.

The remainder of this chapter first examines the signals coming from both President-elect Trump and the JDP leadership on the road to the Trump's inauguration on January 20. Then its focus shifts to Trump's the so-called Muslim Ban and his foreign policy positions in terms of how they were perceived in, and what responses they attracted from, Turkey.

On the Road to the Trump Presidency

Barack Obama's last days were not easy for Turkish-American relations. While the Obama administration maintained its support for the Kurdistan Workers' Party—the *Partiya Karkerên Kurdistanê* (PKK)—and its affiliated Democratic Union Party (PYD) in Syria, Turkey used harsh rhetoric in its anti-Obama statements. On January 3, in his address to the JDP parliamentary group, Prime Minister Binali Yıldırım called on Donald Trump to "put an end to this vileness." What he thought vile was the Obama administration's support for the PYD.[9] As for President Erdoğan, on January 9, he said, "Our relationship with the US is going through a very sensitive period. I believe we will accelerate the dialogue, especially after the new President Trump taking office on January 20th."[10] The leader of the Nationalist Action Party (NAP), Devlet Bahçeli, who had lent strong support to Erdoğan in his quest for a presidential system, said, "despite the Clinton lobby within us, Trump won the election. Clinton's loss shocked all at once. After all is said and done, those who dreamed of a USA without Trump were lost at the ballot box." This is a precise but very interesting expression of a mood in Turkey, as reflected in the large part of mainstream media,

---

adviser-is-lobbying-for-obscure-company-with-ties-to-turkish-government/to-turkish-government/?,%20Liberals; https://www.wsj.com/articles/ex-cia-director-mike-flynn-and-turkish-officials-discussed-removal-of-erdogan-foe-from-u-s-1490380426.

[9] Retrieved from: www.dailysabah.com/diplomacy/2017/01/03/turkey-expects-trump-to-end-obama-administrations-support-to-pyd-terrorists-pm-yildirim-says.

[10] Retrieved from: www.tccb.gov.tr/konusmalar/353/70692/9-buyukelciler-konferansi-vesilesiyle-duzenlenen-yemekte-yaptiklari-konusma.html.

which considered Trump's election success as a victory against the Fethullah Terrorist Organization (FETO).[11]

In the face of these Turkish expectations, the first promising signal came from Rex Tillerson, the former Exxon-Mobil CEO who was President-elect Donald Trump's secretary of state nominee. During his Senate hearing,[12] Tillerson argued that there was a lack of US leadership in the Middle East, which provided Russia with an "open door" to assert its influence in the Middle East. He underlined the need to "re-engage" with Turkey's President Erdoğan and make clear to the Turkish leader that the country's sustainable alliance is with the US rather than with Russia. He blamed the absence of US leadership for Turkey's nervousness in the region and its turn to Russia.

On the road to January 20, the Turkish government had two principal demands of the new Trump administration. First, Turkey wanted the US to cut its support for the PKK-affiliated YPG militia in Northern Syria because Turkey denied any meaningful difference between the PYD and the PKK other than the difference in their names, and so the US needed to stand with its NATO ally in its fight against terrorism. Second, Turkey demanded the extradition of Fethullah Gülen, accused of being behind the *coup* attempt on July 15, 2016.

However, from the day of Donald Trump's inauguration, an ambiguous waiting period began, which could be considered as a defining mark for Turkey of his first 100 days. The Turkish government wanted the Trump administration to clarify its position over Syria, PYD, and FETO. As far as this expectation has not been realized, the gap between expectation and reality has widened, as one prominent pro-Erdoğan journalist indicated.[13] Moreover, giving a positive response to the question whether the "re-engagement" with Turkey that Tillerson promised happened under the Trump administration is highly questionable. Erdoğan and Trump

---

[11] Retrieved from: www.sabah.com.tr/gundem/2016/11/15/bahceliden-avrupali-buyukelcilere-sert-tepki.

[12] Retrieved from: www.atlanticcouncil.org/component/content/article?id=33957:the-tillerson-hearing-what-was-said-about-the-middle-east.

[13] Retrieved from: http://www.hurriyet.com.tr/yazarlar/abdulkadir-selvi/trumpa-sunulacak-pkk-pyd-dosyasi-40357705.

are far from boosting a reset that could start a new era of US-Turkish relations. Trump administration's approach to Turkey has been dubious. This view was also shared by the Republican People's Party (RPP) delegation that met the Trump administration in Washington. Öztürk Yılmaz, the RPP deputy chairman and former diplomat said, "Trump administration's vision of Turkey is not clear yet, it is needed to wait a little more."[14] While waiting for its views on Turkey to become clear, Erdoğan curbed criticism and kept viewing Trump's presidency as a chance to reset relations with the US, which he desperately needed.

Reaction But No Response to Trump's "Muslim Ban"

Among President Trump's many controversial statements and actions, the one that attracted most criticisms within Turkey was the executive order that temporarily prohibits immigrants and visa holders from seven Muslim-majority countries from entering the US—now widely coined the "Muslim Ban." Trump was not the only target for criticism in Turkey, for Erdoğan was also criticized for his silence. This "Muslim ban" was originally a campaign promise made by Trump, which, at the time, did not escape Erdoğan's firing arrows.[15] However, when Trump kept his promise, Erdoğan made literally no statement about it. The government's delayed statements were far from adequately satisfying public opinion.

Main opposition Republican People's Party (RPP) leader, Kemal Kılıçdaroğlu, criticized Trump's executive order and stated that it was a violation of human rights. He condemned Trump's Muslim Ban as being "against universal values, fundamental human rights and the common achievements of mankind that occurred after hundreds of years of struggle."[16] Moreover, the RPP Deputy Chairman and Speaker, Selin Sayek Böke, criticized the JDP government and said, "we have not heard

---

14   Retrieved from: www.chp.org.tr/Haberler/24/chp-genel-baskan-yardimcisi-ozturk-yilmaz-baskanligindaki-heyet-trump-yonetimiyle-gorustu-55006.aspx.
15   Retrieved from: https://www.wsj.com/articles/erdogan-wants-istanbul-towers-to-lose-trump-name-1466855822.
16   Retrieved from: www.chp.org.tr/Haberler/47/chp-genel-baskani-kemal-kilicdaroglu-bir-ulkenin-vatandaslarini-toptanci-anlayisla-teror-suphelisi-olarak-gormek-cag-disi-52865.aspx; www.hurriyetdailynews.com/main-opposition-leader-slams-trumps-muslim-ban.aspx?PageID=238&N

a single word from the JDP government about this open discrimination against the Muslims. This once again showed us that the JDP was not on the side of right, but always stood by powerful."[17] Speaking in the Grand National Assembly of Turkey, a RPP Deputy, Murat Bakan, said, "We learned from the press that the President made a 45 minute phone call with US President Trump. The content of this 'phone call is very important. During this 'phone call, did the President say, One minute! About this ban' to Trump?"—a reference to the words in a speech made by President Erdoğan against Shimon Peres, then-President of Israel, at Davos[18]—"If he did not say it, we say: 'Mr Trump, One Minute! You cannot separate people according to their faiths and religions!'"[19] In a similar vein, Deputy of Turkey's third-largest party, People's Democratic Party, Ahmet Yıldırım, asked similar questions: "I wonder what Erdoğan talked about with Trump last night? Did he ask the problem of the citizens of the seven Muslim countries whose access to the USA is banned? We are really wondering whether Erdoğan dared to ask Trump about the situation of Muslim countries."[20] Former Turkish leaders also spoke out. The former President of Turkey, Abdullah Gül, also reacted to Muslim Ban by saying, "the decision is all about a cheap show which would provide advantage to terrorists."[21] The former Prime Minister, Ahmet Davutoğlu, wrote on February 2, "This Muslim ban will see the institutionalization of Islamophobia as government policy by a superpower."[22]

However, all this time, Erdoğan kept quiet and barely a word of criticism was heard in corridors of Erdoğan's newly constructed presidential

ID=109117&NewsCatID=510.

[17] Retrieved from: www.chp.org.tr/Haberler/11/chp-genel-baskan-yardimcisi-boke-hayir-diyenleri-terorize-etmeye-kalkiyorlar-sera-da-bu-yuzden-hedef-alindi-53016.aspx.

[18] Retrieved from: http://news.bbc.co.uk/2/hi/business/davos/7859417.stm.

[19] Retrieved from: http://www.chp.org.tr/Haberler/4/bakandan-trumpa-one-minute-53249.aspx.

[20] Retrieved from: www.t24.com.tr/haber/erdogan-trumpa-abdnin-musluman-ulkelere-uyguladigi-yasagi-sorabildi-mi,387952.

[21] Retrieved from: www.hurriyet.com.tr/abdullah-gul-karar-teroristlere-avantaj-sagla-40354146.

[22] Retrieved from: http://www.middleeasteye.net/essays/obama-trump-lessons-and-challenges-844775829.

complex. Deputy Prime Minister and government spokesperson, Numan Kurtulmuş, was the first Turkish government official to speak out against Trump's Muslim Ban executive order. He told *Habertürk* in an interview on January 31, "Unfortunately, I am of the opinion that rising Islamophobia, xenophobia and anti-immigrant feelings have a great weight on this decision. Taking such a decision in a country like America where different ethnic and religious groups are able to co-exist is very offensive. This is not right."[23]

At the same time, a debate within pro-Erdoğan media outlets broke out about their attitude toward Trump. Özlem Albayrak, a columnist of *Yeni Şafak*, started one of his columns with the question of "Why are we defending Trump?" She wrote that "even those who identify Trump's fate with Erdoğan's, just because he is against the established order, must see that the US's fast and furious new president is a complete mystery for Turkey and be calm."[24] Against this criticism, the Erdoğan government's silence on Trump's controversial Muslim Ban, Sevilay Yılman wrote in her column at *Habertürk*:[25]

> even though Deputy Prime Minister Numan Kurtulmuş said something in order to appease the masses, I think that was also unnecessary, because it is not our business. Excuse me but are we the fool of the Islamic world? Where are this world's trillionaire oil traders? Even Saudi Arabia, Qatar, Egypt did not say "One Minute!" to Trump, why did it then bother us? Could you tell us what will bring us to take an offense when the man [Trump] has no problem with Turkey and the citizens of the Republic of Turkey?

Another action that did directly affect Turkey was the Trump administration's decision to introduce a ban on electronic devices for passengers

---

[23] Retrieved from: http://www.haberturk.com/gundem/haber/1373595-numan-kurtulmus-kabul-etmek-mumkun-degil-rencide-edici.

[24] Retrieved from: http://www.yenisafak.com/en/columns/ozlemalbayrak/why-are-we-defending-trump-2035806.

[25] Retrieved from: www.haberturk.com/yazarlar/sevilay-yilman-2383/1377156-evet-bana-dokunmayan-trump-bin-yasasin

on nonstop flights originating from 10 airports in the Middle East and Africa, including Ataturk International Airport in Istanbul.[26] Britain, following the US, also forbade passengers from bringing any electronic devices larger than a cell 'phone into the cabin on non-stop UK bound-flights from six countries including Turkey."[27] That Ataturk International Airport (IST) and Turkish Airlines were included in this ban came as a shock to Turkish authorities.

Against the ban, Erdoğan called on the US and Britain to drop what he said were "exaggerated" new aviation restrictions imposed on flights from some airports, including Istanbul. Foreign Ministry spokesman, Hüseyin Müftüoğlu, also criticized the two countries for not consulting with Turkey before deciding on the ban. Müftüoğu said that taking measures "against people that pose a threat instead of punishing normal passengers would be more effective." The spokesman also claimed Istanbul's Ataturk Airport was one of the safest in the world.[28] However, the government's general belief was verbalized by the Minister of Justice, Bekir Bozdağ, who said, "Now those who cannot compete with Turkish Airlines introduced a ban. The passengers of Turkish Airlines cannot take their tablets into the cabin. They cannot compete in quality, in service, in customer satisfaction, in reaching everywhere in the world, but they are trying to block Turkish Airlines with prohibition and restrictions."[29] The US representative of President of the Independent Industrialists' and Businessmen's Associations (MUSIADs) made a similar statement:

> the ban is more of an economic sanction rather than a security measure toward Istanbul, Turkey. The ban certainly will affect the economies of these countries since people can fly from other airports. It is against fair trade.

---

[26] Retrieved from: www.dhs.gov/news/2017/03/21/fact-sheet-aviation-security-enhancements-select-last-point-departure-airports.

[27] Retrieved from: www.bbc.com/news/uk-39343971.

[28] Retrieved from: www.apnewsarchive.com/2017/A-senior-official-says-Turkey-is-taking-steps-to-keep-Istanbul-s-main-airport-and-its-national-carrier-Turkish-Airlines-outside-of-the-scope-of-new-aviation-restrictions-imposed-by-the/id-e74b95c3726c4fe38687148d1241225c.

[29] Retrieved from: http://www.hurriyet.com.tr/bozdag-fetonun-yargiyi-ele-gecirmesinde-chpyi-sucladi-40406050.

As the president of MUSIAD representative in USA, we say that security-justified practices with strategic moves are far from reality, which is an unfair application towards rising global brand like Turkish Airlines.[30]

Even though the ban was presented as a security requirement, it was widely considered in Turkey as not being motivated by security considerations, but as a commercial move with a view to halting Turkish Airlines competitive power.

TURKEY AND TRUMP'S FOREIGN POLICY

Trump, Turkey, and Syrian Crisis

The chief agenda item of the relations between Turkey and the US was undoubtedly what would be the new strategy of Trump administration toward the Syrian crisis in general and the use and arming of Syrian Kurdish YPG militia in particular. Even though Trump's attitude toward the Syrian Kurds was unclear at the beginning, his approach toward the resolution of Syrian crisis was expected to be a radical departure from that of the previous Obama administration. During his presidential campaign, Trump advocated an anti-interventionist approach. He framed the Syrian crisis principally in terms of refugees, fighting ISIS, and as a way of criticizing President Obama and his former Secretary of State, Hillary Clinton. Thus, the US would not intervene into the Syria to oust the President Bashar al-Assad, rather his priority would be to defeat ISIS.[31] He even suggested during a presidential debate that the US should work with Russia and Syria to defeat ISIS.[32]

After he entered the Oval Office, President Trump put the idea of establishing "safe zones" in Syria on the agenda. He said in an interview with David Muir on *ABC News* on January 25 that[33]

---

[30] Retrieved from: www.twitter.com/MusiadUSA/status/844274248759885830.
[31] Retrieved from: http://abcnews.go.com/Politics/trump-syria-assad/story?id=46620156.
[32] Retrieved from: www.rt.com/usa/362184-trump-pence-syria-disagree/.
[33] Retrieved from: www.abcnews.go.com/Politics/transcript-abc-news-anchor-david-muir-interviews-president/story?id=45047602.

I'm gonna be the president of a safe country. We have enough problems. Now I'll absolutely do safe zones in Syria for the people. I think that Europe has made a tremendous mistake by allowing these millions of people to go into Germany and various other countries. And all you have to do is take a look. It's—it's a disaster what's happening over there.

However, he did not give any information about where these areas would be established. The Turkish government took a cautious stance on Trump's statement. Foreign Ministry spokesman, Hüseyin Müftüoğlu, told reporters at a briefing in Ankara, "We have seen the US President's request for conducting a study. What's important are the results of this study and what kind of recommendation will come out." He went on: "Setting up of safe zones is something Turkey has advocated from the start. The best example is in Jarablus,"[34] a town near the Turkish border that was freed from ISIS by Turkish-backed Syrian rebels in August 2016.

Even though the establishment of safe zones within Syria has been a long-standing demand of the Obama administration by Erdoğan, Trump's safe zones statement raised concerns in Ankara because it was not clear where Trump was planning to establish those safe zones. Turkish government doubted that such a move could lead to the establishment of a Kurdish corridor along southern borders of Turkey, which Turkey is trying to prevent. *Hurriyet Daily* reported that Trump's safe zone plan was reminiscent of operation "Poised Hammer", which aimed to protect the Kurds from the attacks of Saddam Hussein in Northern Iraq after the First Gulf War, but ended up creating an autonomous Kurdish entity.[35] A new but related development was the idea of establishing a no-fly zone over the Kurdish areas in Syria, which in turn would make Turkey unable to act in the northern Syria and thus would effectively push Turkey out of the Syrian equation. Even though Trump's proposal for the establishment of safe zones in Syria has never been

---

[34] Retrieved from: http://www.reuters.com/article/us-mideast-crisis-syria-turkey-idUSKBN15A10O.

[35] Retrieved from: www.hurriyetdailynews.com/a-trojan-horse-in-syrias-safe-havens.aspx?PageID=238&NID=109073&NewsCatID=570.

clarified, Russia, Turkey, and Iran signed an agreement for the creation of such safe zones on May 4.[36]

During the visit to Ankara on February 9, the Director of the Central Intelligence Agency, Mike Pompeo, it was reported that, in a response to Turkey's proposal for a joint Raqqa operation, has said, "if you have this alternative in your hand, we will seriously consider it."[37] Turkey's main objective was to affect the Trump administration's new Raqqa plan that was then allegedly being prepared at Trump's request. Ankara had long insisted that the Raqqa operation should be conducted by local Arab forces, possibly with the support of Turkish troops, as opposed to the US-backed Syrian Democratic Force (SDF), a military alliance dominated by the Kurdish YPG militia. Speaking during a trip to Germany, Turkish Prime Minister, Binali Yıldırım, said there would be "serious issues" if the US preferred to go with Kurdish militia for the Raqqa operation against ISIS.[38]

At a meeting on February 18 at the Incirlik air base in Turkey, a key hub for the US-led coalition against the ISIS, Turkish military chief, Hulusi Akar, and his US counterpart, Joseph Dunford, deliberated over alternative Raqqa operational plans.[39] According to *Hurriyet*, Turkey proposed two alternative plans to the US as to how it should carry out a joint military operation to drive ISIS from Raqqa, its *de facto* capital city. Turkish government's first and preferred plan of action envisages Turkish and US special forces, backed by commandoes and Turkey-backed Syrian rebels entering Syria through the border town of Tel Abyad, currently held by Kurdish YPG militia. The plan maintained that the forces would cut through YPG territory, before pushing on to Raqqa, about 100 kilometers (60 miles) south. Such a plan would require the US to convince the Kurdish militia to grant the Turkey-backed forces a 20-kilometer

---

[36] Retrieved from: www.rt.com/news/387105-syria-talks-safe-zones/.
[37] Retrieved from: http://www.hurriyet.com.tr/rakka-yaniti-elinizde-alternatif-varsa-degerlendiririz-40362215.
[38] Retrieved from: http://aa.com.tr/tr/gunun-basliklari/basbakan-yildirim-olursa-abd-ile-iliskilerde-ciddi-sorun-olur/753322.
[39] Retrieved from: www.hurriyetdailynews.com/us-top-general-lands-at-incirlik-air-base-to-meet-with-turkish-counterpart.aspx?NewsCatID=358&nid=109861&pageID=238.

wide strip through YPG-controlled territory.[40] Prime Minister Yıldırım clarified that Turkish forces would not be directly involved in combat but would provide tactical support. Yet both the Turkish and US military would have a ground presence, he added.[41] The second alternative outlined by Akar to Dunford was, *Hurriyet* reported, to push toward Raqqa via the Syrian town of Bab. However, the long journey of 180 kilometers and mountainous terrain make that possibility less likely.[42]

However, despite Turkey's hopes and efforts for a change in the US policy of cooperation with YPG in Syria under the new Trump administration, US Army Lieutenant-General Stephen Townsend, who commands the US-led coalition effort against ISIS in Iraq and Syria, told a Pentagon news briefing that a role for the Kurds was still in Washington's plan. "There are going to be Kurds assaulting Raqqa for sure," he said. "The number, the size of them, and how many Kurdish units are participating...I can't really say right now."[43] There is a saying in Turkish—the huge mountain gave birth to a tiny mouse—that best describes the disappointing results that follow big expectations. At the end of the day, it turned out that there was not much change in the US attitude toward the Syrian Kurds. Trump's so-called renewed ISIS plan turned to be the one that looks pretty much the same with Obama's plan.[44] However, Erdoğan and his JDP government never gave up their insistence on the exclusion of Kurdish YPG militia and kept pressing for a deal that would downplay the differences between the two NATO allies. Trump, however, signed the decision to arm the YPG militia with heavy weapons. Dana W. White, the chief Pentagon spokeswoman, said in a statement that the arming was necessary to ensure that Raqqa could be taken "in the near future."[45]

---

[40] Retrieved from: http://www.hurriyet.com.tr/pydyi-bol-rakkaya-in-40369478.

[41] Retrieved from: http://aa.com.tr/tr/gunun-basliklari/basbakan-yildirim-olursa-abd-ile-iliskilerde-ciddi-sorun-olur/753322.

[42] Retrieved from: http://www.hurriyet.com.tr/pydyi-bol-rakkaya-in-40369478.

[43] Retrieved from: http://www.reuters.com/article/us-mideast-crisis-syria-turkey-usa-analy-idUSKBN169250.

[44] See: http://www.thedailybeast.com/who-invented-trumps-isis-plan-obama; http://www.nbcnews.com/news/us-news/trump-s-secret-plan-beat-isis-looks-lot-obama-s-n735171.

[45] Retrieved from: https://www.nytimes.com/2017/05/09/us/politics/trump-

Erdoğan has not yet lost his faith in Trump because he seems to assume that he will sooner or later persuade him about wrongness of the course of partnering with the Syrian Kurdish militia. However, it could be argued that the exclusion of Kurdish militia from the planned Raqqa operation is not Erdoğan's number one priority. His top priority appears to be ensuring that Turkey has an important place in the US regional strategy, to which end he never brought his criticisms of the US strategy to point that would severe relations with the Trump administration, as he had done with the Obama administration. Therefore, Erdoğan knows when and where he needs to be silent. Despite the contrary expectation in Turkey, Trump's new plan for Raqqa operation did prefer to depend on Kurdish YPG militia, and so it kept its central place in Pentagon's struggle against ISIS.

Trump's missile strike against Syria was by far the most surprising and dangerous development of his early days in office. The strike came after Trump stated that Syria's al-Assad "crossed a lot of lines" with gas attack, referring Obama's infamous "red line" over Assad's use of chemical weapons. At that time, Trump had warned Obama not to get involved in the Syrian civil war. Trump had tweeted in 2013, "President Obama, do not attack Syria. There is no upside and tremendous downside. Save your 'powder' for another (and more important) day!"[46] However, by intervening in the Syrian civil war, Trump threw away his own campaign promise and advice to Obama of adopting a non-interventionist approach. This is one of the most obvious case of Trump's inconsistency, but, at the same time, it was a rare move that prompted Erdoğan on April 7 to hail the attack by the US on a Syrian air base as a positive development, in terms of the future of Syrian President Bashar al-Assad, but it was not enough on its own and "serious steps" were needed to protect the Syrian people.[47] The US's cruise missiles attack at a Syrian airbase was also hailed by the pro-Erdoğan media outlets as well.[48] The leader of Nationalist Action Party, Devlet Bahçeli, also welcomed the attack.

kurds-syria-army.html.
[46] Retrieved from: https://twitter.com/realdonaldtrump/status/376334423069032448?lang=en.
[47] Retrieved from: http://www.reuters.com/article/us-mideast-crisis-syria-erdogan-idUSKBN1791X2.
[48] Retrieved from: www.yenisafak.com/dunya/abdye-destek-yagdi-2640156.

He said, "Assad found his just reward."[49] A missile attack was enough to hastily reawaken the old optimism and strong desire in Turkey.

This enthusiasm of Erdoğan and his JDP government did not last very long. In an interview on April 12 Trump said, "we're not going into Syria."[50] Erdoğan kept doing business as if such an attack had never taken place and as if he never made those follow-up statements calling for USled intervention into the Syrian civil war. For example, Turkey, together with Russia and Iran, signed an agreement on the creation of safe zones, which they defined as the de-escalation zones. Their principal objective was to separate extremist groups, including Islamic State terrorists and Jabhat al-Nusra (Al-Nusra Front), from the moderate opposition. The safe zones include Idlib, Latakia, and Homs, as well as parts of Aleppo.[51]

THE QUESTION OF FETHULLAH GÜLEN AND REZA ZARRAB

Turkey expected Trump not to follow in Obama's footsteps, an expectation that has not been yet been met. This is also the case with respect to Turkey's second main demand of the new Trump administration—the extradition of Fethullah Gülen. During the Obama administration, despite Turkey's formal request after the July 15 *coup* attempt to extradite Fethullah Gülen, the Obama administration had not started any of the necessary extradition legal process. Therefore, the extradition of Gülen is one of Turkey's main expectations of the Trump administration, for which, it has been revealed, Turkey indirectly commissioned lobbyist and, perhaps, covert activities.

On election day, November 8, Michael T. Flynn, the retired Army General cum political lobbyist who became Trump's first National Security Adviser, wrote an op-ed in *The Hill*,[52] in which he called on the next president, whoever that would be, to accede to Turkey's request and

---

[49] Retrieved from: http://www.haberturk.com/gundem/haber/1454019-bahceli-esed-yonetimi-layigini-buldu.

[50] Retrieved from: http://www.foxbusiness.com/politics/2017/04/11/trump-exclusive-were-not-going-into-syria.html.

[51] Retrieved from: http://www.rt.com/news/387105-syria-talks-safe-zones/.

[52] See: http://thehill.com/blogs/pundits-blog/foreign-policy/305021-our-ally-turkey-is-in-crisis-and-needs-our-support.

extradite Fethullah Gülen, the US-based Muslim cleric. Flynn referred to Gülen as a "shady Islamic mullah" and "radical Islamist." His movement—Hizmet—he called a "scam," and argued that the US "should not provide him safe haven." He noted: "Gülen's vast global network has all the right markings to fit the description of a dangerous sleeper terror network." Flynn went on to argue: "We must begin with understanding that Turkey is vital to US interests. Turkey is really our strongest ally against the Islamic State in Iraq and Syria, as well as a source of stability in the region. It provides badly needed cooperation with US military operations."

Flynn's remarks boosted optimism in Turkey regarding Gülen's extradition. Speaking to *Anadolu Agency* correspondent in Rome, Taha Özhan, the head of Turkish Parliament's External Affairs Commission, stated: "Talks on this issue [extradition] can be done once it's February. At this stage this expectation has to be voiced but the US government transition has to go through. Because Trump is [now] president-elect. After Trump assumes his duties, this file [on Gülen] should certainly be sent to him."[53] Yunus Paksoy, a *Daily Sabah* columnist argued, after referring to Flynn's op-ed: "Ankara now expects the Trump administration to work closely with Turkey toward Gülen's detention and his ultimate extradition." Even though the Obama administration distanced itself from the issue of FETO, Flynn hinted at an entirely different approach. Paksoy cited Burhanettin Duran, Director of the Foundation for Political, Economic and Social Research (SETA), who claimed, "Trump is expected to approach the FETO issue more positively for Ankara. He will collaborate more with Erdoğan on this radical group FETO."[54] Flynn's remarks were also picked up by another *Daily Sabah* columnist, Hilal Kaplan. After referring to Flynn op-ed, Kaplan argued, "the reflection of this viewpoint into Trump's policies will contribute to erasing the remnants of the straining Turkey-US relations during Obama's term in office."[55]

---

[53] Retrieved from: http://aa.com.tr/en/politics/feto-leaders-us-extradition-talks-can-start-in-feb/682877.

[54] Retrieved from: https://www.dailysabah.com/war-on-terror/2016/11/11/trump-expected-to-turn-the-heat-on-feto-extradite-gulen-for-better-relations-with-turkey.

[55] Retrieved from: https://www.dailysabah.com/columns/hilal_kaplan/2016/

However, several days after the appearance of Flynn's op-ed in *The Hill*, *The Daily Caller* reported[56] that a consulting firm founded by Flynn—Flynn Intel Group—was hired as a Washington lobbyist by a Dutch company—Inovo BV—owned by Ekim Alptekin, the Chairman of the Turkish-American Business Council, a non-profit arm of Turkey's Foreign Economic Relations Board, so giving it ties with Turkey's government. *The Daily Caller* reported that on behalf of his firm, Flynn signed a contract on August 9, 2016. Six days later, Trump announced that he was naming Flynn as national security adviser. This was a very pleasing development since one of Trump's senior strategic aides would be a person who is aware of the danger that Fethullah Gülen and his terrorist organization pose to Turkey.

But in early February, Flynn was fired after revelations that he had misled senior Trump administration officials, including Vice-President Mike Pence, by not fully disclosing his contacts with the Russian ambassador to the US.[57] It became clear, with Flynn's admission, that he was paid $530,000 for work on Turkey's behalf between September 9 and November 14 when he was one of Trump's principal campaign national security advisers. In the course of this work, it was reported, Flynn also met with Turkey's Foreign Minister, Mevlüt Çavuşoğlu and Energy Minister Berat Albayrak (President Erdoğan's son-in-law) in New York on September 19, 2016.[58] Regarding this meeting, another important allegation was reported in *The Wall Street Journal* on the basis of statements made to it by the former Director of the CIA, James Woolsey. He said that Flynn met with two ministers, Mevlüt Çavuşoğlu and Berat Albayrak on September 19, 2016, to discuss a covert and potentially illegal plan to remove Gülen secretly from the US.[59] In response to this

---

11/11/is-a-clean-slate-with-the-us-possible.

[56] Retrieved from: http://dailycaller.com/2016/11/11/trumps-top-military-adviser-is-lobbying-for-obscure-company-with-ties-to-turkish-government/?,%20Liberals.

[57] Retrieved from: https://www.washingtonpost.com/world/national-security/michael-flynn-resigns-as-national-security-adviser/2017/02/13/0007c0a8-f26e-11e6-8d72-263470bf0401_story.html?utm_term=.e0ebdbaae5ef.

[58] Retrieved from: https://www.nytimes.com/2017/03/10/us/politics/michael-flynn-turkey.html. See also:

[59] https://www.wsj.com/articles/ex-cia-director-mike-flynn-and-turkish-officials-

allegation, Çavuşoğlu said, "He is a former [CIA] director but what he says is total nonsense. We are a state, not a terror organization."[60] Although Ekim Alptekin denied that the contract his company, Inovo BV, made with Flynn was done without the knowledge of the Turkish government,[61] it seems that Turkish government had invested in Flynn, and his firing as National Security Advisor seems to have undermined Turkish government's efforts to persuade Trump not to follow in Obama's footsteps.

At the end of the first 100 days of Trump administration, the current state of Fethullah Gülen case shared the same fate of Turkey's insistence on the US to cut off their support to Syrian Kurdish PYD militia. It is not possible to make a definitive statement about any change in White House's attitude toward Fethullah Gülen's extradition. There were numerous statements of Turkey's Minister of Justice, Bekir Bozdağ, regarding how he and the government were hopeful about new developments occurring in the extradition case of Fethullah Gülen.[62] However, at the end of the first 100 days, this hope was held in vein, as the Trump administration had not yet submitted in a US court the evidence Ankara handed over to them in support for the extradition, and provisional arrest of Gülen.

That we are witnessing a strange time in the relations between Turkey and the US becomes very evident when Trump's firing of Preet Bharara as US attorney in the Southern District of New York attracted even more public attention in Turkey than it did in in the US. Media outlets close to the Turkish government welcomed it. Bharara, as the responsible US attorney, directed the arrest and prosecution of Reza Zarrab, a Turkish national, who allegedly helped run a scheme that funneled billions of

discussed-removal-of-erdogan-foe-from-u-s-1490380426.

[60] Retrieved from: http:// www.hurriyetdailynews.com/turkey-to-suggest-joint-raqqa-operation-to-us-during-secretary-of-state-tillersons-visit-.aspx?pageID=238&nID=111385&NewsCatID=510.

[61] Retrieved from: https://www.nytimes.com/2017/03/10/us/politics/michael-flynn-turkey.html.

[62] Retrieved from: http://www.hurriyetdailynews.com/turkish-justice-minister-to-discuss-gulen-extradition-with-us-counterpart.aspx?pageID=238&nID=109723&NewsCatID=338. See also: http://aa.com.tr/en/americas/turkey-expects-new-developments-on-gulen-extradition/750111.

dollars' worth of gold into Iran, in violation of US sanctions. This prosecution was considered by President Erdoğan and his JDP government to be an act against the interests of the Turkish government. They insisted that Bharara had covert ties with Gülen's FETO network. That is to say, they considered the case against Rıza Zarrab was part of an operation conducted by Bharara in connection with FETO.[63] Rıza Zarrab was a key figure in an earlier Turkish corruption scandal, which Erdoğan denied happened, instead he accused Gülen of orchestrating an attempted "judicial coup" and of building a "parallel state" with extensive influence in the Turkish police and judiciary.[64]

After his arrest, in Miami, Zarrab hired some of the most expensive lawyers in New York. He also hired Rudy Giuliani, a former New York City mayor who had acted as a surrogate for Donald Trump during his campaign, and another prominent lawyer, Michael B. Mukasey, who served as Attorney General in President George W. Bush's administration. Having a legal team with ties with Trump raised the question of whether Zarrab added Giuliani and Mukasey to his legal team in an effort to negotiate a beneficial resolution of his case at the highest levels of the Trump administration. On March 27, *The New York Times* reported that Giuliani and Mukasey held a secret meeting with President Erdoğan in Turkey in February about the case.[65] Richard Berman, the judge, asked that Giuliani and Mukasey provide more information about their role in the case.[66]

The situation became even more complicated with the arrest (in the US) of Mehmet Hakan Atilla, the Deputy General Manager of Halkbank, one of Turkey's largest state-owned banks, in connection with the Zarrab case.[67] The case against Atilla was built on much of the same

---

[63] Retrieved from: http://aa.com.tr/tr/turkiye/adalet-bakani-bekir-bozdag-turk-milleti-kendini-anlayanlarla-yoluna-devam-edecektir/769579.

[64] Retrieved from: http://www.aljazeera.com.tr/haber/cumhurbaskani-erdoganin-ilk-roportaji.

[65] Retrieved from: https://www.nytimes.com/2017/03/27/nyregion/reza-zarrab-iran-sanctions-case-rudolph-w-giuliani-to-legal-team.html.

[66] Retrieved from: https://www.nytimes.com/2017/03/28/nyregion/iran-sanctions-rudy-giuliani-turkish-trader.html.

[67] Retrieved from: https://www.bloomberg.com/news/articles/2017-03-28/halkbank-deputy-g-m-arrested-in-u-s-in-iran-financing-probe; http://www.reuters.com/article/us-usa-turkey-banker-idUSKBN16Z2I4.

evidence—wiretapped 'phone conversations—that was used to charge Zarrab. As in the case of Zarrab, the reason for Atilla's visit to the US is, as yet, unknown. President Erdoğan showed his support to Zarrab and claimed that his arrest and detention in the US is politically motivated. Speaking in Ankara on April 25, Erdoğan said, "Zarrab isn't my father's son but simply a citizen of my country. If he has committed a crime, his files should be sent to our Ministry of Justice, otherwise, if he is arrested under false pretenses [and if we don't protect him], we become a country that doesn't protect its citizens ..."[68] He also added that he would discuss the situation of Zarrab with President Trump.[69] The Turkish Minister of Foreign Affairs, Mevlüt Çavuşoğlu had earlier said that he would raise the issue with his US counterpart, Rex Tillerson.[70] It seems that President Erdoğan and his JDP government are taking the Zarrab case very serious and it is put on the agenda whenever they met with US authorities. As of the end of the Trump's first 100 days, the Zarrab matter became even more complicated with the related arrest in the US of Halkbank's Deputy General Manager, Mehmet Hakan Atilla.

Conclusion

President Erdoğan saw the election of Donald Trump as an opportunity to open up a new page in Turkey-US relations that had been strained throughout the second term of Obama administration over the US support to the Syrian Kurds and its refusal to extradite Fethullah Gülen. It is obvious that none of the recent problems, not to mention the old persistent problems, have been settled during the first 100 days of Trump administration.

In Turkish domestic politics, President Erdoğan has monopolized power and considerably personalized it. A similar pattern may be discerned regarding the formation and execution of Turkey's foreign policy. This

---

[68] Retrieved from: www.sabah.com.tr/ekonomi/2017/04/26/zarrab-babamin-oglu-degil.

[69] Retrieved from: www.sabah.com.tr/ekonomi/2017/04/26/zarrab-babamin-oglu-degil.

[70] Retrieved from: https://www.washingtonpost.com/news/worldviews/wp/2017/03/30/what-you-need-to-know-about-turkey-and-the-trump-administration/?utm_term=.5fcf0d2972ba.

tendency is not a new phenomenon, because Erdoğan has employed back channel or informal diplomacy since he came to power in 2003. As he has become politically stronger within Turkey, his conduct of personalized power has become much more obvious in terms of foreign relations too. Personalization of the conduct of Turkey's foreign relations has crystalized, particularly with respect to Turkey-US relations. It seems that Erdoğan established his strategy for a new *modus vivendi* on the expectation of his personal harmony with Trump. However, his optimistic expectations were not realized by the end of Trump's first 100 days. Indeed, it is hardly possible to indicate any seeds of meaningful change in the US policies toward Syria, the role attributed to Syrian Kurds, and the extradition of Fethullah Gülen. Thus, the current relationship between the two countries is not very promising. It is an open-ended process that it may go better or worse. Perhaps, it is unrealistic to predict that Turkey-US relations will completely break down. However, the events in Trump's first 100 days clearly not a success story for Turkey. For the US, it may well be stated that the Obama's Middle East policy has been revitalized under the Trump administration, particularly in relation to Syria and to the Kurds of Syria. It remains to be seen whether the Erdoğan and Trump administration are able to revise their foreign policy to bring them into a greater degree of alignment.

It may well be concluded that the initial optimism about Trump and his administration among the Turkish political establishments—particularly in the inner circle of the Erdoğan administration—would transform US-Turkey relations—by enhancing the personal relations of the two presidents—has become a stillborn endeavor. That said, does not mean both leaders are not looking for new opportunities to work out new modus vivendi to renew their cooperation. This, too, remains to be seen.

13
"OUT OF AFRICA":
TRUMP'S EARLY IMPACT ON US-AFRICA RELATIONS

John J. Stremlau

INTRODUCTION

Donald J. Trump has never shown much interest in, knowledge of, or empathy for sub-Saharan Africa, a position much like his disregard for the aspirations and wellbeing of 46 million African-American compatriots, most of whom are the descendants of African victims of American slavery. During the initial months of his presidency, he offered only indirect and generally negative hints of how his handling of the presidency might alter the sub-Saharan African countries long-running partnerships with the United States (US). This African region comprises forty-nine states, with the five North African states, and the Sahrawi Arab Democratic Republic also being members of the African Union (AU), and represents more than one billion people. In at least one area of vital concern to sub-Saharan Africa—the continued US mitigation of the damage it is doing to the global environment, along with a commitment to assist vulnerable low-income counties to adapt to climate change—Trump's policies portend dire consequences for Africa.

Trump's 2018 Budget Blueprint would sharply reduce foreign assistance to developing countries, most of them African, and eliminate programs supporting good governance, human rights, and democracy.[1] These have enjoyed unusual bi-partisan support within the Congress and have been welcomed across Africa. The fate of most of these programs is now uncertain, but all must await Congressional budget action. Shortly after Trump's inauguration, Democratic Senator Chris Coons of Delaware, a member of the Foreign Relations and Appropriations Committees, published a detailed review of US-Africa relations and a carefully drawn

---
[1] See: http://www.npr.org/2017/03/16/520379061/read-president-trumps-budget-blueprint.

list of recommendations to sustain the cooperative links forged by previous administrations.[2]

Trump's rhetoric and behavior during his first months as President suggest that as his foreign policies emerge, they will aim to reduce any bilateral and multilateral agreements if they do not produce equal, or advantageous, short-term material benefits for the US. Trump also has a long record of questioning publicly the value to America of its participation in alliances, regional and global organizations, including the United Nations. Policies to cut or eliminate US support would ignore the domestic needs and international priorities of virtually all sub-Saharan African countries. One early sign of South African concern is prominent in the International Relations Discussion Paper for the 5th National Policy Conference (June–July 2017) of the ruling African National Congress. This urges priority attention be given to the question: "What does the election of Donald Trump as President of the US signify, and what lessons can the ANC draw from this?"[3]

This chapter considers only the first half of that question, but from a broader, pan-African—essentially a sub-Sahara—perspective, and is in three parts. The first focuses on the fundamental conflicts of norms, already evident, and likely to strain US-Africa relations for however long Trump is in office. The second summarizes several programs that have defined US Africa policy for the past quarter century, highlighting early signs of how each will probably fare during the Trump era. The third assesses some of Trump's leadership traits, noting their similarities to those of Africa's strong men that should alarm democrats and could comfort autocrats. A short conclusion sees glimmers of hope in the growing US domestic resistance to Trump, which could eventually help to restore better US-Africa relations.

Clashing Norms and the Prospect of Estrangement

Trump's core beliefs of ethnic and economic nationalism are well known in Africa. The first offense against African racial sensibilities began with

---

[2] See: https://www.the-american-interest.com/2017/01/25/u-s-africa-policy-recommendations-for-president-trump/.

[3] See: http://www.anc.org.za/sites/default/files/National%20Policy%20Conference%202017%20International%20Relations.pdf.

Trump's rise to political prominence with the false claim that Barack Obama, America's first African American president, was not really born in America, and his presidency was, therefore, illegitimate.[4] Obama, of course, was American born. And he remains enormously popular throughout Africa.[5] Many Africans, especially in post-apartheid South Africa, therefore, saw Trump's rise as a racist backlash, a view that does not appear to have changed.

A Pew Research Center global survey of public perceptions of the US in July 2015 showed that 79% of Africans had a favorable view of America, a higher percentage than any other region.[6] Some of this enthusiasm might be attributed to the "Obama factor," but Pew polling in the past decade shows America's positive image in Africa was virtually the same during the two terms of Obama's predecessor, Republican George W. Bush.

Since Trump's election, there has been a sharp drop in the world's regard for the US. According to a Pew survey of 37 countries, released in June 2017, there was a 15% drop in positive views of the US (from 64% to 49%) since Barack Obama left office. Confidence in the US presidency under Trump, however, plummeted 42%.[7] Only in Russia and Israel is Trump more popular than Obama. Six African countries were polled and reveal the following declines of confidence in the US presidency since Trump's inauguration: Senegal (−51%), South Africa (−34%), Ghana (−33%), Kenya (−33%), Tanzania (−27%), and Nigeria (−5%).

One of Trump's first executive actions—the controversial travel ban aimed at halting all travel into the US for an initial 90 days from seven Islamic countries, three of them African (Libya, Somalia, and Sudan), reeked of racism. A US court quickly blocked it. But, it provoked a sharp rebuke from outgoing African Union (AU) Commission Chair

---

[4] See: https://en.wikipedia.org/wiki/Barack_Obama_citizenship_conspiracy_theories.

[5] See: https://theconversation.com/barack-obama-an-enduring-legacy-for-advocates-of-democracy-in-africa-73088.

[6] See: http://www/pewresearch.org/fact-tank/2015/07/23/5-charts-on-americas-very-positive-image-in-africa/.

[7] See: http://www.pewglobal.org/2017/06/26/u-s-image-suffers-as-publics-around-world-question-trumps-leadership/.

and South African presidential candidate Nkosazana Dlamini Zuma. In the remarks prepared for the 30 January AU assembly of African heads of state and government she declared: "The very country to whom our people were taken as slaves during the Trans-Atlantic slave trade has now decided to ban refugees from some of our countries."[8]

When the respected 2016 American National Election Study, with its detailed quantitative analysis of voter attitudes, the salience of racism among Trump's most ardent supporters was confirmed.[9] *New York Times* columnist David Leonhardt drew a similar conclusion when he summarized the political forces shaping Trump's first 100 days in office: "Trump won the White House despite—and partly because of—his disdain for Mexicans, Muslims, and African-Americans and his flirtation with anti-Semitic tropes."[10]

A second area of clashing beliefs arises from Trump's economic nationalism and his disregard for multilateralism. Both of these are inimical to Africa's dependence on global trade and aspirations for greater regional integration and a larger role in global institutions, notably the United Nations and its many agencies with extensive operations in Africa. Forecasts, based on extensive and credible scientific research, show Africa for the rest of this century to be highly vulnerable to the vagaries of climate change, forced migrations, and epidemics of deadly diseases that can only be managed through creative, resilient, carefully balanced, and adequately funded multilateralism.

The 2015 Paris Accord on climate change is the most recent and hopeful indication that 195 sovereign states are capable of negotiating, and voluntarily accepting, a complex mix of varying obligations and costs, in the shared hope for the betterment of all. Trust and agreed means of

---

[8] Retrieved from: http://ewn.co.za/2017/01/30/au-chief-us-travel-ban-heralds-turbulent-times-for-africa.

[9] Retrieved from: http://www.electionstudies.org/studypages/anes_timeseries_2016/anes_timeseries_2016.htm.

[10] Retrieved from: https://www.nytimes.com/2017/04/26/opinion/donald-trumps-first-100-days-the-worst-on-record.html?rref=collection%2Fbyline%2Fdavid-leonhardt&action=click&contentCollection=undefined&region=stream&module=stream_unit&version=latest&contentPlacement=21&pgtype=collection.

verification are essential and can be bolstered by credible scientific evidence of needs, and costs and the prospects of redressing them. Africa is, in many ways, the most vulnerable continent, but it is also the most receptive to creative multilateralism, which makes climate change denial by Trump and his key senior advisers so dangerous. On 1 June, Trump announced America's withdrawal from the agreement and cancelled the pledge to fund the Green Climate Fund that will assist African countries to adapt to climate change.[11] Trump generally favors American disengagement and greater self-reliance and disdains multilateral institutions and arrangements. In the view of former Swedish Prime Minister Carl Biltd, Trump's proclaimed policy of "America First" is evolving into a more dangerous doctrine of "America Alone."[12]

The third area of clashing norms and likely estrangement has to do with Trump's apparent distrust of democratic institutions, processes, and values, despite having been elected President. Perhaps reflecting his highly personal, ever suspicious, and entirely transactional—zero-sum—approach to business, Trump shows autocratic leadership traits that are uncharacteristic of, and may well prove to be incompatible with, America's political traditions and politics. They may be perceived in Africa, however, as almost the mirror image of some of the worst characteristics of the colonial, white minority, and post-colonial autocratic governance that has blighted many countries on the continent in the past 50 years. These realities prompted then President Barack Obama, during his first visit to Africa, to declare in his only major public address on the continent that to succeed politically and economically Africa needs strong institutions, not strong men.[13]

The fact that Trump holds a contrary view was made evident in the early months of his presidency by his preference for dealing directly with au-

---

[11] See: https://theconversation.com/africa-is-the-perfect-testing-ground-for-adapting-to-the-anthropocene-epoch-65055.

[12] Retrieved from: https://www.nytimes.com/2017/06/02/opinion/donald-trump-poisons-the-world-html; https://www.washingtonpost.com/news/global-opinions/wp/2017/06/02/the-scariest-part-of-trumps-speech-wasnt-about-the-paris-accord/?utm_term=.5bd60849b01f.

[13] See: http://www.sundaytimes.lk/090712/International/sundaytimesinternational-03.html.

thoritarian strongmen, notably Russia's Vladimir Putin, Egypt's Abdel Fattah el-Sisi, Turkey's Recep Tayyip Erdogan, the Philippine's Rodrigo Duterte, and Saudi Arabia's King Salman and should alarm Africans who may be struggling under very difficult conditions to build and sustain fledgling democracies. For this could reassure Africa's autocrats and oligarchs that their repressive and corrupt practices will be less scrutinized and less likely to be the subject of sanctions imposed by Washington.[14]

Trump disdains past US government support for international programs to advance democracy, human rights, the rule of law, elections, and other elements of good governance, which have been a major focus of US-Africa relations for decades. Many governments have welcomed, or at least tolerated, US support for pro-democracy non-governmental organizations (NGOs). There is no regional consensus on any specific form of democracy, or a sudden resolve to interfere in each other's internal affairs. But, there has been a historic shift in regional diplomatic norms. African governments will no longer be indifferent to abuses of power, including denial of basic human rights, internal conflicts, and violation of constitutionally sanctioned presidential term limits, especially unconstitutional changes of government. These are all seen as early warnings of such conflicts and the dangers to regional stability of forced migration and untold numbers of refugees.

Since 2002, Africa's leaders have formally endorsed the spread and entrenchment of democracy as serving their collective aspirations for sustainable peace, economic development, and as a basis for gradually advancing regional integration. Democratic norms are embedded in the African Union's Constitutive Act of 2002, which supplanted the less politically ambitious Charter of the Organisation of African Unity, a 1963 post-colonial sovereign alliance that precluded involvement in the internal affairs of members. The AU commits all 55 of its member states to "promote democratic principles and institutions, popular participation and good governance" and "to show respect for democratic principles, human rights, the rule of law and good governance."[15]

---

[14] See: https://www.washingtonpost.com/politics/trump-keeps-praising-international-strongmen-alarming-human-rights-advocates/2017/05/01/6848d018-2e81-11e7-9dec-764dc781686f_story.html?utm_term=.5a775c4b7490.

[15] Retrieved from: http://www.achpr.org/instruments/au-constitutive-act/.

To begin implementing the AU's vision of a more democratically inclusive, peaceful, and integrated Africa, AU members also unanimously adopted in 2007 and later ratified the African Charter for Democracy, Elections and Governance (ACDEG). This Charter commits all states to holding regular peaceful democratic elections, open to observation by AU election monitors drawn from other African states. In a report prepared for the Electoral Institute for Sustainable Democracy in Africa (EISA), to commemorate its 20th anniversary in 2016, it was noted that EISA, a pan-African NGO based in Johannesburg, provides technical assistance to all AU electoral observation missions in virtually all AU member states.[16] Quality and credibility vary, of course, but this is a positive development, along with the related constitutional provisions in most African states that set two-term limits for the head of state, although these limits have been overturned in 13 of the 38 states that have adopted them.[17]

Trump has demurred from promoting democracy internationally, including in Africa. During his campaign and initial months in office, he has shown a shocking disregard for America's democratic institutions, the constitutional checks and balances, and the primacy of the rule of law and due process, all of which are so essential in sustaining any democratic experiment.[18] His election and behavior in office should remind leaders and publics in Africa's young and still fragile democracies that no democracy, even the oldest one, is ever fully secure or perfect. As Margret Dongo, a prominent Zimbabwean democrat and former parliamentarian, once quipped: "America is still growing into its Constitution."[19] Trump threatens this growth as never before, raising new fears among Africa's democrats.

Africa, after all, is the world's most ethnically diverse region, where deadly conflicts most often occur within, not between or among states.

---

[16] See: https://www.eisa.org.za/pdf/eisa2016Stremlau.pdf.

[17] See: https://theconversation.com/democracy-is-taking-root-in-africa-but-that-doesnt-mean-it-works-all-the-time-78273.

[18] See: https://foreignpolicy.com/2017/06/09/a-shining-comey-on-a-hill-trump-russia--investigation/?utm_source=Sailthru&utm_medium=email&utm_campaign=New%20Campaign&utm_term=%2AEditors%20Picks.

[19] A remark made to the author.

Democracy, despite its challenges, is increasingly viewed as the best—perhaps the only—way to accommodate this pluralism.[20] Democracy, in theory, should provide ways and means to accommodate and reap the advantages of diversity, while preventing and resolving local conflicts. Trump's rise to political power through the demagoguery of clear and emotional appeals to disaffected and angry white voters, promising them renewed privileges and greater access to national resources, also alarms liberal Africans.

In the past quarter century, despite the general weaknesses in the governing institutions, along with the prevalence of small and undiversified economies and extreme inequalities in many post-colonial African countries, democratic experiments have proliferated throughout sub-Saharan Africa. Acemoglu and Robinson's (2012) global study—*Why Nations Fail*—offers many vital insights into the debilitating nature of extractive state rule in many African countries, compared to the few that have succeeded in developing more inclusive and resilient governing institutions. There are worrying signs that democratic reforms have at least slowed and, in a few countries, been reversed.

Freedom House's latest (2016) index shows barely half of sub-Saharan Africa to be free or partly free and a major 2017 report—*Breaking Down Democracy: Goals, Strategies and Methods of Modern Authoritarians*—adds vital political analysis to the 2016 index.[21] The latest Index of African Governance, produced by the Mo Ibrahim Foundation, surveyed 54 African countries in 2015 and concluded, "overall governance progress in Africa is stalling."[22] The accuracy and fairness of the Ibrahim numerical ranking is debated across Africa and among donor democracies.

Recent research into African governance and economic development issues (Mills et al. 2017) offers a more hopeful picture, citing evidence of a positive causal relationship between economic growth and democratic advancement in 43 sub-Saharan countries, compared with regimes still under military or civilian autocratic rule. This study also stresses the

---

[20] See: https://www.washingtonpost.com/news/worldviews/wp/2013/05/16/a-revealing-map-of-the-worlds-most-and-least-ethnically-diverse-countries/?utm_term=.84720d35d1fc.

[21] Retrieved from: www.freedomhouse.org.

[22] Retrieved from: www.moibrahimfoundation.org.

advantages of democratic over autocratic governance in preventing and resolving domestic conflict and tensions. The African polling organization, AfroBarometer,[23] has shown a steadily rising preference for democratic government between 2002 and 2012, concluding that by 2013, 70% of those surveyed in 34 countries favored democracy over other kinds of government.

Risks remain, however, with tensions rooted in the extractive and autocratic legacies of colonialism and persistent poverty across a region where the main source of income for the majority of the population remains subsistence agriculture and the population is the world's youngest and fastest growing. As former Nigerian president Olusegun Obasanjo warns,[24] sub-Sahara's youth (under 15) will exceed 450 million in a total population projected to double to over 2 billion by 2050. Unless governments acquire greater capacities and economies grow, the youth, Obasanjo warns, will continue to be uneducated, unskilled, unemployed, and frustrated.

It is difficult to know the impact of Trump's presidency on the attitudes of Africa's 18-to-24-year-old population, or even the extent to which his actions trend on the social media. From personal anecdotal evidence of South African university students and visits to campuses in Nigeria and elsewhere, the issues raised above do generate considerable interest and comment. Although Obama was a much bigger draw, Trump's actions also attract attention, most of it critical or mocking, especially when inspired by the satire of a celebrity, notably South African comedian and US television talk show star, Trevor Noah.[25] It is impossible to know how Trump's reign will affect the attitudes toward America of Africa's next generation of leaders or the prospects for US-Africa cooperation, but the fate of the programs highlighted in the next section will likely yield important clues.

---

[23] See: http://www.afrobarometer.org/data.

[24] Retrieved from: http://newafricanmagazine.com/tapping-potential-youth-drive-africas-agricultural-transformation/.

[25] See: https://www.youtube.com/watch?v=2FPrJxTvgdQ; http://www.dailymail.co.uk/video/news/video-1218615/Trevor-Noah-argues-Trump-perfect-African-president.html; https://www.facebook.com/thedailyshow/videos/10153629107981800/.

Trump's Africa Policies

Of more immediate concern to African governments than the political and social undercurrents likely to strain US-Africa relations during the Trump years, is the fate of specific programs and partnerships that have been the mainstay of generally good relations since the end of the Cold War. These include cooperative initiatives aimed at promoting trade, investment, building capacity for more rapid economic development. The US has also championed efforts to advance and entrench good governance, democracy, and human rights. Other US priorities have been improving public health, education, increasing agricultural productivity and resilience, developing alternative sources of energy, and, more recently, expanding efforts to help countries adapt and mitigate the effects of global climate change. Small but extensive military assistance programs have been more controversial, during and after the Cold War, and recently justified as helping vulnerable African governments combat violent extremism and acts of terrorism.

Clues about how the Trump administration might develop its Africa policy surfaced in a *New York Times* report in January 2017—a four-page list of Africa-related questions that was circulating at the State Department and Pentagon.[26] Though the report ascribed authorship to unnamed members of the Trump transition team, US embassy officials in South Africa said the list had been generated elsewhere. It suggested the curtailment of development and humanitarian commitments, in favor of pushing business opportunities. Its substance, however, has not been repudiated and is generally compatible with the tone and tenor of Trump's "America First" rhetoric and the draft budget he sent to Congress in early March. Among the reported questions prominent on the list were as follows:[27]

- How does U.S. business compete with other exporting nations in Africa? Are we losing out to the Chinese?
- With so much corruption in Africa, how much of our funding

---

[26] Retrieved from: https://www.nytimes.com/2017/01/13/world/africa/africa-donald-trump.html?_r=0.

[27] Retrieved from: https://www.nytimes.com/2017/01/13/world/africa/africa-donald-trump.html?_r=0.

is stolen? Why should we spend these funds on Africa when we are suffering here in the US?

- We've been fighting al-Shabaab [a terrorist group operating in Somalia], why haven't we won? We've been hunting Kony [Ugandan terrorist leader] for years, is it worth the effort? The LRA [Kony's Lord's Resistance Army] never attacked U.S. interests, why do we care?

The memo did not address Africa's special trading relationship with the US under the highly favorable terms of the Africa Growth and Opportunity Act (AGOA),[28] a major concern of African exporters of agricultural products and manufactured goods, although not oil and other natural resources. Trump has not spoken publicly about AGOA despite his loud and frequent complaints about most other US trade agreements and policies, which he flatly disparages—without proof or context—as taking unfair advantage of a too pliable US. He promises they will all be renegotiated in the spirit of "America First."

There was much speculation in the South African media about Trump reneging on AGOA or trying to renegotiate terms more favorable to the US. South Africa, as Africa's biggest exporter of manufactured goods, would be especially hard hit. Fortunately, AGOA was renewed for ten years in 2015 and enjoys bi-partisan congressional support and Trump has indicated no interest in challenging it. US proponents of AGOA also point to the 120,000 US jobs that have resulted from expanded trade with Africa, a selling point with Trump. Similar support and presidential silence apply so far to the continuation of the Millennium Challenge Corporation, a President George W. Bush initiative that has led to billions of dollars in investments in partnership compacts with African governments and has been linked to obligations to greater government transparency and democratic accountability.

On March 3, the Trump White House sent Congress its proposed budget priorities for 2018.[29] So far, this provides the most comprehensive picture of Trump's national priorities, which have yet to be debated and

---

[28] Retrieved from: http://trade.gov/agoa/.

[29] Retrieved from: https://www.whitehouse.gov/sites/whitehouse.gov/files/omb/budget/fy2018/2018_blueprint.pdf.

approved by Congress. His total request is for $4 trillion, but his budget priorities only apply to one-third of the total—its discretionary spending component—that includes defense. Congress would have to amend the legislation that mandates how the spending of the larger portion of the budget, for items such as Medicare and servicing America's $20 trillion debt.

Trump also wants major tax cuts for wealthy Americans and corporations. Yet, under current revenue projections, the proportion of the budget over which he has no control will need an additional $487 billion. How he will reconcile these competing priorities is unknown, but this fiscal situation does not bode well for carrying forward America's current programs of development and humanitarian assistance for Africa.

US spending on foreign assistance in 2017 will total about $34 billion, with roughly 21% designated for Africa, while representing only about 0.2% of the total budget, according to CNBC-Africa.[30] The Congressional Research Service[31] uses a somewhat broader definition of foreign assistance, yielding a total of $49 billion or 1.3% of the Federal Budget. In any case, cutting aid to sub-Saharan Africa would represent a tiny fraction of the $54 billion to augment a defense budget already larger than the combined total of the world's next fifteen largest militaries. Perhaps because aid to Africa is so relatively small, the bi-partisan congressional proponents of these programs are likely to prevail. Indeed, two of Barak Obama's biggest Africa initiatives—to improve African agriculture (Feed the Future) and develop alternative sources of energy (PowerAfrica)—are not referred to in Trump's budget outline.[32]

Among US global assistance priorities, just $8 billion was allocated in 2015 for 49 sub-Saharan countries, considerably less than the $11.8 billion given to just four others: Afghanistan, Israel, Iraq, and Egypt.[33]

---

[30] See: http://foreignpolicy.com/2017/03/22/trumps-america-first-budget-puts-africa-last/; http://www.latimes.com/world/la-fg-global-aid-true-false-20170501-htmlstory.html.

[31] See: https://fas.org/sgp/crs/row/index.html.

[32] Retrieved from: https://www.usaid.gov/news-information/fact-sheets/jul-20-2016-president-obamas-commitment-global-development.

[33] See: https://www.foreignassistance.gov/explore.

This aid is, however, prized by the millions of Africans who benefit from it. Whether, and by how much, Trump's first budget will cut the cost of development, humanitarian, military, and other mutually beneficial partnerships with African nations will only become clear when budget bills are finally signed and the Trump administration's Africa policies are articulated and adequately staffed. But were Trump to have his way, the 28% in savings from cutting foreign assistance would not likely come from such strategic priorities as Afghanistan or Israel but from Africa.

More than half of US assistance to Africa in the recent years has gone to bilateral health programs, including the treatment of HIV/AIDS, material and family health and support for government healthcare systems, mainly in Africa. And Trump does propose to maintain current funding of the President's Emergency Plan for Aids Relief (Pepfar), initiated by President George W. Bush. Pepfar is vitally important to South Africa, saving millions of lives there, as it does in many other African countries.

As for aid for the health of African women and families, the budget reflects Trump's earlier executive order defunding organizations that provide family planning assistance. So, in April, the Department of State said it would end support for the United Nations Population Fund (UNFPA), to which the US has been the third-biggest contributor, providing nearly $80 million in 2015.[34] The reason given was that this violates the Trump administration's policies announced during Trump's first week in office, including ending all aid to any organization providing abortion services, information counseling or referrals. The impact is likely to be especially hard on African women, whose mortality during childbirth has steadily declined since 1990. It could also result in an increase in unsafe abortions, which currently account for 13% of all maternal deaths. Major reductions in US contributions to the United Nations Children's Emergency Fund and World Health Organization would, if enacted, hit Africa especially hard.

International humanitarian assistance, much of it channeled through UN agencies for their work in Africa, only accounts for 16% of current US aid. The Trump budget proposes to defund the State Department's

---

[34] See: http://www.unfpa.org/press/statement-unfpa-us-decision-withhold-funding.

Emergency Refugee and Migration Assistance (ERMA) account, used to avert and mitigate disasters such as this year's famine in South Sudan and to help resettle and sustain some 65 million refugees, many of them Africans. The US contribution to such relief represents, at 29%, the world's biggest, although at $6.4 billion it is just a tiny slice of the US budget. Much of this is in the form of agricultural goods purchased from US farmers, which, for domestic reasons, may be the last to be cut. But, Trump's budget targets the UN and its agencies for major reductions of US support, which could include the financial support to, among others, the UN High Commissioner for Refugees. US support for the World Bank and UN Development Program, which have their biggest operations in Africa, are also targeted for large reductions.

Military and security assistance account for 35% of the aid budget and much of this is also spent domestically on purchasing US military equipment, training foreign military personnel, and UN peacekeeping operations. The last category has been targeted for cuts of $1 billion, which will likely be opposed by many in the Congress, but it sends a strong signal to African governments that they can no longer look to the US as a major contributor to UN operations, most of which are currently in troubled states in Africa.

The same cannot be said of US bilateral military assistance linked to Trump's counter-terrorism priority. That, we may assume, will be at the heart of any Africa policy. Much of this assistance is buried in the huge Pentagon budget. Trump may have been unaware of the approximately 1,700 members of Special Forces and other US military personnel undertaking 96 missions in 21 African countries, but it is doubtful he disapproves.[35] The number of countries immediately threatened by violent extremists is, however, much smaller—Nigeria, Kenya, several others in the Horn region, and the Sahelian central Africa.

As for funding the diplomacy necessary to help prevent and mitigate the need for peacekeeping operations and much of the military aid, the State Department, along with USAID, is targeted for a 29% cut in funding. Among all federal departments, this proportion is only surpassed by

---

[35] Retrieved from: http://www.newyorker.com/news/daily-comment/the-enduring-american-military-mission-in-africa

the 31% cut proposed for the Environmental Protection Agency (EPA). Secretary of State Rex Tillerson accepted this cut without protest and maintains that the reason why he has filled few senior policy posts, including that of the Assistant Secretary for Africa, is that it allows him time to restructure his department and, presumably, accommodate a big budget reduction.

The effects of understaffing on US-Africa relations are impossible to measure. Reports that African governments are being needlessly irritated, however, illustrate the problem. One example was the visit of Rwandan President Paul Kagame to Washington in March, during which no one in the Trump administration was available to meet him. Another occurred in late April when Tillerson unexpectedly and inexplicably cancelled a scheduled meeting at the State Department with African Union Commission Chair Moussa Faki Mahamat. This not only reportedly infuriated Mahamat but also surely dismayed senior officials in all AU member states.

A final substantive area of critical concern for African countries is the disruption and dangers posed by global warming. A key element of the Paris Accord, in the conclusion of which the Obama administration played a leadership role,[36] was the creation of a Green Climate Fund, the purpose of which would be to assist the poorest and most vulnerable countries, mostly in Africa.[37] An initial fund of $10 billion was pledged, with the expectation that it would grow to $100 billion annually in order to fund projects and programs to help these countries adapt to global warming. The Obama administration pledged $3 billion, paying out $1 billion just prior to President Obama leaving office.

Trump criticized the Paris Accord process throughout his campaign and his first 100 days in office, appointing climate denialists to key senior posts, including Cabinet Secretary in charge of the Environment Protection Agency, Scott Pruitt of oil-rich Oklahoma, and cancelling a host of earlier executive orders and policies issued by Obama aimed at mitigating the US's production of greenhouse gases. On 1 June, he for-

---

[36] Retrieved from: http://unfccc.int/paris_agreement/items/9485.php.
[37] Retrieved from: http://www.greenclimate.fund/-/african-countries-propose-ambitious-gcf-pipeline-at-cape-town-dialogue.

mally announced the US would withdraw from the Paris Accord and, in particular, would not contribute to or cooperate with the Green Climate Fund, which is so vital to Africa's ability to adapt to global warming.[38]

Africa is the region least responsible for, most vulnerable to, and least able to afford the cost of adapting to, global climate change. Southern Africa is already suffering the effects of severe drought and other extreme weather events as the sub-region is warming at twice the rate of the global mean, as three of South Africa's leading climate scientists show (Scholes, Scholes, and Lucas 2015). Prompt and pervasive international criticism of Trump's actions, including a leaked EU-China joint climate statement that suggests they are prepared to replace the US as climate leaders, do give Africa hope.[39] There are also some early indications that Africans themselves may be prodded by Trump's affront to seek greater national, regional, and international self-reliance and integration, without regard to the US, in meeting their Paris Accord pledges.[40]

Trump's Leadership Traits Resonate Negatively in Africa

There are some important ironies to note regarding Donald Trump's leadership traits. The man who now speaks for the world's oldest democracy conducts himself in office in ways that often appear more characteristic of several of Africa's most notorious autocrats. The most famous comments on these similarities were made during the 2016 US presidential campaign by South African comedian Trevor Noah, now host of America's *The Daily Show*.[41] Among the demagogic traits that Noah noted were:

---

[38] Retrieved from: https://www.youtube.com/watch?v=Q9gf5viOEDg; see also: https://www.washingtonpost.com/posteverything/wp/2017/06/02/trump-will-stop-paying-into-the-green-climate-fund-he-has-no-idea-what-it-is/?utm_term=.91cee8237ce5.

[39] Retrieved from: http://www.climatechagenews.com/2017/06/01leaked-eu-china-climate-statement-full/

[40] Retrieved from: https://theconversation.com/as-trump-smacks-the-climate-worl...mate%20world%20must%20do%20better%20to%20save%20planet.

[41] Retrieved from: http://www.vulture.com/2016/10/trevor-noah-compares-trump-to-african-dictators.html.

- offering people simple and absolute answers to complex issues; and
- appealing to their fear, anger and prejudices in emotionally compelling ways.

Juxtaposing quotes from Trump with virtually identical language used by former dictators Idi Amin Dada of Uganda, Muammar Gaddafi of Libya, and, of late, Robert Mugabe in Zimbabwe made for some sensational television clips, widely available in Africa and wildly popular among US progressives. At that stage, however, the prospects of a Trump victory were low.

Just after Trump's election, however, Noah reprised his African strongman comparison in a much more politically relevant fashion, comparing Trump with South Africa's current president, Jacob Zuma, now mired in controversy related to corruption and abuses of power.[42] Noah's phrase, "when you look at Zuma and Trump it seems like they're brothers from another mother," quickly went viral.[43]

Among the traits shared by Zuma and Trump that are damaging or could damage their countries' international standing and domestic health are the "unclear lines between their children running the family businesses and those kids' access to the government, threatening to prosecute political enemies using government resources [referred to in South Africa as 'state capture'], and vowing to censor the press."[44] Allegations of conflicts of interest arising, in Trump's case, from the business dealings and official extraordinary access enjoyed by his son-in-law, Jared Kushner, are raised when South Africans express concerns about leaked emails purportedly showing comparable conflicts involving President Zuma and his son Duduzane, ensuring that their family's business interests have privileged access to government contracts.[45]

---

[42] Retrieved from: http://www.businessinsider.com/trevor-noah-donald-trump-south-african-president-jacob-zuma-2016-11.

[43] See: https://www.facebook.com/thedailyshow/videos/10153629107981800/; see also: http://www.dailymail.co.uk/video/news/video-1218615/Trevor-Noah-argues-Trump-perfect-African-president.html.

[44] See: https://www.facebook.com/thedailyshow/videos/10153629107981800/; see also: http://www.dailymail.co.uk/video/news/video-1218615/Trevor-Noah-argues-Trump-perfect-African-president.html.

[45] Retrieved from: https://www.timeslive.co.za/news/south-africa/2017-06-02-

The success of Noah's satire, of course, is the kernel of truth it contains. Some further comments on the autocratic attributes of Trump's leadership style and personality may shed light on the less obvious ways in which his presidency could have an impact on the prospects for sustainable democracies in Africa and on US-Africa relations.[46]

Favoring Strong Men Over Strong Institution

Trump has showed little interest in sub-Saharan Africa, aside from placing brief 'phone calls to the presidents of South Africa, Nigeria, and Kenya, which reportedly focused on countering terror and promoting US economic interests. The only African invited to Washington for a state visit during this period was Egypt's dictator, Abdel Fattah el-Sisi, and this defiance of Obama's policy of avoiding such encounters could result in future visits by other African autocrats to the Trump White House. What was not mentioned, but is much discussed in South African foreign affairs circles and, presumably, in other African cities, is Trump's criticism of the previous US administrations' emphasis on good governance and strengthening democratic institutions, including limitations on executive powers. In South Africa, Gumede (2017, 36–37) warns of "demagogue peers," including Trump, Zuma, Erdogan, Putin and Duterte (Gumede 2017, 36–37).[47]

Crony Capitalism

Trump's transactional approach to governing and foreign affairs and the blurred lines between his personal financial interests and those of his former business associates and current members of his Cabinet and family members are the bane of many resource-rich African states. There, the extraction of resources by a small elite precludes the emergence of more inclusive and resilient institutions of governance. America's institutions are comparatively strong, yet Trump's conflicts of economic interests

---

guptaemails-duduzane-emerges-as-middleman-for-zuma-with-foreign-business/.

[46] The following attributes draw upon: https://theconversation.com/trumps-leadershp-traits-are-bad-...its%20are%20bad%news%20for%20democrats%20in%20Africa.

[47] Retrieved from: http://democracyworks.org.za/african-leaders-are-masters-at-post-truth-politics/.

and disregard for institutional safeguards against such practices are bad nationally and bad example for countries where such practices already predominate. Furthermore, Trump's reported history of many financially advantageous dealings with Russian oligarchs may also resonate among Africa's most corrupt and often least democratic governments, where the prospects may suddenly have brightened, with the US more likely to remain essentially a safe haven for illicit financial flows.[48]

Transparency

For decades, American presidents have been pressing African governments to become more transparent for the benefit of their citizens and as a cornerstone of good governance. Trump's persistent refusal to disclose his own financial dealings and taxes and the new restrictions on access to information at the White House and among his Cabinet officials sets another bad example for Africa.

Freedom of Expression

This is an all-too-familiar affliction of African autocrats, which now has many disturbing parallels in the Trump administration's restrictions on press access to the White House, curtailment of press briefings, and strict new limitations on members of the media allowed to accompany senior US officials, including the Secretary of State, on foreign trips.

The Political Art of Lying

Trump's frequent blatant lies are well documented. The *Washington Post*'s non-partisan fact checkers documented 623 false and misleading claims made by Trump during his first 137 days in office.[49] His use of lying, which he often does when claiming others are lying about him, may even be strategic, what a *Washington Post* columnist Dana Milbank calls "verbal jujitsu,"[50] using his opponents' strengths against them. Ly-

---

[48] Retrieved from: http://www.gfintegrity.org/.
[49] Retrieved from: https://www.washingtonpost.com/graphics/politics/trump-claims-database/?tid=a_inl&utm_term=.c1081f9b2c96. On 13 November it was reported that in 298 days Trump made 1,628 false and misleading claims. Retrieved from: https://www.washingtonpost.com/graphics/politics/trump-claims-database/?tid=a_inl&utm_term=.d36a59b8c8df.
[50] Retrieved from: https://www.washingtonpost.com/opinions/of-course-trump-

ing may also reflect East African editor and journalist Charles Onyango-Obbo's warning that "[t]he genius of Trump is that he understands what adept guerrilla leaders figured out ages ago—do that which the opponent thinks is impossible or so unthinkable, that they have not planned how to defend it."[51] Lying in emotionally appealing ways to delude citizens and to discredit opponents and keep them off balance is a familiar strategy of demagogues and African autocrats.

Opinion Over Fact

Trump's preference for his opinion over facts is similar to the fact-free tendencies of African strongmen. His denigration of responsible media reporting and his dismissal of scientific evidence—most notably regarding climate change—have seriously undermined his administration's credibility both at home and abroad. When Zuma defies facts in justifying attacks on foreigners in South Africa, Gumede (2017, 36–37) imagines South Africa's president calling "... in Donald Trump style—for a wall to be built alongside the Limpopo River to keep out those northerly neighbours." Or, in Zuma stirring up popular support and false hopes for "Radical Economic Transformation," Gumede compares Zuma's "layered lies" to those that Trump uses to promote his demagogic slogan, "Make America Great Again!" Zuma and Trump both benefit from uncritical dissemination of their unfounded claims and promises by favored broadcasters financed by their enablers, ANN7 (and the *New Age* newspaper) in South Africa and Fox News, among others, in America.

Infallibility

This is another self-righteous trait Trump shares with African autocrats such as the former Zimbabwean President Robert Mugabe. It means never accepting responsibility and always blaming others. While Trump cannot ascribe his failures to imperialism, as Mugabe does, his citing of all sorts of unproven conspiracies to thwart or unseat him may reassure like-minded peers in African capitals.

---

called-comey-a-liar-thats-his-strategy/2017/06/12/6ff4b4-4a8-4fa6-11e7-91eb-9611861a988f_story.html?utm_term+.026ffla843bf.

51 Retrieved from: https://theconversation.com/idi-amin-and-donald-trump-strong-men-with-unlikely-parallels-78004?utm_medium+emali&utm_campaign%20f.

Repression

Trump does not accept criticism from anyone, whether it be the media, Democrats, human rights groups or other civil society organizations. Repression of these groups has a long and troubling history in Africa and recent closures of Internet access in eleven countries point to a possible resurgence. America's legal institutions have thus far restrained Trump, as they have Zama in South Africa, but their willingness to test and even suppress efforts to hold them fairly accountable rightly alarms democrats there and elsewhere.

Dignity and Equality for Women

Trump's disregard for women's rights, both in his personal behavior and in his early executive actions to restrict their right to access family planning support, safe abortions and anti-discrimination protections, rivals the most orthodox behavior of traditional African leaders. His glamorizing male dominance with a modern gloss, including in nearly all of his Cabinet and other senior appointments, is likely to continue to resonate perniciously in a still overwhelmingly male-dominant Africa.

Tribal Trump

The campaign to "Make America Great" raises the question: great for whom? And one of Trump's few core beliefs and values appears to be the need to reassert the primacy in America of white, Christian men. Ethnic nationalism has a long and conflict-ridden history in Africa. In recent years, constitutional provisions requiring political parties and electoral victories that satisfy various minimal standards of diversity have moderated ethnic nationalism. Norms supporting civic nationalism are also now embedded in the African Union and sub-regional organizations. These norms are also linked to the AU's aspirations for greater national and regional peace and security and for regional integration.

CONCLUSION

If there is a silver lining to Trump's presidency—for Americans and for Africans—it could be the revitalization of civil society and political action in the US to thwart many of his policies and the election of a

Democrat majority to the US Congress in 2018, which could further restrain—even impeach—him. What impact this might have in inspiring, or even abetting, democratic forces in Africa can only be surmised, along with any residual effects on US-Africa relations.

Indeed, in his assessment of Trump's first 100 days, author and activist Eric Liu in the *Washington Post* refers ironically to "one of the greatest surges of American citizen action in half a century as Trump's most striking accomplishment so far."[52] The epic Women's March on Washington following Trump's inauguration was an immediate reaction, prompting demonstrations of solidarity across America and around the world, including in South Africa. Popular reactions and judicial action to halt Trump's Muslim ban were another benchmark of resistance, applauded in Africa's mainstream and social media. If the resistance to the Trump presidency respects constitutional rights and obligations and is fully transparent, this might give hope to those working for sustainable democracy in Africa.

Reports of large spikes in the membership and funding of American NGOs opposed to Trump's various actions are also hopeful indications of democratic revitalization. So, too, are sharp increases in the circulation and advertising revenue of, and hiring at America's leading news media, both print and electronic, many of which have already played vital roles in exposing conflicts of interest and possible obstructions of justice by Trump and several key members of his administration. Trump's mendacity and disregard for factual reporting, scientific evidence, and the sanctity of America's legal institutions and due process, could ultimately lead to Congressional actions that would result in his leaving office before completing his first term.

One can also hope that, in the meantime, public pressures on both sides of the Atlantic will demand greater reliance on facts and scientific evidence, even when honestly and openly contested, in complex critical areas, such as the nature and extent of the risks resulting from global warming, and the likely impact and costs of actions to mitigate and over-

---

[52] Retrieved from: https://www.washingtonpost.com/opinions/trumps-most-striking-accomplishment-so-far/2017/04/24/904f71e2-23b5-11e7-bb9d-8cd6118e1409_story.html?utm_term=.656495893071.

come their effects. This will place ever-greater responsibilities on universities and centers for advanced research in all regions, especially Africa, where the evidence of climate impact is so ominous. This will require more than solid research done by credible well-trained experts. The role of public intellectuals, assured of academic freedom, in countering deceptively simple solutions offered by demagogues in the guise of populism will be critically important. Well-informed popular demands for greater transparency and accountability, locally, nationally and globally can be an antidote to the demagoguery and abuse of power of leaders such as Donald Trump and the best hope for sustainable democracy in Africa as well.

REFERENCES

Acemoglu, D. and J. Robinson. 2012. *Why Nations Fail.* New York: Crown Business.

Gumede, W. 2017. "Post-truth Politics: Down the Rabbit Hole with Jacob Zuma." *The Africa Report*, 90, May, 36–37.

Mills, G., O. Obasanjo, J. Herbst, and D. Davis. 2017. *Making Africa Work.* Cape Town, ZA: Tafelberg.

Scholes, B., M. Scholes, and M. Lucas. 2015. *Climate Change: Briefings from Southern Africa.* Johannesburg, ZA: Wits University Press.

14
KAZAKHSTAN LOOKS AT THE UNITED STATES UNDER DONALD J. TRUMP

Scott Spehr and Aigul Adibayeva

INTRODUCTION

A post-communist, semi-authoritarian country, a major producer of strategic commodities, looks at the United States under Donald J. Trump and sees ... itself.

The recent election of Donald J. Trump as President of the United States (US) has unleashed a global tsunami of speculation as to what his election signifies, in terms of the national mood, and what it portends, in terms of future policy on the part of the world's most powerful actor. In Kazakhstan, however, the response to Trump's election, and anxiety over future US policy, has been rather muted.

The major players in Kazakhstan's neck of the woods are Russia and China, for obvious reasons, ranging from proximity, to political culture, to recent historical ties. The EU and the US play a lesser role, as balancers in some cases, and even then the influence of the EU has been ascendant, as US influences has been in decline for a decade or more. It is not particularly surprising, then, that reaction to Trump's election, and the policies espoused and rhetoric employed during and following his election campaign, has been somewhat underwhelming.

CONTRASTS AND CONGRUENCE

Political Leadership

One reason why alarm about Trump's election has not been particularly forthcoming, either from the general public or from official channels, is that the purported authoritarian, populist, or nationalist tendencies of the Trump presidency are not that alien to the political culture, or the political practice, of this semi-authoritarian state. Indeed, for the last 25 years or so, Kazakhstan has been led by an unchallenged autocrat, Nursultan Nazarbayev, whose authoritarian proclivities make Trump seem like a model democratic leader. And, it should be added, President-for-life Nazarbayev appears to be genuinely popular, perhaps because of his "strong leader" tendencies, in this still rather conservative, traditional society with little experience of actual political opposition, protection of individual rights, freedom of expression, or other similar democratic practices. Nazarbayev, for his part, argues that external realities should be taken into account when judging the legitimacy of less-than-democratic regimes (Putz 2015).

This reflects the notion that circumstances—existential threats to the survival of a regime, for example, or even the threat of significant disorder or sociopolitical paralysis—are justification for, and explanatory of, authoritarian, repressive, or even murderous regimes. Regimes based on the cult-of-personality may reflect this dynamic, in terms of the deliberate construction of an image of an omnipotent, all-knowing, indispensable leader, supposedly the possessor of the charisma that legitimates all of his actions; examples abound—Josef Stalin, Mao Zedong, Kemal Atatürk, even Adolf Hitler. In Central Asia, this pattern, on a somewhat lesser scale, has been emulated to a greater or lesser degree—Saparmurat Niazovin in Turkmenistan, Islam Karimov in Uzbekistan, as well as Nursultan Nazarbayev. As noted by Max Weber, however, charisma is an inborn trait, not one that can be constructed. Hence, the cult-of-personality, as a deliberate construction, is really incompatible with the basic notion of charismatic leadership (see, for example, Epley 2015). In any event, it should remembered, that those post-Soviet republics—Stans—where such deliberately constructed charismatic leaders have been absent—in Tajikistan and Kyrgyzstan—political instability has been frequent.

In Kazakhstan, given the overwhelming centrality of its president to all things political, it is not surprising that the president's party controls nearly all seats in the country's legislative bodies.[1] And, going the Trump president/daughter relationship one better, Nazarbayev's daughter,

---

[1] There is a small "opposition" virtually created, or ordered into existence, to give the system some small semblance of democratic competition, a tactic reminiscent

Dariga, has been a Deputy Prime Minister, and is now one of the president's appointees to the Kazakhstan Senate.² Given the cultural context, it is not surprising then that a recent—unrepresentative and likely unreliable—a Demoscope poll (March 2017) indicated that four times as many Kazakhstani respondents had a favorable opinion of President Trump than an unfavorable one.³

Rule-of-Law and Corruption

The rule of law is very weak in Kazakhstan. The World Justice Project ranks Kazakhstan 73rd out of 113 countries on its 2016 Rule of Law index, whereas the US was ranked 18th.⁴ In terms of corruption, Kazakhstan ranked 131st out of 176 countries and territories in Transparency International's 2016 Corruption Perceptions Index, whereas the US ranked 18th.⁵ The McCain Institute declares "Nazarbayev's family dominates politics, restricting freedom of expression and association, while corruption is widespread."⁶

It is not surprising, then, that legal restraints on the activities of people in positions of political power are widely ignored and are not really expected by the average citizen of Kazakhstan. Thus, it is not surprising that Trump's apparent obliviousness to the constitutional limitations on his president's power, and so his presidential actions that may reflect potential abuse of power when, for example dealing with heads of investigatory agencies such as the Federal Bureau of Investigation, elicits little popular or official dismay or approbation in Kazakhstan. It is also not surprising that charges that Trump is corrupt and has used the Oval Office to advance his business interests has not gained much (if any) attention in Kazakhstan.⁷

---

of Kemal Atatürk's policy in this regard in Turkey.

2   Retrieved from: https://www.neweurasia.info/en/events-and-opinions1/1444-are-political-reforms-afoot-in-kazakhstan-not-so-fast-nazarbayev-will-remain-the-supreme-arbiter.

3   Retrieved from: http://demos.kz/rus/index.php?poll=59.

4   Retrieved from: hxk://data.worldjusticeproject.org/.

5   Retrieved from: https://www.transparency.org/news/feature/corruption_perceptions_index_2016.

6   Retrieved from: https://www.mccaininstitute.org/9460-2/.

7   There is another possible nexus of similarity between Presidents Trump and

Policy Comparisons

There are several areas where fruitful comparisons can be made between the policies articulated, however incoherently or incompletely, by the new Trump administration and those espoused by the Nazarbayev regime—and it is important to note here that Kazakhstan's policies, both foreign and domestic, are largely identical with the wishes of its president.

Foreign Policy

Foreign Policy in Kazakhstan is based on, in large part, cooperation with Russia, or at the very least, on the recognition that Kazakhstan's engagement with the rest of the world must take into consideration Russia's desires and interests. Similarly, Nazarbayev has urged President Trump to seek closer ties with Russia, a policy that Trump promoted during his campaign,[8] and to indulge in cooperative measures to combat global terrorism.

Terrorism is something that the Nazarbayev regime has focused on at home, and equates with Muslim extremism. Trump's "travel ban" policy is compatible with Nazarbayev's frequent pronouncements about the danger of extremists infiltrating from abroad, and the need to exert more control over borders to combat such a threat. Indeed, Kazakhstan's policy initiatives in this regard are compatible with those proposed by the new Trump administration, in the sense of using coercive measures to thwart any possibility of such extremism taking hold inside the borders of the country.

Nuclear weapon non-proliferation is a policy issue upon which Kazakhstan has been a world leader. This is compatible with its status as one

---

Nazarbayev. It could be argued they both believe in the power of money and do not care much for principles and values. They think everybody has a price tag, and can be bought.

[8] Trump told his supporters that the United States "can find common ground with Russia in the fight against ISIS." Retrieved from: http://www.cbsnews.com/where-donald-trump-stands-on-terrorism/; and http://transcripts.cnn.com/TRANSCRIPTS/1608/16/acd.01.html. Of course, after the allegations of collusion between the Trump Campaign and Russia to interfere in Trump's favor in the presidential elections, any such efforts are on hold indefinitely.

of only a handful of countries that have voluntarily given up their nuclear weapons. It must be made clear that Kazakhstan inherited nuclear weapons placed on its territory during the Soviet era. It relinquished such weapons in return for the assurances of its territorial integrity and pledges of assistance from the US and others. In contrast, Trump's stand on nuclear proliferation has been inconsistent.[9] In March 2016, he told the *New York Times*, "Japan and South Korea might need to develop their own nuclear capabilities to protect themselves from China and North Korea in the event the United States is not able to step in."[10] More recently, he has moderated his position. Since taking office, however, he has refrained from the more inflammatory remarks about nuclear weapon proliferation, remarks that were, in large part, campaign rhetoric that may also have been intended to intimidate China and, especially, North Korea, in terms of their own nuclear strategies or ambitions.

Kazakhstan's multi-vector foreign policy assumes a robust global presence for the US, in order to partially offset the influence of Russia and China in Central Asia. According to a CBS news report,[11] President-elect Trump and President Nazarbayev discussed the "importance of strengthening regional partnerships" and shared viewpoints on issues of "stability and security promotion" in Central Asia. However, President Trump's ambiguous pronouncements regarding US foreign policy has caused some anxiety in Kazakhstani foreign policy circles—what exactly does he mean by "America First" in the context of global engagements?

Kazakhstan has evidenced its commitment to inter-governmental organizations. It supports the United Nations, and is currently a member of its Security Council. It very recently lobbied hard and successfully to become head of Organization for Security and Cooperation in Europe. The Eurasian Economic Union—a customs union comprised of

---

[9] See: http://www.courthousenews.com/trump-echoes-putin-call-for-nuclear-proliferation/.

[10] Retrieved from: http://www.courthousenews.com/trump-echoes-putin-call-for-nuclear-proliferation/.

[11] CBS News reported on December 2, 2016: "President-elect Donald Trump spoke over the phone with Kazakhstan's President Nursultan Nazarbayev earlier this week, praising the dictator for the country's "miracle" during his reign, according to a Kazakh readout of the call." Retrieved from:https://www.cbsnews.com/news/donald-trump-kazakhstan-nursultan-nazarbayev-miracle/.

Russia, Kazakhstan, Belarus, Armenia, and Kyrgyzstan—was originally Nazarbayev's idea, but it came to be dominated and heavily promoted by Russia. Nevertheless, Kazakhstan rigorously follows a pattern of promoting its own, and others', involvement in this regional initiative:

> Eurasian integration is increasingly viewed from Astana as a priority focus area of its diplomacy. Thus, Kazakhstan is pledging its continuous support to the Customs Union and the Common Economic Space with Russia and Belarus, since both of these structures will serve as the basis of the future integration bloc. However, Kazakhstani authorities are keen to preserve the country's sovereignty and independence from Moscow, in the context where Russia has been pushing for closer integration not only at the economic level but also at the political one (Voloshin 2014).

Kazakhstan is a member of the Partnership for Peace initiative designed to promote cooperation with NATO to increase regional security. It is a member of the Shanghai Cooperation Organization, a Eurasian political, economic, and security organization.[12] Kazakhstan has also put itself forward as a locus for, and as an "honest broker" in, negotiations to end conflicts, such as the war in Syria.

In contrast, President Trump has not only encouraged developments that do damage to international integration and cooperation, such as Britain's decision to withdraw from the European Union, but he has gone so far as to question the need for NATO, one of the primary agents of US global involvement,[13] while adopting an aggressive tone regarding situations occurring in places such as Syria and North Korea. Indeed, his proclivity to engage in a type of "brinkmanship"[14] in dealing with

---

[12] "The Shanghai Cooperation Organisation (SCO) is a permanent intergovernmental international organisation. ... The main goals of the SCO are strengthening mutual confidence and good-neighbourly relations among the member countries ..." Retrieved from: http://eng.sectsco.org/docs/about/faq.html.

[13] Trump may be using inflammatory rhetoric, referring to NATO as "very bureaucratic, extremely expensive" in order to coerce NATO allies to meet their funding commitment, a tactic very much compatible with his preferred negotiating style.

[14] This raises the interesting possibility that Donald Trump may be, consciously or

what he considers to be rogue nation, apparently without consulting—or even informing—regional allies of US intentions and actions, raises fears in the Middle East, East Asia, and elsewhere of potentially devastating armed conflicts. This "America-alone" approach[15] is at odds with Kazakhstan's preferences regarding cooperative international endeavors.

Despite President Nazarbayev's enthusiasm for international organizations, he resents western interference in Kazakhstan's internal affairs, especially criticism of his regime's shortcomings in regard to Western-style democratic practices. Kazakhstan emulates China in many ways, particularly its practice of encouraging private enterprise while discouraging political participation, and it is the pragmatic approach to foreign policy and investment or economic cooperation, which involves paying little attention to the internal practices of the regimes with which it does business. Trump would seem to be similarly inclined. So, Trump's lack of interest in "nation-building" or "regime change" in places that do not reflect Western norms is very much welcome.[16]

Trade Policy

President Nazarbayev's regime has employed import substitution measures and made use of import duties and border taxes on goods coming from outside the new Eurasian Economic Union, principally from China.[17] This reflects a protectionist trade policy strategy designed to diversify Kazakhstan's economy and reduce its dependency on natural resource extraction. The higher cost of imports or import substitutes also increases inflation but can improve the balance of trade and diversify employment opportunities. Trump's economic nationalism campaign rhetoric has similarly espoused such measures, and has also focused on resuscitating the American manufacturing sector, creating jobs, and improving the balance of trade, particularly with regard to China, although

---

unconsciously, engaging in a type of mirror-imaging, as brinkmanship has long been the preferred negotiating style of the North Koreans.

[15] Retrieved from: https://www.washingtonpost.com/politics/trumps-america-first-looks-more-and-more-like-america-alone/2017/11/11/5cffa150-c666-11e7-aae0-.cb18a8c29c65_story.html?utm_term=.3cc02198b3be.

[16] Retrieved from: https://radiotochka.kz/29931-nazarbaev-peredacha-vlasti-po-nasledstvu-eto-ne-dlya-nas.html.

[17] Retrieved from: http://www.china.org.cn/english/features/fmar/165940.html.

after President Xi's recent visit to the White House, that stance may be somewhat modified.

Refugees, Immigration, and Ethnic Relations

Kazakhstan's laws concerning immigration and the acquiring of citizenship are much more stringent than those of the US, even after considering the Trump administration's ideas about a moratorium on accepting refugees or immigration from some Muslim majority countries. Kazakhstan is very concerned about the spread of Muslim radicalism from Afghanistan or Syria. A recent account notes that as of late 2015, Kazakhstan had taken in only 27 Syria refugees from the over four million Syrian refugees as of the beginning of 2016 (Lillis 2015). This compares to over 18,000 accepted by the US. Kazakhstan is not particularly welcoming of refugees in general. It closed the border with Kyrgyzstan during that country's 2010 political upheavals, fearing an inflow of Kirgiz fleeing street violence. And, it particularly does not want refugees or asylum seekers from China, since it is bound by both the 1951 International Convention on the Status of Refugees and agreements under the Shanghai Cooperation Organization framework to extradite "terrorists/extremists/separatists" to its powerful neighbor. That would quite likely provoke serious protests among ethnic minorities communities, particularly the Uighurs, and their supporters. Kazakhstan has also returned to Uzbekistan a number of Uzbeks who had sought refugee status in Kazakhstan, even though there was ample evidence to suggest they would be subjected to arrest and mistreatment by the repressive regime there if sent back. Additionally, refugees are not eligible for citizenship. It stands to reason, then, that Kazakhstan would be in agreement with Trump's proposal for the establishment a "safe zone" within the confines of Syria, where refugees could seek safe haven.[18]

The Trump administration, in an effort to discourage people, mainly from Mexico and Central America, from entering the country without authorization, supports a revision to citizenship laws. Specifically, the Trump administration wants to change the law that confers citizenship on anyone born within the territory of the US (*Jus Soli*).[19] It argues that

---

[18] Retrieved from: htpp://aljezera.com/indepth/opinion/2017/01/trump-real-estate-approach-safe-zones-syria-170130135423734.html.

[19] It should be noted that the US and Canada are rather unique among ad-

this law is abused by undocumented immigrants to acquire citizenship for their offspring, which, in turn, serves as the basis for allowing the parents to remain in the country as close relatives of an American citizen. These children born in the US are referred to, disparagingly, as "anchor babies" by Trump's supporters and others opposed to unrestricted immigration into the country.[20]

In Kazakhstan, citizenship is conferred on those who can demonstrate that they are ethnic Kazakhs, even if they have never visited the Republic of Kazakhstan and cannot speak the language. Indeed, such people are encouraged to immigrate to Kazakhstan as part of the effort to create an ethnic Kazakh majority. While the same right of immigration and citizenship applies to non-Kazakhs from other former Soviet Republics, no efforts are made to attract them, even if they are close relatives of Kazakhstani citizens, despite the country being officially regarded as under-populated. Quite the contrary, the policy of decreasing the proportion of the population of Slavic origin is scarcely disguised. Data for 2008, for example, regarding immigration to Kazakhstan, indicate that ethnic Kazakhs far outnumbered all other nationalities, with ethnic Kazakhs numbering nearly 14,000, and all others (including 235 Russians, presumably mostly arriving from neighboring Central Asian states) totaling little more than 1,000 (Meshimbayeva 2008). This pattern has held for many years.

One way to discourage immigration from Russia is to disallow dual nationality, a provision that both discourages ethnic Russian Kazakhstanis from staying in Kazakhstan and discourages any actual immigration from Russia to Kazakhstan. Ethnic Russians, at least in the period immediately following the breakup of the Soviet Union, were unsure of their future in Kazakhstan and saw dual nationality as a prudent strategy in the event of ethnic strife. An English translation of official immigration policy reads as follows:

---

vanced industrial countries in being the only ones conferring by law citizenship to all born in the country. See: http://www.npr.org/sections/thetwo-way/2015/08/18/432707866/3-things-you-should-know-about-birthright-citizenship.

[20] Retrieved from: http://www.cbsnews.com/news/donald-trump-anchor-babies-arent-american-citizens/.

application for citizenship acquisition is denied in following cases: [the applicant] is a citizen of other countries. This provision does not apply to citizens of the former Soviet republics, who arrived for permanent residence in the Republic of Kazakhstan, having one of his close relatives—the citizens of the Republic of Kazakhstan, if they applied to the interior authorities a written appeal of renunciation of foreign citizenship.[21]

All of this is not to say that a policy to increase the proportion of Kazakhstanis who can claim Kazakh ethnicity is not understandable. At the birth of modern Kazakhstan, ethnic Kazakhs were a minority in their own country, despite their titular status.

Trump's stress on ethnic nationalism, as opposed to the civic nationalism, is offensive to many in the US as a country of immigrant. Outrage over his ties, via his relationship with Steve Bannon, to the so-called Alt-Right, a movement that is seen as promoting the interests of ethnic Euro-Americans, is evidence of this. But, such sensitivities are not in much evidence in Kazakhstan, where ethnic favoritism, and favoritism shown to family or clan, is standard practice. In all fairness to Nazarbayev, he has been very astute in balancing the notions of a country of many nationalities, with the desires of ethnic Kazakhs to increase their numbers, and to promote their group interests and domination in the cultural, social, and political spheres. Given the acceptability of ethnic favoritism widespread in Central Asia, criticism of Trump-style ethnic nationalism is not to be expected.

The Environment

In the summer of 2017, Kazakhstan hosted Expo 2017, an international event focused on the promotion of sustainable future energy. While considerable rhetoric has been devoted to the efforts to promote alternatives to fossil fuels, according to one commentator, Catherine Putz (2017): "Kazakhstan remains a country firmly married to conventional energy industries." This should not be surprising. Kazakhstan has proclaimed its intention to become a fully developed country by 2050, one

---

[21] Retrieved from: http://egov.kz/cms/en/articles/how_to_become_kz_citizen.

of the top 30 in the world, and the only way to accomplish this formidable feat is to exploit its extensive mineral resources, most notably, oil, gas, and coal. And as has been noted, "despite the intensive and growing burden on the environment, Kazakhstan imposes virtually no ecological costs on production [of minerals]" (Zhukov 2005). That is to say, proclamations about the necessity of protecting the environment and moving away from fossil fuels aside, it is business as usual in terms of the extraction and marketing of the country's mineral wealth.

The compatibility of Kazakhstan's policy, if not its rhetoric, with the Trump administration is very clear. Trump questions the evidence for man-made climate change. After examining the various, often contradictory statements he has made concerning climate change, Lauren Carroll (2017) reaches the conclusion that "on the topic of man-made climate change, he's expressed doubt more often than not." And certainly, his policy positions reflect an unconcern with the effects of the continued extraction and reliance on conventional fossil fuels, as his promotion of, and support for, the coal industry and the burning of coal for energy in the US demonstrates.[22]

Political Rhetoric

Perhaps, the largest gap between the Presidents Trump and Nazarbayev is their political rhetoric. Nazarbayev's public persona is that of an experienced, sober, benevolent father-figure—known by Kazakhs as the "Father of the Nation"—guiding his young nation carefully, as it slowly develops its political, social, and economic systems. Indeed, the President and other top officials in Kazakhstan's government have been referred to as being "image-obsessed."[23] This is in sharp contrast to the bombastic, confrontational, and suspiciously narcissistic image projected by Trump, who is also obsessed with his image. The populism that he tapped to win the presidency is far from being inclusive—at least in terms of those who can expect to benefit materially under his regime—and so is not in accord with the consensual politics as espoused in Ka-

---

[22] See: https://www.washingtonpost.com/news/powerpost/paloma/the-energy-202/2017/06/05/the-energy-202-inside-the-question-of-whether-trump-can-save-coal-jobs/5931927ce9b69b2fb981dc3a/.

[23] Retrieved from: http://foreignpolicy.com/2015/07/30/kazakhstan-cant-get-no-respect-olympics-2022-nazarbayev/.

zakhstan. Certainly, Nazarbayev and other members of his regime brook no real challenge to their stranglehold on power. But, given the potential for ethnic conflict of the type that has occurred in some of the other post-Soviet states (including neighboring Kyrgyzstan), the rhetoric of confrontation that now marks American politics is puzzling to many Kazakhstanis, both inside and out of the government. And it would be potentially far more dangerous to pursue a political agenda of confrontation in a country like Kazakhstan than in America, where strong institutions constrain American presidents. The weak institutional setting in Kazakhstan would make such an agenda far more dangerous.

Nevertheless, like Trump, Nazarbayev is hardly immune to the lure of personal aggrandizement. His image adorns the 10,000 Tenge note, he agreed to the naming of a new, lavishly funded university in the capital of Astana after himself. So far, however, he has resisted calls by sycophant legislators to re-name the capital in his honor. There are Nazarbayev scholarships for foreign university education, too. Similarly, "President's Day" is a national holiday and there has been only one president.[24] Trump can only dream of such adulation.[25]

Relations with the Media

Marvin Kalb, who has been a well-respected journalist for decades in the US, remarked recently in a speech given before the Cosmos Club[26] that Trump seeks to humiliate journalists, to belittle them, so as to discourage their criticism and to emasculate the fourth branch of government[27]

---

[24] It should be noted, however, that by Central Asian standards Nazarbayev is rather modest—Saparmurat Niyazov, the deceased former president-for-life of Turkmenistan—who renamed himself Turkmenbashi or "Father of the Turkmen"—and had dozens of gilded statues of himself erected in his small country, including one that rotated with the sun, so that the father of all Turkmen would always be facing the light.

[25] Retrieved from: https://www.washingtonpost.com/news/worldviews/wp/2016/12/01/trump-may-want-to-learn-a-thing-or-two-from-kazakhstans-dictator/?utm_term=.6fafda8471c0.

[26] This is venerable private club, founded nearly 140 years ago, which has counted a number of US Presidents, Vice Presidents, and three dozen Nobel Prize winners as members, as well as many other notables. Retrieved from https://www.cosmosclub.org/About-the-Club.

[27] "There are three branches of government—executive, legislative and judicial—

as it was once called, to rob it of the legitimacy it used to enjoy among many Americans. Why? because, at the end of the day, the president can govern as he wishes, without the judiciary to impose legal constraints and without the media to raise embarrassing questions or to criticize his policies (Kalb 2017).

Nazarbayev enjoys a media environment in Kazakhstan that President Trump can only dream about in the US. His government controls a system where the media is very constrained,[28] using various tactics against critical media voices, such as charging media outlets with libel and defamation, among other charges, in order to censor and intimidate critics.[29] Kazakhstan is near the bottom of Reporters Without Borders world rankings for press freedom, and violence against independent journalist critical of the government is not uncommon.[30] Freedom House classifies Kazakhstan as "not free" in terms of press freedom.[31]

In short, independent media have little opportunity to criticize or to raise embarrassing questions. Indeed, "Most media outlets are controlled or influenced by members of the president's family, including his daughter and her husband, and other powerful groups. According to the BBC, many of the 1,000-plus newspaper titles are government-run and the state controls printing presses."[32] Donald Trump, his daughter Ivanka, and her husband Jared Kushner have their work cut out for them if they wish to compete with the Nazarbayev clan in terms of countering the power of media in politics and society.

---

that make, enforce and interpret laws and public policy. The media tell the people what the three branches of government are doing. ... Without the media, people would know little about what our elected officials are doing" Retrieved from: https://usatoday30.usatoday.com/educate/elections/elect5.htm.

[28] See: https://www.economist.com/news/asia/21724435-worlds-biggest-landlocked-country-open-business-only-half-ready-it-kazakhstan.

[29] See: https://www.theguardian.com/world/2015/jul/08/kazakhstan-media-crackdown-independent-press.

[30] See: https://www.article19.org/resources.php/resource/38747/en/kazakhstan:-stabbing-of-journalist-must-be-immediately-investigated.

[31] Retrieved from: https://freedomhouse.org/report/freedom-press/2017/kazakhstan.

[32] Retrieved from: http://www.bbc.com/news/world-asia-pacific-15482614.

Fake News

One of the main criticisms Donald Trump has leveled at the mainstream US (and international) media outlets is that they are biased and promote a liberal political and social agenda. He charges that these media outlets slant their coverage of events to denigrate the conservative and traditional perspective, even to the point of inventing news, or exaggerating the significance of events that do take place. In short, Trump's use of the term reflects a particular interpretation of the term bias. According to James Carson, an English journalist, bias is a "selectively-chosen but truthful elements of a story put together to serve an agenda" or "stories where the 'truth' is contentious ... where ideologies or opinions clash ... there is sometimes no established baseline for truth. Reporters may be unconsciously partisan."[33] Traditional news sources employ editors to filter the news—part of their gatekeeping function—can be considered a type of bias. Competition between news outlets should, theoretically, work to counteract bias in reporting. Trump seems to believe that all mainstream news outlets share an ideological leaning to the political left, which these media outlets consider to be objective. Many of his politically disaffected supporters agree with him. Going one better than the US, Kazakhstan has a law against "spreading false information" punishable by fines or even long prison terms,[34] a statute that has been used to intimidate dissident media, usually those that investigate corruption in high places, or are critical of Kazakhstan's shortcomings in regard to democratic governance. President Trump can only dream about having such a statute applicable to all the media operating in the US.

Conclusion

One of the primary differences between liberal democracies and much of the rest of the world is that constitutional and rule-of-law restrictions on the abuse of power act as real constraints on political leaders, elected or unelected. Suggestions that Donald Trump is unaware of, or does not recognize such constraints, have resulted in many voicing fears that

---

[33] Retrieved from: http://www.telegraph.co.uk/technology/0/fake-news-origins-grew-2016/.

[34] Retrieved from: https://freedomhouse.org/report/freedom-press/2016/kazakhstan.

the future of democratic government is in jeopardy in the US. These fears are grossly exaggerated. This may be because democratic, constitutional government in the US has remained without serious threat for over one hundred fifty years. Any deviation from accepted norms of conduct on the part of powerful political actors then can be blown out of all proportion. Outside observers, especially ones from countries with little or no experience of institutional constraints on the politically powerful, may find puzzling such fears, and the anxiety they spawn. In many parts of the world, abuse of power is so commonplace as to be the norm. Bombastic pronouncements of a partisan or even mildly ideological nature, such as those voiced by President Trump—like "America First"—elicit little concern in such political environments. President Trump's narcissistic self-aggrandizement, his self-promotion, his relentless tweeting—at odd hours, often directed at the media or others he sees as his political opponents, and often crude, vulgar, or abusive—all have demeaned the institution of the presidency. This is very unfortunate, but it is not reflective of impending system collapse. It may be that the culture of the US is in the process of becoming ever more coarse and vulgar, or, perhaps more accurately, popular culture is becoming more ever more coarse and vulgar. And the first "reality TV" president and his relentless pursuit of media attention—via bizarre behavior—is reflective of this phenomenon. This vulgarization of the public sphere may or may not reflect a type of "culture shift" (Inglehart 1990). But, the point of this comparison between the US under Donald Trump and Kazakhstan under Nursultan Nazarbayev—a country and a leader not untypical in the world today—is to put the current administration in Washington into some kind of perspective. The Trump administration is temporary. Democracy in America is robust and will survive this challenge, if, indeed, it is being challenged by this most unusual of presidents.

References

Carroll, L. 2017. "Does Donald Trump Believe in Man-made Climate Change?" *PolitiFact*, June 5. Available at: http://www.politifact.com/truth-o-meter/article/2017/jun/05/does-donald-trump-believe-man-made-climate-change/.

Epley, J. 2015. "Weber's Theory of Charismatic Leadership: The Case of Muslim Leaders in Contemporary Indonesian Politics." *International Journal of Humanities and Social Science*, 5 (7): 7–17. Available at: http://www.ijhssnet.com/journals/Vol_5_No_7_July_2015/2.pdf.

Kalb, M. 2017. "Trump's Troubling Relationship with the Press." *Brookings*, February 21. Available at: https://www.brookings.edu/blog/up-front/2017/02/21/trumps-troubling-relationship-with-the-press/.

Inglehart, R. 1990. *Culture Shift in Advanced Industrial Society*. Princeton, NJ: Princeton University Press.

Lillis, J. 2015. "Syrians Find Asylum in Kazakhstan." *EurasianNet's Weekly Digest*, December 1. Available at: http://www.eurasianet.org/node/76356.

Meshimbayeva, A., ed. 2008. *Demographic Data Annual of Kazakhstan*. Astana, KZ: Kazakhstan Agency of Statistics. Available at: https://web.archive.org/web/20100705041402/http://www.stat.kz/publishing/DocLib/Dem_Ezegod_2009%20CD.pdf.

Putz, C. 2015. "Should We Stop Calling Kazakhstan an Autocracy?" *The Diplomat*, September 3. Available at: http://thediplomat.com/2015/09/should-we-stop-calling-kazakhstan-an-autocracy/.

Putz, C. 2017. "Astana Expo 2017: Future Energy and a Kazakh Contradiction." *The Diplomat*, June 2. Available at: http://thediplomat.com/2017/06/astana-expo-2017-future-energy-and-a-kazakh-contradiction/.

Zhukov, S. 2005. "Kazakhstan: The Development of Small Raw-Material Exporters Under the Constraints of Globalization." In *Central Asia at the End of the Transition* (ed. B. Rumer). Armonk, NY: M.E. Sharpe.

Voloshin, G. 2014. "Kazakhstan Adopts New Foreign Policy." *The Central Asia–Caucasus Analyst*, February 5. Available at: https://www.cacianalyst.org/publications/field-reports/item/12904-kazakhstan-adopts-new-foreign-policy-concept.html.

INDEX

Abe, Shinzo 209ff, 264
Abbas, Mahmoud 220
Abdullah II, King 238, 239
Afghanistan 62, 137, 147, 151, 167, 176, 219, 302, 303
Africa: clashing norms and prospect of estrangement 292-9; Trump's Africa Policies 300-6; Trump's leadership qualities resonate negatively with Africa 306-11
Africa-US special trade relationship 301
African Union 291, 293, 296-7, 305, 311
Africans on Trump 293
al-Assad, Bashar 31, 32, 131-2, 199, 200, 228, 279, 283
Albania 158, 166, 173
al-Shabaab 301
al-Qaeda 227, 232ff
"America first" vii, 76, 124, 125, 169, 172, 245, 253, 295, 300, 301
"America first energy plan" 193
American isolationism vii-iii, 205
Amin, Idi 307
Arab Spring 218
Armenia 320
Argentina 62, 103
Asia 123, 199-200
Atatürk, Kemal 316
Australia 30-1, 42, 62, 123
Authoritarian leadership proclivities,

Trump's: mirror authoritarians in: Africa 295-6; Central Asia 315-17
Balkan states 157-8; 173
Baltic states 143, 151, 157, 172, 189n
Bandwagoning diplomacy, Japan's 209
Belarus 167, 189n, 191, 320
Bilateralism vii, 163, 165, 166, 169, 165, 166, 169, 171, 176, 182, 254, 292
Biltd, Carl 295
Bolivia 103
Bosnia-Herzegovina 166, 173, 181
Brexit 84, 119, 121, 122, 123, 124, 126, 132-3, 134, 135, 144, 151, 158
British on Trump 119, 128-9, 133, 134-5
Bulgaria 144, 157
Bullshit 17
"Buy American and hire Americans" 89
Canada 30, 89, 92, 96: benign neglect and in difference 79-80; environment and energy tensions 74-6; rhetoric without accomplishment 80-1; security and border tensions 76-8; US constitutional impediments 82-3; trade tensions 71-3
Canadians on Trump 70-1, 83-4
Capitalism, crony 308-9
Central and Eastern Europe (CEE) 125, 137, 145, 147: CCE in the international arena 172-4; Balkan states 157-8; managing risk and

uncertainty 163-9; US-CEE relations, non-confrontational asymmetry and security dilemmas 160-3; pro-EU states 157; pro-Western states 157; risks of uncertainty 169-71; Trump and Key CEE states 174-81; US interests in 158-60. See also Poland

Central Intelligence Agency (CIA) 147

Chile 103

China vii, viii, 32, 52, 133, 134, 196, 199-200, 205, 210-12, 230, 240, 315: North Korean problem 261-4; Trump and China, the early days 256-61; Trump's caution when dealing with China 264-6; Trump's China foreign policy objectives 253-6; US-China relations before Trump 251-3; US-China relations, future outlook 266-7; Xi's dream form China 246-51

Climate Acord, Paris 40, 41, 74, 75, 82, 135, 194, 197, 202, 203, 294-5, 305-6, 312

Clinton, Bill 33, 58

Clinton, Hilary 33, 211, 271, 272

Conspiracy theories 33

Crimea 148, 149, 151; 180, 198, 203

Croatia 158, 167, 177, 182

Czech Republic 139, 140, 144, 157, 170, 171-2, 179-80, 182

Defence mechanisms, Trump's 23-4

Deferred Action for Childhood Arrivals (DACA) ("dreamers") 107, 110

Democracy 45, 254, 329

Democratization 146, 148, 158, 159, 166, 191, 196-7: in Africa 291, 295, 296-9, 300, 312, 313

Deregulation 40

Donut, the Oscar Wilde 83, 84

Duterte, Rodrigo 82, 196, 296

Economic nationalism 292, 294

Egypt 30, 168, 169, 203, 219, 224, 238, 239, 277, 296, 302, 308: important US partner 236-8

Egyptians on Trump 218

el-Sisi, Abdel Fattah 217, 218, 223, 237, 239, 296, 308

Erdogan, Recep Tayyip 82, 271ff, 296

Estonia 141, 157, 167, 173

Ethnic nationalism: African perspective on 292-3; Kazakhstani perspective on 322-4

Europe 29, 84, 103, 123, 165, 197

European Union (EU) 29, 119, 121, 122, 123, 129-30, 133, 137, 138, 139, 144, 151, 157, 160, 164-5, 167, 170, 173, 191, 197, 202, 204, 303, 306, 315: Two speed Europe with Eurozone core 164

Fake news 42, 327

Federal Bureau of Investigation (FBI) 19, 31, 64-5, 79, 130, 317

Foreign assistance (aid) 291, 295, 300, 302-4

France 42, 52, 62, 130, 167, 198

Gaddafi, Muammar 307

Georgia 147, 149, 151, 171, 190, 191, 203

Germany 42, 52, 62, 77, 103, 130, 143, 144, 148, 167, 189n, 197, 198, 251,

266, 280, 281
Ghana 293
Grabar-Kitarovic, Kolinda 178
Greece 141, 158
Gulf states 218, 237
Gülen, Fethullah 271, 271, 274, 287, 288, 289, 290
Hezbollah 223
Hitler, Adolf 316
Human rights 30, 92, 104, 106, 109, 110, 187, 189, 191, 193, 196, 199, 204, 217, 237, 254, 257, 275, 291, 296, 300, 31
Hungary 148, 157, 159, 166, 172-3, 176-7, 182
Hussein, Saddam 146, 280
Immigrants, illegal 40, 90, 100, 106-10
India 62, 246, 252
International Monetary Fund (IMF) 132
Iohannis, Klaus 179
Iran 32, 33, 147n, 195, 199, 201, 202, 218, 223, 225, 230-1, 236: nuclear agreement (the Joint Comprehensive Plan of Action) 51-2
Iraq 121, 137, 140, 147, 151, 167, 195, 302
Ireland 123
Israel 30, 52, 200, 203, 218, 220, 221, 223, 224, 237, 302, 303: biggest winner in the Middle East 222-2; Palestinian-Israeli conflict 238-40
Islamic State (ISIS) 232, 239, 240, 279, 281, 282, 284: fight against 232-6

Islamic Sunni alliance 223-4
Islamic terrorist groups 147, 165, 176, 201, 220, 226, 227, 234, 238, 300
Italy 62, 130, 167
Japan 30, 255, 264, 319: Japan prior to Trump 210-11; initial phase, sigh of relief 211-12; second phase, fears and expectations 212-14; third phase, orgy then apathy 214-15
Japanese on Trump 209
Jerusalem 222, 239, 241
Jordan 132, 224, 237, 238, 239
Kagame, Paul 305
Karimov, Islam 316
Kazakhstan: contrasts and congruence: political leadership 315-17; rule of law and corruption 317; policy comparisons 318-25; political rhetoric 325-6; relations with the media 326-8
Kenya 293, 304
Kim Jong-un 31, 42, 79, 168, 213
Kosovo 158, 166, 173, 181
Kyrgyzstan 320
Kurdish militia, Syrian 233, 272, 279-284, 285
Latvia 157, 173
Libya 147, 195, 293
Lithuania 157, 173
Lies 18-19: Trump's 52, 59, 309-10
Macedonia 158
"Make America Great Again" vii, 40 125, 127, 192, 245, 253, 310, 311
"Make America Safe Again" 103
"Make America Strong Again" 138

Mao Zedong 316

May, Theresa 84, 119ff

Merkel, Angela 29, 77

Mexicans on Trump 88, 89-90, 94-5, 102, 111-12

Mexican (Southern Border) wall 33, 40, 60, 82, 99-104, 113, 194-5, 201

Mexico 32, 71-2, 113, 82: domestic political challenge 88-90; migration and security 104-6; preparing for the worst 91-5; rescuing NAFTA 95-9; supporting illegal migrants 106-10; wall and border security 99-104

Middle East viii, 13, 132, 168, 191, 200-1, 203, 248, 272, 278, 290, 321: implications of Trumps Middle East policies for Russia 224-5, Islamic Sunni alliance 223-4; Palestinian-Israel conflict 238-40; Trump's Middle East rhetoric and actions 225-6; White House visits by Arab leaders 220-1

Middle East's reaction to Trump 219-20

Missile defense systems 139, 140, 151, 179: Ballistic Missile Defence 139-40; European Phased Adaptive Initiative 139; Ground-based Midcourse Defense 139

Moldova 167, 173, 190n, 191

Montenegro 158, 173, 199

Moon Jae-in 264

Mugabe, Robert 307, 310

Multilateralism vii, 164, 165, 182, 189n, 190, 193, 198, 254, 292, 294, 295

Muslims 40, 181, 195, 294

Nazarbayev, Nursaltan 316ff

Nepotism 52, 54

Netanyahu, Benjamin 30, 218, 221, 222, 238

New Cold War 141, 150, 158

New Silk Road 248

Niazovim, Saparmurat 316

Nieto, Enrique Pena 71, 87ff

Nigeria 293, 299, 304, 308

Non-confrontational asymmetry international relations 160-3, 175-6

North American Free Trade Agreement (NAFT): Canadian perspectives 71-3, 80, 81, 83, 131; Mexican perspectives 89-90, 92, 95-9, 104, 111, 112

North Atlantic Treaty Organization (NATO) 29, 76, 124-5, 126, 127, 129-31, 132, 137, 141-2, 142-44, 147-8, 149, 151, 157, 159-60, 163-6, 171, 167, 171, 169, 170, i71, 172, 173, 178, 181, 202, 203, 282, 320

North Korea vii, 7, 31, 33, 42, 79, 140, 142, 165, 168, 176, 199, 200, 202, 203, 210, 210, 230, 240, 245, 255, 259, 261-2, 319, 320: nuclear missile threat 7, 31, 79, 140, 165-6, 176, 199, 200, 202, 211, 212-13, 214-5, 258, 259: North Korean problem 261-4

Nietzsche's übermensch 24-7

Nuclear weapon non-proliferation 318-19

Obama, Barack 19, 29, 33, 41, 52, 53, 58, 60, 61, 62, 66, 69, 73, 74, 75, 76, 84, 107, 130, 131, 134, 137, 138, 139, 143, 144, 147, 164, 165, 168,

211, 217, 218, 221, 222, 224, 228, 238, 240, 251-3, 261-2, 271, 2272, 273, 279, 282, 283, 290, 293, 299, 305, 308

Obamacare 40, 79

Offshore balancing 146

One China policy 256

Orban, Viktor 176-7

Organization of American States 103

Pahor, Borut 178

Palestine 224, 238: Palestinian-Israel conflict 221, 238-40

Philippines 42, 82, 196

Poland 157, 166, 168, 172, 173, 178, 182: on Trump's defense policies 138-42; on Trump's engagement with NATO 142-44; Trump and Polish foreign policy 144-6; US-Polish relations 146-9; US-Russian relations 149-50

Poles on trump 137, 145, 165

Putin, Vladimir 31, 82, 125, 131, 141-2, 144-5, 173, 179, 194, 195, 203, 204, 205, 211, 224-5, 296

Refugees 31, 60, 76, 77, 78, 82, 128, 150, 158, 176, 177, 180, 195, 202, 239, 263, 279, 294, 296, 304, 322-4: Refugee crisis 150n

Romania 139, 144, 157, 168, 170, 173, 178-9, 184

Russia vii, viii, 18, 31, 42, 43, 125, 127, 130, 131-2, 134, 140, 141, 142, 143, 144, 148, 149, 150, 151, 157, 158, 159, 163, 164, 167, 171, 173, 174, 177, 178, 179, 180, 181, 185ff, 211, 224-5, 227, 228, 230-1, 232, 235, 240, 252, 255, 274, 279, 280, 284,

286, 293, 315, 318; foreign policy objectives 187-91 182; meddling in 2016 US presidential election 6, 31, 50-2, 64-5, 78, 79, 176, 201-2, 216; sanctions on 142, 148, 151

Senkuku and Diaoyu Islands 211, 212

Salman bin Abdulaziz Al Saud, King 296

Saudi Arabia 62, 132, 200, 201, 203, 222, 226, 227, 231, 233, 234, 236, 237, 254, 277, 296; another winner in the Middle East 222-3

Senegal 293

Serbia 158, 173, 177, 181, 203

Scandinavia 62

Selfhood, Trump's currency of 22

Self-identity (ego), fragility of Trump's 23, 32

Slovakia 157, 159, 172-3, 182

Somalia 195, 293, 301

South Africa 292, 293, 299, 300, 301, 303, 306, 308, 310, 311

South China Sea dispute 256

South Korea 30, 62, 167, 169, 200, 203, 211, 255, 258, 264, 319

Soviet Union, collapse of 137, 158

Spain 103

Spratly Islands 212

Stalin, Josef 316

Sudan 195, 293

Sweden 295

Switzerland 62

Syria 31, 32, 33, 76, 79, 131, 176, 195, 196, 197, 202, 213, 219, 223, 225, 226, 279, 283, 320: the US bombing of 227-30; reasons behind US attack

230-2, 273
Taiwan 256
Tanzania 293
Terrorism 29, 30, 32, 77, 120, 132, 147, 171, 179, 234, 239, 274, 276, 284-5, 286, 300, 318: War on terror 30, 131, 137, 146-7, 159, 165, 223, 232, 237, 304, 306, 316
Transatlantic Trade and Investment Partnership (TTIP) 124, 132-3, 197
Trans-Pacific Partnership (TPP) 40, 41, 65, 96, 199, 202, 205, 209, 215
Trudeau, Justin 30, 69ff, 91
Trump, Donald J.: presidential: accomplishments 59-67; appointments 41, 62-3; candidature 39, 52-3; reflections on 55-9; traits 39-40; entrance on the international stage 41-2; public personality 1: agreeableness 9; conscientiousness 4; extraversion 6; neuroticism 10; openness 2; speculation 12: narcissist 12; psychopath 12-13; sociopath 12; rise to power 43-4: America's special circumstances 44-9; Republican build up to Trump 49-50; view of the world 28: "good guy" countries 29-31; "bad guy" countries 31-2; moral compass 28, 32; worldview 15: existential epistemology 16; existential individualism 21; hermeneutic agency 27: blind spots 28
Trump's foreign policies: issue-based policies 193-7; geographic-based policies 197-201; domestic and international challenges 201-2; US-Russian relations, implications for Trump 202-4

Trump's "rocking horse presidency" (Fareed Zakaria) 70-1, 84
Truth, 17: and Trump 32, 53
Travel bans, selected Muslim countries 41, 76-7, 107, 120, 128, 135, 195, 201, 212, 219, 275-9, 293-4, 312, 318
Tsai Ing-wen 256
Turkey 42, 82, 128, 223-4, 225, 231, 235, 236, 240: on the road to the Trump presidency 273-5; silence on Trump's Muslim Ban 275-79; Turkey and Trump's foreign policy 238, 279-84; the Gülen and Zarrab cases 284-9
Turkes on Trump 273-4
Turnbull, Malcolm 31
Twitter 66-7
Ukraine 138, 139, 142, 144, 148, 149, 150, 151, 167, 171, 174, 179-80, 190, 191, 197, 198, 202
Ukrainian crisis, 2014 141, 142-3, 149-50, 158, 172, 173, 179-80
United Kingdom 29, 42, 52, 240, 141: NATO summit 129-31; post-Brexit US trade agreement 132-3; Prime Minister's White House visit 125-9; threat to NATO 124-5; trade a vexing issue 123-4; Trump's seesaw approach to foreign policy 131-2; US-UK special relationship 121-3
United Nations (UN) Security Council 129, 221
Xi Jinping 200, 214, 230, 245ff, 322: Xi's dream for China 246-51
World Trade Organization 197, 266
Yemen 195, 217, 219, 220, 223, 226,

231, 234, 326, 241: US strike on 226-7

Zartrab, Reza 287-9

Zeman, Miloš 179

Zuma, Jacob 307, 310, 311

ABOUT THE EDITORS AND CONTRIBUTORS

The Contributing Editors

John Dixon is a Professor of Public Administration in the Department of Political Science and Public Administration at the Middle East Technical University in Ankara, Turkey. He was the Distinguished Professor Public Policy and Administration at KIMEP University (2009–2015) in Kazakhstan. He is an Emeritus Professor of Public Policy and Management at the University of Plymouth in the United Kingdom. He is a fellow of the British *Academy of the Social Science* (nominated by the British Social Policy Association) and an honorary life member of the American *Phi Beta Delta Honor Society for International Scholars* (nominated by the Policy Studies Organization and the American Political Science Association). He has published very extensively with 38 books, and 93 refereed articles, and 51 book chapters in the fields of international public and social policy and administration. Selected research publications have been translated into *Chinese, Spanish, Russian, Japanese,* and *Hebrew*. His last authored books are *The Public Administrator: Contenders, Contentions, and Tensions* (Westphalia Press, Washington DC, 2015) and *The Idea of Neoliberalism: The Emperor Has Threadbare Contemporary Clothes* (Westphalia Press, Washington DC, 2016).

Max J. Skidmore is University of Missouri's Curators' Distinguished Professor of Political Science and Thomas Jefferson Fellow at the University of Missouri-Kansas City. He has been Distinguished Fulbright Lecturer to India, and Senior Fulbright Scholar at the University of Hong Kong. He has published very extensively with dozens of books and edited journals, and more than 100 articles and book chapters widely varied subjects. His books on the presidency include: *Presidential Performance: A Comprehensive Review* (McFarland, Jefferson, NC, 2004); *After the White House: Former Presidents as Private Citizens* (Palgrave Macmillan, New York, 2004); *Maligned Presidents: The Late 19th Century* (Palgrave, New York 2014); and *Presidents, Pandemics, and* Politics (Palgrave, New York, 2016). He also has published books on other subjects, such as American political thought, politics in Hong Kong, political ideologies, poverty, the effects of language on politics (*Word Poli-*

tics (James E. Freel and Associates, Palo Alto, CA, 1972); and *Politics and Language*, with Andrew Cline (Cambridge Scholars Press, London, 2007); and on America's systems of Social Security and Medicare: *Medicare and the American Rhetoric of Reconciliation* (University of Alabama Press, Tuscaloosa, AL 1970 and Questia Media, 2000); *Social Security and its Enemies* (Westview Press, Boulder, CO, 1999); Bulwarks *Against Poverty in America: Social Security, Medicare, and the Affordable Care Act*, (Westphalia Press, Washington, DC 2014); and *Securing America's Future* (Rowman and Littlefield, Lantham, MD, 2008).

The Contributors

Mexico

María Celia Toro is a professor-researcher at the Centro de Estudios Internacionales oat El Colegio de México, and coordinator of its Mexico-US-Canada program. She has written on drug trafficking in the context of US-Mexican relations; the transnationalization of US police and justice; and intergovernmental networks as a dominant form of governance. She is author of *Mexico's War on Drugs. Causes and Consequences*; "The Internationalization of Police: The DEA in Mexico"; "Mexican Policy Against Drugs: From Deterring to Embracing the United States". She is currently writing on US-Mexican relations after NAFTA.

Canada

Frédérick Gagnon is the Raoul Dandurand Chair in Strategic and Diplomatic Studies, and Director of the Center for United States Studies in the Department of Political Science at University of Québec in Montreal. He teaches American Politics and US foreign policy. He has been a Fulbright grantee at University of Massachusetts in Amherst (2005), a Visiting Scholar at the Canada Institute of the Woodrow Wilson International Center for Scholars, and at the Center for American Politics and Citizenship of the University of Maryland (2006), and a Visiting Professor at the Center for Canadian-American Studies at Western Washington University (2008). He has also held Fulbright Canada Visiting Research Chairs at State University of New York, Plattsburgh (Fall 2014), and at University of California, Berkeley (Spring 2015).

United Kingdom

Kevern Verney is a Professor in American History and Associate Dean in the Faculty of Arts and Sciences at Edge Hill University (UK). He has a wide range of publications on American history. From 2010 to 2014, he was co-organizer for the Barack Obama Research Network funded by the UK Arts and Humanities Research Council. The Network held a series of public events and interdisciplinary symposia assessing policy formulation and political developments as they unfolded during the Obama presidency. He is a regular media commentator on the United States and co-editor of *Barack Obama and the Myth of a Post-Racial America* (2013).

Charlie Whitham is a Senior Lecturer in American History at Edge Hill University in the United Kingdom. He undertook his masters in History at the University of the West of England, Bristol (1990–1993) and his doctorate at Swansea University (1994–1999). In essence, his research is concerned with how US power was conceived and articulated in a global context as it rose to 'superpowerdom' during the critical mid-twentieth century. He has won fellowships at the Franklin D. Roosevelt Library (New York), Harry S. Truman Library (Missouri), and George H.W. Bush Library (Texas), and has given papers at conferences in the UK, France, Portugal, Germany, Holland, and the United States.

Poland

Karol Bieniek is an Assistant Professor in the Institute of Political Science at the Pedagogical University in Krakow. His MA (2006) and PhD (2011) are in the field of political science and he holds an MA (2009) in Turkish philology. His research interests include Turkish foreign policy, domestic policy and party system of the Turkish Republic, Turkish and Muslim minorities in Europe. He is an author of several scientific papers and two books (*Turkish Foreign Policy towards the Balkan States* (in Polish, 2008) and *The Party System of the Republic of Turkey in the 1950–2011 Period* (in Polish, 2013).

Grzegorz Nycz, Ph.D., is an Assistant Professor in the Department of European Studies at the Institute of Political Science at the Pedagogical University in Krakow. He successfully defended his doctoral thesis (*Between Persuasion and Intervention. American Policy of Promoting Democracy after 1989*) in 2009 at the Institute of Political Sciences and International Relations at Jagiellonian University. He specializes in the analyses of US foreign and security policy (theory and practice), including strategic race of arms and the outreach of the United States, NATO and EU as pillars of democratic peace. He is a Member of Polish Society of International Studies.

Eastern Europe

Bohdan Szklarski is a graduate of the English Institute at Warsaw University and the Department of Political Science, Northeastern University, Boston. In his almost 25 years of teaching, he has taught at numerous American and Polish universities. He has been at the American Studies Center (ASC) since 1992. His research interests include political leadership, the presidency, political communication, interest groups, and political participation. At the ASC, he offers courses in domestic and foreign policy and political culture. He frequently appears in the media as a commentator on American and East European political events.

Russia

Maciej Herbut is an Assistant Professor at the University of Wroclaw's Faculty of Social Sciences. His research focuses mostly on the issues of democratization, international relations, and political systems. His research has recently broadened to include international relations theory, small states (such as Georgia and Moldova) facing the expansionist policies of the Russian Federation, Consequently, the Russian Federation's rebuilding its former hegemonic status.

Karol Chwedczuk-Szulc holds PhD in political sciences and MA in sociology and international relations, teaches at the University of Social Sciences and Humanities in Warsaw, Poland. Currently, his research focus is primarily on EU-US comparative studies. He was a research fellow at the American University in Washington DC in 2015/2016. His latest publications are on the potential of social constructivism in forecasting, EU-US comparative studies, and future of EU.

China

Klaus Larres is the Richard M. Krasno Distinguished Professor at the University of North Carolina in Chapel Hill, NC. He was educated at the University of Cologne in Germany and the London School of Economics and Political Science in the UK, where he worked for almost 18 years. He was, among other professorial appointments, a Professor of International Relations at the University of London. He is a Fellow of the Royal Historical Society (UK) and the American Academy of Political Science. He is also a Fellow of the Institute for Advanced Study at the Princeton University. Recently, he also worked at a Berlin-based think-tank and advised German policy makers on relations with the US and with China. He lectured at Tongji University (Shanghai).

Japan

Tetsuya Sahara is a Professor in the Faculty of Political Science and Economics at Meiji University. His field of research is modern and contemporary history. He has studied various topics, including late Ottoman Empire, Macedonian question, Bosnian Civil War, and Japanese militarism. His major works are, *An Eastern Orthodox Community during the Tanzimat* (TUFS, Tokyo, 1998), *Bosnian Civil War: Globalization and Chaos* (in Japanese) (TUFS, Tokyo, 2008), *What Happened in Adana 1909* (Isis Press, Istanbul, 2013), "Making of 'Black Hand' reconsidered," *Istorija 20. veka*, 34/1, 2016, "Japanese views on WWI and the rise of "Asianism": the ideology of Japanese fascism," *Almanach VIA EVRASIA*, 4, 2016.

Egypt (Middle East)

Magda Shaheen is a Professor of Practice and Director of the Prince Alwaleed Bin Talal Bin Abdulaziz Alsaud Center for American Studies and Research in the School of Global Affairs and Public Policy at the American University of Cario (AUC). She is a career diplomat. Her former embassy posts include Bonn Attache, New York Counselor, Geneva Deputy Chief of Mission, Egyptian Ambassador to Greece, as well as Assistant Minister of Foreign Affairs for International Economic Relations. She has been a member of the Egyptian Missions to the United Nations in Geneva and New York, as well as chief negotiator in the World Trade Organization. Since joining AUC in 2011, she has set about enacting her vision of building cross-cultural connections between Egypt, the United States, and the Middle East.

Turkey

Mustafa Türkeş is a Professor of International Relations at the Middle East Technical University (METU). He has a BA (History, Hacettepe University, 1995), an MPhil (Near Eastern Studies, University of Manchester, 1990), and a PhD (Middle Eastern Studies, University of Manchester, 1993). He was an Invited Professor to the Top Scholar Programme of Meiji University, Japan (June–July 2016). His primary areas of research expertise are International and regional order, the Balkans, European Security, Black Sea Region, Turkish Foreign Policy, Cyprus Question, Turkey-USA Relations, Turkish Politics, and Kemalism. He is the author of *Ulusçu Sol Bir Akım: Kadro Hareketi* [A Patriotic Leftist Current: The Cadre Movement] (İmge Yayınları, Ankara, 1999) (Awarded by Turkish Historical Society as the best book of the year 2000).

Tolgahan Akdan is a doctoral candidate in the Middle East Technical University's International Relations doctoral programme. He graduated in 2008 from METU's Department of International Relations, and then he completed an MSc in International Relations at METU in 2014, his thesis was entitled "A Systemic Analysis of the Cold War and Turkey's post-War Drive to the West". His primary areas of research interest are Cold War History, History of the Soviet Union, Russian Politics, Russia–United States relations, and Liberal International Order. He has published a chapter entitled "Miscarriages of Revisionist Analysis of the Cold War" in *Thinking Beyond Capitalism* (eds. Aleksandar Matković, Mark Losoncz, and Igor Krtolica) (University of Belgrade, Institute For Philosophy and Social Theory, Belgrade, 2016).

South Africa (Africa)

John Stremlau retired as a Professor of International Relations at the University of the Witwatersrand, where he was the Head of its Department of International Relations (1998–2006) and is now a Visiting Professor. He returned to the University of Witwatersrand after nine years as Vice-President in Charge of Peace Programs at the Carter Center in Atlanta, Georgia. Earlier in his career, he was an officer of the Rockefeller Foundation (1974–1987), then he worked briefly in strategic planning at the World Bank, before serving as Deputy Director for Policy Planning for US Secretaries of State (1989–1995), leaving to join the Carnegie Commission on Preventing Deadly Conflict. His publications are mostly about Africa's international relations.

Kazakhstan

Scott Lawrence Spehr, B History, M Political Science, PhD (Political Science), is an Associate Professor and the Head of the Department of International Relations and Regional Studies at KIMEP University. He has published on subjects that focus primarily on the relationship between culture\identity and attitudes\behavior, especially as they relate to political conflict and its amelioration.

Aigul Adibayeva holds a Bachelor degree in International Relations and a Candidate of Sciences degree in Political Science. She is an Assistant Professor in the Department of International Relations and Regional Studies and the Associate Dean of the College of Social Sciences at KIMEP University. Her publications are in the areas of Central Asian studies, national processes in the Republic of Kazakhstan after independence, political parties, political transformation of the Central Asian states.

Made in United States
North Haven, CT
26 May 2022

19564455R00202